The Furies of Indian Communalism

By the same author

The Painful Transition: Bourgeois Democracy in India

The Furies of Indian Communalism

Religion, Modernity and Secularization

ACHIN VANAIK

verso
London · New York

First published by Verso 1997
© Achin Vanaik 1997
All rights reserved

Verso
UK: 6 Meard Street, London W1V 3HR
USA: 180 Varick Street, New York NY 10014–4606

Verso is the imprint of New Left Books

ISBN 1–85984–921–0
ISBN 1–85984–016–7 (pbk)

British Library Cataloguing in Publication Data
A catalogue record for this book is available from the British Library

Library of Congress Cataloging-in-Publication Data
Vanaik, Achin.
    The furies of Indian communalism : religion, modernity, and
secularization / Achin Vanaik.
        p.   cm.
    Includes index.
    ISBN 1–85984–921–0 (hardback). — ISBN 1–85984–016–7 (pbk.)
    1. Communalism—India.   2. Hindus—India.   3. Muslims—India.
4. Secularism—India.   5. India—Ethnic relations.   I. Title.
DS422.C64N36   1997   96–50055
320.954'09'045—dc21   CIP

Typeset by CentraCet Limited, Cambridge
Printed by Biddles Ltd, Guildford and King's Lynn

For Suresh

Contents

PART III

Acknowledgements

This study was only possible because of a Research Fellowship awarded to me by the Centre for Contemporary Studies in the Nehru Memorial Museum and Library (NMML), New Delhi. My grateful thanks first of all to Professor Ravinder Kumar, eminent historian and Director of the NMML. The Centre as a community of scholars has been a relaxed and stimulating place to work in and for this much credit has to go to Professor Kumar's supervision and commitment. I am also indebted to him for many insights about modern Indian history and historiography. There are many other people I would like to thank for their helpful comments. But before coming to fulfilling that pleasant if obligatory responsibility, I would like to clarify one presentational point. I have sought to handle the question of gender-sensitivity in the language of the text by sometimes using the male form of pronouns or nouns, sometimes the female form, and sometimes both.

I am particularly grateful to Mike Marqusee (whose passion for cricket and enthusiasm for leftwing politics is rivalled by his deep interest in India), Javeed Alam, Kamal Mitra Chenoy, Sumit Sarkar and Gopal Balakrishnan for their detailed comments on various parts of the book. Justin Dyer did a fine job of copy-editing. Others who took time from their busy schedules to listen to my ideas, offer comments and suggest changes and sources include Rajeev Bhargava, Aijaz Ahmad, Zoya Hasan, Mihir Desai, Satish Saberwhal, Pamela Philipose, Neeladhri Bhattacharya, Sumit Guha, Romila Thapar, Prakash Upadhyay, Joya Chatterjee, Mushirul Hasan, Rustom Bharucha, Tanika Sarkar, Sarah Joseph, Ritu Menon, Anuradha Chenoy, Neera Chandoke and Praful Bidwai. They will not all have agreed with everything I've said, indeed some have sharp differences. But they have all helped to improve the text. My thanks to all of them. Responsibility for the remaining deficiencies is mine alone.

The politically formative period of my adult life were the fourteen

ACKNOWLEDGEMENTS

years (1964 to 1978) I spent in England, where I was radicalized by the anti-racist and anti-imperialist movements of the time. There I formed some political and personal relationships which have endured even after my return to India. Indeed, these links have helped to connect in a small way anti-communal struggles here with the anti-racist struggles of the Indian diaspora in Britain, in places like Southall. A divisive communalism greatly weakens the struggle against racism in Britain as black anti-racist militants know full well. One among those dedicated militants who has spent two decades and more in that struggle (and continues the battle) is Suresh Grover, director of the Southall Monitoring Group.

It was also in my years in England that I discovered one abiding lesson – comradeship and friendship are not the same. Indeed, they rarely fuse completely. But when they do, it is something special. Therefore, I would like to dedicate this book to Suresh Grover, closest comrade and dearest friend.

PART I

— 1 —

Introduction

In 1997, India celebrates fifty years of independence. Born in the fires of a communal holocaust (Partition) in which millions died, it was the fervent hope of that generation of freedom fighters that never again would Hindus and Muslims be so bitterly divided. The Indian state's official commitment to secularism was seen as the guarantor of communal amity and national unity, themselves considered the pre-requisites for pursuing the goals – democracy, prosperity, social justice and cohesion – of successful modernization. For nigh on two decades the country seemed on course at least in the respect that communal tensions had subsided and riots were rare.

Then matters unravelled. In the last twenty-five years, the communal phoenix has risen from the ashes and spread its wings to cast a growing shadow over India's body politic. The hopes of our founding generation seem to have been belied – have we learnt nothing over half-a-century? Yes we have, and all is far from lost! We were naive in the ways we thought about modernity and communalism, religion and secularism; we cannot afford to remain so. The new urgency created by the rise of communalism has forced many to think for the first time, others to think anew, so that we may all be better equipped to tackle this ugly beast. This has been the spur to writing this book at this time.

There is no single running argument in the volume, but the essays collected here, written over the last five years and focusing on the constant theme of communalism's effect on Indian society and polity, are strongly interconnected. Except for the first essay (the one following this Introduction), all the remaining four in Parts II and III, while they can be read as self-contained pieces, were from the beginning conceived of as parts fitting together to make up a larger whole, this book.

Six years ago, when I had just completed my overview of contemporary India's economy, polity and society (*The Painful Transition*, Verso, 1990), I confided to a friend who had helpfully commented on the

3

book, particularly on the chapter 'Communalism and Hindu National-ism', that in the near future Indian intellectuals would play a major role in raising the quality of the general debate on secularism above existing theoretical and political levels even worldwide. This would be likely if for no other reason than because the problem of communalism (and therefore the issues of secularism/secularization/the secular) was so acutely and urgently felt in India, which was also more fortunate than many other third world countries in having a large body of capable scholars and scholar-activists already working in and around 'the field'.

I can confidently say this prediction has been partly fulfilled. The last six years have seen a burgeoning of theoretical interest in communalism, fundamentalism, secularism and associated themes, and an outpouring of quality analyses in newspapers, magazines, academic journals and books. Some new historical studies of the colonial period and the rise of communalism have made self-consciously theoretical and methodolo-gical explorations. The Bombay-based *Economic and Political Weekly*, in many ways a unique journal, has been particularly important for conducting this debate. But perhaps it is unfair to single it out. Other print forums have served as such mediums, though they are less well known abroad. The contributors have been largely though not exclu-sively from within India. India scholars of Western origin (mainly in the USA and UK) as well as intellectuals of Indian origin teaching in academia in the Anglo-Saxon world (USA, UK and Australia) have also intervened to definite effect.

A significant portion of intellectuals, at home and abroad, have emerged as critics of one sort or the other of secularism and the secular Indian state. Both have been put in the dock, as it were, and blamed partly or fully for the rise of communalism and fundamentalism. On closer inspection, one can usually trace here the strong influence of both post-modernist and anti-modernist strands of thinking. However, even among those concerned to defend secularism, secularization and the secular, the focus of attention has been mostly on the character, practice and ideal of the secular state, on its laws and its affirming ideology. Much less has been written about the secularization of Indian civil society – its advances and retreats, its possibilities and obstacles, its desirability or undesirability. That there is a secularization process going on 'in the background' is generally conceded, but it is the secularity of the state and the ideology of secularism (demanding the separation of the political and the religious) that have been foregrounded in most intellectual discussion. It is generally here that theoretical advances and new insights have been provided.

No doubt, the recent rise of religious fundamentalisms, nationalisms and communalisms in the East – all with a strongly political thrust towards existing state structures – gives such preoccupation with the state a particular urgency. But the longer term battle to defeat communalisms and fundamentalisms will be waged on the terrain of civil society where the democratic process must be stabilized and secularization deepened. Historians and sociologists in Europe have provided illuminating narratives of Europe's secularization process. There is no equivalent to this so far in the sub-continent. Instead we have either those who, perceiving secularization as the 'gift of Christianity', deny its applicability to geographical India, or we have straightforwardly secular histories, or, more recently, histories tracing the rise of communalism – but not narratives of the secularization process as such.

One major reason is that while the sociological approach to the study of religion is now well established in the West, this is not the case in India, certainly not with regard to its premier religion, Hinduism. There has been more emphasis on sociological and anthropological studies of Hindus, which has led to more interest in folk Hinduism and caste practices. But philosophical approaches still dominate the study of Hinduism and its place in Indian life. The larger sweep which could be provided by a sociology of Hinduism remains a rarity for studies of modern India. This book does not compensate for this lacuna, but the essays here have sought to shift the balance of theoretical and analytical attention a little more towards civil society, towards less talk about the importance of the secular and secularism and more about the importance of secularization.

If this is an attempt on one score to rectify a perceived imbalance, on another score I could be said to be deliberately endorsing an imbalance. This book discusses Hinduism, Hindu nationalism and Hindu communalism, but makes only peripheral references to minority communalisms, to Islam or Islamic India. But apart from an unnecessarily defensive attempt to establish appropriate liberal credentials by 'balancing' my preoccupation with majority communalism by a study and condemnation of minority communalisms, I doubt that very much would be gained by a study of this type. My main obsessions are the secularity of the Indian state and the secularization of Indian civil society. India cannot become an Islamic state; it can certainly become a Hindu state. If secularization – understood as relative decline in religious influence and in the importance of religious identity – is to proceed apace, then it must address above all that religious system, Hinduism, which purports to describe the beliefs, rituals and practices of the overwhelming majority of the population.

The issue of minority communalism, its sources and directions, becomes more obviously relevant in studies whose focus lies elsewhere, e.g. Kashmir and Punjab and their impact on the rest of the Union, or studies about the current turmoil within very significant sections of Muslims in India. But I would admit to one serious lacuna even in this type of study. No practical perspective for combating majority communalism can be complete without insisting simultaneously on combating minority communalisms, particularly Muslim communalism. Any perspective on *how best* to combat Muslim communalism would be greatly enhanced by an in-depth historical and sociological analysis of Muslim communalism and its complex relationship to lived and doctrinal Islam.

This is outside the purview of this book and beyond my own competence. Such a major exercise is important not just for the reason stated above but also because of the new pressure exerted by powerful circles in the West to carry out a demonization of Islam. Islam-baiters both in India and the West push a set of common themes – Islam is basically intolerant; Islam shapes the Muslim mind more than anything else; an Islam in crisis is creating an increasingly monolithic *Ummah* or worldwide community of believers. These pressures intersect with the academic study of Islam and Islamic societies by scholars in, and of, the West. One is not suggesting that all such academic studies are thereby tailored to such pressures, though there is a lot of that as well. But even more scrupulous scholarship, past and present, can be inflected with new meanings and made to serve as new justifications, though never originally intended to play such a role.

Those academic studies of Islam and Islamic societies making broader generalizations about the role and place of Islam in modernity or as a global phenomenon have also been dominated by Western scholars. Only now is this changing and one result is greater awareness of the complexity of lived Islam, the limitations of concepts like *Ummah*, the multiple interpretations of what supposedly constitutes doctrinal Islam, and the many kinds of Islamic fundamentalisms. It is also striking that those scholars most apt to generalize about global Islam, such as Clifford Geertz, Ernest Gellner, Bernard Lewis, have rarely studied India or, by extension, South Asia where over 40 per cent of all Muslims in the world live. Scholars like Gail Minault, Peter Hardy, David Gilmartin, Barbara Metcalf and Francis Robinson who have studied India/South Asia either do not make such generalizations or, if they do, meet with strong challenges from scholars particularly within India, like Mushirul Hasan and Imtiaz Ahmed.

The late Ernest Gellner, a confident theorist of global Islam, for example, knew little about India or Indian Islam. He wrongly dismissed Hinduism as only a folk religion, and subscribed to a 'pendulum' view of Islam before modernity. That is to say, there is oscillation between High and Low Islam (the Great and Little Traditions) because of the tribal and segmentary character of original Muslim society contrasted to urban Islam, which is dominated by the Great Tradition and accommodates itself to state power. In modernity the pendulum swing or overall state of balance is broken. There is now a more or less linear expansion of High Islam as state power becomes so much greater. There is a greater singularization of Islam and a stronger tendency towards uniformity in the *Ummah*.[1] The severe monotheism of Islam which is testimony to its greater rationality as compared to other world religions actually makes it more compatible with modernity. Gellner said this because of his Weberian belief in rationality (therefore rational religion–monotheism) as the driving force of history. But this compatibility makes Islamic fundamentalisms (variations played on the same key of Reformist High Islam) more powerful and likely to prevail than the movement towards a progressively more secular state and society.

There is some truth in this argument, not so much in his pendulum theory (which is highly debatable) but in his claim that the balance is broken by the advent of modernity. The social bases of folk Islam are decisively altered, e.g. by capitalist industrialization, which does promote the greater singularization of Islam and the construction of a more self-conscious and wider sense of belonging to something called a Muslim community. But it is another thing altogether to argue that this stronger sense of Muslim belonging extends across nations and nationalities in the direction of pan-Islamism. It is in countries where Muslims are in a minority that pan-Islamic sentiments tend to be stronger. The process that has been gathering strength recently is the thrust towards *different kinds of Islamic nationalisms*. This is a result not of its general compatibility with modernity but of specific reactions to the crises and problems of late modernity. Even here there can be significant deviations from this norm. The Indian experience can still refute the thesis that High Islam is now stronger than lived Islam and gaining ground at its expense. Since the formation of Pakistan there has been no all-India Muslim political party, nor is any likely to emerge.

Moreover, the tendency to greater singularization of Islam is more than compensated for by its *relativization* and *evacuation* in ordinary and

7

political life, itself testimony to the power of the secularization process attendant upon modernity. This judgement is not refuted but actually affirmed by current revivalisms. As Perry Anderson put it in his criticism of Gellner on this point, Islam,

> a traditional religion ... is bound to be decommissioned by contact with modern science and mass consumption, like every other such faith ... ending up like them in the symbolic rather than effective economy of belief. Intercontinental hysteria over blasphemy expresses not unusual congruence with modernity but exceptional fear of it. With good reason: there will be no special reprieve for the integrity of the Koran.'[2]

In the mood dominant today such sober voices are unfortunately in a serious minority. Gellner, after all, was a genuine and respected liberal with wide intellectual influence and anything but a rabid Islam-baiter.

*

But now to matters of commission rather than omission: this book has been divided into three parts of two essays each. Part I comprises this Introduction and an essay which reworks an article, 'Reflections on Communalism and Nationalism in India', which originally appeared in the *New Left Review* No. 196, (November–December 1992). I have consciously resisted the temptation to revise in any major way the article as it appeared. But three years later, with the intensity of earlier forebodings diminishing, I have become more critical of the Congress and its unwillingness to oppose Hindu communalism. In some important respects the value of this originating essay is undiminished. It attempted an overall synoptic view and I would continue to stand by the basic contours sketched then. Even my programmatic perspective stressing the importance of the anti-caste struggle as a counter to Hindu communalism has been strongly vindicated by subsequent developments.

This essay also first broached most of the major concepts and some of the more important lines of thought which guided my subsequent research. In the course of revising this essay I have added a narrative of the political rise of Hindu communalism, including more details about its crucial Ayodhya campaign. I have also replaced the earlier postscript with a conclusion assessing, over a time-span amenable to reasoned speculation, the prospects for India's liberal democracy. The chapters in Parts II and III, though developing, refining and elaborating themes first presented in this essay, are not enlarged versions of it but are very different essays standing by themselves in terms of distinct thematic structures and purposes.

The shameful destruction of the Babri Masjid (mosque) on 2 December 1992 by the Rashtriya Swayamsevak Sangh (RSS) or National Volunteer Corps and its cohort organizations had all the drama and impact of an occasionally predicted but still unexpected political earthquake. Suddenly the Indian state and Constitution were under siege by the forces of darkness as never before. This gave rise to an apocalyptic mood. Things could swing *decisively* one way or the other and they would do so *quickly*, or so it looked at the time. One lesson of that shock endures. The short-term battle to save the Indian state from the clutches of political Hindutva had now to be given temporal priority over the more difficult and longer-term struggle to de-communalize Indian civil society. But India also has a way of surprising all who write about it. Time and again, the same lesson gets driven home. Things are rarely as bleak or as positive as they seem at the time. The complexity that is India provides remarkable resources of hope as well as sources of despair. The period over which to judge whether there will be or has been a decisive shift in the 'relationship of forces' regarding the drive of the Bharatiya Janata Party to political power is a more prolonged one than earlier perceived.

Vesting hopes in the Congress to confront effectively the BJP is not warranted. A more sober assessment of Congress capacities and infirmities is, it is hoped, provided in the two chapters making up Part III. The acuteness of the 'crisis of the Congress party' is much more visible now than at the end of 1992, just as there is more understanding of the degree of complicity (even approval) in the Congress regarding the BJP's actions and directions.

*

Part II constitutes the theoretical heart of the book. The first chapter in Part Two is on 'Religion, Modernity, Secularization' – note *secularization*, not secularism. Although communalism is made possible by the modernizing–secularizing process, there is an undeniable sense in which secularization and secularism are antidotes to the communal disease. But to understand secularization the key point of reference is not communalism but religion. However, amidst contending notions of secularization, one has to choose one's alignments and explain why. I have sought to defend the classical notion of secularization – relative decline in religious influence – as a *fact* in modernity everywhere. Its further deepening in societies like India is a definite *possibility* but will

9

have to be fought for. Finally, I endorse the *desirability* of such relative decline in religious influence and in the importance of religious identity. I did not start out with the idea of launching such a defence but was more concerned to understand the field better so as to become clearer about where I stood. My defence emerged out of the study, it did not guide it.

In time it became clear that to defend the classical view of secularization required one not just to grasp what religion is and does, but also to clarify one's understandings of culture and society and of certain permutations – the various claims about the relationships between religion, culture, society, as these have been changed in and by modernity. This chapter is perhaps the most abstract and self-consciously theoretical one but it is indispensable to the architecture of the book. I have contested those who argue that even in modernity religion is necessarily central to culture and to society, and, therefore, beyond a soon-to-be-reached or already reached point, the secularization-as-decline thesis cannot apply. Religion and modernity, they say, must be strongly conjoined for the good of human society.

This chapter builds in an abstract and theoretical (but not historical) manner a plausible case for the validity of the secularization-as-decline thesis. It does so by distilling and then contesting the 'strong' arguments of those who are its opponents. Of course, the most convincing way to establish that substantial secularization of Indian society is already an indisputable fact and that further secularization is a real possibility is to provide a *historical* narrative of the secularization process in India. But unlike in the case of Europe nobody has done this in and for India. We have secular histories of India but not specifically histories of the secularizing process in India. What I have written, therefore, is something like an abstract prolegomenon to this still unfulfilled responsibility which at least calls attention to its need and importance.

While a sub-section in the chapter deals with the Marxist understanding of religion-as-ideology, I have not felt particularly beholden to that tradition in my effort to 'understand religion'. Religion always has ideological functions. Given this it has become something of a Marxist convention to bring in Gramsci because of his remarkable insights into 'hegemony' and 'ideological domination'. His observations on religion emerged from his studies on Italian Catholicism and its place in the construction of an Italian national culture. But the strength of the Marxist approach is also its weakness. Religion has ideological functions but it is and does much more than this. Of course, immortalizers or near-immortalizers of religion ignore, soft-pedal or deny this ideological

10

dimension and it is here that the Marxist approach remains a useful reminder of the ever-present link between religious discourses and practices and social and political power.

But there is also much more to be said and on these terrains the contribution of the Marxist tradition is much more limited. So Gramsci features in my survey but in a minor role. He had a core understanding of religion that was deep and broad but his thoughts on the matter took a specific direction because of his preoccupation with the how and why of fascism and fascist ideology, and of course with what to do about it. The influence on me of another Marxist intellectual–activist closer to our own times, Raymond Williams, has been more important.

In the religion–culture–society relationship, the middle term is the pivot. The later Raymond Williams worked with a notion of culture – as a 'realized signifying system' – contrasted with his earlier, more anthropologically inclined 'whole way of life' notion which remains the best starting point for investigating modern, complex societies, at least for my purposes. Williams also later dropped his treatment of 'culture in common' and 'common culture' as synonyms. Common culture was now contrasted with essentialist notions of culture as would be suggested by the term 'culture in common'. Cultural essentialism is a basic assumption of those who would contest the value of secularization and secularism for India, and must be opposed and refuted.[3]

Earlier drafts of 'Religion, Modernity, Secularization' were discussed at a number of seminars. One common criticism was often voiced. I had not attempted to deal with the issue of modernity with the same care that I was prepared to devote to the issues of religion and secularization. This is true, but I do not think it constitutes a serious handicap given the purpose of the chapter in question.[4] The disputes about the nature and meaning of modernity revolve around three axes. There are three crucial points of reference for the notion of modernity – tradition, capitalism, post-modernity. For the chapter in hand, it is the relationship of modernity to tradition that is the most important. Certainly, the orientations one has towards the latter two points of reference, capitalism and post-modernity, do impinge on the perspectives discussed. But they will have less effect on the question 'What basically happens to religion in modernity?' than on the more programmatic questions of 'What should we be wanting and fighting for now?' and 'What is it feasible to want and fight for now?'

One of the key issues in the historical discussion of modernity has always been whether it is industrialization which happens to be capitalist, or *capitalist* industrialization that constitutes the fundamental process of modernity as it has unfolded. Marxists correctly insist on the latter, e.g. Perry Anderson and Robert Brenner.[5] Theorists of power, e.g. Anthony Giddens and Michael Mann, hold to the former view, as also do the theorists of rationality and cognitive transformations as the driving force of modernity, e.g. Max Weber and Ernest Gellner.[6] But all these six names would subscribe to what Gellner called the 'Big Ditch' view of a profound and decisive *rupture* created by the advent of modernity in the trajectory of specific societies and in the processes of world history itself. They would have many shared understandings of the relationship of modernity to tradition, which is really the principal terrain of investigation in this first chapter of Part II.[7]

This question of 'rupture' is fundamental for anyone wishing to situate herself in the modernity–tradition debate in India. There are three possible lines of argument. India, it can be claimed, is still basically a traditional society.[8] A second view is that India is a society in transition between tradition and modernity. A third view, to which I strongly subscribe, is that India has long been pursuing its own trajectory of modernity, different from that in the West but not understandable without reference to it. It is not that 'traditional' institutions, beliefs, values and practices do not exist but that they no longer can do so in the 'old' way, and that this itself constitutes a decisive change. Even in the long history of pre-modernity there is always change as well as continuity but ordinary people's 'lived experience' of both (of time and space) is so very different then from what happens after the impact of modernity. Now ordinary life becomes living in a whole new world and being a very different kind of person.

Modernity destroys tradition but also reworks and 'preserves' it, hence providing the objective basis for many intellectuals reflecting on modernity, to adopt a Nostalgia Paradigm. This paradigm is characterized by its sense of history as decline, a feeling that there is now a loss of wholeness and autonomy. These are, in fact, new feelings created by new times. But the essential point is that traditions recently invented and older ones reworked continue to *be important* in modernity itself, at least until late modernity, when the destructive and inventive dimensions of 'sustaining' traditions reach qualitatively higher levels than ever before. Traditions in the pre-modern sense are always linked to localism and local communities, which is why over any wide territorial expanse, e.g. pre-modern India, the existence of a traditional society is always the existence of traditional societies *in the plural.* In late modernity, this crucial local contextualism in which tradition thrives is undermined as never before by its principal characteristic – capitalist globalization![9]

India escapes none of the processes of modernity in its different phases. It simply experiences them in its own uneven and combined way. The idea of India still being basically a traditional society is simply an absurdity. The idea of it being in transition between tradition and modernity is not much better. India's encounter with modernity came via colonialism. It is only in the earliest phase of this encounter that it is legitimate to talk of a *truly indigenous* resistance. During this initial contact there is 'primary' resistance to protect recently affected lifeways. But once indigenous society is irrevocably changed, there can only be 'secondary' resistance – a resistance within the terms of modernity, even when it seeks to refute it.[10]

Those who rework tradition after this encounter with colonialism are themselves influenced by criteria brought to India by colonialism. The 'internal criteria' of Indian tradition never suffice for the necessary reworking. The reinterpretations–reworkings are carried out by members of the elite but popularized in ways never available or tried before and therefore large masses of ordinary people begin to develop new awarenesses of, and allegiances to, what are supposed to be their enduring traditions.[11] The first serious reworkings of tradition in response to modernity took place in a context (colonialism) marked by a sense of defeat. This meant that there was strong pressure on those carrying out this reinterpretation–reworking both to rationalize the colonial victory, and to find distinctive and relatively untouched sources of 'Indian superiority' in its traditions.

It is one thing to insist that India and other societies outside the advanced industrialized world have long since been 'condemned to modernity' and therefore to insist on finding modernist solutions to contemporary problems. It is another thing, however, to ignore the inadequacies and uglinesses that accompany this modernity. Here its *capitalist* character becomes a crucial source for explaining its evils, and understanding this helps us to better explore ways to overcome them. Neither pre-modernist indigenisms nor post-modernist meanderings offer much in this respect. They only serve to obscure and disarm. Since both the anti-modernist and the post-modernist see industrialism, science–rationality and the rise of the nation-state as the principal characteristics of modernity, capitalism itself is let off the hook. Following from this, socialism and Marxism are dismissed as having no relevance to their respective projects. For the post-modernist the issue isn't even the evils of modernity anymore. The way to counter the advocacy of these false trails cannot be a simple argument for the value of an unproblematic modernity. It has to be the defence of a *critical* and *modest* modernity in which a critical and modest Marxism assuredly has a place.

The second chapter in Part II explores those concepts which are the bread-and-butter terms of discourse on Hindutva (roughly translated as 'Hinduness') and communalism. These include terms like 'Indian civilization', 'Indian culture', 'Hinduism' and 'caste'. Even those who line up on opposite sides in their attitude to Hindutva or secularism often share similar understandings of these key concepts and of their inter-relationships. Consequently, all too often there are unwarranted concessions to votaries of Hindutva and to anti-secularists (those who oppose both Hindutva and 'Westernized' secularists).

I dispute the idea of a centuries-enduring Indian civilization and of some essentialist Indian culture beholden to Hinduism. I further dispute the view that Hinduism is a 'single, religious fabric' or 'comprehensible whole' even though it has undeniably been subject to a process of singularization in the last two hundred years which is currently gathering pace. Caste as a pan-Indian phenomenon is also relatively recent, so neither Hinduism nor caste can be said to constitute the essential elements of a putative Indian civilization and culture of long standing. Such essentialism is usually accompanied by an exaggeratedly benevolent rendering of Hinduism (its 'mystique of tolerance') and even of the caste system.

There is a brief deconstruction of the ideological structure of Hindutva discourse. The way the forces of Hindu communalism manipulate cultural, political, social and economic themes of various kinds to construct *practical* and *mobilizing* ideologies at different points of time for different purposes and for different audiences is always a highly flexible, mobile and complicated, indeed sometimes erratic, affair. I have confined myself to the much simpler task of portraying the relatively inflexible 'chain of reasoning' that makes up the intellectual construct of Hindutva that then informs and guides the more practical forms taken by ideological arguments and claims.

Unlike the crude construct of Hindutva, the arguments of the proponents of anti-secularism and anti-modernism are often highly sophisticated. The way their influence in elite public discourse, among NGO activists, in academia at home and abroad has grown is not a function of their organizational and political power as it is in the case of the forces of political Hindutva. It is much more directly a function of the persuasiveness of their ideas in a milieu marked by the decline of Marxist intellectual influence, the rise of post-modernist thinking and the current dilemmas of liberal modernism. I have devoted considerable

14

space to criticizing the views of the anti-secularists and of the strident anti-modernism of psychologist Ashis Nandy, who is undoubtedly the key figure in this respect. This section is the most directly polemical one in the book.

The anti-secularists are decidedly unhappy with even the liberal democracies, not because these systems are capitalist or insufficiently democratic but because their 'liberalism' enshrines a conscious separation of private meaning and public legitimacy. A primarily political language of legitimation has emerged in contrast to the pre-modern, supposedly more wholesome inseparability of the private and public orders of meaning. For the Indian anti-modernist taking his cue from Gandhi, the sources of evil in modern life rest not on social factors but in a view of the ultimate purpose and meaning of man. Modern civilization is said to be based on a false theory of man.[12] Ancient civilizations, where a religious culture was allowed proper sway, were soul-centred. They had a spiritualism at their core anchored by a notion of the transcendent and thus did not suffer from the debilitating dichotomies of mind–body/soul–body characteristic of modern man.

Gandhi's judgement of modernity was not historical or sociological but psychological–moral–philosophical, though he made no serious attempt to understand philosophy or psychology. This is where a relatively uncritical defender of Gandhi's thought (being uncritical actually reduces the complexity and stature of a figure like Gandhi) like Nandy can step into the breach. Furthermore, the growth of communalism (not in the first twenty years after Indian independence but later) is seen by the anti-secularists as evidence of the increasing divorce of the Indian political and social elite from the masses. This Westernized and secular elite speaks a different language from that of the authentic Indian found for the most part in the villages.

This is a truly surprising claim. Actually, Indian democracy in action has produced a form of democratic culture more imbued with an indigenism which can be appropriated by communal forces. Sudipta Kaviraj has perceptively observed that

> since the sixties, Indian politics has seen a massive alteration in style, language, modes of behaviour, reflecting far more the actual cultural understandings of rural Indian society rather than the Westernist cultivation of the elite which inherited power in the Nehru years.[13]

One can attribute the origins of communal politics not simply to tradition, nor simply to modernity, but to changing patterns within modernity.

The arguments of the anti-secularist and anti-modernists are both false and dangerous, not least because they legitimize the proposition that a 'religious community', which is insufficiently differentiated internally, is a vital, operative, bottom-line 'political unit'.[14] Further support for this view has now come (not altogether surprisingly) from another important source – some leading lights of the Subaltern Studies School or Group, notably Partha Chatterjee, its most important theorist now that the founding figure and original inspirer of the Subaltern Studies Group, Ranajit Guha, has withdrawn from active editorial involvement in the preparation of the volumes published under that name. Guha provided the original theoretical rationale for seeing Subaltern Studies as a distinct school within the wider field of Indian historiography, and for defining its purposes and ambitions. His *Elementary Aspects of Peasant Insurgency in Colonial India* was the first book-length study representing this new historiography.[15]

Partha Chatterjee's *Nationalist Thought and the Colonial World: A Derivative Discourse?* and *The Nation and Its Fragments: Colonial and Post-colonial Histories* were the major book-length studies that emerged from and expressed the *theoretical* trajectory taken by later Subaltern Studies. Chatterjee's 1994 article in the *Economic and Political Weekly*, 'Secularism and Tolerance', continued along the direction set by his last book.[16] It confirms how close he has now come to the indigenism of Nandy and to his programme for organizing religious tolerance but without quite accepting Nandy's anti-modernism. A common and unbalanced hostility on both their parts towards the nation-state, Enlightenment rationalism and liberal rights discourse lies behind this convergence.

Chatterjee's article is the closest that any self-avowed member of the Subaltern Studies School has come to a direct and sustained assault on the Enlightenment view of secularism. I have therefore devoted some space to evaluating it. Hitherto, any criticisms of secularism and India's secular state from members of the Group have been of an occasional and tangential nature. Even then the focus has been on the general problematicity of any liberal-humanist discourse (rather than on the specific infirmities of Indian secularism) and has therefore tended to endorse the validity of a post-modernist perspective in grappling with India's colonial and post-colonial histories. Dipesh Chakrabarty, and a more recent adherent to the Group, Gyan Prakash, have been the main figures pressing for such an orientation. Another contributor, Gyan Pandey, has also chipped in with a defence of the value of a history of fragments in opposition to all meta-narratives.

These five figures – Ranajit Guha, Partha Chatterjee, Dipesh Chakrabarty, Gyan Pandey and Gyan Prakash – have in the main assumed responsibility for theorizing the importance of a Subaltern Studies school of historiography. They have not put forward any commonly shared understandings of the key concepts and themes discussed in this chapter – civilization, culture, Hinduism, caste, Hindutva, secularism, modernity. Nor are they ever likely to. But given the direction that Chatterjee, Chakrabarty and Prakash in particular would like Subaltern Studies to take, one should not be surprised if in the future there is stronger convergence of post-modernist and anti-modernist motifs against the common enemy – Enlightenment-inspired notions of modernist possibilities and potentialities in India.

Given the current status of Subaltern Studies and the likelihood that its influence is likely to grow both in the West and in India, albeit unevenly (reception in India has been and will continue to be more restrained and critical), a historical sketch of the evolution of Subaltern Studies should prove salutory and informative. It would be a serious intellectual misfortune if the anti-historical critique of secularism and secularization in India by anti-modernist anti-secularists like Nandy and his supporters is now reinforced by an influential current claiming to ground itself in a superior grasp of Indian history itself, be it the 'fragmented' histories of various 'subalterns'. This is why my critique of Partha Chatterjee's views on secularism has been preceded by just such a sketch.

The last part of Chapter 4 takes up the task of clarifying the distinctions between religious fundamentalism, religious nationalism and communalism. Although the most dangerous forces of Hindu communalism (the rightwing reactionary formations of the RSS and its front organizations, and the BJP) explicitly espouse a Hindu nationalism, there are a range of Hindu nationalisms. Theirs is the most pernicious kind, posited as it is on hostility to the Muslim 'Other'. Moreover, the danger represented by this Hindu Right is not just cultural or directed only against Muslims or other religious minorities, but is political and directed against the majority of ordinary Hindus themselves.

By identifying themselves as Hindu nationalists, these forces of the Hindu communal Right clearly wish to disguise their wider and deeper danger. A major part of their overall project is a Hindu nationalism and there is no real problem in referring to it as such *provided* this larger danger of the Hindu communal Right is clearly recognized and the multiple sources for its resurgence properly analysed.

*

The two essays in Part III argue respectively about how not to perceive
the forces of Hindu communalism, and how better to situate it in the
overall context of economic, political and social changes in India. The
first chapter in Part III is probably the most iconoclastic as far as the
Indian Left goes.[17] Easily the dominant view within the Indian Left and
among Indian Marxists is that in the Hindu communal Right we are
witnessing the rise and growing danger of an Indian fascism. I do not
deny that the Hindu Right has certain fascist characteristics but otherwise I dissent from this general view. How one characterizes and
understands the enemy affects the long-term conduct of the struggle
against it. It all depends, obviously, on what one understands by fascism,
and this is by no means straightforwardly answered. Most sensible
Marxist and bourgeois approaches to trying to 'understand fascism'
involve serious investigation–reconstruction of the histories of 'actually
existing fascism'. To be thorough this investigation–reconstruction
would have to be comparative. And it would have to start with what is
universally accepted as the primary raw material – the histories of fascist
movements and regimes in inter-war Europe, the proper study of which
would in part entail delving into the pre-war and late nineteenth-century
histories of the countries and the continent in question. This approach
is not the special insight of 'dialectically inclined' Marxists but simple
common sense.[18]

But hereafter differences emerge. There is no simple positivism that
operates in such historical investigation–reconstruction. There is already
a framework of assumptions and biases – which, at least for those more
self-consciously aware of this and wanting to be internally consistent,
constitutes a coherent operating paradigm – that guides this research
and decisively shapes the final assessments. It matters a great deal
whether it is a Marxist or non-Marxist who is doing the historical
reconstructing, and if a Marxist, what kind of Marxist she is. Such prior
alignments shape the scope and method of historical research, the
directions of investigation, the weights assigned to different causal
factors, and the generalizations that emerge from such a study. Either
one is more self-conscious not only about the varied methodologies
concerning the historical study of fascism between Marxists and non-
Marxists but also about the differences among those calling themselves
Marxist, or one is not.

Greater self-consciousness on this score encourages sensitivity to the
value of another, secondary level of discussion about fascism. This looks
at the wider field of studies on fascism, seeks to grasp the guiding
frameworks behind different approaches, tries to understand why there

are different theories of fascism, why different thinkers–writers theorize the way they do (and why they think they are right), and, finally, whether or not it is possible amidst contending understandings to set up accepted standards of adjudication. Discussion of this sort leads to a greater awareness of the *difficulties* in *convincingly* theorizing a point of view or perspective on fascism, to a better *self-location* of one's own basic orientation on the issue, and to a greater degree of self-criticalness and modesty in presenting one's own argumentative claims. These are some of the reasons why I have engaged in such a discussion in this chapter.[19] But the most valuable purpose of such an exercise is that one becomes much more aware of the problem of *competing* 'fascist understandings' or 'fascist minimums' or 'fascist essences' or 'generalizations about the nature of fascism' and that one must have good reasons for choosing one's own alignments.[20]

Of course, most good studies of inter-war actually existing fascisms, whether of bourgeois or Marxist provenance, provide generalizations about the *essential* nature of the fascist beast. This can be called establishing the basic dynamic of fascism or the proper dialectic of the international and the national, or defining its key characteristics, or whatever. The point is that this is regularly done and in turn becomes a crucial guiding frame for investigating other possible fascisms in differ- ent times and places. But how do we adjudicate between different Marxist understandings of contemporary 'fascist threats'? The crucial reference point remains *historical* fascism and the subtlety and power with which this was analysed by outstanding Marxist thinkers and activists of the time – the classical Marxist tradition.

There are certain defining elements of that understanding. Fascism was not merely linked to the contradictory workings of capitalism in the imperialist era, and therefore is a recurring tendency or possibility as long as capitalism and imperialism exist, but was a highly *distinctive*, indeed extreme, form of resolution of not just any or many kinds of capitalist crises but of the most exceptionally acute form. The fascist state was not just a very authoritarian form of rightwing reactionary nationalism in power but a very special kind of authoritarian state representing the most *extreme form of political centralization* (the 'political expropriation of the ruling bourgeoisie') necessitated by the excep- tional severity of the crisis faced by capitalism in the country concerned. Hence both the *rarity* of fascist victory and the profound *qualitative* impact of even such a rare victory.

Fascism is not just the strongest form of national reaction but the strongest form of *international* reaction. That is what historical fascism

19

was and it is astonishing that third world Marxists subscribing to the notion of fascism in third world countries can so flippantly and casually ignore this. Fascism's victory and its years in power represented the consolidation of a most dramatic rightwing shift in the relationship of class forces not only nationally *but also internationally*. This could only be so because the terrain on which that victory took place – the national territories of Europe – included advanced *imperialist* countries. Hungary and Romania, where strong fascist movements existed in the inter-war period, might not qualify as imperialist countries but their movements were part of the penumbra of European fascism, whose umbra (Italy and Germany) was imperialist and thus gave the fascist threat its distinctive character. Victory for these movements in Hungary or Romania would have constituted regimes better characterized as semi-fascist or something similar, thus registering their different and lower order as compared to Italian and German fascism.

In my own text I have sought to emphasize the *qualitatively* different *global* impact in this respect of, say, a fascism victorious in the USA and a supposed clerico-fascism in Iran. The impact of a 'fascism' in a backward country is so enormously different from and weaker in depth, scale and consequences for human history than fascism in an advanced country that it makes no sense, indeed bad sense, to see them both as species of the same genus.[21] The classical Marxist tradition had a powerful sense of the great importance of this point, hence its recognition that fascism proper was a phenomenon of imperialist countries only.

The dominance of the Stalinist and Maoist tradition in India has been so strong that one should not be surprised that respect for the classical Marxist tradition generally is that much weaker. If the theory of Socialism in One Country (even a backward country) has not been repudiated, then why not also a Fascism in a Backward Country! At least some Indian and third world Marxists have sufficiently respected the power of the classical Marxist analysis of historical fascism to talk not of Indian fascism but of a semi-fascist or quasi-fascist, etc., danger. In my chapter I have queried even these usages. They are certainly preferable to talking of the danger of an 'Indian fascism' but if used should be used as only a rough descriptive label.

The key issue in all this has to do with the forms that fascism can take. Can we talk of fascism taking different forms? Obviously and certainly we can! Can we talk of fascism taking a great many different forms? This is much more problematic, indeed highly dubious. Can we talk of there being virtually no limit to the forms fascism can take? Since capitalism is universalizable is not fascism also, at least potentially, to all and any capitalist country? This is an absurdity. It is to so stretch the concept of fascism as to render it worthless. It is, in fact, to disregard the actual historical meaning and significance of fascism.[22] A theory that universalizes the possibility of fascism and believes itself to be Marxist constitutes a fundamental revisionism of the classical Marxist view. Such revisionism should not, in and of itself, be automatically judged wrong. But too many in and around the major Left parties in India who carry out this revisionism either do not believe or do not know that they are so engaged. Or if they do know, they are unconcerned about justifying it in relation to the classical view. This classical view does not rule out the temporal extension of the fascist danger beyond the inter-war period, tied as it is to the crisis-prone rhythm of world capitalist accumulation. But it does rule out its spatial extension to backward, dependent capitalist countries. I strongly endorse this circumspection.

I have also suggested that the use of the fascist paradigm to understand contemporary rightwing threats even in the advanced capitalist and imperialist countries is questionable. Some reasons have been given for this but here I am more open to changing my assessment if sufficiently convincing counter-arguments are given. I suspect, however, that whether arguing for its growing irrelevance or for its continuing relevance in understanding what is happening in imperialist countries there are *objective* reasons for this difficulty in exercising a decisive persuasive appeal either way.

The period of original fascism was the period of the most serious crisis ever, globally speaking, of modern capitalism. One is referring here to the crisis of its *internal* dynamic of capital accumulation not to such matters as its impact on the global ecological balance. As Eric Hobsbawm has forcefully reminded us, only if we recognize the unique depth of this crisis can we understand why this period saw the first successful proletarian revolution and the rise of powerful Communist movements and parties across the industrialized world *and* the emergence of fascism on such a scale.[23] Fascism represented not just the most polarizing counter-force to Communism – which had emerged as the antidote to capitalism, thereby lending its own impetus to this very crisis – but also the most serious danger ever to liberal-democratic capitalism and the most advanced values born of the great bourgeois revolutions and the Enlightenment. According to Hobsbawm, actually existing fascism was so much greater a danger than actually existing backward Communism in Russia to liberal-democratic advanced capitalism that

21

only a 'bizarre' alliance between liberal democracy and Communism could (barely) save the day.[24]

Clearly, the inter-war period suffered a very distinctive kind of structural crisis of capitalism, had very distinctive forms of conjunctural crises, giving rise to distinctive forms of barbarism and reaction, and calling forth distinctive forms of resolution of those crises. It is now common currency on the Marxist Left (and elsewhere) to point to a three-phase pattern of capitalist evolution in this century.[25] Indeed it is the structuring principle for making those kinds of political–ideological generalizations that Marxists are wont to make. But this particular pattern of Great Depression–Long Boom–Long Downturn was never *anticipated* by Marxists. More precisely, no Marxist ever anticipated or predicted the years of the Long Boom or the Golden Age. All analysis of this was in some way *post facto*.

This failure has some bearing on current discussions about the 'fascist danger'. It suggests the existence of serious problem areas in the Marxist analysis of capitalism–imperialism regardless of the fact that it is almost certainly superior to alternative analyses of the 'nature of the epoch' or of world capitalism. Many Marxists fared much better when it came to explaining why the Long Boom would not last and predicting its end. Thus there has been little dispute that since the early seventies world capitalism has entered a Long Downturn, whatever its shorter-term cycles of accumulation and growth, and that this Downturn lays the foundation for the likely rise of a new period of widespread political and ideological reaction.

Again, no Marxist ever anticipated or predicted the *speed* or *manner* of Communist collapse, caused above all not by external pressures but by internal failings of the Communist societies. The international capitalist context ensured that backward socialisms (if they did not extend to advanced countries) could only be 'holding operations' – but not when or how they would stop holding. Too much should not be made of such 'grand' predictive failures, which were, after all, no Marxist monopoly. But they do suggest at the mildest that there are some significant weaknesses in the Marxist understanding of the current phase of imperialism.

Without adequately grasping this new phase of imperialist downturn, simply to assert that there are new forms of fascism that correspond to this new phase of imperialist accumulation means little. Some will agree, some will not. Others, including myself, will suggest that the period of political reaction that we are now in has given rise (and will give rise) to new kinds of barbarism which, because they share some characteristics with old forms of barbarism (fascism), tempt some to consider them as fascisms. Even the concrete 'dialectic' of international–national elaboration which is supposed to explain why there exists a fascist danger in a given country presumes exactly that level of competence which Marxists should be highly cautious about claiming – that they have a sufficiently adequate grasp of the 'international context' and of the nature of current neo-imperialism.[26] Our Marxist predecessors in the inter-war period, by contrast, had a much surer and superior grasp of the nature of their period!

Of course, political struggle cannot 'wait' for sounder analysis of the nature of the enemy before commencing. It is not only in studying but also fighting it that one better understands the enemy. The last part of Chapter 5 addresses precisely this issue, in general, and specifically in relation to India. The question this section raises and seeks to answer is simple and directly programmatic. What difference does it make to strategic and tactical perspectives of struggle against the enemy whether we consider it fascist or not, and what should these perspectives be?

The last chapter in Part III is a survey of the contemporary political scene. It highlights four fundamental processes as marking out the general terrain on which the political battles now and in the immediate future will be fought. These four ongoing processes are: (1) the communalization of the Indian polity, for which the forces of political Hindutva bear the greatest responsibility; (2) a new Muslim ferment, which, while it does not constitute an aggressive political assertion, does constitute an ever clearer recognition by significant sections of Muslims that fighting the growing danger of Hindu communalism means putting their own house in better order (opposing the traditional clerical leadership and their own fundamentalists) as well as seeking secular political alliances and representation; (3) the continuing 'forward march' of the backward castes; (4) finally, the new Dalit ('Downtrodden' in preference to the usual term of 'untouchable') assertion.

Indian politics is in flux as never before. If the trajectory of the current global situation is so filled with uncertainty even ideologically (contrary to the teleologists of capitalist liberal democracy[27]), then how much more uncertain is India's? The bourgeois democratic character of the Indian polity is under strain as never before. However, doomsday analyses and fears should be put into proper perspective. The natural social and cultural heterogeneity of India, the very history of a working political democracy (whatever its multiple failings) and the rise of the intermediate and scheduled castes are powerful factors militating against the imposition of an iniquitous form of political uniformity.

India is still one of the few countries where mass Communist parties exist and where a far Left presence is not insignificant. Since the struggle against communalism in my view is also linked to the struggle for radical social transformation, it seems natural to devote some space to evaluating the current state of health and the future prospects of the likely agencies for such a transformative project. The agencies focused upon here are the two mainstream Communist parties, i.e. the Communist Party of India (Marxist) (CPM) and the Communist Party of India (CPI); with additional reflections on the far Left and on the Indian women's movement. Within the 'new social movements' the women's movement has self-consciously sought to address the problem of communalism.

This last chapter ends with its hopes for progress pinned on the institutionalization of a New Social Democracy. The time-scale for achieving socialism is now considerably extended as a result of a whole host of developments over the last decade. There is also the obvious necessity to rework in part the very vision of socialism itself. Thus the shorter term practical perspective that is being advocated here is not the politics of transition to socialism: it is the politics of the transition to that transition! Whether something like a New Social Democracy can emerge we will have to wait and see. But of course, the possibility of it emerging is directly connected to the struggle to bring it about. It would be an abrogation of our own moral and political responsibilities if we simply 'wait and see'.

Notes

1. J. Alam, 'Tradition in India Under Interpretive Stress: Interrogating its Claims', in the *Theses Eleven* issue on 'India and Modernity: Decentring Western Perspectives', No. 39, 1995. Alam argues that there is a shift in favour of High Islam in India. He does so on the basis of a much more solid grasp of Indian society and history than Gellner, but he would still avoid the larger pan-territorial generalizations of the latter. E. Gellner, *Postmodernism, Reason and Religion*, London, 1992.

2. P. Anderson, *A Zone of Engagement*, London, 1992, p. 201.

3. R. Williams, *Culture*, London, 1981, and *Resources of Hope*, London, 1989.

   There is another kind of essentialist claim different from cultural essentialism. Will religion always be essential for most or many people no matter how much success there is in the construction of the desired socialist future? This question is not broached in the chapter, but, given the now increasingly widespread view that religion will easily outlive

Marxism and even socialism, some observations may not be amiss. Even if the relationship of religion to culture and society in the course of modernity is accepted as historical and contingent, what about the *spiritual* dimension of human existence and religion's relationship to this?

To theorize the spiritual is even more difficult than to theorize the religious or the religious experience. But clearly the spiritual experience is not congruent with the religious experience, though it may take that form. A spiritual feeling is probably not capable of full description or theorization. It is experienced as an exceptionally heightened sense of self in relation to something, so heightened that in some key respect it is ineffable or indefinable. It is not for Marxists to deny the existence of the spiritual experience but to point out that its sources can be and are many, and that a positive and healthy modernity enhances the sources and the possibilities of the spiritual.

It can be experienced in a religious form, so a fully atheist Marxist Utopia is neither necessary nor desirable. But it also has other sources and forms – the sense of awe a scientist may have in the course of his explorations, the impact a piece of music may have, the intensity of an emotion experienced in a relationship of friendship or in love, the sense of wonder at nature's beauty. If there is no warrant for the Marxist to deny all value to religion and the religious experience, there is also no warrant for the immortalizer of religion to insist on a *privileged* relationship of the religious to the spiritual.

4. A more serious weakness, I believe, lies in the failure to deal with the implications of the 'mediaization of modern culture'. Production and diffusion of symbolic goods is much more institutionalized and extends over time and space as never before. All this is key to the creation of a *mass* culture. In late modernity is the mediaization of culture more important than the secularization of culture? See J.B. Thompson, *Ideology and Modern Culture*, Oxford, 1992.

5. The Anderson–Brenner riposte to neo-Weberian arguments about the separation of 'power accumulation' from 'capital accumulation' is a powerful one. In feudalism it is precisely the form taken by production relations that necessitates power accumulation in order to enhance capital accumulation. P. Anderson, *Lineages of the Absolutist State*, London, 1974; R. Brenner, 'The Social Basis of Economic Development', in J. Roemer (ed.), *Analytical Marxism*, Cambridge, 1986.

6. In the Indian context Gandhians and neo-Gandhians like the anti-modernist Ashis Nandy, Director, Centre for the Study of Developing Societies, New Delhi, hold a similar view of modernity as industrialism–rationalism abstracting from its capitalist character. The 'enemy' then is science, rationality, Western materialism. Mahatma Gandhi saw colonialism as flowing from Western materialism rather than from capitalism.

7. The answer to the question 'What is the duration of tradition?' can be variable. Also, what is supposed to represent the continuity of a tradition from pre-modernity to modernity depends on what is defined as essential to tradition and on who does the defining. Historically what was defined as tradition was decided by its custodians and thus inseparable from questions about the distribution of social and cultural power. In modernity the essentialism of tradition is also decided by the 'observer' of tradition. So modernity also has its traditions.

   Tradition is a special way of organizing time (and space). In pre-modern society the historical sense is less linear (it is not absent) and depends more on the organization of collective social memory. As Giddens points out, the 'authenticity' of tradition comes not from its accuracy in capturing the past – the most traditional societies are oral cultures which can never accurately capture a true past. Instead it comes from the fact that it is 'the very medium of the "reality" of the past'. It is this status of tradition that is disrupted. A. Giddens, U. Beck and S. Lash, *Reflexive Modernization*, Oxford, 1994, pp. 93–4.

8. This is a stand an anti-secularist/anti-modernist like Nandy would take. It is a stand shared by an eco-feminist indigenist like Vandana Shiva, Director, Research Foundation for Science, Technology, Ecology and Natural Resource Policy, Dehra Dun.

9. Giddens emphasizes the globalization not the capitalism. But he is right when he claims that this globalization runs directly counter to tradition, which 'controls space through its control of time'. Instead, globalization controls time through its control of space. A. Giddens, U. Beck and S. Lash, *Reflexive Modernization*, p. 96.

10. See R.G. Fox, 'Gandhian Socialism and Hindu Nationalism', in S. Bose (ed.), *South Asia and World Capitalism*, Delhi, 1990; and S. Sarkar, *'Popular' Movements and 'Middle Class' Leadership in Late Colonial India*, New Delhi, 1983.

11. See J. Alam, 'Tradition in India under Interpretive Stress', for a subtle analysis on this point.

12. See P. Chatterjee, *Nationalist Thought and the Colonial World: A Derivative Discourse?*, Delhi, 1986, Chap. 4. Chatterjee sees Gandhi as critiquing civil society rather than Western modernization. In fact, at a deeper level evident in Chatterjee's own analysis, Gandhi's critique rests on a theory of man himself.

13. S. Kaviraj, 'Religion, Politics and Modernity', in U. Baxi and B. Parekh (eds), *Crisis and Change in Contemporary India*, New Delhi, 1995, p. 313.

14. Even a critic of anti-secularists/anti-modernists like Akeel Bilgrami has conceded to this. A. Bilgrami, 'Two Concepts of Secularism: Reason, Modernity and Archimedean Ideal', in *Economic and Political Weekly*, 9 July 1994.

15. R. Guha, *Elementary Aspects of Peasant Insurgency in Colonial India*, Delhi, 1983.
16. P. Chatterjee, *Nationalist Thought and the Colonial World* (see note 12); *The Nation and its Fragments: Colonial and Post-colonial Histories*, Delhi, 1994; 'Secularism and Tolerance', in *Economic and Political Weekly*, 9 July 1994.
17. An earlier draft titled 'Situating the Threat of Hindu Nationalism: Problems With the Fascist Paradigm', in *Economic and Political Weekly*, 9 July 1994, preceded the writing of Chapter 4 of this book. This chapter further clarified my own thinking on the differences between religious nationalism and communalism. In the light of that subsequent discussion I have changed the title of Chapter 5 and made minor amendments to the text of the *EPW* article, frequently substituting the terms 'Hindu communalism' or 'Hindu communal right' for the term 'Hindu nationalism'.
18. Strangely, Aijaz Ahmad seems to think this is the preserve of the former. See his 'Structure and Ideology in Indian Fascism', in *Germinal*, Vol. 1, 1994, p. 34.
19. Ahmad fails to appreciate the value of this level of discussion. Ibid.
20. This effort reinforced my respect for the classical Marxist understanding of fascism which emerges from studies by major Marxist thinkers of the inter-war period, and the work by those Marxists coming later who chose fidelity to that tradition, such as the late Ernest Mandel. It is precisely this respect that makes me so sceptical of the value of, certainly, a spatial extension of the fascist paradigm to backward and dependent countries.
21. Would a 'fascism' in India really have a qualitatively weaker impact historically and globally than a fascism in a smaller Western European country? Of course it would! A serious fascist threat in one Western European country is conceivable only in the context of a wider and deeper scale of fascist threats and upsurges in Western Europe. A victory in one such country would have huge consequences in the rest of Western Europe and in the world precisely because of the much more integrated character of the Western European economies, of their 'national' class struggles, and of Europe's importance in the world economy and in determining the international relationship of class forces.
22. A striking example: 'Every country gets the fascism it deserves.' A. Ahmad, 'Structure and Ideology in Indian Fascism', p. 34.
23. E. Hobsbawm, *The Age of Extremes*, London, 1994.
24. Quite the weakest part of Hobsbawm's book (ibid.) is his inadequate treatment of Stalinism. The other side of his determination to emphasize the importance of this 'bizarre' alliance and of the historic role of Stalinist Russia in defeating fascism is the inadequate emphasis on

Stalinist culpability in enabling the rise of fascism to power in Germany and in Europe generally, at least up to the 1935 Comintern turn towards popular frontism. Nazism could have been defeated by a united left in Germany and in that process Germany might have become ripe for proletarian revolution. Even for Spain, Hobsbawm has not adequately addressed Stalin's reactionary and disarming role. That is why Trotsky was right to emphasize that the period of fascist possibilities was also necessarily and simultaneously the period of revolutionary possibilities.

25. So for Hobsbawm there was The Age of Catastrophe (1914–1945), The Golden Age (1945–1973) and The Landslide or Crisis Decades of 1973 and after.

26. Being sceptical of the contemporary existence of grave fascist threats, especially in backward countries, is one thing; having satisfactory alternative analyses about the nature of contemporary rightwing reaction is another. The difficulties in both respects are rooted in the common objective difficulties in understanding the contradictions and possibilities inherent in the period as a whole. I am far from fully satisfied with my own use of the term 'the politics of cultural exclusivism', even as a mere description of the nature of current political reaction.

27. F. Fukuyama, *The End of History and the Last Man*, London, 1992.

— 2 —

Reflections on Communalism and Nationalism in India

The spectre of growing communalism haunts India today. In the battle for the soul of Indian nationalism three positions have been staked out. First are those who insist that Indian nationalism must rest on cultural and psychological foundations of an impeccably Hindu provenance. Second are those who insist that Indian nationalism must derive from secular principles. Notwithstanding the problems of precise definition, the term 'secular' does possess an agreed meaning: state neutrality with regard to religion. In multi-religious India, this can mean either a fundamental separation of the state from religious activity and affiliation, or impartial state involvement on issues relating to the religious interests of different communities. In practice, 'Indian secularism' has been a mixture of the two: an unsatisfactory attempt to reconcile essentially incompatible approaches.

The third position has, to date, a narrower field of operation, confined mostly to academic rather than activist or popular debate. Nevertheless, it has been claiming an increasing number of adherents, especially among NGO activists, and its influence on the public debate is growing. It holds that because secularism is in origin a profoundly Western, or at least un-Indian, concept, it is at odds with the reality of non-Western/non-Christian existence in general, and with the Indian genius in particular. What is needed is not secularism, nor Hindu nationalism, but an anti-secularism which opposes factitious attempts at separating religion from politics/state and instead encourages the use of the 'authentic' resources of faith to sustain a socio-political culture with a deeper tolerance of diversity and pluralism than 'Western secularism' can ever generate.

Religion itself is the key resource in the struggle against communalism. State-centred theories of how to engineer the social good (the modern secular state) are themselves the problem, the stimulus behind communalism. To these must be counterposed the resources of a

29

religiously suffused and plural civil society. Indian anti-secularism can to some extent join forces with post-modernist celebrations of difference, diversity and pluralism, likewise located in civil society and threatened by the technocratic state.

These competing claims provide the context for the following reflections on communalism and nationalism. To fight communalism we must understand what it is and how it grows. To fight it in the name of a secular nationalism requires us to understand nationalism as well, to know what it does and does not share with communalism.

The Pattern of Modern Nationalism

There is a consensus that nationalism is a modern phenomenon attendant upon the emergence of capitalism, though its longevity has undoubtedly surprised those who thought the globalizing tendencies of late capitalism would render nationalism increasingly anachronistic. But what are 'nationalism', the 'nation', 'nationality'? Up to post-1945 decolonization nation formation and the emergence of nation-states has mostly taken place in four ways. There was first what Benedict Anderson has called creole or settler nationalism of the New World, where language was not the *differentia specifica* of nationhood and nation-state formation.[1]

Then came the linguistic-based territorial nationalisms of Western and Eastern Europe, where national yearnings were related to the dissolution of the Habsburg, Ottoman and Tsarist multinational empires. In this century came the tide of anti-colonial nationalisms, whose boundaries of resistance coincided in almost all cases with the seemingly artificial border demarcations of colonial administrative convenience. In these 'new' nations, nation-state formation was more clearly connected to the existence of self-conscious national movements intent on expressing a distinct national culture and history which could not always, or often, be congruent with the spread of some single indigenous language or ethnic group.

More recently, we have seen not only the resurgence of the supposedly resolved 'older' nationalisms but also the emergence of post-colonial nationalisms whose *raisons d'être* are new and cannot be ascribed to the distorting legacies of colonial rule. Such is particularly the case with South Asia – Bangladesh, the national movements in Pakistan, Tamil nationalism in Sri Lanka, and the secessionist struggles in India's northeast, Punjab and Kashmir.

There is an important lesson here: there is no single feature or identifiable factor common to all nationalisms, to all nations, to all nation-state formations. Though many cultural characteristics occur in different nationalisms, they never combine in any immutable package of 'national markers'. Furthermore, no single characteristic is ever indispensable. Nations (and nationalisms) are *not* intrinsically secular categories. They can rest on exclusivist racial, tribal or religious claims. Indeed, in India religious groups have been among the strongest candidates for nationhood – as testified to by secessionist struggles in Kashmir and Punjab and in the fact of Partition itself.

The early stirrings of Indian nationalism (whether as political movement, national identity or national ideology) owed much to the 'Hindu Renaissance' of the nineteenth century. Hindu nationalism was important in promoting a national identity, though it was not the only factor and was contested by wider-ranging interpretations of Indian culture and history. There is always a cultural struggle involved in the creation of a nation or nationality, which is best understood either as Anderson has defined it – an imagined political community – or better still as Kohn understood it: as a cultural entity, lodged above all in consciousness, striving to become a political fact.[2]

This cultural struggle is sharper for the 'new' nations where nation-formation is more directly tied to a national movement intent on fostering a national identity based on indigenous cultural roots. It is this latter capacity that has given nationalism the edge over socialism, largely explaining why successful socialist revolutions have taken root by way of a nationalism either anti-colonial or anti-imperialist in thrust (Japanese imperialism in the case of China, American imperialism in the case of Cuba and Nicaragua).

The purpose of this brief excursus into the nature of the newer nationalisms in general and into Indian nationalism in particular is to establish on *prima facie* grounds the plausibility of the following proposition: the period when an anti-colonial national identity was being forged was also the period when the Indian polity was being communalized, and the Congress-led National Movement cannot escape most of the responsibility for this. This conclusion stands opposed to those currents of Indian historiography that insist on the essentially anti-communal character of the Indian National Movement.

Here Gandhi's role comes into dispute. How central was his use of religious idiom and his personal 'saintliness' to generating a mass following for the Congress? Was his religiosity peripheral or central to the forming of a winning political strategy for independence – a

Gramscian 'war of movement' hinging on an escalating series of compromises? Was it the source of a mere communal tinge? Or did he speak the 'language of the masses' with a force that no one else could approximate?

Gandhi did not so much speak the language of the masses as speak *in* the language of the masses. The distinction is fundamental. Gandhi helped to create an important 'Congress link' between local-level grievances and the pan-Indian struggle against a centralized colonial state. But it was a link over which he did not exercise much control. Historians of the subaltern have pointed out the frequent discrepancies between what Gandhi espoused and the way his exhortations or directives were interpreted to fit popular perceptions of the meaning of their struggles.[3] Since the socially oppressed of India are no more naturally prone to permanent non-violence towards, and class conciliationism with, their social oppressors than the socially oppressed elsewhere, Gandhian principles of *ahimsa* (non-violence) and 'trusteeship' (class paternalism) were in part forged precisely to serve as control mechanisms.

The link also provided for a two-way interpenetration of identities. Most historical work has stressed the seeping downwards of a 'national identity' so that obscure villages and unknown villagers could come to identify themselves with the National Movement as Indians as well as retaining their more spatially restricted identities. Sandra Freitag has been one of the few who have emphasized the opposite process: how local-level identities generalized and spread upwards to influence even the character of the National Movement.[4]

In the north, contrasted to the west and south (where linguistic and anti-Brahmin caste identities were rather more important), the dominant community identity was often religious in character. Here the development and expansion of a common religious identity was not the passive product of colonial machinations but was imbricated in local cultural and political practices, themselves undergoing change in a dynamic socio-economic and political context. Even before Gandhi, Congress efforts to widen its local support base meant building on existing cultural cleavages and perceptions consolidating religious identities. That the Congress-led National Movement did have an important secular dimension tied to leadership aspirations is not in dispute. But the growing weight of historical evidence would strongly suggest that any easy separation of nationalism and communalism during the colonial period is frankly untenable.

Communalism

If the characterization of nationalism as a modern phenomenon is unproblematic, the same cannot be said of communalism. Nevertheless it is best understood in this way and thus as qualitatively different from the politico-religious tensions and conflicts of pre-modern/pre-capitalist/pre-colonial times. The idea that the separation of the political and religious is a viable proposition had to await the emergence of generalized market relations (generalized commodity production) which enabled a decisive separation of the political and economic spheres of existence making possible an autonomous civil society.

That political life and whole areas of social existence become relatively autonomous of each other marks a decisive transition, providing the foundation for the *relative* decline and compartmentalization of metaphysical and religious thought. The private world of 'meaning' and the public arena of 'legitimacy' were substantially separated. Secularism is itself a modern ideology promoting the notion that the separation of the political and religious is a positive ideal.

It is because of this pre-established point of reference – the secular ideal – that communalism has a distinctly negative connotation, itself testimony to its more modern character. Communalism may not be straightforwardly counterposed to nationalism, but it is more easily contrasted with secularism. There is another more important reason for emphasizing the modernity of communalism. In the era of modern mass politics, religious politics has a strength qualitatively greater and more dangerous than its equivalent in the pre-modern era. The distinguishing characteristic of modern politics is the decisive significance of mass mobilization, mass appeal and popular legitimization of elite rule.

This is not something found only in the democracies. It is crucial for authoritarian and quasi-democratic regimes as well. Here the capacities for mass mobilization are weaker and the relationship between popular sanction and elite governance less direct. But even dictatorships must pay attention as never before to moulding and influencing popular perceptions. Centralized control over key networks of communication is the *sine qua non* for political monolithism. Ruling classes, whether by coercion and/or persuasion, justify their dominance in the name of maintaining or extending 'national popular interest'. This stands in contrast to the legitimations sought by the absolutisms and monarchisms of the past. The politics of communal appeal today

33

are in an altogether different register from the politics of religious appeal in the past.

Having affirmed communalism's modernity, what then of its meaning? The term 'communalism' was first used by British colonialists to describe colonies like India and Malaysia, where substantial religious minorities existed alongside a religious majority. The colonial use of the term gave it a negative connotation of bigotry, divisiveness and parochialism, thus helping to justify its civilizing mission. It was also a way of understanding Indian history as colonialists saw and lived it, apparently corresponding to its pattern of expansion – defeat of the Mughal Empire, of Hindu princely kingdoms, of Ranjit Singh's Sikh empire.

Indian nationalists adopted the term, accepted its negative significations, but saw it as a colonial, post-British phenomenon not a pre-colonial circumstance that the British inherited. Since, contrary to earlier hopes, communalism did not fade out after Partition and independence, searching for a deeper understanding of it has assumed new urgency. The most sustained theoretical discussion on this issue has been within the Indian Left. The most influential argument has maintained that communalism is essentially an ideology. The variant meanings or complex layers of this cluster concept have been left aside in favour of an unproblematic understanding of ideology as sets of beliefs which in this case *falsely* represent the interests of a social group.[5] Here religion as such, even religious ideology, has little or nothing to do with communalism. Communal politics is the politics of religious identity; but beyond marking out the social category in question, it has little to do with the phenomenon of communalism. Such an understanding is modular and can characterize other forms of communitarian 'false consciousness', such as casteism or regionalism.

Communalism becomes a species of manipulation. This approach endorses an instrumentalist understanding of the relationship between religion and communalism and advocates the propagation of a counter-ideology of anti-communalism not just as one dimension of struggle but as the *central* terrain of combat. But if communalism is an ideology and a modern one at that, then what of its structural anchors in modern capitalist society? To what extent can the struggle against communal ideology be divorced from the struggle against its social underpinnings, whether classes, castes or institutions?

How important is it to deal successfully with the alienations associated with capitalist modernity, which foster collective identity crises that in turn promote identity politics based on essentialist notions of culture and biology? Can all this be perfunctorily acknowledged but brushed under the carpet while one prepares for a decisive ideological onslaught on communalism? Are one's *strategic* allies to be found among all those political formations which, whatever their communal practice, avoid programmatic endorsement of communalism?

Another approach that sharply criticizes the view that communalism is above all else an ideology situates communalism (in ideology and practice) as an aspect of ruling-class politics.[6] The merits of this description are two-fold. It insists on the deep connections between class and power relations and the phenomenon of communalism, and following from this it stresses the indissoluble linkages between the struggle against communalism and the wider struggle against the prevailing social order and for socialism. However, this approach also has weaknesses. For one thing it is an overly political understanding leaving little space for grappling with the more 'non-political' sources and directions of communalism. For another it is strongly biased towards a functionalist explanation of the relationship between the reproduction of social power and the reproduction of communal relations in India, and thus suffers from all the usual problems of functionalist argument.

I would venture another approach.[7] But first there must be some prior exploration of the meaning of secularism and secularization. There is no single, universally accepted definition.[8] Though secularization usually implies some attack on religious power or reach, the acceptable degree and scope of this 'assault' is disputed. One view is of coexistence between the domains of the secular and sacred – the state and the 'public' falling within the ambit of the former, and the 'private' within the latter. This is, in effect, a rationalization of the history of secularization of the state, and much of civil society, in post-feudal Western Europe. Here the consolidating processes of capitalist modernization, bourgeois democratization, nationalism and reform Christianity moved more or less in the same direction, despite substantial regional variation in the way these processes combined.

Another view of secularism and secularization has stressed, in the name of a universalist humanism, the need to centre existence on humanity and human autonomy, and therefore to reject comprehensively the sacred, mythological and metaphysical world-views associated with religion. Secularization here means a many-sided process involving the progressive decline of religious influence in the economic, political and social life of human beings, and even over their private habits and motivations. A Marxist view of secularism, while not coterminous with this tradition, sits firmly within it. But whatever one's understanding of secularism, for the secularist, communalism must imply some degree of de-secularization.

Communalism in a religiously plural society is a highly complex phenomenon which it is risky to try to encapsulate in a single definition. But it is among other things a process involving competitive de-secularization (a competitive striving to extend the reach and power of religions), which – along with non-religious factors – helps to harden the divisions and create or increase tensions between different religious communities. Here greater importance is granted to religious forces, religious identity, religious competition, religious ideologies and to religious imbrication in popular, folk and elite cultures. The development of a strong collective religious identity among Hindus, Sikhs, Muslims and Christians is a necessary though not a sufficient condition for the growth of communalism. Non-religious factors are not excluded as important causal factors, but are often misperceived in religious terms. A comprehensive examination of both the religious and secular in Indian society is required if we are to properly comprehend communalism.

Communal Politics

Focusing on the specific problem of communal politics, we are immediately confronted with two broad questions. First, what lies behind the communal appeal? Though the identity crisis of an urban middle class undergoing modernization and partial Westernization has made them receptive to such appeals, the origin of such appeals has usually been elitist and their purposes secular. There is considerable authority in the instrumentalist argument that religion, whether in the form of faith or ideology, has little to do with the formation of such appeals – beyond the obvious point that some of its symbols, myths and devotional themes are selectively misappropriated.

Here a 'materialist' analysis of the sources of communalism would reveal the role of the colonial state in deliberately exacerbating the communal divide. Competition for jobs created tensions between Hindu and Muslim urban middle classes and elites. In post-independence India, attention would no doubt be focused on the socio-economic changes that have taken place in many northern Indian towns possessing a sizeable Muslim population as a result of Gulf remittances, the growing export demand for handicrafts and artisanal products, and other expressions of uneven development that have clearly disturbed traditional patterns of dependence between Hindu traders and Muslim artisans. Similarly, Green Revolution effects in Punjab are not without communal resonance for the Sikh kulak and Hindu trader. Then again, there is the upward economic and political mobility of the agrarian bourgeoisie, of the upper echelons of the intermediate castes having its social and emotional reflection in a greater striving towards association with a broader Hindu identity. There is nothing wrong with such explanations, but, though important, they are only part of the story.

There is also a second question: why the success of the communal appeal? Here it becomes impossible to maintain any artificial separation between 'true' or 'folk' religion on the one hand and communalism on the other. For what unites 'folk' and 'elite' religion, its 'authentic' and 'inauthentic' forms, is something intrinsic to the nature of all the main world religions – Judaism, Islam, Christianity, Buddhism and Hinduism. We are here on the socio-psychological terrain of identity, of the relationship (never static) between religious belief and the socio-psychic need to affix one's senses of self, or more correctly one's senses of selves.

Among the many functions of religion and religious belief, this is now arguably the crucial one, and is common to all believers from whatever social strata. While the claims of a religious philosophy or ethics can be universalist, this function of identity fixation/affirmation must *always* be particularist. A believer is Hindu or sub-Hindu, Christian or sub-Christian, Islamic or sub-Islamic, and so on, even if this particularist identity can itself be an expansive one. The communal appeal thus derives much of its formidable character not just from the resources of power accumulated by the one making the appeal, but also from the importance of religious identity in the psychic health of the receiver. This is not to invest it with incontestable powers.

The importance of religious identity is historically and socially variable. Where substantial secularization of state and civil society has taken place, religious identity in social – and psychic – life is less important, and the communal appeal correspondingly less attractive. Since the formation and expansion of religious identity 'from below' takes place largely in civil society; secular emphasis concerning state and civil society needs to be inverted.

Outside of the advanced West, in much of West, South and Southeast Asia there have been far more complex patterns of development in the relationship between modernization/secularization and de-secularization. Even in those social formations dominated by the capitalist mode of production, no single pattern of evolution explains the overall process

of secularization of different social formations. Particular social formations possess specific combinations of the secular and non-secular
emerging from their specific histories.

In the later modernizing societies of the post-colonial countries,
where the state played a more important role in carrying out a forced
industrialization, there is all the more reason to expect sharper dispari-
ties between the modernizing–secularizing pretensions of the state and
the slower-changing realities of civil societies. In Iran under the Shah,
efforts to secularize the state and its laws, while not without merit or
effect, did not so much reduce overall religious influence as *displace* it
onto civil society, in certain respects reinforcing its power there. It
remained a latent force fully capable of resurfacing and encroaching on
the state domain, as the post-Shah Iranian experience shows. Post-
Communist Poland is perhaps another more qualified example.[9] In
Turkey, the Kemalite revolution resulted in significant displacement of
religious influence and not just overall decline.

In India, a non-denominational state with substantially secularized
laws, resting on a secular Constitution, coexists with a civil society where
religious influence is pervasive. It is a situation that gives rise to a
profound tension. Even the flawed secularity of the Indian state makes
it a crucial bulwark against the growing tide of communalism. Its
secularity must be strengthened. But the crucial challenge lies elsewhere, in civil society itself. In this respect one is struck by the contrast
between the USA and the UK. The USA's secular Constitution (with its
'wall of separation' between religion and the state) compares favourably
with the theocratic trappings of the British state. But British civil society
(with the exception of Northern Ireland) bears no comparison to
America, where church membership is growing and church influence
on government/community/social life is far more pervasive and
powerful.[10]

Even in Western secular societies, there is considerable variation in
the extent to which different states and civil societies are secularized. If
in Protestant Western Europe church membership is declining overall
(though religion retains its importance for the life-cycle rituals marking
birth, the transition to puberty, adolescence, adulthood, marriage/
procreation and death), in the USA, Ireland and Eastern Europe it is
probably increasing. The possibilities of further secularization would
seem to be intimately tied to the fate and future of civil society.

The progressive decline of religious influence in this realm (as in
much of Western Europe) does not signify its progressive abandonment
in personal and family life. In that respect the expectations of many

mainstream sociologists in the fifties have not been borne out. But insofar as religious identity occupies a decreasingly significant role in everyday life, in those collective endeavours that form such a large part of people's economic, political and social routine, the politics of religious identity loses much of its purchase. Where this is not the case, secular gains could over a longer time-span prove more ephemeral. The relationship of secularization–desecularization, of state and civil society, and what it implies for a practical programme of struggle against communalism in India, is something we will return to after a brief look at Hindu nationalism and the anti-secularism that would take its distance from it.

The Hindu Nationalist and the Anti-Secularist

The Hindu nationalist both misunderstands and understands the nature of nationalism. She is wrong to see nationalism as a natural entity. Since the nation is a 'collective state of mind striving to become a political fact', it possesses an inherent fluidity which makes it capable of dying out, metamorphosing, standing on a variety of cultural foundations. The historical debate on the nature of Indian culture – whether it is essentially Hindu, whether it is possible to establish the essentially Hindu, whether it is religiously composite – both stands apart from Indian nationalism and is importantly connected to it.

It is connected because a sense of national identity is partly constructed from competing interpretations of the raw materials of history. It stands apart because Indian nationalism is not 'logically' constructed out of some notion of 'accurate' history. Indian nationalism is *not* naturally Hindu nationalism; nor, incidentally, is it naturally a composite or secular nationalism. It may be *desirable* to rest it on composite cultural foundations which also have their own traditions, but that is something else.

Secular nationalism derives its legitimacy not from History or the past but from its promise, not from origins but from its desirable effects. A social order which is to be progressively humanist and democratic *cannot* simultaneously be Hindu nationalist or communally founded. This is sufficient to define the legitimacy of secularism. Indian nationalism's cultural–emotional content must be fought for.

Here the Hindu communalist understands full well his task. To make the case for his extreme form of Hindu nationalism persuasive, individuals and groups have launched a cultural, ideological, social and political onslaught, primarily from their positions in civil society. Part of this onslaught involves recourse to a systematic distortion of history, to the dogmatization and territorialization of Hinduism – centring Hinduism on specific texts, gods and goddesses, places of worship, myths, symbols, and so forth, that are to made pre-eminent and widely acknowledged as such. To the extent that this is possible it serves psychologically to 'unify' the diverse Hindu community in a way which the Hindu communalist hopes will substantially diminish the relevance of other identities like class, gender and caste. These identities can form the basis for mobilization around demands which erode this unity and promote organization across religious divides. This is a Hindu communalist perspective and effort whose prospects for success are crucially premissed on the psychic and social power of religious identity.

Is the anti-secularist better able than the 'Westernized' secularist to meet the challenge of communalism in general and of extreme Hindu nationalism in particular? The anti-secularist certainly thinks so. Her attack on secularist positions is philosophical and political. Philosophically, the anti-secularist is often a cultural relativist who will not usually hesitate to launch a broadside against the 'conceptual colonialism' of Enlightenment and Rationalist thinking, with its universalist notions of Progress, Reason, Science (and Secularism).

Some of the criticism has substance. The arguments are by now well rehearsed and did not originate with the anti-secularists. The problem of 'cultural translatability', for example, is a very real one. For a society that knows no linguistic, cultural or conceptual equivalent to the notion of secularism, how is such an idea to become meaningful beyond the circle of a narrow, Westernized elite without imposition – which, understandably and legitimately, would evoke popular resistance?[11]

However, it is one thing to raise the question: 'How can one judge societies and cultures from outside their own terms of reference, norms and meaning?' It is another to replace this serious if plaintive query with the close-minded, aggressive reprobation: 'How dare one judge cultures from the "outside"?', as the Indian secularist is presumably wont to do. Such extremism allows no space for willed and purposeful societal change, brought about in part by universal capacities to judge, discard and select from a range of human practices, beliefs and values – which becomes broader as more cultures meet, cross-fertilize and even clash.[12]

Each history and culture provides meaning to a notion of change by way of a common horizon of reference involving a notion of 'progress' with a small 'p'. And surely histories now flow into and diverge from History! We no longer live in a time of parallel, isolated histories, and there is much to be gained, for example, from the universalization of ideas and practices associated with the goals of mass political democracy, gender and racial equality. Where cultures, in the name of their distinctive traditions, oppose such processes, they are likely to lose out in the long run, not due to alien imposition but because each society possesses a critical self-awareness. People do *learn* from their own history and, when it becomes possible, from the cultural, historical Other.

Should secularization be considered a desirable universal? The anti-secularist says No! She would eschew the extravagant quest for under-standing and appreciation across religious divides and settle more modestly for the 'mutual tolerance' that emerges out of the 'lived relations' between different religious communities.[13] But does this answer anything? How is the communal challenge to be met? By counterposing to it a 'positive' anti-secularism? As a tactical perspective, the use of faith as the main resource against communalism might seem appropriate and necessary in the Indian context. But as a strategy it is disastrous.

The anti-secularist, like many a secularist, insists on retaining an instrumentalist view of the relationship between religion and commun-alism. She must separate religion into its tainted and untainted parts, using the latter against the former: i.e. the *ethical resources* of religion constitute the most important armoury of weapons for resistance to communalism. It is the 'good' politics of religious appeal versus the 'bad' politics of religious appeal, and isn't the Mahatma an exemplar of the effectiveness of this strategy?

As well as over-valuing Gandhi's effectiveness and ignoring the issue of how to 'institutionalize' anti-communalism, this is a fatal strategy. It argues and fights on the terrain of the Hindu communalist. The communal appeal will prove stronger for reasons that go to the heart of the function and purpose of religious faith. Humans do not believe because above all else they wish to be good but because above all else they wish to find a home in the world and cosmos. No doubt because religion is a world-view providing more than ontological solace (a moral ethic, an epistemology), its ontological function by association becomes even more powerful. Religious morality gives power to religious identi-fication, but it is the latter which is primary. Communal politics tries to link itself explicitly to the deepest psychic needs of identity enhance-ment and securement, besides which questions of religiously sanctioned good or bad behaviour cannot have the same power and appeal. The anti-secularist, by refusing to outlaw the 'politics of religious identity' as a strategic goal, helps to extend and consolidate its legitimacy.

41

Both the communalist and the anti-secularist are moved to take their respective approaches partly because of a shared exaggeration of the power and importance of religion. A world completely without religious faith may be inconceivable, contrary to certain versions of Utopia. But even at its strongest point – the issue of identity – religion has retreated. To venture a global generalization subject to spatial and social variation, the most important contemporary form of a 'social we', is not religion, caste, ethnicity, gender or any 'primordial' identity. Nor is it class. It is nation and nationality. The most powerful is not the same as the most enduring. Like all historically constituted identities, it is subject to transcendence, decline and death.

But germane from our point of view is the question: why is the power of nationalism so great? Numerous forms of transnational identification and mobilization – class, gender or sisterhood, racial or black solidarity, Third Worldism, the pan-religious loyalties of an earlier era – have all suffered ignominious defeat when they have sought to confront nationalism head on. We have yet to develop an enduring and widespread internationalist sentiment or sense of belonging that goes beyond the emotions of charitable concern and vague fellow feeling.

The Hindu 'revivalist', it should be noted, cannot dare to challenge nationalism in the name of a higher or stronger allegiance to a wider pan-Asian Hinduism. The references to an ancient geography of Hinduism stretching from the Middle East to the Southeast Asian archipelago can focus emotions on the 'Muslim Betrayal' via Partition (the 'rape of Mother India') and on the expansive 'grandeur' of Hinduism's past. But, basically, it is ammunition to help culturally redefine the foundations of the Indian Union. The Hindu 'revivalist' does not confront nationalism in the name of a *greater* religious loyalty but seeks to co-opt it.

This exceptional character of nationalism surely lies in its unique combination of politics and culture, of civic power (e.g. the importance of citizenship) and identity. The nation-state for the first time invests ordinary people (through the principle of equal citizenship rights) with an authority and importance that is historically unique. To date the zenith of popular individual empowerment is political citizenship, whose frame of operation is the nation-state or multinational state.[14] Does this contain a clue as to how we can more effectively tackle communalism in India today? Of how the struggle for socialism and secularism are to be linked? I think it does. But first a brief survey of the rise of Hindu communalism and its relation to the democratic process since independence.

The Political Rise of Hindu Communalism

For the first two decades after independence the considerable success of India in institutionalizing democratic rule and in carrying out a degree of welfarist industrialization enabled the Congress to survive as the dominant political institution. Indeed, the Congress and its leadership oversaw this period of successful transition to a relatively stable democracy. A variety of factors were responsible for the subsequent emergence of the peculiar paradox of India's polity – endemic political instability encased within a framework of remarkable democratic durability. A democratic political system had been institutionalized with strong mass commitment to its preservation. But there was the partial decay and mutation of a variety of democratic institutions such as the legislature, civilian bureaucracy, judiciary and press.

Above all, the principal overseer of political stability, the Congress had entered a period of slow but steady decline. For decades a Congress alliance with rural landed elites had assured it decisive control over the countryside while it also carried a populist appeal among the poorest sections. Given the enormously segmented character of Indian society – no other country in the world is criss-crossed by such a range of community affiliations and identities – the Congress was the centrist formation par excellence, the one party appealing to the widest cross-section. To be stable, Indian political democracy could not rest on some unachievable two-party competitive system, but seemed to require the constant popularity of a dominant centrist formation.

Challenges from above and below undermined Congress dominance. Historically, the electoral base of the Congress were the Brahmins and forward castes, along with the 'core minorities' of Muslims, Dalits (untouchables) and tribals. The very success of Indian development in the first two decades transformed the situation. New rural elites from the middle or backward castes, as they were also called, emerged and pressed for their aims both within and outside the Congress party. At the same time growing expectations made the support of large sections of the core minorities for the Congress increasingly volatile. The Congress itself had also transmogrified. In the first two decades after 1947 the Congress had moved from being a mass movement and organization to being an increasingly corrupted party of governance and patronage. Organizationally, it had become an electoral machine to be cranked up around the time of various local, regional and national elections.

43

The crisis of Congress hegemony became obvious and therefore the inauguration of the era of endemic political instability took place in the late 1960s, when for the first time in its post-independence history the Congress party split, with Mrs Gandhi's wing proving triumphant. Ever since, the basic dilemma has remained. On the one hand there is the historical and historic decline of the Congress in that its status as the centrist focal point of Indian politics cannot be taken as assured. On the other hand there has been the consistent inability of any other political formation to replace it as a dominant and stable point of reference.

The Emergency is best understood as Mrs Gandhi's failed attempt to resolve this endemic crisis through an authoritarian transformation of the polity. But this failure has only meant that one is clearer on how not to tackle the problem of instability. Six of the seven general elections since 1971 have been referendum-like in character. In the absence of any clear and convincing ideological perspective from any side the electorate has been presented with issue-based differentiation between the main claimants to power. This has only recently begun to change with the rise of the strongly ideological BJP, and the RSS behind it. The 1996 elections were not like a referendum.

In those six elections either the Congress or a centrist alternative – usually a patchwork formation united by anti-Congressism rather than by any positive principle – came to power. The Congress lost twice but the alternative to it did not last a full term. Congress victories by massive seat majorities in the first-past-the-post system in 1971 and 1984 (when Mrs Gandhi was assassinated) were themselves, ironically enough, indicative of the growing volatility of voter support, which could swing massively from one referendum-like election to the other. In 1990 the Congress for the first time in its history came to power as a minority government. A specifically parliamentary instability had been added to the general problem of endemic political instability, until the Rao government engineered the necessary defections. This new pattern of parliamentary instability was reaffirmed in the 1996 elections, in which the Congress was ousted but its replacement – a United Front government of non-Congress, non-BJP parties – could only rule with outside Congress support.

By the late 1970s and early 1980s the Nehruvian Consensus itself had come to be increasingly regarded as a failed project. But its basic principles were not yet questioned. That would come with the rise of political Hindutva, whose principal components were, first, the steady expansion of RSS influence in civil society through the extension of *shakas* (neighbourhood chapters where cadres are recruited and given

44

physical training and a politico-religious catechism) and, second, the political rise of the BJP and its forerunner, the Jan Sangh.

It was the Emergency and the mass-scale anti-corruption movement that preceded and partly provoked it that gave these forces an unexpected lease of life. The cadres of the RSS found a cause – opposing corruption and then the Emergency – that gave it mobilizing experience and public legitimacy on a much greater scale. The Jan Sangh, hitherto a fringe rightwing party, by becoming a part of the political coalition called the Janata Party which overthrew Mrs Gandhi and the Emergency regime in the 1977 elections, secured more seats for its chosen candidates standing under the common Janata banner (over 90 in a Lower House of around 540) than it had achieved in all previous elections put together. It also secured practical political power for a time, using this to place adherents and sympathizers in various positions in the bureaucracy.

The Janata Party was to break up over the unwillingness of the Jan Sangh to sever its links with the RSS, an extra-parliamentary organization with no commitment to the Janata Party as such. This led to the formation of the breakaway party, the Janata (Secular), in mid-1979. In the 1980 elections, won by Mrs Gandhi's Congress, the Janata (S) got 41 seats. The Jan Sangh remained part of the rump Janata Party, which got 31 seats. Out of these the Jan Sangh got 16, fewer than the 93 it won in 1977 but closer to the 22 it got in 1971. Between 1980 and the next general elections in 1984 the dilemma facing the Jan Sangh (which had reconstituted itself as an independent party) was the classic one. Given the sectional and segmented character of Indian society, how could any non-centrist party hope to win, or even fare well electorally? Should the BJP weaken or strengthen its links with the RSS, whose agenda could not be the same as that of a political party, even one with a commitment to Hindutva? The RSS would support even the Congress (as it has done on occasions) if it felt that this would promote the advancement of Hindu cultural nationalism of the kind it desires in civil society. Should the Jan Sangh try to be the party of the 'Great Hindu Rally/*Rassemblement*', or should it try to be the Hindu equivalent of a rightwing Christian Democratic party of Western Europe – only more Hindu than Christian Democracy is Christian, and less democratic? Should the Jan Sangh move towards the centre of the Indian political spectrum, thereby diluting its Hindu nationalist and communalist message? Or should it swing towards a more aggressive and communalist posture, tying itself more strongly to the parent cadre organization, the RSS, and accept in the final count the latter's authority?

Between 1980 and 1984 the Jan Sangh sought to weaken its links with the RSS, to move to the centre and to dilute its ideological message through advocacy of a largely incomprehensible 'Gandhian Socialism'. This eventually gave way to 'Integral Humanism', a covering label coined by Deen Dayal Upadhyaya (a Hindu nationalist leader of less self-confident times), and then to an aggressive, extreme and open form of Hindu nationalism. The 1984 elections were the turning point. The Jan Sangh fared dismally, getting only two seats. L.K. Advani replaced the 'moderate' A.B. Vajpayee; there was a change of orientation; and even of name, to the Bharatiya Janata Party (BJP).

Between 1984 and 1989 the BJP was to achieve remarkable success in spreading its pernicious message. Since Muslims are only 12 per cent of the population and are disproportionately represented amongst the poorer and illiterate sections of Indian society, a message of direct domination by Muslims over Hindus cannot be sold. Instead the focal point of attack has been different. The (weakly) secular Indian state has been attacked for 'appeasing' Muslims, and thus treating Hindus 'unfairly'. In selling this message the forces of Hindu communalism have been abetted by the fact that the Indian state has not so much appeased Muslims as appeased *all* communalisms.

Thus the absence of a Uniform Civil Code (UCC) of even an optional nature has been a concession to a Muslim fundamentalist leadership adamant about the sanctity of a conservatively interpreted Sharia. Meanwhile, a refusal of governments to carry out a purge of predominantly Hindu paramilitary forces which have themselves attacked Muslim communities has been the other side of the picture. In 1986 the issue of a UCC came up when the Supreme Court insisted that the provisions of the Indian penal code on maintenance take precedence over Sharia for an elderly Muslim divorcee, Shah Bano, who had petitioned it. The Congress government's decision to legislatively over-turn the ruling in favour of preserving Muslim Personal Law sparked mobilization by Hindu communal forces and counter-mobilization by fundamentalist Muslim leaders. This transformed what was essentially an issue of women's oppression by personal laws of all kinds into a battleground of identity politics between 'appeased' Muslims and 'aggrieved' Hindus, although the victims of such a government decision were Muslim women and children.

To counter-balance this concession to Muslim communalism, the government appeased Hindu communalists by lifting the locks of a disputed shrine in Ayodhya, giving Hindu devotees full access to worship while Muslims, rightly regarding the shrine as a mosque which had long been desecrated by the surreptitious placement of Hindu idols, were denied such access. In the early 1980s religious front organizations of the RSS, most notably the Vishva Hindu Parishad (VHP), had carried out a series of mass mobilizing pilgrimages of a semi-religious/semi-cultural nature aimed at consolidating a common Hindu identity. The forces of Hindu communalism were the only formations confident of carrying out such mass mobilizations. But missing was an issue that could not only focus with some degree of plausibility on the state's 'appeasement' of Muslims but simultaneously also arouse a strong sense of Hindu deprivation and grievance.

The government provided it with just such an issue with its action in Ayodhya, the mythical site of the birthplace of the Hindu God-king Rama. For decades there had been a localized belief, unsubstantiated by any serious empirical evidence, that a temple dedicated to Lord Rama had been destroyed by the first Mughal Emperor, Babar, in the sixteenth century and a mosque built in its place. Local disputes after 1947 had led successive governments to restrict entry to the disputed shrine in the 'interests of law and order', though elementary justice demanded full restoration of its status as a mosque which had been defiled by nocturnal introduction of idols in December 1949.[15]

The 1986 decision of the government to open up the locks on the shrine in Ayodhya enabled the RSS, BJP and VHP to spearhead a remarkable campaign for the destruction of the mosque and its replacement by a new temple dedicated to Lord Rama as a symbol of respect for 'Hindu wishes' desecrated by past 'Muslim perfidy'. All those, including the state, opposing this were 'appeasing' Muslims and were contemptuous and hostile to 'Hindu sentiment'. This campaign was among the most significant in India's post-independence history. It polluted the political and democratic atmosphere of Indian society, delivering huge political and social dividends to the forces of Hindu communalism, though in time it was to offer diminishing returns.

By the time of the 1989 elections, which were won by the Janata Dal (headed by V.P. Singh on an anti-corruption platform – Rajiv Gandhi's involvement in the Bofors arms sale scandal), the BJP had clearly become a powerful new actor on the political stage. The peak of its Ayodhya campaign and the unmasking of the Sangh Combine's ruthlessly authoritarian, communal and anti-secular face was yet to come. Nonetheless, by 1989 the BJP *going it alone* in the elections won 88 seats, propping up a minority Janata Dal government that it would soon enough bring down.

The V.P. Singh government depended on both the Left (consisting primarily of the Communist parties) and the BJP for its survival. The BJP had by then identified the mosque/temple issue as a high-priority item on its agenda. The elevation of the mosque/temple issue also expressed a qualitative change in the relationship between the party and its 'sister' organizations in the Sangh Combine, the Vishwa Hindu Parishad, the Bajrang Dal and the Rashtriya Swayamsevak Sangh, especially the VHP. The VHP is the broad religious–cultural front organization set up in 1964, and the Bajrang Dal is a recent addition to the 'family'. For obvious reasons the Combine calls itself 'Sangh Parivar' or 'Sangh Family'.

The VHP launched the Ayodhya campaign in the early 1980s and controlled it until 1988. The BJP's adoption of the campaign meant that the VHP, a rag-tag coalition of assorted sadhus, leaders of obscure Hindu sects and plain fanatics, had become much more important within the RSS-led 'family'. The RSS consolidated a particularly close relationship with the BJP from the mid-1980s onwards. At the RSS's goading, the BJP astutely exploited the potential the mosque/temple issue offered, first to mobilize people politically on a mass scale, and, second, to combine non-parliamentary activism with its parliamentary work, thus bringing the pressure of its mass campaign to bear on the weak V.P. Singh government. By mid-1990, numerous forms of mobilization by the Sangh Combine could be identified: collection of 'consecrated' bricks from villages and towns in a symbolic gesture of support to the planned construction of a Rama temple on the alleged birthplace/site of Lord Rama (Ram Janamabhoomi) at Ayodhya; public meetings where fiery anti-Muslim rhetoric would flow freely; and processions of *Ram jyotis*, literally oil lamps dedicated to Rama, which would be organized late at night often in a provocative fashion to threaten violence and aggression to Muslims in the neighbourhood.

In parts of north India, an overtly militant and particularly menacing form of mobilization was organized: the wielding and brandishing of the *trishul*, or trident, Lord Shiva's weapon, and its use as a symbol of a new militant Hindu consciousness. A whole industry manufacturing propaganda material – posters, stickers, mini-trishuls as well as colourful and fanciful accounts of ancient and medieval Indian history – mushroomed.

In the autumn of 1990, the BJP multiplied the scale of mobilization many times over and imparted to it a particularly aggressive edge in the form of L.K. Advani's *rath yatra* – literally a chariot tour, which covered more than half of the country. The chariot – an imitation of ancient horse-drawn carts from the *Mahabharata* (in reality a decked-up Toyota van) – took Advani to more than twenty communally sensitive cities as well as to hundreds of small towns and villages, where volunteers could drum up support and organize rallies and public meetings on an overtly anti-Muslim platform of hatred and vituperation. Advani boldly displayed the election symbol of the BJP – the lotus flower – on the *rath* and made no effort to conceal the link between the *yatra*, religion and politics.

The *rath yatra* left a trail of violence and devastation in its wake. From the beginning the *yatra* was calculated to provoke: there were accompanying rituals using human blood; the most horrifying and belligerent chants and slogans were raised; and Muslim-owned shops and names were openly targeted. V.P. Singh came under pressure from the Left and the secular sections of the media to ban the *yatra* because it was deliberately provoking violence.

Singh dithered, vacillating between promise of tough action and trying to placate the BJP leadership. Ultimately and belatedly, Advani was arrested and his march halted – not by the central government, but by the government of Bihar, then also under Janata rule. As soon as Advani was arrested the BJP announced that it was withdrawing support to Singh in Parliament. By September, the government was tottering and counting its last days. Then in October the VHP launched another offensive, this time in Ayodhya itself. It organized a *karseva*, or voluntary service, to make a symbolic beginning to build a temple. Unwilling to prevent it although it was in blatant violation of court injunctions against a change in the site's status quo, the government allowed *karsevaks* to gather in large numbers right next to the Babri mosque. On 30 October, a frenzied mob climbed over the compound wall of the mosque, and some volunteers planted saffron flags on one of the domes. A weak and vacillating government had allowed the forces of extreme rightwing communalism to score a victory. No one was prosecuted for this criminal act.

The V.P. Singh government was followed by an unstable Congress-supported regime which soon made way for elections in May 1991. The Congress party returned to power in a minority government without Rajiv Gandhi, who was assassinated during the election campaign. The new prime minister, Narasimha Rao, was a weak compromise candidate never known for firmness, and in favour of a 'soft Hindutva' rather than a principled secular approach.

The BJP made handsome gains: it won 119 seats against 88 in 1989. Its share of the national vote rose to over 20 per cent, way beyond expectations, breaking all previous patterns of sudden spurts in electoral support. Thanks to the fragmentation of the rest of the non-Congress vote between factions of the splintered Janata Dal, the BJP emerged as the single largest party of opposition in the lower house of Parliament. It also took power in the state of Uttar Pradesh where Ayodhya is located.

Rao's greater proclivity towards appeasement, his dependence on non-Congress MPs in crucial parliamentary votes, and his weakness within the ruling party were cynically exploited by the BJP's leaders, who extracted concession after concession. A situation of collaboration or informal alliance/understanding between the BJP and the Rao faction of the Congress soon emerged permitting the BJP to tilt the scales in its favour time and again.

An important factor sustained this informal alliance. In mid-1991, the government embarked on a new rightwing-oriented economic policy, which was strongly opposed by the Left. The BJP by and large endorsed the policy, which meshed well with its own orientation, although some of its hardcore RSS leaders had reservations about its emphasis on liberalization of foreign investment and trade. Rao came to depend more and more on the BJP for support for his policy in and out of Parliament. By 1992, the BJP commanded a degree of political influence far in excess of its actual weight in Parliament, politics and society. It used this influence deftly, through the media and the bureaucracy, to advance its Ram Janamabhoomi campaign, calculating that the effete and vacillating Rao government would not be willing or able to stand its ground and resist the Sangh Combine's strategy of physical encroachments into Ayodhya.

In July 1992 the Sangh undertook a *karseva* to construct a platform on a plot of land within the mosque complex, as part of its temple construction campaign. The government's response to this patently illegal and provocative move was supine. It allowed the platform to be built, thus legitimizing the encroachment, and pleaded with obscure religious leaders/sadhus to counsel reason upon the leaders of the agitation.

The post-July run-up to the demolition of the Babri mosque on 6 December 1992 is a story of retreat after ignominious retreat by the government; further intrusion by the BJP; negotiations and special pleading with an unrelenting Hindu communal leadership; disinformation and dissimulation by the government; deception, manipulation and rogue tactics on the part of the BJP and its allies. Subsequent disclosures make it plain that the government had adequate warning from its own intelligence agencies as well as from the Hindu communal leaders with whom it was negotiating, of a planned assault on the Babri mosque on 6 December. However, it failed to take precautionary measures, to deploy adequate central paramilitary troops, secure injunctions from the law courts or to arrest BJP–VHP leaders, who were engaged in a conspiracy to destroy the mosque. The carnage (demolition and anti-Muslim riots) of 6 December sent shock-waves throughout the country. The BJP parliamentary leadership's first response was apologetic: Advani resigned as Leader of the Opposition in the Lok Sabha and the chief minister of Uttar Pradesh also quit. However, the party soon moved to a more defiant militant posture justifying what had happened and blaming the lethargic legal system for its inability to resolve the Ayodhya dispute.

December 1992 marked the peak of the BJP's militant activism. After the demolition it has proved much more difficult for the BJP to maintain a steady upward swing. It cannot comparably mobilize over constructing a temple as over destroying a 'hated symbol'. Instead its regional spread has been subject to reverses and partial recuperations. The most significant barrier to its spread has been the emergence of multi-caste alliances related to lower caste assertion in the north of India. This is a historic political trend which started in the south in the 1930s and has now reached the north. It has been an integral part of the social reform movement in the country. Given the growing awareness of their rights among Dalits and OBCs (Other Backward Classes, or backward or middle castes as they are known in Constitutionalese) this trend seems irreversible.

It got a big boost in 1990 when the New Delhi government under V.P. Singh announced the acceptance of a 1978 report of the Mandal Commission (named after its chairman) on OBCs, which recommended that 27 per cent of all government jobs be reserved for OBCs in addition to the 15 and 7 per cent respectively provided for the Dalits and tribals by the Indian Constitution. Singh's announcement of the implementation of the Mandal Report touched off a furore in the north, with upper-caste Hindus taking to the streets. The agitation had the side effects of both protecting the existing pattern of reservations for the Dalits and tribals from being seriously attacked (a tendency that had been developing before the Mandal furore) as well as alarming them sufficiently to explore connections with the political representatives of the OBCs. The practical effect of implementation was very limited, e.g. some 45,000 new central government jobs would have been affected annually. The real significance of the Report lies in its symbolic impact and message.

Thus political formations of the lower and middle castes received a great fillip. Such a caste alliance pays powerful electoral dividends *provided* it can be sustained. Muslims, OBCs and Dalits represent roughly 12, 45 and 15 per cent of the Indian population. If even half of them back a party or alliance formation, it can expect to win. The *rath yatra*, which so polarized Indian politics, was launched by the BJP partly as a fearful response to the impact of the Mandal Report, which would set lower against upper castes thus enormously weakening the effort to establish a consolidated Hindu vote.

The anti-caste struggle, then, is vital to the effort to de-communalize and transform Indian society in a more, secular, humane and socialist direction.

Secularism and Socialism

Although civil society in India is weak, its institutions are developing. It is an area of contestation where consciously secular forces are weak and lack backing from the state, which has not sought to challenge seriously the expansion of religious influence outside its domain. The struggle lies between, on the one hand, an expanding, self-confident political Hinduism and an orthodox Islam engaged in a powerful operation of retrenchment within a psychologically besieged Muslim community, and, on the other hand, the secular mechanisms of expanding market relations, modern technology and science, corporate and non-corporate bureaucratization, urbanization, and class divisions and struggles in industry and agriculture. In crucial areas of civil society, like education, health, recreation, welfare services, the private media, even trade unions and political parties, secularization has been extremely slow and uneven. In the face of all this it is disturbing that Indian secularists in the main are prepared to ignore civil society in favour of a one-sided stress on strengthening the secular nature of the state, supplemented perhaps by mass ideological campaigns in support of a secular interpretation of Indian nationalism. This is vital, no doubt, especially after 6 December 1992, but it still avoids confrontation on the terrain where communalism's deployments are strongest.

What was possible in the West is not possible in India. The struggle to defeat communalism decisively, to eliminate it as a danger, is inseparable from the struggle to dismantle capitalism and replace bourgeois democracy with a deeper socialist democracy. Why should this be so? Is this claim not a retreat to a Marxist dogmatism that has been clearly refuted by reality – a return to a Utopian millenarianism that has been in practice the source of a tragic ideological and political totalitarianism?

These are large issues, and to make a case for a Marxist vision of socialism in the last decade of the twentieth century – after 1989 and all that – would take us far from our immediate area of investigation. Suffice it to say that the most powerful assault on the idea that liberal-democratic capitalism is the 'end of history' cannot but take recourse to the wellsprings of classical Marxism, to its analytical resources and to its alternative vision of the future. Far from being outdated, the quest for a global alternative to capitalism is made more urgent than ever by the global ecological crisis.

In India, the connections between its specific forms of capitalism, liberal democracy and communalism are so strong that progressive secularization can no longer be confidently visualized as the more or less inevitable outcome of an Indian 'long march' of capitalist moderni-zation and liberal-democratic consolidation. Under capitalism a neces-sary though by no means sufficient condition for secular advances in civil society, especially in the fields of health, education, child care, recrea-tion, is the creation of a strong welfare state on the model of the best of the Western European countries, though these welfare states have now themselves run into deep trouble. Strong welfare states were never a gift from above by a prospering capitalist or ruling class, but everywhere represented the fruits of the pressure that a well-organized and united labour movement could bring to bear on a given state or ruling-class order. In the countries of advanced capitalism, where the relationship of forces between capital and labour has been historically inclined in favour of the former (e.g. the USA), welfarism has been the weakest.[16]

In India, which has claim to one of the most fragmented labour movements anywhere, state welfarism, to the degree that it was encour-aged, was the result of the Nehruvian social-democratic vision. That era is now gone for good, and in the new climate of 'market-friendly' economic development even a prolonged Indian economic miracle may not lead to a substantial 'welfarism from above'. What if the Indian economy does not take off as a result of the dramatic policy changes recently instituted, but instead carries out a rerun of the Latin American experience?

In that case the existing division of responsibilities between the capitalist state and religious institutions in civil society will be strength-ened. Religion as a social power has always derived much of its strength from its ability partially to redress material–secular needs. Such an order reinforces particularist religious (and caste) loyalties. Hindu communalism has the material infrastructure of the Rashtriya Swayamsevak Sangh (RSS) and its offshoots; orthodox Islam has its own infrastructure of religiously controlled schools, sports clubs, cultural organizations, presses, credit agencies, work cooperatives, and so on.

If capitalism knows how to utilize existing divisions to ensure its reproduction and stabilization, bourgeois democracy reinforces communal divides since effective political competition means subordinating normative ideals to the practical task of successful organization of pressure. It means moving along the path of least resistance, mobilizing on the basis of existing identities and given levels of consciousness. If caste and religious community feelings and structures are already strong and socially effective, then these are likely to be reinforced by the way in which electoral competition operates. This has been the Indian experience, where even centrist, 'secular' parties have sought to work with, rather than against, more overtly communal bodies.

A long-term programme for de-communalizing India must give the highest priority to the building of secular counter-institutions in civil society and to promoting a more secular popular culture.[17] To erode in this way the social importance of religious identity is to seek democratization in its classical rather than 'liberal' sense. It implies the progressive erosion of power differentials between individuals and between groups, be this power social, economic or political in form and be the groups classes, castes or other communities.

If the limited form of empowerment provided by national citizenship can be so corrosive of religious loyalty, or so effective in pushing religious and religio-political structures into a more wary and respectful appreciation of it, then it is not unrealistic to believe that qualitatively higher levels of such empowerment can further narrow the space of religious loyalty – or else push it in a direction where the value of religious loyalty, fervour and belief becomes increasingly based on its commitment to an egalitarian universalism that is not essentially ideological or transcendental in character. This would be nothing short of a profound secularization of the religious mission itself – as is the case with liberation theology.[18]

This really is to tie the anti-communal struggle to the struggle for socialism. India is one of the few countries in the world where Communism remains a mass force. While Communist state governments and leftist social movements have secular achievements to their credit, they sometimes compromised with caste and even communal appeals and have yet to embrace an integral socialist democracy. This question lies at the heart not just of the socialist project in India and elsewhere, but also of the project for carrying out a progressive secularization of Indian life. How to bring about a socialist transformation in a liberal-democratic capitalist order is still the most important unresolved strategic problem. But an indispensable part of such an overall strategy is the building of democratic *and secular* counter-institutions in civil society through a multiplicity of localized struggles and single- and multiple-issue movements coordinating and uniting such struggles through appropriate structures, programmes and action networks.

Since no realistic assessment of these times can ignore the fact that the mass appeal of socialism is weaker than at any time since 1917, is it the case that anti-communalists in India are doomed at best to carrying out a long-term holding operation for secularism? To argue that capitalism and bourgeois democracy in India cannot be the preconditions for the eradication of communalism is not the same as arguing that there is no other scenario for the future than communalism's progressive escalation or India's inexorable descent into a communal–authoritarian nightmare. Shorter and even medium-term prospects for the future of India's liberal democracy are not so bleak. The last sub-section in this chapter provides a brief résumé in this regard. It is quite conceivable that weakened but enduring bourgeois-democratic structures will coexist with communal tensions and more institutionalized patterns of discrimination against non-Hindu minorities, in much the same way as racism and bourgeois democracy in the West have coexisted, though this analogy should not be stretched too far.

Moreover, such a perspective presumes that the challenge posed by the forces of Hindu communalism will at least be contained. The short-term task of de-communalizing the purely political terrain and preserving the secular state has become all-important. The BJP and the organizations behind it must not stabilize themselves in power at the Centre. Unless secular political forces prevent such a denouement, the longer term and more fundamental task of successfully secularizing civil society is hardly conceivable.

If the high stakes involved here prioritize forthcoming electoral struggles, this does not mean ongoing efforts to secularize civil society must come to a halt. Much of the power of Hindu communal forces (and Muslim communalists), even for the purposes of successful electoral mobilization, comes from their entrenchment here. On this terrain as also on the electoral front, the anti-communal struggle, especially the fight against Hindu communalism, is crucially bound up with the anti-caste struggle.

Caste is an identity more deeply felt than class and has an emotional resonance stronger still than that of religion, because the social roots of caste oppression are deep and its social consequences all too real. The Hindu nationalist ideology of Hindu communalism can offer psychological uplift by its invocation of a wider Hindu unity resting on uniform affiliation. But it has no real answer to the material foundations of this intra-Hindu oppression.

The stronger the mobilization around caste, the more damaging it is to the communal advocates of Hindu nationalism. A substantial majority of Hindus suffer caste discrimination and social disadvantage vis-à-vis the upper castes. But the post-Ayodhya developments have shown that Dalits (untouchables) and the numerically large lower echelons of the backward castes are alert and constitute a potent resource to build upon, one which gives hope that a more decent Indian future can be built.

Conclusion: Prospects for Indian Democracy

In the former colonial world, India's experiment has been unique. No other country has had such an enduring democracy, albeit violent and weak relative to those of the advanced democracies. In assessing the continued durability of Indian democracy, especially in the light of the communal challenge, the historical and structural sources of this uniqueness must be understood.

The main historical features belong to both the colonial and post-colonial period. There was the distinctive character of British rule with a mere 100,000 troops controlling the fortunes of a sub-continent for over a century. Such rule was simply not possible without an administrative infrastructure manned largely by Indians themselves to help govern the country in the name of the Crown and its proclaimed ideals. This also affected the character of the National Movement for independence. Only the Chinese and Vietnamese national liberation struggles bear any comparison with the National Movement of India in longevity and in the scale of mass support and mobilization.

However, in the Indian case the struggle was essentially non-violent and dedicated to the transfer of power from, rather than overthrow of, the institutions of colonial rule. Through a prolonged process of demanding greater rights for Indians within colonial rule which gradually moved up to the demand for independence, the instruments of self-governing and democratic rule were built up – the rule of law and an independent judiciary; a 'depoliticized' steel frame of an administrating bureaucracy; a military apparatus kept separate from the liberation struggle and subservient to political command and authority; the elements of a Westminster-style legislative system. Of course, the pre-1947 legacy of the Congress itself was paramount but has now systematically eroded to the point where its impact can no longer be deemed significant. It is the post-independence historical factors that must henceforth be given decisive weight.

Since independence there has been a combined and complex process of both further institutionalization and de-institutionalization of Indian bourgeois democracy which has given it a distinctive character. Hence the unique paradox of endemic political instability encased within a quite remarkable democratic systemic durability. Some important aspects of this de-institutionalization process have been remarked upon, above all the decline of the Congress itself. But quite the most important institutionalized force behind the sustenance of Indian democracy must also not be forgotten – the absorption of a democratic ethos and commitment to preserving its basic institutions through the real awakening of the lowest classes and castes of Indian society.

It would be romanticism, of course, to believe that this alone could ensure the preservation of the democratic system. But when this is allied (among other things) to the most important structural feature of Indian society, then we do arrive at a more important basis for democratic durability. This latter feature is the single most powerful 'negative' obstacle to the establishment of a centralized and national authoritarian structure. The extraordinarily segmented and sectionalized character of Indian society makes extremely difficult both 'unity from above' (amongst the dominant classes, castes and parties) and 'unity from below' (of a kind that can promise revolutionary social change). Indian society is both strongly resistant to centralized macro-authoritarianism and very open indeed to the institutionalization and spread of micro-level authoritarianisms.

The segmentation of Indian society is a 'permissive', not an 'efficient', cause of its democracy. It is not sufficient to guarantee its durability. Indeed, the overall trend line of Indian political life has been opposite to the general trajectory of third world politics, which, though subjected to considerable variation, country-wise and even region-wise, has been towards greater democratization. The greater economic marginalization of a large part of the third world counteracts and diminishes the political consequences of the drift towards quasi-democracy or near-democracy. But it does not alter the fact of such a political drift overall; nor of the specific benefits of greater political rights and freedoms of various kinds, even if rights understood only as civic and political rights remains an unsatisfactory and far too narrow conception.

In India, compared to the past, the centre of gravity has shifted to the right, and for the worse, in three crucial spheres: the economy, secularism and democracy. Regarding the economy, the New Economic Policy inaugurated in 1991 virtually guarantees the institutionalization of a deeply iniquitous dualist economy. *Such a rightwing economic shift greatly increases the need for a correspondingly rightwing political representation for ruling elites that breaks from the traditional populism of Indian politics.* This growing space (within limits) for rightwing political formations means a space not for the equivalent of conservative–liberal parties of the Western European or OECD type, but for more anti-democratic, reactionary rightwing formations.

Regarding secularism, enough has already been said about the communal challenge to Indian democracy. From the late 1960s/early 1970s onwards perhaps the most accurate characterization of Indian politics was that there was a clear drift towards a more 'authoritarian democracy'. But given the paradox of the polity, it was necessary to equally emphasize both the authoritarianism and the democracy. One could still feel secure that although the brush fires of authoritarian practices and developments were increasing in size, frequency and intensity, they were still brush fires unable to come together on a really system-threatening scale. The social and political preconditions for such conscious organization of national-level and centralized authoritarianism were still absent.

The general argument presented here is that this can no longer be so confidently assumed; that such preconditions have been in the making. At the same time the emergence of countervailing forces and the strength of the existing structures opposing a generalized authoritarian involution of the Indian polity must not be underestimated. The situation may be summed up by saying that where once in characterizing the overall drift towards an 'authoritarian democracy' it was necessary to maintain a parity of emphasis on both terms in this apparent oxymoron, now it would be more accurate to emphasize the first term more strongly. On the continuum between strong democracy and strong authoritarianism India continues to lie on this side of the critical point separating varieties of democracy from varieties of authoritarianism. But it is closer to this critical point of transition than it once was.

The basic democratic mould of Indian politics established since 1947 has not been broken. But it has been shaken, cracked and patched up in places with glues of uncertain strength. In Kashmir, independent

India faces its strongest ever secessionist movement. But so many are the variables in operation, national and international, that only the foolhardy would confidently predict that this will lead either to a break-up of the Union or to generalized repression. Secessionist pressures remain confined to the geographical periphery of India. A more serious problem is the possibility of an anti-secular reaction in other parts of India to Islamic militancy in Kashmir and the more general anti-democratic and brutalizing effects of a state repression legitimized in the name of 'national unity'.

Perhaps the best vantage point to take in judging the future prospects of Indian democracy is to remember that within the catch-all term of the 'third world', meant to signify a collective unit sharing some common characteristics, India is both the most and least third world of countries. It is among the most third world in the character of its mass poverty and in the various forms of extreme social backwardness. But in the general sophistication of its economic and political structures it is in so many ways much closer to the advanced industrialized democracies than to developing countries.

Is there reason then to be more than a little hopeful about the future survivability of Indian political democracy? One might tentatively suggest that there is and that this might be of some comfort to socialists as well. After all, hopes of realizing a progressive form of an Indian socialism also rest on the survivability of such a historic gain.

Notes

1. B. Anderson, *Imagined Communities*, London, 1983.
2. H. Kohn, *The Idea of Nationalism*, New York, 1944.
3. R. Guha and G. Chakravorty Spivak (eds), *Selected Subaltern Studies*, New York, 1988. See especially G. Pandey, 'Peasant Revolt and Indian Nationalism'; and S. Amin, 'Gandhi as Mahatma'.
4. S. Freitag, *Collective Action and Community*, Oxford, 1989.
5. B. Chandra, *Communalism in Modern India*, New Delhi, 1984.
6. R. Singh, 'Communalism and the Struggle Against Communalism: A Marxist View', *Social Scientist*, August–September 1990. 'Communalism in contemporary India, as ideology and practice, is above all an aspect of the politics of the ruling classes in a society with a massive feudal–colonial inheritance, deep religious divisions, and undergoing its own, historically specific form of capitalist development' (p. 19).
7. A. Vanaik, *The Painful Transition: Bourgeois Democracy in India*, London, 1990. See Chapter 4 on 'Communalism and Hindu Nationalism'.

8. The definition of secularism (either as a state of affairs or as an ideology) and of secularization is tied to one's definition of religion and the 'religious', not always deemed synonymous. The first problem for any general conception of secularization is how to define religion in a broad all-inclusive way, so as to fit all sets of religious beliefs and practices. What is the irreducible essence of religion that separates it decisively from what is thought to be secular? Such attempts at a broad inclusive definition should be avoided; they would only lead to a conceptual quagmire. For our purposes it is enough to focus on the 'world historic religions' which share preoccupations with 'salvation' and 'transcendence', and to discuss the secularization thesis in regard to them. Confucianism is then excluded as a religion and seen as a secular creed.

Combining the insights of Weber and Durkheim, many sociologists of religion see the religious as an eternal category. We are in essence religious animals. This renders 'secularization' nugatory except for limited conceptual purposes and geographical spaces. Since the religious can never progressively decline or disappear, it can only change its forms; secularization is not the embodiment of religious decline but the registration of these changing forms – e.g. routinization–secularization in the functioning of churches in the USA, or the rise of a pluralist religious market where competing religions, sects, cults, and so on, sell their respective therapeutic wares. See P.L. Berger, *The Social Reality of Religion*, London, 1969; P. Glasner, *The Sociology of Secularization*, London, 1977. Alternatively, the thesis of secularization-as-decline is accepted, but it is frankly denied that secularization is a significant trend anywhere outside Europe, and even there its 'achievements' are said to be grossly exaggerated. See D. Martin, *The Religious and the Secular*, London, 1969.

Generally, those who reject or strongly qualify the secularization thesis seek to conjoin religion and modernity. Indeed the idea of the religious being eternal and religion being coterminous with culture replaces the issue of how, why and to what extent religious influence is declining with the issue of where religion or the religious stops. Where it was once fashionable in the USA to overstress the secularity of American life, it has become more fashionable since to overstress its religiosity. Such a position is usually based on the following premises: (1) its advocates have a strong sociological bias towards theories of social order and stability than of conflict; (2) religion is deemed crucial for providing the normative foundations for social order; (3) its advocates share Weber's view of the relationship between the Protestant Ethic and the rise of capitalism; (4) they see secularism/secularization as the 'gift of Christianity', especially of Protestantism.

These premisses are disputed by, among others, B.S. Turner, *Religion and Social Theory*, New Delhi, 1991; S. Amin, *Eurocentrism*, New York, 1988; S.N. Eisenstadt, 'The Protestant Ethic Thesis', in R. Robertson (ed.), *Sociology of Religion*, Harmondsworth, 1969; R.K. Fenn, 'Religion, Identity and Authority', in R. Robertson and B. Holzner (eds), *Identity and Authority*, Oxford, 1980.

9. The relationship between secularization and de-secularization need not be 'dialectical', i.e. two moments of the same process. It can also be one of adjacency or juxtaposition with minor feedback loops. These two processes can respectively pertain to distinct spaces, state and civil society; or to distinct ethnic groups, Britons of Asian and non-Asian origin; or to dominant and dominated classes. (B.S. Turner, *Religion and Social Theory*).

10. Durkheimian sociologists who believe that the USA in some sense holds the mirror to the future of secularization elsewhere have developed the notion of 'Civil Religion', i.e. the American Way of Life which binds the country. This is an ethos encompassing those of the three main faiths, Protestantism, Catholicism, Judaism, yet is significantly shaped by them, particularly Protestantism. For criticisms of the civil religion argument in its strong version, see B.S. Turner, *Religion and Social Theory*, R.K. Fenn, 'Religion, Identity and Authority', and, from another angle, D. Martin, *The Religious and the Secular*. See also Chapter 3, pp. 109–11.

11. T.N. Madan, 'The Concept of Secularism', paper presented at the National Seminar on Secularism in India, organized by the Indian Academy of Sciences and the Tata Institute of Social Sciences, 25–7 September 1989.

12. See the excellent critique of relativism by S.P. Mohanty, 'Us and Them: On the Philosophical Bases of Political Criticism', in *Yale Journal of Criticism*, Vol. 2, No. 2, 1989.

13. The Indian experience shows that the relationship between religious pluralism, individualism and secularism is much more complicated than in the standard US-based model where religious pluralism has strong connections to the privatization of religious concerns, the absence of church–state conflict, and the immigrant nature of American society. Interestingly, where some American sociologists see Christianity as the source of secularization and democracy, some Indian scholars see Hinduism as the source of secular and democratic impulses in India. If Christianity is the master key to world history, Hinduism is the master key to Indian evolution! Both modern Christianity and modern Hinduism call attention to their 'innate tolerance'. It has been said that Christian ecumenicalism is the laying of ground rules to rationalize intra-Christian religious competition. In the past, Hinduism's renowned 'tolerance' was the result of its lack of self-consciousness and the very absence of a 'Hindu' coherence or any notion of a 'Hindu community'. Caste (an expression of social intolerance) was the organizing principle.

Today's self-consciously avowed claim of tolerance by Hindus is more often than not the intolerant expression of feelings of religious superiority to the Semitic faiths, especially Islam.

14. Supra-nationalism, to be stable and enduring (Western Europe), must retain the institutional foundations of this popular empowerment. If it is to survive, it cannot go backwards. Indeed, it will have to offer more than what has so far been achieved if it is not to be merely another label for a loose confederation of national structures of political power only slightly diluted by the requirement to come together in this way. A truly supra-national unified Europe will have to be more secular, not less.

15. A detailed history of the dispute is provided in S. Gopal (ed.), *Anatomy of a Confrontation*, New Delhi, 1991.

16. Turner (*Religion and Social Theory*) is among the few writers to have stressed the structural differentiation in respect of 'existential dilemmas', of how religious responses to 'meaning of life' questions tend to be more intellectualized for dominant classes and more mundane – related to questions of health, terrestrial power, security and wealth – for socially more insecure and oppressed classes. His 'corporeal sociology of religion', influenced by Foucault, insists on linking existential questions to the biographical history of our bodies. The theory and practice of health is thus linked to the theory and practice of religion.

17. Popular culture and recreation in India are segmented along religious and caste lines. One big exception is sport. It is not at all surprising that anti-communal groups, in their propaganda efforts to promote communal amity, should have made references to the composite character of, for example, the national cricket team. An effective poster brought out by the Bombay-based anti-communal group Ekta ('Unity') featured photographs of four Indian cricketers: a Sikh, Maninder Singh; a Hindu, Kapil Dev; a Muslim, Mohammed Azharuddin; and a Christian, Roger Binny. The poster, in Hindi, Marathi and English, read 'We can play together, we can live together'.

18. The Indian anti-secularist has not hesitated to cite Christian liberation theology in her support. But a chasm separates the two. For the anti-secularist the principal lines of demarcation are between believers and non-believers, the secularist and the non-secularist, the indigenous and the alien. At no point is she prepared to appropriate as her fundamental line of demarcation the operative principle of liberation theology at its best: the *social* divide between rich and poor, oppressor and oppressed. Characteristically, liberation theology sees Marxism as a valuable resource and Marxists as actual or potential allies, while the anti-secularist sees Marxism and Marxists as opponents or at best as irrelevant.

PART II

Religion, Modernity, Secularization

Four Notions of Secularization

Etymologically, the word 'secular' comes from the Latin *saeculum*, which first meant 'age' or a 'great span of time' or the 'spirit of the age'. Later it acquired another meaning, of belonging to 'this world'. There existed two worlds, the secular and the religious–eternal, temporal and spiritual, each with distinctive practices and institutions. This was the birth within Christian discourse of the notion of relative separation or disengagement. However, it was the spiritual order that ultimately remained decisive. The term 'secularization' emerged after the Peace of Westphalia in 1648 and originally referred to the transfer of ecclesiastical lands to civic control. By the nineteenth century and in the still powerful flush of Enlightenment values, G.L. Holyoake of Britain coined the term 'secularism' to define an ideology and movement wherein social (and individual) morality, hitherto determined by the transcending principles of religion, were now to be determined by reason, and anchored to the good of man or woman in this life. Agnostic or indifferent to religion, this version of secularism acquired a more atheistic slant through Holyoake's disciple, Charles Bradlaugh. But secularism as a rationalist movement, either agnostic, indifferent or atheistic, soon stalled. It ignored rather than confronted religion or religious discourse.

Capitalist industrialization, the rise of science and of the Enlightenment, the emergence and consolidation of civil society, in short modernity, posed the question of religion anew. How did religion, specifically Christianity, relate to modernity's emergence? What was its place in the new dispensation? 'Religious change' in the West (originary location of capitalist modernity and the secular state) was an incontestable fact and the notion of secularization was the registration of this. Broadly speaking, to this day three notions of secularization have vied, singly or in combination, for controlling emphasis.

There is the concept of secularization as decline, of religious institutions, beliefs, practices and consciousness losing social significance. There is the concept of relative separation. Other terms to signify more or less the equivalent process are disengagement, differentiation, compartmentalization. Here there is lateral shrinkage in the social space occupied or influenced by religion, also an implied reallocation of religious functions in polity, society and culture. The third notion is intimately connected to the growing importance of rational thought and activity. This dynamic implies newer claimants to intellectual and moral authority other than the traditional religious systems. It implies growing bureaucratization and routinization in forms of organization. Secularization here means greater rationalization of thought and behaviour. This kind of secularization can take place within as well as against religious systems, e.g. the view that Protestantism is a more secularized form of Christianity.[1]

The last two notions are to be distinguished from the first.[2] Those subscribing to the first notion of secularization as religious decline can accept the second and third as complementary facets of the secularization process. Those subscribing to the second and third notions need not (and many sociologists of religion do not) accept the first notion, either definitionally or as an accurate historical evaluation.[3] Intellectually, a great deal is at stake in this conceptual divide – nothing less than one's understanding of the general place of religion in modernity, society and culture, of the very nature of humans, culture and society, and therefore of the possibilities of future social and cultural change.

What is generally not in dispute is the fact of some overt shrinkage in the social space occupied by religion at least when compared to the past; the concomitant fact of greater influence in everyday life of rational processes unknown or less used in the past; and the fact or desirability of substantial, indeed decisive, practical separation of government/state and religion.[4] However, this consensus does not concede either the fact or desirability of separating religion from *all* politics, nor the fact and desirability of the decline of religion in civil society.

Moreover, the emergence of a secular state in Western democracies was more a practical consequence of a specific historical experience than an institutionalization of an abstract secular ideal. It represented the lessons learnt by both church and state from a history of debilitating religious–sectarian strife when such separation was not operative. What *is* in dispute is the meaning of secularization of civil society (outside the domains of formal political governance) and of culture. Contending notions of secularization are here inseparable from contending notions of religion. The difficulties in defining, discussing or agreeing about secularization are clearly related to the difficulties in defining, discussing or arriving at a consensus about religion.

But before skating on the treacherously slippery ice of 'understanding religion', a more recent fourth notion of secularization must be taken up. This Indian contribution is the product of its specific history. In a context where there was no equivalent to the Enlightenment experience, where the values associated with liberal democracy and nationalism were imported, secularism was perceived as the unifying principle mediating between and collating different religious communities in order to forge a common struggle for national liberation. Secularism was the invocation of the principle of religious tolerance, itself romanticized as constituting the cultural or spiritual essence of an ancient and enduring Indian civilization. Here secularization was not a registration of religious change. Unlike in the West, where secularization and secularism are related but not congruent terms, secularization was all too often treated here as more or less a synonym for secularism. Both terms were used to characterize 'a state of affairs', an enduring feature over time rather than a coming to terms with any process of religious change. The Indian usages of the terms 'secular', 'secularism', 'secularization' invoked images of an unchanging religio-spiritual–cultural essence.

Like its Western democratic counterpart, the Indian secular state would be religiously impartial. But this impartiality would be ensured not by abstinence from religious affairs but by its 'fair' involvement on India's multi-religious terrain. In actual practice and in constitutional provision, the difficulties in successfully institutionalizing such a notion meant that the Indian state did not represent that sharp a contrast from the broad Western model. The secularity of the Indian state is correctly characterized as something of an admixture both in theory and practice. It institutionalized separation in law while endorsing some degree of state intervention in religious affairs in the interests of 'public order, health and morality'.[5]

But its political practice all too often involved an active balancing of favours to various religious communities quite at odds with the model of behaviour of the Western secular state. Legal sanctions regarding the degree to which the state can intervene in religious affairs vary. This reflects different specific histories. It is not a refutation of the general principle of a basic (if never complete) separation of state/government from religion. There is even in the most secular states some small overlap.[6] The permanent invariant is that in cases of conflict between religion and the state, faith is not above law. Final powers of arbitration are given to the state.

In the Indian context the overdetermination of the notion of secularization by the idea of tolerance did mean that the question of secularization of civil society was never posed in the same way as in the West. Whether Indian civil society was, could be or needed to be secularized were effectively non-questions since for most, the tolerance (i.e. secularism) of Indian society was treated as axiomatic, despite the communal horrors of Partition. It is only in recent years, with the fragility of Indian secularism revealed, that the issue of secularism and secularization has been seriously inserted into the intellectual–theoretical agenda.

The political importance of this debate is obvious. How can one hope to fight successfully for something unless one is clear what one is supposed to be fighting for? Amidst contending notions one must choose and explain why. It is my contention that the classical concept of secularization – the declining influence of religion – needs to be strongly defended as something that has happened, and whose furtherance is desirable (though not certain) in countries like India. I talk of secularization rather than secularism because the key referent of the latter is the state whereas my greater preoccupation is civil society. The substantial and enduring secularization of civil society is itself the best way to preserve and deepen the state's existing secularity; and to secure wider acceptance of secularism as a political doctrine. Since, in the short run, maintaining and deepening the secularity of the Indian state is also vital, there can be no gainsaying the importance of those discourses concentrating on secularism, as distinct from secularization.

To understand communalism it is necessary to understand secularization. But to understand the latter it is crucial to understand religion and its role and place in society: specifically in the era of modernity. As the title of this chapter indicates, religion, modernity, secularization, therefore have to be the central themes that must undergo investigation. Having pointed out that there are contending views on secularization, I have also suggested that there are contending notions of religion to which these are connected. So there is a definitional issue of some importance.

However, it would be a serious error to select and then defend at all costs any particular definition of religion. What is more important is (a) to understand the pitfalls of certain definitions or ways of understanding religion – what I have called, respectively, the assassination and immortalization of religion; and (b) to recognize that modernity introduces everywhere a decisive shift in the relevance of religion from a social to a more personal domain of human existence. It is not that the personal and the social are easily separable, but persevering readers will get my drift when they come to the appropriate sub-section in this chapter.

Any defence of the feasibility and desirability of further secularization has to try to expose the inadequacies and limitations of religion. In particular, it must successfully argue against the view that religion is unavoidably central to culture and/or society. Religion, culture, society (and their inter-relationships), in our times must also, therefore, be scrutinized. The sub-section on 'Culture and Society' (preceded by an assessment of the not solely Marxist notion of religion as ideology) explores this terrain. Those who subscribe to the 'religion is central to culture/society' thesis (hence what price secularization?) have very little choice but to subscribe to some kind of Social Coherence or Social Cement thesis of society where religion is the key cementing agent. But those who subscribe to a Social Cement thesis have more flexibility. They don't have to subscribe to the view that religion is unavoidably central to culture/society. I've suggested that all coherence models of society are less plausible compared to other approaches grappling with the 'problem of order' in society. This conclusion simultaneously strikes a body blow against the centrality of religion thesis and powerfully reinforces the view that further secularization, understood as religious decline, is indeed feasible!

Yet another temptation has been to deterministically understand the relationship between culture and society. There is thought to be either the 'cultural programming of society' (in which religion is often seen as the key cultural programmer) or the 'social programming of culture' (the 'dominant ideology' thesis is the Marxist variant of this approach). Since an appropriate understanding of culture is vital for engaging in this discussion, I have had to clarify my own thinking. Clearly, the term 'culture' has variable meanings, which is its strength. How best to understand it depends upon what one is trying to explain or distinguish between, e.g. art and culture, market and culture, or, as in this case, culture and society. I have been decisively influenced by the later Raymond Williams. Cultural essentialism of any kind – and most immortalizers of religion tend to be cultural essentialists – is the bane of any serious attempt to understand the increasingly complex and dynamic nature of the relationships between religion, culture and society in modernity.

The next sub-section on 'Religion in Modernity', explores the basic role of religion today. Here it is the question of identity that becomes paramount. It becomes necessary to focus on the religious identity and its relationship to other identities, to point also to the peculiarities and limitations of religious identity. Further secularization means the further decline in the importance of religious identity. This is both possible and desirable. Religion should become more privatized and religious affiliation more of an optional choice. But I do not claim that it must or should become progressively more marginal or should or will disappear. The view that religion reasserts its centrality to human society in modernity but differently from its pre-modern past, i.e. through some unique capacity to stabilize the human personality, is also rejected.

Other arguments against the secularization-as-decline thesis are also taken up, while the final sub-section returns to the inadequacies of the specifically Indian notion of secularism–secularization as 'tolerance'.

The Definitional Issue: Assassins and Immortalizers

Modernity has been the most formidable challenge yet to religion. Religious systems have responded by carrying out internal reforms in beliefs and practices so as to reassert their contemporary relevance. They have also responded by adopting modern means to pursue traditional goals and values. But perhaps the most striking tribute to the power of modernity is the spawning of the study of religion itself. Religion has come to be seen as a distinct entity distinguishable from the less religious spheres of existence, and a new mass awareness of it existing in different forms as different religions/religious systems.

Religion not God(s) is the focus of such self-conscious scholarship. There is more than an echo here of Nietzsche's 'God is dead, long live religion'. In Weber's striking observation, the modern man or woman seems no longer able to live with religion or to live without it! She now needs to name and understand it where once there was unreflective acceptance of its reality, indeed of it *as* reality.

The definitional issue, then, can hardly be dodged. Seeking definitions of such complex, multidimensional phenomena as religion is always a risky affair. Definitions chop reality up in different ways. They can be too broad or too narrow. They can bring too much into their field of vision or leave too much out. They draw boundaries in the dark with more than a hint of arbitrariness. It may well be more fruitful to 'talk about' religion or to recognize that in the overlaps between different definitions are the most interesting insights. This refusal to make too much of definitions is wise.

But what other way than by adopting, however cautiously, working definitions is there of securing some more or less useful entry point into the domain of inquiry? Weber explicitly stated that a definition of religion would be the end result of his monumental comparative researches into the world religions. But he, too, had to begin with an implicit definition and a distinctive approach, *verstehen*, understanding from within, religion as the meaning in a meaningless world, sociology as the interpretive study of society. The real problem here with definitions is that, useful as they may be as points of entry, they may too strongly fix the points of exit. They may assign or invite conclusions and evaluations in an excessively deterministic manner.

Peter Berger, one of the most respected modern theorists of religion, warned against 'assassination by definition'.[7] He had in mind those negative definitions which easily lend themselves to abusive ideological usage: religion as 'the disease of language' (Max Müller), or as 'false consciousness' (many Marxists though not Marx), or as 'imperfect philosophy' (Tylor and other nineteenth-century positivist anthropologists), or as 'the childhood of man' (Freud). For Berger such biased approaches consistently fail to preserve that necessary balance in the assessment of what religion is and does; of its involvement in the relationships between humans and nature and between humans themselves.

Yet the very same charge can be levelled against Berger. Like others he was prone to immortalization through definition. This would apply to all those definitions which ultimately root religion in the anthropological condition, i.e. the notion that in our essence we are inescapably religious animals. For Durkheim and many influenced by his sociology this immortalization is routed through society. We are social animals and the sacred–religious is the ineradicable form of the social relationship between the individual and the group, constituted, as it has to be, as a 'moral community'. Other immortalizing definitions see human–social existence as inconceivable without 'overarching values' and anything providing this is a religion. Or whatever confers a strongly solemn sense of identity is religion. Or the capacity to transcend one's biology is religion.[8]

Immortalizing religion effectively renders the idea of secularization-as-decline as, at best, of very limited value. Its bias towards endorsing a 'strong coherence' model of culture and society should be obvious.[9] To investigate religion is to investigate what it is and what it does. There can be two ways of defining what it is. Real definitions look for an

71

essence. They are evaluative and ask to be judged by their truth. While this may be appropriate for the study of some or many religions, it seems impossible to establish an essence common to *all* religions or worshippers. Nominal definitions are descriptive. But description can be from the outside or inside. Outside descriptions are more likely to be non-evaluative and cautious in assessing religion's relationship to society and culture.[10]

Insider descriptions generally belong to the hermeneutic–phenomenological school. 'To believe is to understand, to understand is to believe.'[11] The religious experience or faith must be understood in its own terms. Historians of religion and cultural anthropologists often favour this approach but it has also received considerable impetus from philosophy's 'revolution of language'. Religion and culture have come to be seen as, above all, symbolic orders, meanings embodied in symbol systems. For example, religion is perceived as sacred symbols synthesizing the 'ethos' of a people's culture.[12] Humans are said to have a natural propensity to symbolize. Symbolic systems are said to substantially constitute reality. The way is cleared for over-valuation and near-immortalization of religion. Here religion is said to provide meaning and order. What is ignored is that religion is in part an 'ideology' and operates not simply on the terrain of meaning but on the *intersections* between meaning and power.

The idea of religion as above all 'the religious experience' or 'faith' raises at least two problems. It generally forecloses further investigation into experience or faith itself. The individual subjectivity, the religious actor/believer, is at the epicentre of the religious enterprise. To grasp religion is to understand (as much as one can) through empathy the subjective purposes, feelings and responses of the believer, not to judge them. The religious experience is beyond truth and falsehood. Yet this claim cannot be secured beyond all doubt. The notion of experience *is* open to cognitive investigation. Experiences and identities have epistemic status. What goes into them – beliefs, values, desires – has epistemic status. There can be better or worse, truer or falser experiences judged by a 'weak' principle of objectivity – not complete freedom from error but nonetheless more accurate, more explanatory, more humane in their reading of the world since an experience is a 'pattern of salience', one way of 'processing information'.[13]

Faith is not simply to be accepted as given and impenetrable to the outsider but must itself be theorized as much as possible. There is bad faith and good faith and it is an abnegation of intellectual, moral and political responsibility *not* to argue with faith, especially if it is bad faith.[14] It is one thing to stress the difficulties of this; or to recognize that even in bad faith there is a component central to faith which must be acknowledged and respected even when it makes bad faith so resistant to change. But it is something else to so elevate the importance of faith as to deny the necessity and usefulness of its interrogation, or to assume this can *only* be done from a position of sympathetic detachment from within.[15]

The second problem is a paradox. The outsider supposedly can only go so far in the effort to understand from within, especially when this is across cultural and religious divides. If the problem of cultural untranslatability precludes all but the hermeneutical approach, how is the claim to correctness of this tradition of scholarship to be validated? How is one to confirm that it is a religious experience in the first place? Some level of translation always takes place, otherwise meaningful communication across linguistic divides would be impossible. Once acknowledged, the thin end of the investigative wedge has been inserted. There can be no logical objection as to why better translation and better understanding of not just the individual actor but of her context should not be possible. Given competing translations and competing understandings even *within* a cultural or religious system, what reason is there to assume that decisive arbitration here must rest with the religious actor alone?

Durkheim, father of the functionalist definition, said the importance of religion lay in what it does, not in what it says or claims. A distinction must be made between its manifest and latent functions and it is the latter that are decisive in the proper comprehension of religion. Religious practice (e.g. rituals) were much more important than beliefs or doctrine. Religious doctrine and beliefs could be false but the heart of religion, its role, could not be. Durkheim's functionalist approach was a paradigm shift. It profoundly altered twentieth-century thinking on religion. The centre of gravity shifted from the philosophy to the sociology of religion.[16] Its great flaw was that it left out the subjective dimension. What about religion's relationship to the ultimate conditions of individual existence – the problems of pain, suffering, death?

Unlike Durkheim, Weber did address 'meaning of life' questions. So most modern sociologists of religion have sought to wed the approaches and insights of Weber and Durkheim. They have sought to elaborate on what religion is and what religion does, to deal with substantive as well as functional issues. The real line of division in the definitional issue seems to be between the substantivist and functional approaches, each having either a psychological or sociological bias.[17]

Where psychological substantivists talk of the 'religious experience', sociological substantivists make one such experience, e.g. belief in supernatural beings, the cornerstone of their definition. Psychological functionalists stress religion's role in cognition (explaining the unknown) or see religion as a compensatory mechanism or as human projection come to life (alienation/reification). This is either rooted in the anthropological condition or in social need. Sociological functionalists view religion as that which has ultimate significance for a social group or which integrates it. This integration can be system cohering where the system is culture and/or society. Alternatively, religion as a form of ideological discourse can be seen as legitimating oppression. In the first case, religion is usually seen as helping to create a universe or canopy of meaning where meaning-creation and organization is also the creation of 'order'.[18]

Obviously this division between substantivists and functionalists is not sharp. Who doesn't believe in some social function of religion? Many if not most substantivists (Berger supported the phenomenological approach) have strong functionalist accents. But the reverse is less likely to hold for functionalists. Not surprisingly, in our post-Enlightenment era of greater scepticism about the 'divine order of things' and 'divine will' notions, religion is more often asked to justify itself by reference to what it does. A *general* defence of religion must focus on the similarities among religions and this is what functionalism does. Functionalist definitions promote large-scale theories of religion and open up the prospect of comparative studies. Substantivists have shorter range theories; they provide more focus on differences among religions and are more empirically oriented. But functionalist definitions can encapsulate substantivist ones. They see as religion all that substantivists do (ideology, value system, etc.) and more, sometimes too much more.[19] Substantivists, then, are also likely to be 'moderate' functionalists but rarely non-functionalists or 'extreme' functionalists.

Immortalizers or near-immortalizers of religion, however, cut across the substantivist–functionalist divide. Marx, a substantivist (religion as ideology), and a psychological functionalist (religion as alienation) was not an immortalizer. Freud, a psychological functionalist, was not an immortalizer. Admittedly, sociological functionalists, in their overwhelming number, are. Religion presumably has crucial immortal or near-immortal properties because its role is *irreplaceable*, not because it necessarily plays a great many roles. The question of religion's immortality and omnipotence is in the end dependent as much on one's broader understanding of culture and society as it is on one's specific

74

understanding of religion. For Marxists that relationship has been mediated by the concept of ideology.

Religion as Ideology: Marxists and Others

The common thread among Marxists is that religion is an ideology, though what different Marxists mean by ideology is not uniform. Nonetheless, in seeing it as ideology, Marxist discussion is conducted on the terrain of ideas, doctrine, discourse, etc., and their impact on individual and society. This is in contrast to the Durkheimian function-alist emphasis on practice/ritual as the heart of religion. Thus certain Marxist approaches come quite close to modern non-Marxist cognitive understandings of religion.

Marxist historical sociology, which has sought to explain the riddle of Western superiority or why capitalism first emerged and flourished in Western Europe and then extended itself globally, has also taken in the study of world religions. What was the role of specific religious systems in encouraging or obstructing the emergence of capitalism out of the pre-capitalist incubator? This was also Weber's project, but because he gave an un-Marxist primacy to the world religions as the 'switchmen' who decided the tracks along which civilizations would move (though powered by the engine of 'social interests'), he would seek to carry out major comparative studies of the world religions themselves.

Marxists, though they studied Islam and the Islamic world (Maxime Rodinson) as a counterpoise to colonialist and orientalist historio-graphy, were never tempted to emulate Weber in the same way. The empirical foundations for Marxist theorizations about religion have been either anthropological studies of tribal religions/magic, the Judaeo-Christian biblical tradition or the rise and spread of Christianity. It is only more recently that one can talk of Marxists making sketches on a wider canvas. In the Marxist tradition as it stands, the specifically Christian experience constantly risks being transmogrified into the general characteristics of religion per se.

Most Marxist work on religion has been of two types.[20] It has consisted of commentaries on or developments of Marx's and Engels's approaches. Or of applications of these to specific cases, e.g. Kautsky's study of Christianity. But more recently, and clearly motivated by liberation theology and radical Christian grassroots movements in Latin America (the only large area that was both overwhelmingly Christian *and* colonized), there has been a deeper effort to appreciate the utopian and redemptive dimensions of religious thought and doctrine. Thus there has been an attempt to recover within the Marxist tradition those currents which drew some inspiration from the Romantic rebellion against the excesses of Enlightenment Rationalism and anti-clericalism or saw important positive convergences between Marxist and Christian millenarianism or stressed the compatibility of the moral philosophy of religion and Marxism.[21]

Marx's own understanding of religion was in important respects different from that of Engels. 'False consciousness' is used by the latter, never the former. Marx was more of a Hegelian, understanding the origin of religion as alienation, while Engels was more of an anthropological positivist, seeing the believer as a failed rationalist, i.e. the origin of religion in the misunderstanding of nature and its forces.

Early Marx saw religion as alienation, later Marx as ideology, but did not abandon his early notion.[22] Ideology concealed alienation. Insofar as Marxists continue to see religion as a strong or the 'basic' form of alienation, they and immortalizers/near-immortalizers often have strikingly convergent views about the power and importance of religion. Peter Berger's alienation model of religion involving the dialectic of externalization, objectification and internalization of man's own thought-products is explicitly Hegelian. For him 'religion is the audacious attempt to conceive of the entire universe as meaningful.' It is the positing of a 'sacred cosmos' which transcends and includes man and 'locates his life in an ultimately meaningful order'.[23]

But no matter how positive this positing of a sacred cosmos might be (and for Berger it is highly positive), it remains a mystification and falsification of the world, a human thought-product *given* reality by man through alienation–reification. 'All human productions are, at least potentially, comprehensible in human terms. The veil of mystification thrown over them by religion prevents such comprehension.'[24] Gramsci in one of his formulations described religion in a way that has a definite affinity to Berger's view of religion as an 'audacious' project. 'Religion is the most gigantic utopia, that is the most gigantic "metaphysics", that history has ever known, since it is the most grandiose attempt to reconcile in mythological form, the real contradictions of historical life.'[25]

But Gramsci's emphasis on religious reconciliation of the 'real contradictions of historical life' shows how Marxist approaches depart from Berger, Durkheimians and even Weberians. For he is saying that it performs an ideological function as well and at least implicitly serves specific social interests and relations of power. It is the notion of religion as ideology that links the Marxist understanding of religion to questions of social power and social order. But this social order is understood not merely or primarily in terms of how the *individual* is to relate to society and the cognitive presuppositions for this, i.e. the 'ordering of meaning', society and culture being 'universes of meaning', but in terms of how specific social groups, e.g. classes, *impose* their social order or control social conflict, and the intellectual–ideational preconditions for the dominance of these groups–classes. This, in fact, is the most important insight provided by the Marxist approach to religion.

Religion is many things and plays many roles. But it also has ideological functions which are *negative*, i.e. which serve oppressive group interests. The ordering of meaning in society, or *nomization*, is never neutral or wholly positive but mediated through social relations. We are not simply individuals alone in the cosmos; each one of us is also an 'ensemble of social relations'. All attempts to understand religion and the religious quest which insist on the *individual* mind being the decisive point of departure are likely to be dangerously misleading because they obscure this ideological dimension.[26]

Whatever the *origin* of the religious impulse and whatever the unprecedented existential dilemmas of the modern individual (faced with alternative forms of cosmization, nomization and social legitimation to those of a religious system), religious systems, for most of their lifetimes, have confronted humans as a *given*. Their power over humans is not the result of an individual *choice* to 'order meaning' or 'make sense of her society or the world' in a religious way, but more the expression of that individual's existence as an 'ensemble of social relations'. Over these religiously legitimated social relations – their power distribution, their durability and strength – that individual has no say. Over their reproduction or transformation she has some say.

For Marx, religion was a *form* of ideology and ideology was a 'specific mode of being of ideas'. Ideology is always ideas but ideas are not always ideologies. Marx had a negative and restricted conception of ideology.[27] It is negative because ideology is a distortion of real contradictions in the world. It is restricted because there are many more distortions and errors than ideology can cover or speak of. So the relationship between ideology and non-ideology is not a simple positing of falsity to truth. Moreover, ideology distorts real contradictions in different ways. It denies contradictions, misunderstands them, displaces them or dilutes them, and by doing so serves the social interests of those who benefit from this general misrepresentation.

Marx does not have an interest theory of ideology or interest theory of religion. He does not have a functionalist *explanation* of ideology or religion. He does not claim that the origin or purpose of ideology or religion is to serve special interests. He simply points out that it *also* has this function. He *attributes* this role; he doesn't *explain* ideology or religion by this function.

Marx's understanding of ideology develops further complexities. Ideology is the inversion in consciousness of an inverted reality. It is the 'inverted reflection of an inverted reality which results in negation of the latter inversion'. Inverted reality comes about through alienation. Alienation is the inversion of an objectified social practice. Ideology is the further distortion – inversion in consciousness of this already inverted reality. It is in this sense that religion is the basic form of alienation and the first form of ideology. And it is in this sense that the critique of religion must, above all, be the critique of the conditions (inverted reality) that give rise to it in the form of alienation and ideology.

Marx and Engels believed that the era when religion could play a progressive role was over. There was, therefore, little reason for them to devote too much further effort to investigating either religion in general, or specific religions. They took this view for two reasons. First, they held a negative conception of ideology in which ideology itself was to be rejected or exposed as distortion. Therefore religion as a form of ideology could not provide resources in the struggle against ideology. Religion was an *obstacle* to progress, it could not be a *weapon* of progress.

Second, this view fitted their understanding of the transition from pre-capitalist societies to capitalist ones. This was a movement from societies where relations of dependence and exploitation were transparent and therefore more in need of sacralizing legitimating systems (religions), to a mode of production where such relations were obscured and no longer transparent. This facilitated the emergence of other kinds of non-religious, non-sacralizing ideologies. Secular bourgeois ideologies would become more important and their most important counterpoint would be secular socialist ideas (not socialist 'ideology'). Religious discourse would have little role or place in this new battlefield of ideas and social forces. Where religious ideology sought to *justify* the existence of hierarchy and dominance, bourgeois political ideology sought to obscure and deny the existence of this dominance.

It is likely that the rise of mass working-class parties in Europe promoted a positive or neutral conception of ideology. Corresponding to its growing class strength, the notion of a 'class point of view' became more important. Clashes of ideas sharpened and the notion of confronting a ruling-class ideology by a working-class counter-ideology became increasingly legitimate among socialists. Whatever the explanation for this shift from a negative to a positive or neutral concept of ideology, it is complete by the time of Luxemburg, Lenin and Trotsky and finds its most fruitful developments in the thought of Gramsci, where 'hegemony' and 'ideological subordination' become closely related concepts.

As far as the issue of religion is concerned, this shift has had a generally beneficent impact. Marx's restricted concept of ideology promoted a restricted conception of religion. It tended to ignore the importance of religious practice and its significance in symbolic–cultural life. It certainly promoted too one-sided an emphasis on religion as illusion, as distorted consciousness. However, Marx's concept cannot be reduced simply to false consciousness (though Engels and many other Marxists were not as subtle). For Marx, religion was the expression of real needs but it misconstrued those needs and then 'answered' these misconstrued needs in a way which helped to perpetuate both the needs and their misconstrual.

Religion thus reproduced its conditions of existence and its role. Religion did not posit a false world as an *alternative* to the real world but posited a way of relating to a real world through belief in a false world. To risk an oxymoron, religion was not a false consciousness but a false real consciousness, a false way of experiencing real lived relationships. Experiences are always real in that they exist; but can still have false epistemic status.

The sophistication Marx could extend to the notion of ruling-class ideas (not ideology) was effectively denied to religion. Whereas the ideas of the ruling class could be undistorted (if self-serving) expressions of practice, ideology and religion as a form of it could only be distorted expressions of practice. But even a notion of religion as more than ideology, as belonging to the set of ruling-class ideas, is clearly insufficient. This would sociologically limit the concept to the ruling class, just as Marx's notion of religion as ideology epistemologically limits it to distorted ideas.

The strong criticism of Marx's concept is (a) that it sees religion as primarily a form of knowledge; and (b) that it distinguishes too sharply between different forms of knowledge, ideology and non-ideology, science and ideology, ruling-class and subordinate-class ideas. Religion, even understood as a form of knowledge, cannot be so easily compartmentalized.

Though Marx and Engels paved the way for a study of religion in relation to social power, their negative definition links it more strongly to oppressive social groups. The idea of religion as a social opium could suggest that religion legitimates oppressive-class rule by enveloping it in hazy mystification; and that it simultaneously acts as a palliative for the oppressed classes. What is lost from view is religion's capacity to provide a Utopian motivation to rebel, something that Engels was quite willing to admit when talking of religion in the past. Liberation theology is a sharp reminder that religious belief, doctrine or sensibility can still inspire progressive social movements. Religion, even as a form of knowledge, belongs to a wider domain of ideas or 'signification'.

According to the more positive or neutral conception of ideology, this field of signification can be the domain of ideational conflict. This looser, more general conception of ideology frees the study of religion from the corsets imposed by a restricted and negative conception to allow something more closely approximating religion's truer place in the realm of human affairs. But the critical edge of the Marxist approach to religion can also be lost in this loosening of epistemological and sociological stays. Retaining a fundamental emphasis on the relationship between meaning and power and on ongoing conflicts in the field of signification is essential.

There is much to be said for linking ideology to asymmetrical relations of power, of understanding ideology as 'meaning in the service of power'. Meaning is understood not as beliefs but as signification. So ideology is much more than a belief system and not necessarily as coherent. It belongs to the realm of language and discourse rather than to the realm of beliefs and is embodied in everyday practices and routines.[28]

Those Marxists seeking to defend Marx's notion of religion have had to greatly broaden the notion of ideology itself. In doing so they risk so expanding its conceptual boundaries as to make it less and less different in scope and nature from culture. Furthermore, what is distinctive about religion tends to get lost.[29] These are real dangers not always avoided.[30]

At most, ideology should connect meaning and power but not necessarily in a relationship of 'service'. Ideology is in-between 'explicit doctrine' and 'lived experience'. There is an *ideological formation* which can be looked at from many angles. This formation is multi-layered and criss-crossed, having more as well as less articulated levels. Religion is one such (part of an?) ideological formation, a 'way of bringing to bear the most fundamental questions of human existence on a uniquely individual life'.[31]

There is a tendency among modern Marxists to exaggerate the

importance of ideology and culture, a mental reflex among socialists towards capitalist stabilization and the general absence of revolutionary working-class behaviour in the advanced capitalist countries. But the linguistic turn in philosophy makes a more generous re-evaluation of the role of ideology and cognition in social life unavoidable. The point is: how far to go? Overgenerosity here can make a mockery of the Marxist insistence (howsoever subtly qualified) on the primacy of the economy.

And what of the ideological terrain itself? Is it not occupied by various ideologies (in the plural)?[32] These are not unitary class ideologies but different discourses (ideologies are 'clusters' or 'discursive chains' coexisting, partially merging, and competing with each other). An ideology constructs individuals as subjects and also ideological communities with or without the help of a systematized, explicit body of doctrines. Here, religion is once again a kind of ideology and ideology is a subset of culture. Culture is a system of symbols, so religion/ideology are *aspects* of this symbol system. The key aspects here are those which interpellate subjects (affix identity) and construct imagined ideological communities. Ideologies may or may not have political significance, depending on whether they help to sustain existing relations of power. The more disinterested or natural the ideological community appears, the more it overrides the contradictions of social life. Nationalism is perhaps the most powerful example of such an ideological community, the inheritor of this mantle from kinship loyalty and the religious community of the past.

The notion of religion as a form of ideology, then, is a reasonably productive and defensible one, provided a positive or neutral conception of ideology is employed. Later Marxist understandings are to be preferred to earlier ones. The Marxist approach offers a launching pad for a serious investigation of the connection between social position and religious beliefs and experiences, and of the relationship between religious discourses and the preservation of social and political power. But since religion is also more than this, there are important aspects of its role and impact which tend not to be treated with sufficient sensitivity. In developing a better understanding of religion in modernity, of religion in culture and society, one has to think through and beyond the Marxist tradition.

But whether ideology should be understood in a critical sense or in the positive–neutral sense, or whether one can abstain from so choosing and leave it to be determined by context, are not matters that hinge on the question of how best to understand religion. They hinge much more on the relative analytical usefulness of critical and positive conceptions of ideology for more general purposes. They depend more on how ideology understood in these contrasting ways can be separated from and used to understand culture and society. To make ideology near-coterminous with culture damages such endeavours and risks immortalizing religion. Here it may well be that the critical conception of ideology as 'meaning in the service of power' proves more useful. If this view were adopted, then it would be necessary to make adjustments to the conceptualization of religion and of its relationship to ideology. But there would be no 'loss' to speak of. Religion would now simply straddle ideology and culture rather than be immersed in culture (and society) via ideology. The really important questions concern the relationship between religion, on the one hand, and culture and society, on the other.

Culture and Society: The Problem of Order

Immortalizing religion would not be so questionable a procedure if its advocates were only suggesting that religion is likely to endure for ever because for some or many it will remain the most desired way of coping with the individual's ontological dilemma, that the more individualized functions of religion will endure even as modernity renders its social functions more tenuous and problematic. Immortalizers, however, generally claim much more.[33] They assert religion's inescapable *centrality* to culture and society. Religion is either coterminous with or at the heart of any and all human cultures. Furthermore, religion is crucial to society because it is indispensable to the securance and maintenance of social order.

This is the most common form of the 'Social Cement' thesis. Three types of relationships are involved here: religion and culture, religion and society, culture and society. Culture and society are analytically (though not empirically or actually) separable. But more often than not, proponents of the Social Cement thesis do not rigorously explicate the analytical difference between the two.

For some (usually sociologists and social anthropologists) society is the decisive term and intrinsically human: culture is subsumed by it. For others (most often culturalists and cultural anthropologists) culture is the ultimate human reality and society its vehicle. Some understand religion as the human capacity for symbolic self-transcendence beyond biology, an understanding which eternalizes religion, making it effectively coterminous with any symbolic conception of culture itself.[34] Others are more qualified. *Culture* is the capacity for such symbolic self-transcendence.[35] The fact of mortality is the important source of 'culture, that huge and never stopping factory of permanence.'[36] Culture is seen as basically beyond reason. So far religion has been *the* cultural practice. In modernity, it is conceded, this undergoes some change and philosophy can replace religion. Changing cultural responses to the problem of finitude means the value and importance of the specifically religious antidote can diminish. Religion is but one *form* of that capacity.

Theoretically, this allows for the possibility of non-religious kinds of culture. But hardly any better substitute is envisaged. Culture subsumes society. Society comes out of but is then the condition for culture's production/reproduction. There can be no question of disorder in society because society *is* order. Society's key purpose is nomization (the ordering of meaning) and its stability is best attained when cosmization (ordering of the cosmos) reinforces nomization. Religion as a mode of cosmization is exceptionally powerful and stable because it is reverential, sacred and evokes awe. It is a 'sacred legitimation' that unites nomos and cosmos. Dharma then, far from being unique (as claimed by innumerable savants of Brahminical Hinduism), is but the 'high' Indian version of religious–sacred cosmization–nomization. What is distinctive about dharma is its incredibly detailed and elaborated character. Dharma, along with the karma–samskara complex, provides a unique way of handling the theodicies of suffering and happiness, enclosing it with complete symmetry, providing a *simultaneous* legitimation of the conditions of all social strata. This is the most *conservative* form of high religious legitimation of social hierarchy yet devised.

Whether or not religion is inescapably central to society, then, depends on whether alternative modes of cosmization–nomization, alternative legitimations, are possible and as effective. Berger, the foremost proponent of this view, recognized that religious theodicies have become more implausible in modernity and thus religious forms of cosmization–nomization are weakened. There are alternative modes (e.g. science) but they are not better. If modernity makes it *possible* for religion no longer to be central, society is likely to imperil itself if it thinks it can find an adequate non-religious replacement. Hence Berger's ambiguous attitude to modernity and his fear and scepticism about secularization if this is taken to suggest a continuing process of religious decline. Not only is society order, but order is also human nature.[37] In true Durkheimian fashion the only serious conflict allowed for is that between individual and society. Intermediate social groups and their conflicts don't come into the picture.

From a substantivist perspective Berger was as deeply committed, indeed more so, to a social coherence model as any Parsonian functionalist who sees religion as providing the normative order cohering society. Only the routes are different. Functionalism sees society's normal state as a healthy equilibrium like that of a biological organism. Disturbance sets off a dynamic which has its wellspring in shared moral values/ norms that aim to establish a new equilibrium. Most functionalists see religion as the main source of this but some accept that another mechanism besides religion can do the job.[38]

Others would say another kind of religion needs to emerge, e.g. American Civil Religion, where the relationship is inverted. Culture is no longer based on religion but religion on culture. This is a convoluted way of recognizing the declining influence of religion in the USA yet preserving its claim of social centrality. What is noticeable in the functionalist approach (where religion is linked to society) and the phenomenological–hermeneutic approach (where religion is linked to culture) is that an unshaken commitment to the Social Cement thesis is accompanied by a distinctly shakeable consensus on religion as an essential or major component of that cement. Modernity has created uncertainty about religion's social role even among those seeking to conjoin religion and modernity.

The 'religion is central to society' formula is generally the result of a double fusion. Religion is fused with culture and culture with society. The latter fusion is the source of the Social Integration or Social Cement thesis – the cultural programming of society. The former fusion establishes religion as the key cultural programmer.[39]

The fusion, an intellectual one, is inscribed in the conceptual tools developed and deployed, even though these may be empirically legitimized through anthropological field study or sociological survey. Raymond Williams points out that a general conception of culture only emerges after the Industrial Revolution as a reaction to the general character of change and to the increasingly felt need for general designs.[40] Seventeenth- and eighteenth-century Romanticism, with its rejection of strong notions of progress and reason, fostered a notion of culture 'beyond reason', as in part symbolically expressive of a people's basic and enduring values, perhaps best captured through recognition of the 'informing spirit' of its religion–culture. Nineteenth-century anthropology, with its notion of culture as a 'whole way of life', made culture coterminous or broader than society. This reinforced the idealist tenor of Romantic conceptions of culture which by the late eighteenth century treated it no longer as a noun of 'process', of 'tending' ('to cultivate'), but as a noun of configuration or generalization of the 'informing spirit'.[41] This was now extended to a whole way of life. But it also stimulated a *descriptive* conception of the whole way of life, its artefacts, habits, customs, etc., that promoted comparative cultural studies and systems of classification.

The most important twist was supplied in the 1960s after the decline of behaviourism. Recognizing that human action was not so much a response to external stimuli/constraints as the result of internal representation of the external environment was an advance. From being 'out there', culture came to be seen more as 'in the mind'. Ever since, a cognitive conception of culture, in particular a semiotic or symbolic conception, has dominated the field of culture theories.

Allying itself to the anthropological notion of a whole way of life, a strongly idealist conception of culture has resurfaced at a considerably higher level of sophistication than before. Symbols are seen as not just partly but substantially or overwhelmingly constitutive of reality itself. The problem lies not with a symbolic conception of culture but with the exorbitation of the Symbolic Order. Society is seen no longer as a nexus of economic, political and cultural–ideological relationships or as their structured totality, but as an *organized* meaning system to be decoded via an understanding of the 'shared system of symbols/meaning', itself organized by a unifying principle which is discoverable. Culture has a unity, a definite patterning, even an essence, or at least a distinctive ethos, rooted for the most part in collective tradition. This is a more developed cousin to the more traditional Durkheimian view of society as a 'structure of social ties informed by a moral consensus'.

Such a sweeping notion of culture–society–the Symbolic Order is strongly inclined towards endorsing the indispensability of religion as its particularly powerful if not decisive axis. Religious–sacred symbols 'condense' the values of a culture. What is important is not faith in God(s) but faith in faith, and the role of faith–worship in society. The self-consciousness and self-questioning of modernity may lead us to question God but if society is to cohere we must encourage the 'worshipping of our worshipping'. What is lost sight of here is that religious symbols do not just 'condense', they also 'refer', i.e. make truth-claims and serve legitimating functions. The Social Cement thesis repeatedly de-emphasizes, where it does not altogether ignore, the epistemological status of religious claims as well as religion's functions in legitimating prevailing social relationships of power.

In all such notions there is little place for cultural contradictions and inconsistencies. Insofar as they exist they are supposed to do so at a secondary level in a framework of overall cultural coherence. Otherwise, by definition, neither culture nor society could survive or reproduce itself. The more segmented, fractured, layered, complex and *messy* our notion of a culture or of a cultural space or zone, the more difficult to sustain the view that religion's relationship to culture is essential and permanent, rather than contingent.

To believe in the contingency of this relationship does not mean that religion has not been and cannot be crucial and enduring. It is only to contest the claims of religion to complete ubiquity and incorrigible omnipotence. It is to refuse to close off possibilities and to be open to the prospects and consequences of cultural change and transformation. It is to have a more *dynamic* notion of culture and it is hardly surprising that more static notions of culture *prima facie* should seem more appropriate to pre-modern cultures and societies. A give-away about the close relationship between the notion of religion and the *static* concept of a culture is provided by the striking fact that no pre-modern religion (certainly not the world-religions) has had a strong concept of terrestrial progress before Enlightenment thinking impacted upon it.

Raymond Williams was more aware of these problems than most. Williams, like others, also held to a cognitive/symbolic concept of culture. But where he was inclined to see culture as 'process', others had a broader and more static vision of culture as a 'class of things shared', a 'state of affairs'. Williams moved away from an earlier, more anthropologically inclined view of culture as a whole way of life to a more restricted one which he felt was more appropriate at least for modern societies.

The sources for this shift lay in his greater sensitivity to the very distinctive problems posed by modernity of *complexity* and *change*. Culture was better seen not as a whole way of life but as a 'realized signifying system' which is not so all-encompassing as just a 'signifying system'. A 'realized signifying system' included 'manifest signifying systems' or the more obviously cultural practices. But it also incorporated the inter-relationship between 'manifest' and 'non-manifest' systems. Either more manifest cultural practices were dissolved in less manifest ones whose main purposes were not cultural but nonetheless had an inescapable cultural dimension, or 'other' practices were dissolved into manifest cultural practices, lending it certain non-cultural dimensions.[42]

Whatever the difficulties and ambiguities here it was his way of distinguishing between the more and the less cultural, of grasping how the more cultural can shade into the less cultural into the almost non-cultural. It was Williams's way of insisting on the inescapability of a cultural materialism and of a materialist culture, of, for example, the culture of the economy and the economy of a culture. In contrast, the whole way of life notion or any too exaggerated notion of the cultural–symbolic order created at least two major problems.

How is one to speak of the more or less cultural, if, in a parallel move to Foucault's dissolution of the notion of power, everything everywhere is cultural? Similarly, what then lies outside culture? The only answer could be nature. The result is a radically polarized conception of the relationship between culture and nature when in fact modernity renders even more complex and multifaceted their relationship in comparison to the already multilayered relationship between the two in all but the most primitive (pre-tribal) of societies. Implicitly, Williams was warning of the dangers of an analytical conflation or near-conflation of culture with society, and of an essentialist or too homogeneous view of culture itself; a view encouraged by the thesis that there is a fusion of religion and culture.

To talk of a cultural zone or space is to employ a heuristic whose worth is guided by the specific purposes of the project for which the heuristic is chosen. Any cultural area always comprises many cultures coexisting, connecting, repelling and clashing, thus creating a shifting balance of cultural forces. One can talk of the tone or ethos of a culture provided it is kept in mind that this is always the temporary resultant emerging out of a cultural field of force always subject to transformation and change; that within that space there are ethoses as well as ethos. Any cultural space comprises 'dominant, residual and emergent' cultures and generational, temporal and spatial tensions of a cultural kind. To talk of a culture as if it were largely sealed, uniform and a long-enduring entity is to risk mistaking the heuristic for the real thing, which is always characterized by far more complexity, openness and flux, especially in modernity.[43] For our times there can be few more plausible understandings of culture, cultures and cultural spaces than those proposed by Williams. His approach also focuses attention directly on issues concerning asymmetries in cultural power and the desirability of cultural democratization.

What of the difference between culture and society? Or between a cultural and a socio-cultural system? Especially after the ascendance of a cognitive concept of culture, the crucial difference is that society consists of persons and their inter-relationships, culture does not. Nor

87

does culture comprise thoughts, for only persons have thoughts. Thoughts and feelings are culturally determined but do not belong to culture as such. Culture comprises propositions or meanings abstracted from particular individuals, encoded in symbols. The cultural system does not have a knowing subject, the socio-cultural system does.[44] Persons, however, are involved in asymmetrical relationships of power having their institutional embodiments which help create a territorial space over which such power hierarchies operate in a structured and not merely haphazard way.

The geographical shape or boundaries of such societies have never been easy to establish. So much so, that some historical sociologists would do away altogether with the notion of society before the advent of modernity and prefer to talk of 'overlapping socio-spatial networks of power'. Accordingly, this network has distinct dimensions of ideological, economic, military and political power.[45] After the emergence of an international system of nation-states, societies have become more visibly bounded and are largely congruent with the territorial boundaries of a given nation-state. Certainly, it is this 'national-territorial totality' that most of us have in mind when using the term 'society' today.[46]

Whatever clarity of definition or degree of resolution a society has, it seems to owe it more to political–administrative factors than to cultural ones. To understand how society exists, survives and reproduces itself one must look at a whole complex of variables and levels of human existence and human relationships, especially at the political level. One cannot simply assume that the key to the whole construct lies in the domain of the cultural or, even more narrowly, in the domain of religion.

The search for the sources of order or stability in a society is to be conducted at the level of the *social* itself or in the socio-cultural system as a whole, and not purely or primarily at the level of the cultural system. Social order is not a simple or straightforward function of meaning. It has as much, if not more, to do with issues of power, and therefore with matters of social tension, dominance and conflict, as it has to do with issues of cultural–moral norms, values and beliefs. One should expect cultural tensions and contradictions (including religious differences) to have some discernible relationships to social stratification and conflict, which indeed they do and have always done.

Existential dilemmas are not uniform or the same for everyone. They bear a definite relationship to social position: religious needs differ and the poor probably have always been more concerned with problems of health, wealth, security, solace and self-respect in the face of deprivation and therefore with what religion has had to offer in these respects.[47] The more ethereal visions of 'religious essence', the abstract enunciations of its 'morally binding' character over society have generally been connected to elitist conceptions of society and to justifications for elite dominance.

When there is downward conflation of the cultural system with the socio-cultural system, then social integration is identified with cultural integration. This promotion of the Myth of Cultural Integration of a society is an untenable move because the cultural system (which excludes persons) can have only a logical not a causal coherence. There are only logical relations in a cultural system (including logically inconsistent relations) but no causal relations. It is illegitimate to read off from logical coherence in a cultural system causal coherence or consensus in a socio-cultural system.[48] The 'grip of tradition' over a society, insofar as it can be said to exist, comes from social factors not from cultural integration.

Structural functionalists believed that value patterning through role expectation led to this cultural integration, though they might differ on whether or not religion functionally integrates the other parts (morality, art, philosophy, etc.) in a cultural system (and therefore in society). For functionalists, coherence is established through practices/activities. Structuralists in the twentieth century believed in invariant properties of the mind. Such invariant properties cohere culture which coheres society. Here, the organizing mechanisms are located in the mind, in the unconscious, e.g. myth. Religion, then, is a 'necessary myth' since social mythology is vital to cohering society. Religion, it can be and is argued, will be a better, more humane kind of Social Cement than non-religious forms of social mythology, because of its transcendent dimension.[49]

Whatever the case for pre-modern societies with low social differentiation and slower rates of change, for modern societies there are grave problems with the standard forms of social coherence models. Empirical evidence alone suggests a much more complex picture of reality. Most people have beliefs which are inconsistent and often incoherent and behave in inconsistent ways. If culture is related to how we think and behave, then cultural inconsistency, contradiction and incoherence is a widespread and irrefutable fact of life. It is also true that there is popular allegiance to certain symbols, values and beliefs which favour the status quo and, therefore, stability (on elite terms) of society.

But the overall picture is much more contradictory, far less uniform, and evinces far less 'committed' consent than suggested by Social

Cement or consensus models which ignore power relations. Such models do not explore the *origins* of normative agreement. They disregard or de-emphasize questions concerning *who benefits* from this social order. They clearly favour the status quo in thrust and direction.

In truth, the Social Cement 'mixture' can have varying compositions. The adhesive strength of the mixture or the degree of consensual attachment it creates can vary from the strongly active to the weakly passive. Legitimation requires a strongly active form of consent. The role of religion in legitimating the public order has indisputably though unevenly declined. Even third world theocracies or confessional states are, in a longer historical view, on the defensive now that republican and democratic alternatives exist and are clearly feasible.

In general, the strength of Social Cement is a function of (a) the degree of development of the infrastructure of communication; and (b) the existence of options regarding morals, values, beliefs. If in the pre-modern era the weakness of the first was compensated for by the relative absence of the second, in the modern period, the rapid development of the first and the 'mediaization of modern culture' is compensated for (and its homogenizing tendencies countered by) the substantial flowering of the second.[50] There were more chances of getting away with the idea of a cultural essence harmonizing society on some higher Olympian plane of spirituality when those tensions and conflicts were class struggle, wars and revolutions, i.e. largely political and economic in character. But today in the second half of the twentieth century, the notion of a harmonizing culture is all the more out of place when the terrain of culture – language, value, identity, experiences, life-styles, etc. – is criss-crossed by tensions and conflicts as never before; when the 'politics of life choices' has joined the 'politics of life chances' on the stage of human struggle.[51]

There are four possible sources for social order: consensus, rational choice, coercion or fear of consequences, lack of *unified* dissensus. Undoubtedly all elements are present in some measure. But models of social stability differ sharply in the weights they assign to each component. The object of criticism here – consensus models (which are the only ones prepared to give religion such a central role) – are convincing neither on theoretical nor on empirical grounds, even in the more stable, advanced capitalist democracies where there has been most empirical testing of such claims.

The average person, it seems, is more likely to have a stretched value-system with a low degree of commitment to all values. Moreover, there is a clear difference between the abstract and the situational. The more abstract and far removed from familiar routines the values and beliefs in question, the more likely that the average person will go along with dominant views. The more situational and directly relevant the values or beliefs in question, the stronger the correlation between that person's views and his social position, and the more likely that these will be in dissonance with or only weakly supportive of dominant views.

The rational choice argument sees social order as the result of interactional bargaining between self-maximizing agents. Compliance here is based neither on fear nor on consensus but on pragmatic assessments of self-interest. But this 'exchange theory' model of social order does not explain why interests are what they are because it does not consider context – they just are, and are taken as such. Its methodological individualism assumes what must be explained. The result is a form of tautological reasoning. Why do people tailor their interests and ambitions so as not to challenge a social order in which the majority are disadvantaged? They don't challenge because it pays them not to. How do we know it pays them not to ? Because they don't challenge!

The third source – coercion, or fear of punishment – is at best a very partial explanation of social stability or order. It is when this is combined with the fourth source that we reach the most plausible perspective. Most people do not see themselves as victims most of the time. To do so would be to block avenues of self-respect which make life liveable and in some sense worthwhile. People are not self-pitying sufferers nor straining at the leash as it were, constrained only or primarily by fear. It is not so much active consensus as the passivities born of routines and habits or the 'dull compulsions of economic life' that help secure social order and social reproduction.

It is not that society has core values (which may or may not be anchored by religious practice and belief) over which there is consensus but that whatever consensus about values/beliefs exists pertains to specific roles.[52] This is a vision of society as more like an orchestra whose members are 'trained' (through socialization processes) and 'persuaded' (through sanctions and rewards) to play their respective parts, than of society as a choir happily singing the same song. But the training is never complete and the persuasion is never irresistible. What keeps society in some sense together is not consensus but a lack of a unified dissensus, i.e. no counter-consensus challenging the social order. For normal functioning, active agreement is not necessary. Passive acceptance of the existing order of things is enough. The weakness of negative factors is more relevant to the explanation of social normality and order than the strength of positive factors.

The Marxist variant of the Social Cement argument is the Dominant Ideology thesis, a form of upward conflation of the socio-cultural system with the cultural system. Instead of normative consensus there is a 'manipulated' cultural consensus. Instead of the cultural programming of society there is the social programming of culture. Ruling-class solidarity leads to a wider social solidity. Another Marxist variant with less affinity to Durkheim and more to Weber is Critical Theory's argument about the diffusion and dominance of technocratic consciousness in advanced capitalist societies.

The Dominant Ideology thesis, however, is available for application over a far wider range of societies, geographically and historically. The severest critique of the Dominant Ideology thesis has been that of Abercrombie, Hill and Turner.[53] It has been an important brake on the slide of Marxist thought in the last two decades along a pronounced culturalist slope. Abercrombie, Hill and Turner do not deny that there is a (or are) dominant ideology (ideologies), only that it does not have the power that its proponents, following the Marx of *The German Ideology*, claim. Abercrombie, Hill and Turner employ theoretical and empirical criticisms. Certainly the empirical evidence in post-war advanced capitalisms supports the notion of a highly 'contradictory consciousness' among the working class.

Theoretically, the Dominant Ideology thesis has too many loose ends. It is much easier to talk of its existence than to specify accurately what it is – its full content and range. Though the dominant ideology is said to incorporate and pacify dominated classes there is, unsurprisingly, considerable disagreement over the degree of incorporation and pacification. Finally, the mechanisms for transmitting the dominant ideology and carrying out a more or less unidirectional indoctrination are not as impervious to the social tensions and cultural contradictions of capitalism as the Dominant Ideology thesis must assume.

The dominant ideology is strong enough to be a significant obstacle to the construction of a collective counter-ideology of the oppressed but no stronger. This is akin to the claim that the putative Social Cement is not much more than slightly toughened social plaster, which nonetheless is generally sufficient to make difficult or prevent collective mobilization and unification amidst the numerous scatter points of dissent in society.

Marxist critics plausibly suggest that the dominant ideology has always been much more important in solidifying the dominant class or social bloc than it has been in incorporating subordinate classes. In feudalism the weakness of communications infrastructure ensured this. In late capitalism there is greater diffusion of the dominant ideology and perhaps greater assent to some of its themes among subordinate classes, i.e. greater partial incorporation. But the role of the dominant ideology in solidifying the dominant class or ruling bloc itself is considerably weakened. This is because differentiation within the ruling bloc is greater and when added to the pressure of over a hundred and fifty years of class and ideological contestation makes the dominant ideology more incoherent.

In rejecting the extravagant claims of ideology, religion and culture in society, Abercrombie, Hill and Turner argue that they are actually following in the footsteps of Marx (*The German Ideology* was an aberration), and even of Durkheim and Weber. Others will not agree. Durkheim, after all, is the progenitor of the original Social Cement thesis. But he did also believe that with the advent of modernity one was moving from the realm of 'mechanical solidarity' to that of an 'organic solidarity' in which the functional division of labour counted for much more than the notion of core values or '*conscience collective*'.[54] Certainly in his tracing of the evolution of legal codes and systems he was also tracing the growing disjunction between morality and religion even as he held to the view that in some basic though perhaps minimal sense the two were inseparable.

Probably the safest approach is simply to accept Durkheim's work as being located at a point of transition, a coming to grips with the challenge of modernity for society and religion, with the ultimate direction of his own thought processes still open and unclear. Even as he emphasized the centrality of *some* notion of religion to society he acknowledged the diminished role in modern life of religion as recognized till then. We cannot know if he would have been in sympathy with the direction taken by subsequent Durkheimians. But Abercrombie, Hill and Turner are on strong ground in claiming that Parsons's more determined commitment to the centrality of the normative consensus became the symptomatic and most influential interpretation of the Durkheimian legacy.

The case of Weber is more straightforward. He may have felt Calvinism explained the origins of capitalism. He would not claim, however, that it or any other religious creed would explain the maintenance and reproduction of capitalism. The world was being progressively disenchanted through the rise of technocratic–bureaucratic rationality. Human society and culture was being progressively compartmentalized.

The decline of religion meant the effective loss of culture's gyroscope – the source of stable definitions of society and the self. The dilemma of the modern woman or man was loss of meaning and a deepening sense of inauthenticity.

If Weber and Durkheim seem to have had a strong sense of the historical firebreak created by modernity, this sense has not always been so manifest in their followers. Howsoever central or stabilizing religion may have been to culture and society in the pre-modern era, modernity is characterized by a rate, scope and depth of change which must upturn all arguments which emphasize modernity's basic *continuity* with tradition and traditional societies. The upshot must be a profound re-evaluation of the relationships between religion, culture, society; a recognition that these are much more likely than not to be qualitatively different from the relationships claimed for these three terms in the past.

We have seen that the social coherence or consensus model is singularly unimpressive in understanding modern societies. That alone is enough to strongly dispute the claim of immortalizers or near-immortalizers of religion about the *unavoidable* centrality of its role in culture and society. Of the past, with its slower rhythms of change, we might concede the fact of such centrality. But even there we do not know enough empirically (and may never know enough) to arrive at confident conclusions. Much of what we do know is from sources (textual) which are strongly biased towards elitist versions of the power, importance and meaning of specific religions and religious systems. If it is plausible that in much of pre-modernity each religion was more thickly integrated into a culture or cultural space, it is also plausible to acknowledge that the space over which such thickness operated was much smaller. So there is a greater expansion of Christianity over pagan Europe in the era of industrialization than before. The greater thinness of religion's connection to culture is the obverse side of the greater spread of a particular religious system. As modernity progresses there is a halt even to this lateral spread.

Raymond Williams suggested that one should not look for a universal schema to explain the relationship between culture and society.[55] The force of this proposition, if accepted, is a real and powerful one. Openness and change are thereby marked on the scroll of the future. There is no fixed relationship between religion and culture, religion and society, culture and society. Even if such fixities were true of the past, they need not be so of the future. Hopefully enough has been said already to persuade that it is not true even of the present.

Religion in Modernity: The Question of Identity

If modernity forces a change in the role of religion, as it assuredly does, then what is the direction of this change? It is the more individual functions of religion rather than its social functions that become increasingly important, even as we acknowledge that there is no easy separation between the individual and society. The manifest function of religion (salvation) becomes more important than its latent function (social binding).[56] Religious influence on the individual, especially in late modernity, is no longer necessary for binding her to society. Nor, indeed, is it any longer so important to control sexuality (women's bodies) through religious sanction for assuring transmission of property rights, since family-owner capitalism has been overtaken to a greater or lesser extent by corporate capitalism.[57]

In the most industrialized/urbanized societies today religion is not so much the 'texture' of life as a 'filling up of the interstices'. In countries like India, the picture is much more combined and fuzzy. But it nonetheless constitutes a significant break from its own past. Neither India nor other third world societies have escaped modernity's powerful impact. The more important individual functions of religion in modernity have to do with questions of identity (individual and group) and meaning. It is the relationship between religion and individual subjectivity that becomes paramount *but* subjectivity itself changes along with modernity.[58]

The modern personality is in crucial ways different from the premodern personality. The impact of modernity on identity-availability and identity-formation is new. The nature and place of religious identity in society is different. So what is identity? Given the connection between identity and culture, a cognitive approach to culture makes it virtually incumbent to adopt a cognitive theory of subjectivity and identity. This approach links identity to an interactional concept of consciousness where consciousness is a world of meanings but 'is less something "within" us than something around and between us'.[59]

A good starting point is Erik Erickson's definition: 'The term identity connotes both a persistent sameness within oneself (self-sameness) and a persistent sharing of some kind of essential character with others.'[60] This 'essential character' which is *held* or *shared* (sameness within oneself cannot be sameness in all respects but has to be some *relevant* notion of sameness) refers to what consciousness is about, namely beliefs, values, desires.[61] It refers to some set of these held and shared. A variation on

95

this cognitive definition is the point made by the Canadian philosopher Charles Taylor, that to be a person or self is to exist in a space defined by distinctions of worth, that is, against a background of strong evaluation. Human beings are strong evaluators and identity is intimately connected to issues of self-worth, hence the particular sensitivity with which one must handle it even in casual discussion and argument. Identity involves *commitment* in a framework of values. Identity is not the same as belonging because belonging *comes* from what is held and shared.

This is clearly a socio-psychological conception of identity. But there can be a difference in bias towards either a more sociological or a more personality-centred understanding.[62] The above definitions as they stand are too mentalist, leaning too much towards a Cartesian separation of mind and body, mind and brain. They benefit from qualification in two respects. A more physicalist concept of identity is required. This would not refute or replace the cognitive concept of identity but be a necessary addendum.

Each person's psychological make-up comprises a core psychological domain having minimum mental capacities for reasoning, emotion, etc., which are universally shared; and a distinctive psychological domain comprising the distinctive elements of consciousness, e.g. beliefs, values, desires. Both together help to make up personal identity.[63] But what makes these capacities and their exercise in forms of consciousness one's *own* cannot be the capacities or forms which are available to and shareable with others, but their physical emplacement in one's *own brain*. An exact biological clone having my exact capacities and beliefs, values, desires, is still not me. The cognitive theory of identity makes it totally interactional and states that there is no 'I' that is not at the same time, actually or potentially, 'part of a we'. The physicalist conception of identity is a reminder that there is a part of 'I-ness' which is *not* shareable. There is no complete merger of the individual and society. There is *an* irreducible element of I-ness which is materially (physically) not ideationally or 'spiritually' located. Even so, the construction of personal identity is always simultaneously the construction of a social identity. And once the physicalist case is accepted, the really interesting things to investigate are best dealt with in and by the cognitive approach.

The second qualification has to do with recognizing the three separate aspects of the self–society relationship. There is an individuation dimension as well as an individuality dimension in the construction of subjectivity. There are conferred identities as well as more freely chosen and constructed ones. Individuation is strongly related to social control and authority (authority figures, authority symbols). Insofar as a sense of self first emerges from a sense of separateness on the part of the infant from the mother which is coupled with a sense of dependency, then individuation is the name of this process. An infant has desires, it does not have beliefs and values. The transition from infancy to childhood to adolescence to adulthood is also a movement on the individuation–individuality continuum towards the latter pole.

There is identifying one's environment, being identified by one's environment, and identifying *with* one's environment.[64] The second (having identity or identities conferred) can come before the first, e.g. at the point of birth.[65] The first is the infant individuation process and the third is where the individuality dimension of identity construction is most prominent. All social identities are, of course, place- and thing-related.

A strong individuality theory of subjectivity is more appropriate for the post-infant than for the infant phase in the human life-cycle. It is also more appropriate for the modern personality than for the pre-modern individual, because the transition from traditional life to modernity also sees a qualitative leap in the individualization of person-ality related to the qualitatively greater range of beliefs, values and desires available, and the greater possibilities of choice from them that now exists. This is not the least nor the only impact of modernity on identity.

Identities are rational and theoretical constructs having epistemic status. There can be false and bad identities, because what makes up identities has epistemic status. Identities act as psychic filters. They are ways of reading the world. They make sense of our experiences and shape them, but are also inputs into the construction of experiences.[66] Identity is located at the juncture of individual and environment. Sociology emphasizes the socialization process, i.e. the internalization of social mores in the individual to stabilize society. Identification theory in psychology is the view from the other side with the emphasis on internalization of mores and identity construction to meet individual needs.[67]

Humans *must* have identity for psychological well-being and stability. There is a *need* for identity or identification which is as powerful as any other human need or instinct. [68]And it is a need that is *always* answered in some form or the other through situational–cognitive processes. Between identity and action/behaviour is motivation. Identities moti-vate, the *need* for an identity does not.[69]

This need for identity exists for personal–social *not* for cosmic-meaning reasons. Religious identity per se is neither inescapable nor essential, identity is! Psychological security comes from having an identity. It does not presume anything more than that. It does not presume a stable social or cosmic order. It does not presume *particular* identities or world-views. Incoherent world-views might do. Infant individualism *is* closely connected to external reliability, predictability and order.

But the transition from individuation to individuality is also the realization of the ability to live and cope with uncertainty and unpredictability. There is no automatic nor necessarily desirable relationship between stable cosmos–stable society–stable personality or psychic order. The modern Age of Doubt does not imply a stronger tendency to psychic disorder (but newer forms of psychic disorder, e.g. newer forms of compulsive behaviour), nor a weakening of the resources for securing psychic order. It does imply a more continuous and frequent process of psychic reordering, a more frequent and multiple negotiation/renegotiation of identities that make up the self. There is a 'structured totality' of identities that make up the self, not, as postmodernists would have it, a fragmented self. But this structured totality is not fixed. It is endlessly revisable.

The new *revisability* of identities on a scale, depth and frequency unknown before is yet another tribute to the impact of modernity.[70] Just as society is uniquely dynamic the self too is uniquely dynamized. But this does not necessarily mean more psychic disorder or greater fragility of identities. Humans are both objects and subjects. The very notion of subjectivity carries this dual meaning. We are subjects–actors, we are subjects–objects of more powerful actors. Identity's object dimension relates to the boundary question. To have a particular identity is necessarily to establish difference from other identities, to be defined by this difference over which one has no control. The subject dimension is related to matters of trust and commitment, an active investment of oneself in an identity involving the anchoring of emotions. It is this active investment that gives such power to strongly held identities. Yet modernity forces more frequent negotiations and affirmations, with respect to both the boundary question and the trust dimension.

There *are* distinctive identity problems of modernity, but these have to do not with the brittleness or fragility of modern identities but with their flexibility and revisability.[71] Modern identities can be as *deeply* held as those of the past. They are not more fragile but more changeable because of the greater self-reflexivity of the individual today.[72] Identities in modernity are not more unstable but are stable identities worn more lightly (if need be, more insistently and regularly), in innumerable hues, 'cut' in a great variety of ways, composed of a greater range of 'fabrics'.

Charles Taylor marks the emergence of the modern identity in the seventeenth century.[73] Pre-modern cosmologies saw the world as conferred with meaning and morality. The world is as it is because it is as it should be: strong certitude arising from a closed order. The world's existence was the fulfilment of some scheme, divine or transcendent. It had a teleologically established rhythm or order which wars, plagues, etc., did nothing to disrupt.

Modernity destroys the certitudes of custom and tradition. But contrary to Enlightenment hopes it does not replace these with certitudes of its own that are as strong. Knowledge and reason have led to growing uncertainty, indeed to the institutionalization of radical doubt, to a multiplicity of claimants to authority. The claims of these authority systems are partial, and religion, the system which has come closest to making a claim to *absolute* authority, must itself lose some ground and reduce the scope of its own claims to a less absolute or complete level. God may not after all have made the world in seven days. Brahminism's cosmic clock (our time of degeneration or *kaliyug*) may best be taken as philosophical metaphor rather than as an empirical claim about the actual historical process. There is a relativization of the role of religion in modernity but the existence of uncertainty also creates a space for religion's resurgence as a form of psychological reassurance. However, this refutes neither the fact of religion's relativization nor its inability to play the same role as in the past or to the same intensity.

In modernity the connection between nomos and cosmos is greatly weakened. Social order and cosmic order, personal or social meaning and cosmic meaning are no longer so strongly connected. Personal and social meaning are elevated in importance while the domain of cosmic meaning suffers relative demotion. This is not just because science and rationality emerge as an alternative explanation of the cosmos. It is even more the consequence of the emergence of new notions of control and progress. Society perceives new vistas of possible and actual progress while the self glimpses a new horizon of fulfilment. The challenge to religion in respect of cosmization is paralleled by challenges in respect of nomization.

There are more and newer ways of making sense of both society and the cosmos. And new notions of progress and fulfilment create a new and stronger preoccupation with the social rather than the cosmic order, encouraging new hopes of moulding society and the self in desired directions. This is partial compensation for Weberian despair over the 'loss of meaning'. Not only does the meaning-of-life-in-society question become more tenuously connected to the meaning-of-life-in-cosmos question, it also becomes the more important question, the major testing ground where religion must prove its modern efficacy. And there is more than just the religious means of meeting the former need. Traditional, usually religious, ideas connecting personal life to cosmic happenings such as notions of *fate* and *destiny* come under new pressure and to some extent or the other buckle under.

The 'who am I?' question is, of course, connected to the 'how am I to live?' question. Humans are *naturally* moral. Not in a biological–genetic sense but in the sense that their common minimal rationality leads them to ask the 'how am I to live?' question. Humans do not simply want to believe that they are good but want *truly* to be good. Identity is connected not just to meaning but also to morality, but the two are not completely congruent. Identity is more is-ness, morality is ought-ness. The more complex a society, the more general becomes its moral value system and the more detachable from any specific identity such as the religious identity. The average tax-dodging yet devoutly Hindu shopkeeper suffers few qualms of conscience and the believing Catholic is more inclined now to question Papal Infallibility. The ability of religious systems to provide a powerful, encompassing and convincing moral canopy weakens decisively in the transition from pre-modernity to modernity and in the progression of modernity itself.

It is more true today than ever before that humans believe (in religion) not so much because they want to be good or because they want to search for the truth but because, above all, they want to locate themselves in society and the world. Both identity and morality move from the realm of the external to the realm of the internal. An external transcendent system gives way to a more internal referential system of morality, knowledge and power. In the past where identity had a more unreflective character, it was more an external horizon. For the individual today, identity is more an inner horizon; not external authorization but self-authorship. Personal fulfilment and authenticity becomes more important. One must be 'true to oneself'. One is more concerned about 'feeling good' than striving to 'match a cosmic pattern' or fulfilling one's dharma. Individual failure to live up to the standards explicit or implicit in these respective referential systems arouses different kinds of emotions and concerns. In the past preoccupations and anxieties about such failure led to conjectures about fate, condemnation and to feelings of guilt. In the present the dominant emotion as a result of comparable failings is not guilt but shame. 'The more self-identity becomes internally referential, the more shame comes to play a fundamental role in the adult personality.'[74]

While the philosophical and ethical dimensions of different religious systems can in theory find some common ground and thus claim near-universality, the most important modern function of religious systems – its identity affirmation and affixation – is inescapably particularist. Is this not fundamentally divisive and therefore an enduring obstacle to the Enlightenment aspiration of universalizing the deepest respect for a common humanity? Universalism cannot be counterposed to particularism but is only achievable through it. 'There is no way of being human which is not *a* way of being human.'[75] Particularism must be the concrete expression of universalism. All identities have boundaries and divide along certain lines but the relationship between particularism and universalism can differ.

How impermeable or resistant to entry and exit are the boundaries of different identities? How respectful of equality despite difference are they? Progressive equality across classes and castes requires the progressive disappearance of classes and castes. If complete success here is considered Utopian, great advances in this direction are not. The white person cannot become black, nor would most men or women ever physically want to change their sex, but racial and gender differences can in time cease to matter that much in respect of preference or self-evaluation. The Spanish speaker can learn Hindi and be equally proud. Particularisms remain but are conducive to universalist goals through growing acceptance of the principle of equality across differences. But can we ever look to a time when a Muslim can become a Hindu or a Hindu become a Christian in relationships of equality with this ceasing to matter that much for the communities in question?[76]

Any hopes that this can come about must mean that the case for free choice and complete revisability of religious identities be increasingly accepted and respected. And this requires a more modest self-appraisal by religious systems of their place and role in the world. Religious affiliation must increasingly be seen as an option, not as a requirement; one among a range of possible loyalties freely chosen and freely left, without dishonour felt by the community of believers in question. This is not an ecumenism which lays the ground rules for religious coexistence and competition but one where competition itself ceases to matter, where conversion between faiths and towards or away from faith is seen neither as collective affront nor as collective vindication.

This goes largely against the grain and tone of religious communities and systems as they currently stand, certainly of the world religions and

101

their community of believers. It is also incompatible with any notion of the centrality of a particular religious system to a particular culture. It becomes a feasible outcome when the religious function is increasingly privatized, and a desirable one when such privatization is accepted as a positive advance; when religious affiliation becomes, above all, an individual choice. The more secularized and democratic a society, the more chances there are of such a notion of religious modesty and religious equality flourishing.

Identities are psychic filters that shape experiences and emotions. The stronger and more expansive the identities in question, the more they will shape experiences and emotions. Strong experiences can and do help to reshape identities, but not all identities in specific societies are *equally* open to revisability in the light of new experiences. Gandhians can say that the strengthening and expansion of religious identity in civil society through a strengthening and expansion of religion's role will foster a stronger and wider sense of moral decency. Others, more critical, say that it is much more likely to shape experiences in ways which divide religious communities and erect barriers between them. This would lead to a stronger 'Hindu point of view' or 'Muslim point of view' when this should *not* be the prism for looking at many things.

Gandhians presume a strong link between morality and religious identity which is precisely what has weakened in modernity. Moreover, the religious identity being sacralized by reverence, it has a distinctive component of dependency, of near-surrender sometimes akin to masochism. This makes it somewhat more resistant to rational evaluation and justified criticism of its workings. In a context of religious conflicts and tensions, strengthening and expanding the importance of religious identities in civil society is much more likely to create more not less hostility and intolerance.

But what of Weberian despair at the loss of even private meaning in a disenchanted world? Is not the perdurance of religion the result of its faithful provision throughout the ages of meaning to an otherwise meaningless world? And is this not the guarantee of its permanent presence and power now and in the future? Religion, in fact, is not the indestructibly hardy answer to the dilemmas of meaninglessness but a non-answer! It has been, throughout pre-modernity, effectively a way of preventing the issue of meaninglessness and meaningfulness being put on life's agenda!

This problem of meaning must be separated from the problem of securing an antidote to the trauma of mortality, of coping with the inescapable transience of a human life. The effectiveness of religion in coping with the fact of mortality did not lie so much in its ability to give meaning but was more decisively related to the timelessness and repetitiveness of life; its closed and continuous rhythm. As aptly put, 'the timeless world did not prompt questions about the meaning of life, since what is obvious (unchallengeable, without alternative) is neither meaningful nor meaningless, but stands outside the realm of meanings.'[77]

Concern with meaning was pointless. Life was not in the hands of the living. It was not 'a task'. 'Life just *was*...." Religion removed meaning-of-life questions from life's agenda, it didn't answer them. Only in modernity does a serious *search* for meaning begin.

> 'Meaning is what is *meant*; there is no meaning unless action is intentional, preceded by a move addressed to a purpose. And there is no meaning where there is no freedom of choice between motives nor between purposes, and thus no responsibility for the choice eventually made. Having taken life out of the hands of the living, religions endorsed the world which had no room for the vexing questions of meaning.'[78]

With the advent of modernity what stands revealed is not the inadequacy or unsatisfactory character of religion as the answer to the newly perceived problem of meaning but the revelation that religion has been the *absence* of an answer. What most sociological functionalists and most immortalizers and near-immortalizers of religion seek to do is to *make* religion play a *new* role, even as they insist it is but a continuation of an older role. It is to push religion forward as the best answer or at least a good answer to the 'problem of meaning' in our Age of Doubt.

To look for meaning is akin to searching for a truth or essence behind appearances. Each of the paradigms of tradition/religion, of modernity, and of post-modernity have a distinctive relationship to the notions of progress and meaning which cannot be combined. One has to choose between these three competing paradigms about the contemporary human condition and their views about the desirable and likely direction of its future.

Pre-modernity–tradition–religion lacks any serious notion of progress. Modernity is seriously committed to progress, even if it has learnt not to be too arrogant about its claims and ambitions. Post-modernity con-sciously rejects the notion and value of progress altogether. Pre-modernity–tradition–religion largely eliminates the problem of meaning from life's agenda. Modernity is the inauguration of a serious search for meaning. Post-modernity is the rejection of such a quest altogether:

appearances are all we have. In the first there is the absence of a strong individuality theory of subjectivity. In the second there is the affirmation of the self-reflexive subject. In the third there is the denial altogether of subjectivity and the self. Different though they are, the first and the third paradigms can be, and often are, uneasy allies in the common assault on the modernist project, what it stands for, what it aspires to. It is a futile assault. The past cannot be restored and the post-modernist vision is but a dangerous chimera.

To briefly recapitulate: modernity affects identities in distinctive ways. In modernity we have considerably more and newer identities, not just of language group, kin, religion, caste or even class, but of belonging to the educated, being consumers, internationalists, nationalists, and so on. Our identities are sharper. The sheer advance in the means of communications and the emergence of census-taking provides a sharper sense of difference, between, say, Muslims and Hindus, a clearer sense of belonging to a religious minority or majority. Our identities are more flexible and revisable. Our identities compete, clash, repel, overlap and combine in new and complex ways.

The religious identity escapes none of these processes. It is relativized by the emergence of more and newer identities. It is sharpened by the collapse of purely localist perceptions and the recognition of other and different religious identities. Its power is qualified by the new potential for self-revisability of identities. It seeks to coexist with or combine with those identities it would not confront, e.g. nationalism.

The conclusion is inescapable. The decline in the power and importance of religious identity relative to its own past and relative to other identities (whatever be the unevenness of this within and across societies) is a *fact*. Its continuing relative decline is a *possibility* inherent in the nature of the modern condition. It is also *desirable* that religious systems be more modest and recognize their reduced role in society. Such self-modesty is also a precondition for the emergence of a *genuine* religious ecumenism that is compatible with a truly democratic life and with real religious equality. The privatization of religious affairs is the other name for this modesty. The conclusions arrived at here – the fact of, the further possibility of, and the desirability of religious decline – clearly affect the plausibility of the defences that can be erected for the various contending notions of secularization.

Secularization Once Again

Historically, secularization (and the ideology of secularism which inter-twines with this process) emerges in Europe in the context of the transition from feudalism to capitalism, the rise of the Enlightenment and of partial de-Christianization. The general understanding of the issue of secularization has ever since been marked by this historical background, with different people assigning different weights to how capitalist modernization, Enlightenment values of humanism, rational-ism and materialism, and Christianity relate to the nature and potential of secularization even today.

Of the three notions of secularization originating from the Western experience, the basic dispute concerns the secularization-as-decline thesis. But it also touches on the other two notions of secularization as relative separation, and as growing rationalization, since the decline thesis incorporates these notions as well.

First, is secularization-as-decline a fact? Much of the argument in preceding pages has been directed at showing that this is undeniable at least for the transition from pre-modernity to modernity. Additionally, that the claim of religion to centrality in modern life is quite implausible. How have opponents reacted? The twin argumentative strategies of immortalization/near-immortalization of religion, and of insisting on its centrality to culture/society have already been discussed. Their other arguments are largely pivoted on the issues of 'base-line', 'permeation' and 'rationality'.

The idea that modernity brings with it secularization-as-decline, it is said, must assume a base-line whence societies of the past were presum ably more religious. This, it is claimed, is the 'myth of the pious primitive'.[79] How do we know this to be so? How can we generalize so extravagantly across the centuries merely from anthropological studies with all the problems of reading these complex societies as 'primitive' exemplars of *our* past?

There is clearly a problem of accumulating proper and decisive historical evidence. But this does not prevent us from intelligently speculating. The base-line argument is something of a formal, technical and abstract objection. Historical evidence (or lack of it) may not convince beyond all doubt about the greater religiosity of past societies, but it certainly does not convince one that the past was more likely to have been less religious. Also, the main critics of the secularization-as-decline thesis try to establish a basic divide between magic and religion along Durkheimian lines, which must be considered unconvincing, to say the least. In the choice between these two assessments (allowing for spatial and temporal variations) it is obvious which is the more likely conclusion for students of history.

The base-line criticism thus needs to be bolstered by its upholders with other arguments concerning permeation and rationality. Older, less complex societies do seem to be more permeated by magic–religion than later, more complex societies and civilizations. Modern societies are quite clearly less permeated. There is at least overt shrinkage in the social space occupied by religious influence whether in institutionalized or non-institutionalized forms. If, in spite of this, it is argued that the secularization-as-decline thesis is wrong, then this claim can only be validated by redefining secularization to mean something other than decline.

This enables one to reject the decline thesis yet accept that secularization (understood only as a form of religious change) has taken place. Declining permeation means growing institutionalization of religion. This, then, is a kind of secularization process which has been taking place long before and right up to the advent of modernity. Then a significant development takes place. The very process of institutionalization (reaching its apogee in Christianity and embodied especially by the Papacy) becomes the precondition for the separation of church and state and the emergence of the secular state. This, it is usually argued, is probably a positive development.[80] But it does not mean there has been overall decline of religious influence and power in civil society, or in society as a whole (society comprising state, civil society, family, economy, etc.).

There has merely been reallocation of religious functions, even a secularization of religious practices. So Protestantism–Calvinism was the generalization of elite asceticism (of monks) to the laity. The Catholic confessional is replaced by the privileged confessional relationship between lawyer and client, doctor and patient. The practice in India of darshan (a respectful sighting) of religious leaders can be transferred to political leaders or leaders in other social fields, e.g. entertainment, sport, etc. The Guru–shishya (disciple) relationship is similarly applicable elsewhere.

Is such reallocation merely a change in the form of religion which only apparently declines? Or is there an actual reduction of the domain under religious control of any kind, not merely of religion in its institutional form? The answer depends on how one understands this transference of function. Is the fact of such transference enough to

106

confirm the loss of religious power or are these needs (howsoever institutionally satisfied) sourced in us as religious animals?

Pre-modern relationships and religious systems have always been imbued with principles of strong hierarchy and dependency. Insofar as modernity also brings in a *new* conception of equality it clearly has the *potential* to undermine and destroy older relational patterns, e.g. the confessional format. The doctor as God is a notion itself under pressure. Even Berger, uneasy, ambiguous and increasingly hostile as he became to the decline thesis, was prepared to concede the fact of *some* secularization of this kind. 'Secularization can be defined as a shrinkage in the role of religion, both in social life and in individual consciousness . . . secularization is a progressive loss of plausibility to religious views of reality.' [81]

The attack on presumably modernist concepts of rationality comes, of course, from other quarters, e.g. post-modernists and anti-modernists, than the one occupied by critics of secularization. But much of the furniture of argument is the same. How can pre-modern or even 'primitive' thought or religious thought be considered irrational compared to modernist thought? And if it is, so what? Is it not the arrogance of the rationalists which leads them to dismiss the importance of the irrational, or of what is beyond rationality and thus of systems like religion? If we cannot talk of past, religiously suffused/permeated societies as irrational or less rational, then what is left of the thesis that in part secularization means *growing* rationality brought about by more secular systems of knowledge like science? The question of secularization is clearly linked to the debate about rationality and cultural relativism.

Basic to the decline thesis (and not only to this notion of secularization) is that religious systems of thought are less rational than scientific ones, and that modern societies are in some sense more rational because of the impact of the scientific–Industrial Revolution. Is this defendable? Obviously it depends on how we understand rationality. But the simple answer is Yes! We have come a long way from the strong foundationalism of the Enlightenment view of Reason. We have learnt to be more modest. We talk of rationality with a small 'r' and of rationalities in the plural. 'Primitive' thought is not so much irrational as another kind of rationality comprehensible in its context. But do we simply leave it at that? Are different rationalities and cultures beyond comparison and judgement?

Rationalities do not simply coexist, they compete and clash. They are what Charles Taylor calls 'incommensurables' which 'somehow occupy the same space'. Insofar as they are incommensurables and obey different rules, they cannot be compared. Insofar as they lay claim to the same space, they can. Magic–religion and science are different kinds of rationalities not comparable. But insofar as the former makes epistemological claims (which it does), e.g. explaining why rain falls, it can be compared and judged inferior to scientific explanation.

To be rational is to explain. To be more rational is to better explain. To explain is to lay out in best or 'in perspicuous order', and this is often (though not always) best done through a 'disengaged perspective', i.e. in a 'theoretical' way. Modern societies are more theoretical than those in the past and to that extent are more rational.[82] This is not merely an abstract virtue. The proof of the pudding is that explaining better is inseparable from having a better handle to 'shape' the world.

The contrast is not between irrationality and rationality but between different and competing rationalities, which forces choice and judgement according to standards. There is the less rational and the more rational and the possibility of *growing* rationality. Irrationality is generally culture-specific. It is an *inconsistency* which can only be gauged *within* a framework of accepted standards, a contextual irrationality. But there is also *logical inconsistency* based on universal standards, e.g. laws of identity, contradiction, negation, just as there are some minimum universal human capacities. Cutting across different rationalities is a common minimum rationality which allows for cultural translation, rational judgement across cultures, change in consensually agreed directions, and 'weak' notions of universal objectivity and progress. Better explanation, i.e. progress in rationality, is generally discipline-specific.[83] Knowledge in specific disciplines *does* grow over time and across cultures. Secularization *has* taken place in the transition to modernity.

The real ire of Berger and other sophisticated critics is not directed at refuting the *fact* of secularization-as-decline. What they are really against is this idea being seen as a master-trend, a continuing if not irreversible process. This is a well-taken objection provided not too much is read into it. It certainly does not refute the view that continuing decline of the importance of religious influence and religious identity is *possible.*

Nor does it mean that substantial secularization has not taken place in non-European societies; or that even if there is some degree of reversal, it is possible to restore religion to its pre-modern status in culture and society.[84] What it does represent is a salutary caution against (a) assuming that non-European societies will easily or eventually replicate the European secularization experience; and (b) assuming that the existing balance of secular–religious influences is not reversible or that, in the long-run, secularization *must* assert itself.

Within the limits of modernity the question of further secularization in civil society and the family is more open-ended. It is not clear if the critics of the decline thesis would dispute that, as far as the state is concerned, its secularization might after all be a master-trend. This is connected to another conjecture. Is the democratic state in the long run a master-trend, a process that can claim still more conquests and whose energies are yet to burn out fully?

Instead of a uni-directional process, more complicated combinations of de-secularization–secularization, of the secular and the religious in society, are clearly possible. This could pertain to different spaces such as state and civil society where the strength of religious influence in the latter is strong enough to threaten the secularity of the state. As in the early phase of the Kemalist revolution in Turkey, Iran under the Pahlavi Shah's 'White Revolution', or Poland under Communist rule, the secularization (of state)–de-secularization (of civil society) could be two moments of the same process. Elsewhere, as in India, the secular and the non-secular simply exist in separate spaces in a relationship of tension. Indian civil society is much less secular compared to the civil societies of other democracies. The hitherto diffuse pressure of anti-secular forces in civil society is now being politically organized with such force as to threaten to undo decisively the secularity of the Indian state and government.

The secularization–de-secularization combination can also apply to different spaces within civil society (different sectors of social life) or to different groupings. In the UK, for example, there is uneven spread of religious influence among different ethnic groups. It is growing among British Hindus and British Muslims but declining among white British Christians and perhaps stable among 'British West Indians'.[85]

American civil society is less secular than British civil society. This simple observation tends to be obscured by advocates of secularization as something other than decline. The secularization of consciousness and religious pluralism (as part of a general pluralization of society) are said to go together. American religious pluralism emerges out of the privatization of religious affairs. It reflects the individualism of modern life. In fact, marketization of religion to meet private, therapeutic needs has reached unprecedented levels. According to them, America is more religiously suffused *and* more secular than Britain because privatization and pluralization are greater. This apparent paradox, they can claim, is resolvable only if we discard the thesis that secularization represents religious decline. Some American Durkheimians have gone on to argue that America has a strong Civil Religion decisively influenced by the Big Three faiths: Protestantism and (a somewhat Protestantized) Judaism and Catholicism.

Certainly, secularization does mean that religion becomes more private, optional and problematic, and privatization does signify decline relative to the past. But it does not necessarily follow that the more 'privatized' and marketized religious affairs are, the more secularized that society. A public culture dedicated to consumerism means not simply a more privatized society but also a more consumerized culture, a homogeneity of heterogeneity. This is in part the 'accomplishment' of American religious life, of its consumerization of religion. More than elsewhere, America's federalized democracy resembles the market model where strong consumer lobbies are very active. Religious consumer lobbies there have a social influence foreign to more secularized societies like Britain, regardless of the formally more secular character of the American state and Constitution. The centre of gravity of mainstream American life can swing to religious conservatism more easily and abruptly than in Britain – one of the dangers of having a less secular civil society.

Yet, the religiosity of American public life should not be exaggerated.[86] Changing demographic patterns – the USA is becoming less white and less Protestant – will no doubt further weaken the attractions of the Civil Religion thesis. Certainly, there are few pertinent lessons for India. The USA as we know it today is almost wholly a modernist construct. Its religious and social life embody modernist values as few other societies do.

Religious pluralism in India is not in the least connected to the secularization–rationalization of consciousness and the privatization of religious affairs. Both Americans and Indians equate religious pluralism with tolerance and secularity. But the mediations stressed are fundamentally different. In the USA, secularism is seen as a modernist ideal centred on individual freedom. In India secularism is seen as an ancient ideal and most assuredly not centred on Westernized notions of individual freedom.

The threads of religious pluralism in the USA can be woven into the fabric of a Civil Religion which it is then claimed covers society. In India, the nature of religious pluralism, the history of religious conflict, the weakness of secularization in civil society, even the weakness of the secular state compared to that in the USA, all make the idea of an Indian equivalent to America's Civil Religion ludicrous. The virtue of the American Civil Religion was that it was more an invocation of God in its common symbols and forms than a sectarian invocation of Christ. In India the conscious attempt to construct a binding Civil Religion will be another name for, or variant of, an aggressive and intolerant Hindu nationalism.

Secularism as Tolerance

The popular Indian view that secularism means or should mean tolerance is deeply misleading. We know how and why this view emerged.[87] This notion of secularism/secularization rests on three misconceptions: (1) It assumes that serious religious decline has not and cannot take place. Indian society is said to be permeated by religion. Moreover, the idea of secularization-as-decline is said to be intimately and ineluctably connected to the nature of Christianity and to its historical trajectory. (2) Its notion of tolerance is utterly inadequate. (3) It involves a sociologically and historically misleading representation of Indian culture and more specifically of Hinduism.

No third world society and certainly not India can escape nor retire from the project of modernity. This is most obvious on the economic and political levels where the market and the apparatuses of the nation-state increasingly sweep aside the pre-modern structures which are obstacles to it, or push them to mutate or transform themselves in order to survive and flourish. On the cultural level the overall results are more 'mixed' and the range of possibilities greater than in the case of the levels where market and state operate. But here, too, the impact has been profound. What has been said about the relationships between religion, culture, society, identity, in the era of modernity applies (in its general thrust and principles) to India as well. There *are* important specificities. They *qualify* the fact of secularization and its further possibility; they do not *negate* either. If anything, the desirability of greater secularization in India is stronger than for other countries. No country comes close in having a similar scale or depth of religious variation or stands to suffer more from a serious reversal and failure of secularization. There are no guarantees against this but the very durability of the Indian democratic and secular state (howsoever weak the democracy and the secularity) is evidence of the strength of modernist strivings and processes. Can Indian civil society be further secularized?

There can be no deterministic answer, but the goal remains something to be fought for. The clear evidence of the growing institutionali-

111

zation of Hinduism is also in its own way a testimony to the declining permeation of religion in society. Neither Hinduism nor Islam will follow the trajectory of Christianity. But unless one believes that Christianity is both the father of secularization in all its main nuances (decline, disengagement, rationalization) *and* the necessary correlate for its sustenance, there is no logical reason why secularization must be a failure or an impossibility in India. If that were so then the best that could be hoped for is a permanent tension between a substantially secularized state and a civil society which cannot be further secularized. While the idea of 'separation of spheres', of the temporal–secular and the spiritual, does emerge and develop in pre-modern Christian discourse, the notion of secularization-as-decline comes much later, in the run-up to modernity. This particular seedling is not the unique gift of Christianity but is much more the result of the emergence of an increasingly autonomous civil society.

If secularization first took place in Christian Europe, can it survive transplantation elsewhere? How strong is the relationship between Christianity and the secularization process? Even in explaining its origin, how much weight should one give to Christianity–Reformation; to the developing capitalist mode of production; and to the Renaissance–Enlightenment? In what way were these processes linked? Weber's Protestant Ethic thesis assigned decisive impetus to Christianity–Reformation, an eminently contestable claim.[88] For all its insights, if Weber's basic claim falls, then Christianity is not quite as strong a source of secularization–modernization–rationalization as made out. The weight of Perry Anderson's explanation, for example, falls on 'the concatenation of antiquity and feudalism'; on the linkage between the Renaissance revival of the rationalist legacy of Hellenism and the special dynamism of Western European feudalism.[89]

Christianity may have had seeds of secularization within it, but so what? Hellenism surely had stronger such seeds and similar seeds can be found in ancient Indian philosophy and religious discourse. Many religious systems, insofar as their engagement with reality has led to developed doctrine, would almost certainly have such seeds. Peter Berger's claim that the seeds of secularization lay in the Old Testament to be revived by the Reformation is extraordinary. According to him, only Christianity had the combination of ethical rationalism, severe monotheism and institutionalized church that could lead to secularization. Christianity is the master-key to modern history, the source of secularization, individualism, democracy itself![90]

Since so much hinges on Weber's Protestant Ethic in explaining the 'riddle of the origin of capitalism' and thus the origin of secularization–modernity, one would have thought that most Indian scholars believing in the Christian incubation of secularization (therefore its alienness to India) would evaluate rigorously the adequacy of the Protestant Ethic thesis. But there is too much to lose in such further exploration. The idea of secularization as the gift of Christianity is largely taken as given. If it should appear more plausible that capitalist modernization (whose original impetus is not derived from Protestantism) is the real force behind secularization, then the intellectual case for the inapplicability of the decline thesis to India is weakened. Indian society will escape substantial Christianization. It cannot escape the uneven and combined process of capitalist accumulation. Furthermore, the weaknesses of secular–rationalist modes of thought may owe more to the absence of the equivalent of the European Renaissance than to the absence of Christianity.[91]

Yet even if one conceded for the sake of argument that the origins of secularization lay in Christianity and that the Protestant Ethic argument is correct, Weber himself would have recognized that, even if not the original driver, capitalism had taken over the driving seat. Capitalist modernization, not Christianity, would be the key source of pressure pushing for further secularization–rationalization. Where capitalism goes, some significant measure of secularization will also follow, no matter what our reservations about its durability in, or adaptability to, non-Christian climes.

The second and third misconceptions will be taken together and the treatment will be brief. A long excursus into the 'nature of Hinduism' will be avoided. It is only after the rise of individualism and individual rights that the terms 'pluralism' and 'tolerance' obtain a strong positive connotation. This comes about *specifically* in modernity. Yet the two terms have been effectively hijacked to describe a set of pre-modern circumstances where such positive resonances simply do not fit. Pluralism as a principle of social and political organization emerges in the second and third decades of this century as a late Enlightenment reaction to absolutist theories of the state and sovereignty, and in the context of democratic and socialist ideas about and demands for autonomy. It had nothing to do with the absence or presence of centrally organized religions. Pluralism was related to ideas of 'social intentionality' and 'social design'.[92]

Segmentary, traditional societies are plural, decentralized and static, possessing a certain balance in their structures. Community social life is usually governed by rules of kinship or ritual. There is an ancient pluralism. But modern civil society has a different pluralism which is based on an individualist moral culture which is also secular. The institutional complexes of pre-modern societies are profoundly different from those of modern societies. The new kind of balances required among structures in today's civil societies cannot be achieved without the construction of secular institutions. The alternative in India would be institutions characterized by 'religious patrimonialism'.[93]

To talk of the ancient Indian or more specifically Hindu heritage of pluralism is to give a modernist and positive tone to a description which historically cannot bear this weight. Sudipta Kaviraj is perfectly right in saying of this traditional pluralism that it was not much more than the registration of variety.[94] To use his analogy: plant life is plural, it is not thereby tolerant. Tolerance in its positive sense means much more than coexistence.

Also, in ancient or medieval India, the absence of church–state conflict meant that states only had to relate themselves to different religious groupings – hence peaceful coexistence of a passive type which promoted a certain kind of religious tolerance. The source for this was not just the nature of Indian society but the character of state behaviour. All states, including Islamic and the British, followed some version of religious neutrality. Religious segregation in society was the norm and this was the basis for the tolerance–coexistence that prevailed.

Pluralism cannot mean positive tolerance except through conceptual slippages. Religious pluralism of a doctrinal and ritual kind is most strongly characteristic of what has been given the compendium label Hinduism. To imply that Indian tradition and culture always had a heritage of pluralism is really to imply that this is overwhelmingly moulded by Hinduism – a notion of culture which has already been criticized earlier on. But even if one were to ignore this near identification of Indian culture with Hinduism, another series of unwarranted jumps in logic are carried out.

The plurality of beliefs, practices and rituals, i.e. ritual and *doctrinal* pluralism, is not equivalent to religious–doctrinal tolerance. And religious–doctrinal tolerance is neither equivalent to nor automatically leads to *social* tolerance. The most that can be said about the presumed doctrinal tolerance of Hinduism and the presumed doctrinal intolerance of the Semitic faiths is that both, if true, are stimulants (how strong has always to be historically and concretely discerned) to the emergence of different mixes of social tolerance and intolerance. If the monotheism of the Semitic faiths has an exclusionary thrust, it also has a thrust towards egalitarian universalism (the formal equality under God of all believers). If the multiplicity of gods/goddesses and forms of worship in Hinduism encourages a measure of ecumenism, such multiplicity is also a precondition for the existence of the caste system. This is an elaborated system of social hierarchy (intolerance in any modern sense of the term, or tolerance on terms set by superiors) in which moral–religious relativism flourishes.

Of pre-modern India, Kaviraj had this to say: 'Coexistence of numerous local communities which would have liked to impose their ways on others had they the power to do it, is not equal to a situation of pluralism–tolerance. It is a pluralism which represents a powerless intolerance.' For Kaviraj the internal structure of Hinduism is 'marked more by ineffective intolerance than an ideological tolerance of a positive kind. It led to peevishness and irritation more than mass violence.'[95] The agglomerative, absorptive and glutinous character of what has come to be called Hinduism should not be misconstrued as implying either a natural inclination to syncretism or a natural propensity to dialogue with other doctrines/religious systems, or a natural bent towards tolerance.

The danger of accepting this elision of modern and pre-modern ideas of tolerance is the political disarming of our ability to fight against modern-day religious intolerances. While the myth of Hinduism's intrinsic and unique tolerance sets up an ideal to which one can appeal to 'good Hindus' to reject Hindu nationalism in the name of saving the essence of Hinduism, there is also the danger that Hindu communalism will be explained away as basically a *reaction* to other religious communalisms since tolerance is supposedly the heart of Hinduism. We can fail to grasp the seriousness of the religious intolerances wracking contemporary India just as we exaggerate the strength of our historical–cultural–religious resources to fight it.

The seriousness of the danger can be exemplified by taking up certain arguments employed by Hindu communal forces. Two apparently winning arguments of Hindu chauvinists have been (a) the need to rectify the humiliation felt by Hindus about the destruction of temples in the past by Muslim rulers;[96] (b) that given the enormous number of such temples despoiled, the destruction of the Babri Masjid and even a few more mosques hardly balances the historical scales of justice.

What is left out here is any reference to the decisive changes wrought by modernity. In the past any temple despoiled affronted those loyal to the temple in question. Given the caste-ridden and segmented character of Indian society, most temples so desecrated were places of worship for specific sects, castes and categories of worshippers, though a few had much more open access and wider fame. But weakness of communication systems alone meant that the scale and depth of the humiliation felt at such acts was controlled and limited. Certainly, it could not compare with what is possible today. Both the scale and depth of anger and humiliation felt by Hindus in India (and even in the Indian diaspora in the West) is incomparably greater than *at the time* when such temple desecrations actually took place. Mass communications, the sharpening of identities and a host of other factors enable the construction of mass anger and emotion on a scale never imaginable before.

The same point applies to the second argument. No matter how many temples Muslim rulers may have destroyed in the past, all of them put together did not and could not have welded mass emotions among Muslims *against* Hindus in the way that the single campaign for the Rama temple and the destruction of the Babri Masjid has done in respect of Hindu sentiments *against* Muslims. No past act of temple destruction was ever perceived as, and could have hoped to serve as, a mass rallying cry, a platform for identity affirmation on such a mass scale for Muslims against the hostile or threatening Other, the 'harbi kafir'.

The reason is simple enough. Modernity is, as never before, the era of mass politics, most certainly since the beginning of this century. Mass energies, mass collectivities and mass campaigns are forged as never before. Precisely because of the uniquely mass character of identity politics in the present there is simply no comparison between the politics of symbolic humiliation in the past and that of today; between the politics of shrine destruction in the past and of today; between the politics of religious identity in the past and today. There is a profound and qualitative difference in the intolerances of the past and of today. The possibility for mass transformations for human good is also of a qualitatively different order to possibilities in the past. In this century both the meridian of mass political good (the institutionalization of political democracy) and the nadir of mass political evil (the horrors of Nazism) have been on display. They are testimony to the uniqueness of modernity and its double-edged potential.

If the intolerances of the present are of such a different order to those of the past, it is elementary wisdom to recognize that the tolerances of the past (negative tolerances at best) cannot seriously be expected to cope with the intolerances of our time. We need to construct new, more robust tolerances. India has its special heritage and its distinctive strengths. It would be foolish indeed not to use those resources. But it will not do to take refuge in extravagant claims about the unique power of the Indian genius, its culture and tradition. The struggle to cope with the problems of modernity will have to be fought on the terrain of modernity itself and for the most part with the weapons forged in modernity.

We must be clear about our goals and assess properly our means. The notion of secularism or secularization-as-tolerance is neither a proper goal nor an adequate means. The secular state in India must mean a basic separation of state and religion, strengthened by further seculari-zation of state laws, state apparatuses and state policies. The effort to secularize civil society in India must mean striving to reduce religious influence in civil society, reduce the importance of religious identity in much of the pursuits of everyday life, and the increasing privatization and optionalization of religious commitment. Overcoming obstacles to these goals is another story altogether. But knowing the direction we must take is some part of the battle won.

Notes

1. Where Catholicism is all-encompassing, Protestantism shrinks the scope of the sacred. Christianity is divested of 'mystery, miracle, magic'. There is God on one side and fallen humanity on the other and the only miracle is grace. Protestantism, especially Calvinism, reduces religion to its 'essentials'. See P. Berger, *The Social Reality of Religion*, London, 1969.

   Larry Shiner's typology of concepts of secularization (decline, this-worldliness, disengagement, transposition, desacralization) is effectively reducible to the three outlined above. See L. Shiner, 'The Concept of Secularization in Empirical Research', in *Journal for the Scientific Study of Religion*, Fall 1967.

2. This is Weber's 'disenchantment of the world'. Durkheimians accept this but need not accept that this means an overall decline in religious influence. Reallocation of religious functions can mean loss of breadth but also an increase in depth.

3. Two among the most forceful opponents of the secularization-as-decline thesis are P. Glasner, *The Sociology of Secularization*, London, 1977; and the books of D. Martin: *A General Theory of Secularization*, Oxford, 1978; *The Dilemmas of Contemporary Religion*, Oxford, 1978; *The Religious and the Secular*, London, 1969. For a more recent restatement of Martin's views see 'The Secularization Issue: Prospect and Retrospect', in *British Journal of Sociology*, September 1992.

4. Even in the USA, with its sharp separation of church and state, laws grant a few special favours, e.g. in regard to taxation, to religious personnel. This is true also in Western Europe, where there is often a formal affiliation to the church.

5. Article 25 of the Constitution guarantees freedom of conscience, propagation and worship subject to 'public order, health and morality'. Lack of clarity and agreement over the meaning of secularism ensured that the word 'secular' was deliberately excluded from the (1949) Constitution and was inserted only in 1976. Partly because of political compromises with Muslim religious leaders, the Common Civil Code was brought into the Constitution but put under the Directive Principles.

   There was an ongoing dispute about education in the National Movement period between those like Bal Gangadhar Tilak, who felt a Hinduized educational syllabus was essential to establish cultural nationalism and anti-colonial pride, and those like Mahadev Govind Ranade, Gopal Krishna Gokhale and Gopal Ganesh Agarkar, who wanted a modern science-related education to overcome debilitating superstitions and to make progress. Gandhi effected a compromise embodied in Articles 28 and 38, whereby all minorities, including religious ones, could set up educational institutions of their choice and apply for state funding. Only those schools *wholly* maintained by such funding would, as a principle, avoid religious instruction.

6. This being the case, there is an excessive enthusiasm among many Indian secularists for tightening up on certain kinds of state behaviour, e.g. eliminating religious inauguration ceremonies at state functions, ending media relays of religious music, functions, etc. Some forms of such behaviour can be curtailed or eliminated. But to do so is *not* to make the Indian state significantly more secular. In fact misplaced zeal for using the secular broom in this way can also be counterproductive.

7. P. Berger, 'Some Second Thoughts on Substantive versus Functional Definitions of Religion', in *Journal for the Scientific Study of Religion*, Vol. 13, No. 2, June 1974.

8. R.N. Bellah, 'Religious Evolution', in A. Robertson (ed.), *Sociology of Religion*, Harmondsworth, 1969; H. Mol, *Identity and the Sacred*, Oxford, 1976; T. Luckmann, *Life-World and Social Realities*, London, 1983. For a general survey, see B. Wilson, *Religion in Sociological Perspective*, Oxford, 1982.

9. This is a strongly contested claim, and if these critics are right then a significant scepticism is cast over the validity of that notion of religion which the coherence model presumes.

10. Two examples of such outsider descriptions are those by Giddens and Southwold. According to Giddens the characteristics of all religions are *symbols* evoking *reverence/awe* among *believers* who practise *rituals*. However, Giddens seems to accept Durkheim's unconvincing attempt to sharply separate magic from religion. His definition would also exclude non-ritualistic religions like the early forms or more austere

currents of Hinayana Buddhism. A. Giddens, *Sociology*, Oxford, 1991, Chap. 14.

Southwold, unlike Giddens, eschews any attempt to establish properties fitting all religions. Using the distinction between a monothetic class (where all members share a common bundle of attributes) and a polythetic class (where all members have some but not all the attributes belonging to that class), he places religion in the latter class. He lists some twelve attributes, a few of which, like belief in supernatural beings and ritual practices, are near universal. (1) Central concern with godlike beings and human relations with them. (2) A dichotomy of sorts of the world into the sacred and profane and central concern with the sacred. (3) Orientation towards salvation from 'mundane' existence. (4) Ritual practices. (5) Beliefs not logically nor empirically demonstrable but held as a matter of faith. (6) An ethical code, supported by such beliefs. (7) Supernatural sanctions on infringements on that code. (8) A mythology. (9) Body of Scriptures or an exalted Oral Tradition. (10) Priesthood or specialist religious elite. (11) Association in a 'moral community'. (12) Association with an ethnic or similar group. M. Southwold, 'Buddhism and the Definition of Religion', in *Man*, Vol. 13, 1978.

Apart from the purposes of formal classification, such descriptive definitions hardly help further investigation into the really interesting questions regarding religion. What, for example, are its more important dimensions: which, where, when, why?

11. See Morris's discussion of the hermeneutic approach to religion in B. Morris, *Anthropological Studies of Religion*, Cambridge, 1987. Also J.A. Saliba, *Homo Religiousus in Mircea Eliade*, Leiden, 1976.

12. C. Geertz, 'Religion as a Cultural System', in R. Bocock and K. Thompson (eds), *Religion and Ideology*, Manchester, 1985.

Geertz's definition of religion is '1) a system of symbols which acts to 2) establish powerful, pervasive, and long-lasting moods and motivations in men by 3) formulating conceptions of a general order of existing and 4) clothing these conceptions with such an aura of factuality that 5) the moods and motivations seem uniquely realistic.'

His definition of culture is 'an historically transmitted pattern of meanings embodied in symbols, a system of inherited conceptions expressed in symbolic forms by means of which men communicate, perpetuate and develop their knowledge about and attitudes towards life' (pp. 3–4).

13. S.P. Mohanty, 'The Epistemic Status of Cultural Identity', in *Cultural Critique*, 24, Spring 1993.

14. This point was particularly significant in the context of the reactionary rightwing Hindu nationalist political campaign over the Ram Janamabhoomi–Babri Masjid issue. Historians, many from the Jawaharlal Nehru

University (JNU), mostly liberal and Left, provided strong historical evidence and argument against the idea that Babar had destroyed any temple (let alone one that had been constructed to worship Ram) in order to build a mosque. These JNU historians were attacked not only from the Right but from sections of the Left as pursuing a typically leftist, insensitive and elitist initiative. These historians were daring to argue with faith, although the faith that a Ram temple existed and had been destroyed was itself *constructed* and had become a mass belief only over the last decade.

The point is not that such a 'rationalist exposure' could by itself (in the absence of mass political counter-mobilization against the forces of Hindutva) check the construction of bad faith, or even play a major role in this. But that this effort was a morally, intellectually and politically important one necessitated by the very deliberate and systematic construction of bad faith on such a wide scale.

See also J.V. Spickard, 'For a Sociology of Religious Experience', in W.H. Swatos Jr (ed.), *A Future For Religion?*, Delhi, 1993. Spickard puts forward a typology of different notions of religious experience. He concludes that religious experiences/emotions–feelings cannot be separated from the ideas and context by which they are explained. For example, one doesn't first speak in tongues and then join an assembly but the other way around. Quite his most interesting idea is '[e]xperiences are inner patterns of time', and these patterns/experiences can be learnt and shared.

15. This was certainly the inclination of Mircea Eliade. For a sensitive and subtle exploration of the question of faith in the Indian context, see R. Bharucha, *The Question of Faith*, 'Tracts for the Times' series, New Delhi, 1993. Bharucha is justifiably more sympathetic than I am in his treatment of the issue of faith, because his basic orientation is different. My own more limited programme is to attack the *exorbitation* of faith and the refusal to recognize its inescapable imbrication with issues of ideology and power. Bharucha takes this imbrication as given, but wishes to explore, nonetheless, the variability in the relationship between religion-as-faith and religion-as-ideology, and is more concerned to understand the 'ambivalences of faith' and the 'enigmas of faith'.

Whereas my political project is to defend a particular notion of secularization-as-religious decline, and therefore contest the idea of the *social centrality* of religion (including its 'faith' and 'other' components), Bharucha's political project is to establish the necessity of fighting for the secular on the terrain of religious discourse itself, a project requiring a more sensitive appreciation of religion–faith and its resources. I concur with his view about the need to fight for the secular on the religious terrain itself. But I am less sanguine about the *degree* of usefulness of such a project. I would certainly subordinate it *strategically* to the struggle for secularization outside the terrain of religious discourse.

16. Indian studies of Hinduism seem to have quite escaped this paradigm shift. Most are overwhelmingly obsessed with the philosophy of Hinduism supposedly embodied in the Vedas. Between contemporary anthropological studies of Hinduism and caste, and Vedantic philosophizing, the historical sociology of Hinduism has been almost completely ignored. Romila Thapar's writings within her time frame of ancient India constitute a magnificent exception.

17. T. Luckmann, *Life-World and Social Realities*. This is a fine insight of his.

18. P. Berger, *The Social Reality of Religion*.

19. T. Luckmann, *Life-World and Social Realities*.

20. M. Löwy, *Marxism and Liberation Theology*, Notebooks for Study and Research, No. 10, Amsterdam, 1988.

21. M. Löwy, 'Revolution against "Progress": Walter Benjamin's Romantic Anarchism', in *New Left Review*, No. 152, July–August 1985. Also references in M. Löwy, *Marxism and Liberation Theology*. E. Bloch, *L'athéisme dans le Christianisme*, Paris, 1978; L. Goldmann, *The Hidden God*, London, 1955; L. Boff and C. Boff, *Théologies de la Libération*, Paris, 1985; C. Gutierrez, *Théologies de la Libération Perspectives*, Brussels, 1974.

22. J. Larrain, *Marxism and Ideology*, London, 1983.

23. P. Berger, *The Social Reality of Religion*, p. 26.

24. Ibid. p. 90.

25. A. Gramsci, *Selections from the Prison Notebooks*, eds Q. Hoare and G. Nowell Smith, London, 1971, p. 405.

26. I have adopted Berger's (*The Social Reality of Religion*) terms of nomization (ordering of meaning) and cosmization (ordering of the cosmos) as useful shorthands. Berger's own individual–social dialectic is unsatisfactory. His triad of externalization–objectification–internalization sees society as externalization–objectivation, and internalization as 'reappropriation in consciousness' of society. This is what Roy Bhaskar calls a dialectical model of 'society forms individuals forms society', which, he argues convincingly, fails because individual and society are *not* related as in a dialectic. Society comes first for any given individual and confronts him as a given. This is precisely the point about religion. See R. Bhaskar, *Reclaiming Reality*, London, 1981, Chap. 5.

27. J. Larrain, *Marxism and Ideology*.

28. J.B. Thompson, *Studies in the Theory of Ideology*, Cambridge, 1984, and *Ideology and Modern Culture*, Oxford, 1990.

Thompson's notion of 'meaning in the service of power' is thus brought closer to Althusser's understanding of ideology as more a matter of habit than conscious thought. But where the latter saw ideology as affixing identities (interpellations), the former links it more strongly to specific social groups. Thompson's conception is broader than Marx's, but, like Marx's, is also determinedly critical. It is episte-mologically lenient but sociologically strict. However, if Thompson's view is accepted, then religion clearly cannot be a *kind* or *form* or *sub-set* of ideology. It is more than that, though it obviously has ideological functions.

29. S. Feuchtwang, 'Investigating Religion' in M. Bloch (ed.), *Marxist Analysis and Social Anthropology*, New York, 1975.

For Feuchtwang, ideology is Althusser's 'lived relations' and religion is a kind of ideology. 'The study of religion is part of the study of ideology, indeed it is part of that study which represents it par excellence' (p. 66).

'[R]eligion "is a shared reality", it is both a system of ideas about reality and a means of communicating those ideas' (p. 62).

Feuchtwang criticizes the 'subjective idealist' sociology of religion, e.g. the hermeneutical school, and himself seeks to provide a wider 'theory' (ideology) from which the 'concept' of religion can be derived. In the end, however, he admits that he has not been able to show what is peculiar to religion as a kind of ideology.

30. Eagleton prefers to remain agnostic about epistemological and sociolo-gical approaches to understanding ideology, only railing against too narrow or too broad definitions of ideology. Different definitions have their differing values and purposes and that, he says, is often good enough. There is no essentialist notion of ideology. By accepting different conceptual usages we recognize that we are dealing with a category whose variant meanings comprise a family of resemblances. T. Eagleton, *Ideology*, London, 1991, p. 50.

31. On the same page Eagleton tries to clarify further. 'Religion consists of a hierarchy of discourses some of them elaborately theoretical (scholas-ticism), some ethical and prescriptive, others exhortatory and consola-tory (preaching, popular piety); and the institution of the church ensures that each of these discourses meshes constantly with the others, to create an unbroken continuum between the theoretical and the behavioural.' Christianity seems to figure inordinately as Eagleton's model of an organized religion, and it is far from clear how useful his approach is compared to others. Ibid., p. 50.

32. K. Thompson, *Beliefs and Ideology*, London, 1986.

33. To allow that a few may escape the hold of religion altogether is to let in the thin end of the wedge. The few can become some can become many, and the argument of eternality is weakened. Better to insist dogmatically that the atheist or the self-consciously non-religious or anti-religious individual is nonetheless a religious animal.

34. T. Luckmann, *Life-World and Social Realities*.

35. P. Berger, *The Social Reality of Religion*, and Z. Bauman, *Mortality, Immortality and Other Life Strategies*, Oxford, 1992. '*Transcendence* is what, everything having been said and done, culture is about. Culture is about

expanding temporal and spatial boundaries of being, with a view to dismantling them altogether' (p. 5).

36. Z. Bauman, *Mortality, Immortality and Other Life Strategies*, p. 4.
37. P. Berger, *The Social Reality of Religion*; N. Abercrombie, 'Knowledge, Order and Human Autonomy', in J.D. Hunter and S.C. Ainlay (eds), *Making Sense of Modern Times: P.L. Berger and the Vision of Interpretive Sociology*, London, 1986.

    See P. Berger, *The Sacred Canopy*, New York, 1967. 'The anthropological presupposition for this is a human craving for meaning that appears to have the force of instinct. Men are congenitally compelled to impose a meaningful order upon reality' (p. 22).

38. See discussion of Merton in R.A. Wallace and A. Wolf, *Contemporary Sociological Theory*, Englewood Cliffs, NJ, 1986.
39. There is also the 'social programming of culture'. Where this is the central emphasis as in the Dominant Ideology thesis among certain Marxists, we have a weaker and much less religiously inclined version of the Social Integration argument.
40. R. Williams, *Culture and Society*, Harmondsworth, 1971, concluding chapter.
41. R. Williams, *Keywords*, London, 1988, pp. 87–93.
42. R. Williams, *Culture*, London, 1981.
43. K. Thompson, *Beliefs and Ideology*, Chap. 4. He uses the metaphor of 'the archaeology of culture'. 'The notion of an archaeology of culture is useful in so far as it suggests that it is necessary to excavate different layers of culture which are in a sense discontinuous. Culture studies have frequently lapsed into a "wholistic" and deductivist approach which views the parts of culture as explicable and decodable as parts of a whole, totality, or system. Find the principle that binds the whole, the code that unlocks the system, and the elements can be explained by deduction' (p. 106).
44. M. Archer, *Culture and Agency: The Place of Culture in Social Theory*, Cambridge, 1988.
45. M. Mann, *The Sources of Social Power*, Vol. I, Cambridge, 1988.
46. See Fred Halliday for the term 'national-territorial totality' in 'State and Society in International Relations: A Second Agenda', in *Millennium*, Vol 16, No 2, 1987.
47. B.S. Turner, *Religion and Social Theory*, London, 1991; and *Body and Society*, London, 1984.
48. M. Archer, *Culture and Agency*. In fact all kinds of combinations are possible, e.g. high logical consistency in elite culture can coexist with a society of low causal consensus.
49. This is the view of David Martin, perhaps the foremost opponent of the secularization-as-decline thesis. See, particularly, *The Religious and the Secular*.

The 'socially necessary myth' argument tends to confuse the social power of *belief* in illusions with the social power of illusions themselves. Some Durkheimians avoid this by focusing on practice not beliefs. Others who take a substantivist view are more prone to this confusion. Symbols stand apart and exercise power. But precisely because they are humanly made and because belief in them is retractable, they are not so stable a source of power in modernity.

50. J.B. Thompson, *Ideology and Modern Culture*.
51. A. Giddens, *Modernity and Self-Identity*, Oxford, 1991.
52. J.B. Thompson, *Ideology and Modern Culture*.
53. N. Abercrombie, S. Hill and B.S. Turner, *The Dominant Ideology Thesis*, London, 1980.
54. Ibid. Abercrombie, Hill, Turner draw attention to and give more importance to Durkheim's *The Division of Labour* than to his *The Elementary Forms of Religious Life* in the general structure of his thought.
55. R. Williams, *Culture*.
56. B. Wilson, *Religion in Sociological Perspective*.
57. B.S. Turner, *Body and Society*.
58. R.N. Bellah, 'Religious Evolution'. Bellah presents an evolutionary schema of religion as a symbol system that evolves historically and linearly in relation to the growing 'concreteness of the self'. The causal mechanism behind this is the impact of growing structural complexity on the self, on the sense of its relationship to nature and society. The measure of this (the criteria of religious change) are symbols, forms of action, types of organizations. Each of these changes character in the evolutionary progression from primitive religion to archaic to historic to early modern to modern religion.

In primitive religion – mythical symbols, no separation of real and mythical worlds, fluid organization, 'acting out'. In archaic religion – more specification in the mythical symbol system, more active in the real world, hierarchical organizations/cults, new 'ways of seeing'. In historic religion – simplification of myth, religious action for salvation, differentiated religious communities and growing tensions between them. In early modern religion – symbolic concentration on direct relation between believer and transcendence, internal qualities of believer more important than acts, simplified organization into the collectivity of the 'elect' and those outside. In modern religion – Kantian revolution and possibilities of religious symbolization made infinite, atrophy of religious organization, individual formulates own religious solution.

Bellah is committed to the eternality of religion because of its unbreakable link via symbols to the 'ultimate' values of humans. But others sympathetic to his schema (Luckmann, *Life-World and Social Realities*) do admit that in modernity these 'ultimate' values are important with respect to the *private* individual. Bellah's schema is inflexible and glorifies Christianity as the religion most compatible with modernity because it is world-affirming rather than world-renouncing. He seeks to establish a *continuum* with respect to changes in subjectivity, which certainly underestimates and possibly aims to deny the *ruptural* character in the transformation of personality caused by the emergence of modernity. But he is not wrong to historicize the question of subjectivity and its relationship to religion, nor to claim that the 'sense of the self' is not the same but can change decisively with decisive changes in social structure.

59. T. Eagleton, *Ideology*, p. 194.
60. E. Erickson, *Identity and Anxiety*, New York, 1960, p. 30. Also, *Identity and Life Cycle*, Indiana, 1959. 'Ego-identity, then, in its subjective aspect, is the awareness of the fact that there is a self-sameness and continuity to the ego's synthesising methods and these methods are effective in safeguarding the sameness and continuity of one's meaning for others' (p. 23). In Erickson's psychoanalytic approach, identity is ego-identity.
61. See R. Bhargava's talented exposition in 'Religious and Secular Identities', in U. Baxi and B. Parekh (eds), *Crisis and Change in Contemporary India*, New Delhi, 1995.
62. 'Personality' remains an unresolved and disputed term in psychology.
63. See in particular P. Unger's discussion of 'dispositional psychology' in *Identity, Consciousness, Value*, Oxford, 1990. Perry Anderson, in talking of Derek Parfit's studies, suggests that it is the material background of genetic engineering not the ideational background of the 'instability of language' that influences Parfit's concept of identity. This is certainly so of Unger, who acknowledges Parfit's strong influence on him in his development of a physicalist–naturalist concept of identity. P. Anderson, 'A Culture in Contraflow', in *New Left Review*, No. 182, July–August 1990.
64. C.F. Grauman, 'On Multiple Identities', in *International Social Science Journal*, Vol. 35, 1983.
65. Ibid. Being identified is to have ascription from others. The two most powerful forms of such conferred or ascribed identities are those that 'make one belong' and those that 'make one responsible'.
66. S.P. Mohanty, 'The Epistemic Status of Cultural Identity'.
67. For a fine exposition of Identification Theory, see W. Bloom, *Personal Identity, National Identity and International Relations*, Cambridge, 1990.
68. A. Giddens, *Modernity and Self-Identity*. Giddens talks of 'ontological security' for psychic normality – the first process of infant individuation whereby it develops a 'protective cocoon'. This comes about only through an initial and fundamental act of *trust*.

Given that there is a biological drive towards identification, is it primary or secondary? George Herbert Mead's view was that it was

125

primary, i.e. biologically programmed and awaiting a trigger. For Freud it was secondary, i.e. emerging out of the infant's experience of dependency and the discovery that identification is the way to ensure primary gratification and resolve primary anxieties. Either way, identification is unavoidable.

69. Gerry Cohen is quite right on this score. The motivating power of identity (identities), he points out, bears some proportionate relationship to the strength of the need(s) filled by that identity or those identities. G. Cohen, *History, Labour, and Freedom*, Oxford, 1988, Chap. 8.

70. This revisability brings in the question of history and its vital relationship to identity. To have a sense of where one is, is connected to a sense of where one is coming from. Hindu communalism, in seeking to establish a new sense of 'Hinduness', must necessarily seek to revise history.

71. H. Mol, *Identity and the Sacred*. Religion strengthens the 'fragile frame of identity'. Mol makes the false claim of greater brittleness of identity in modernity because he wants to make a case for the necessity and importance of religion in modernity through its relationship to subjectivity. For Mol, religion is the sacralization of identity or its affixation/affirmation, which is carried out through the anointment of that identity with the *awe*-some power of reverence, i.e. sacrality. It is thus the best guarantee of psychological well-being, the best or among the best answers to the distinctive identity problems/crises of modernity. The stabilization of society (nomization) is decisively connected to the stabilization of the cosmos (cosmization).

There are distinctive identity problems of modernity, but Mol's approach is not the best way to grasp or cope with them. His is a nostalgia for a world that can never return, and this is revealed most starkly in his warranty for 'close-mindedness'. Identity defence, he says, requires strong boundary defence and this in turn involves prejudice, i.e. pre-judging. Such close-mindedness is good because it preserves order.

72. A. Giddens, *Modernity and Self-Identity*. Self-reflexivity is a new kind of self-consciousness expressing itself in (a) heightened self-monitoring and; (b) self-revisability in the light of new knowledge, which in modernity is a continuous and highly speeded up process. Identities are much more likely to be 'adopted' rather than 'handed down'.

While journals, travelogues and diaries are certainly a feature of the past, 'It is generally accepted among historians that the writing of autobiographies (as well as biographies) only developed during the modern period' (p. 76). For the autobiography is 'not merely a chronicle of elapsed events' but a self-monitoring/self-reflexivity, i.e. 'corrective intervention into the past' (p. 72).

73. C. Taylor, *Philosophy and the Human Sciences (Philosophical Papers–2)*, London, 1985.

126

74. A. Giddens, *Modernity and Self-Identity*, p. 153.
75. G. Cohen, *History, Labour, and Freedom*, p. 146.
76. Religious tolerance in the positive sense is not as evident in the USA as made out. When public threat perception is strong, religious intolerance comes to the fore. So intolerance has been exhibited to Mormons, Jehovah's Witnesses and Black Muslims, and has receded when the perception of their threat to 'mainstream values' has receded. The example of the Jehovah's Witnesses is interesting because a similar controversy was raised in India in the early eighties.

   Just before Pearl Harbor, when Jehovah's Witnesses' children refused to salute the American flag at school (in India they had refused to sing the national anthem), there was a major public outcry. In 1940 the Supreme Court condemned the position of Jehovah's Witnesses. Three years later when American national confidence was much greater, the Supreme Court reversed its earlier ruling.

   Religious tolerance should also mean respect for atheist behaviour. Central to Cold War mythology (for domestic consumption), however, was the pitting of God-fearing and 'God's own country' America against godless and atheistic Communism.
77. Z. Bauman, *Mortality, Immortality and the Other Life Strategies*, pp. 91–2.
78. Ibid., p. 92. Belief in life after death is now an option. The meaning and purpose of death itself change. Death now has *causes* to be *tackled*. Death is rationalized and segregated. Death is given meaning and made palatable if it comes *after* a 'fulfilling life'. In the West most deaths take place in hospitals. For the urban Indian middle class this is becoming more common but most deaths still take place at home. Nonetheless, increasingly, death is rationalized as coming after a meaningful and fulfilling life and not just seen as an unavoidable point of transition in an endless cosmic cycle.
79. M. Douglas, 'Primitive Thought Worlds', in R. Robertson (ed.), *Sociology of Religion*, and 'The Effects of Modernisation on Religious Change', in *Daedalus*, Vol. III, 1982. Also the discussion in B. Morris, *Anthropological Studies of Religion*, on the structural approach to religious symbolism of Lévi-Strauss and Douglas.
80. Most Western opponents of the decline thesis would accept this. Indian opinion is much more divided even on this narrow issue of state separation from religious influence.
81. P. Berger, 'Some Second Thoughts', p. 132.
82. C. Taylor, *Philosophy and the Human Sciences*.
83. A. Gilbert, *Democratic Individuality*, Cambridge, 1990.

   Gilbert makes the important point that knowledge is not just culture-specific it is also discipline-specific and open to disciplinary progress and assessment. Aristotle's political and moral philosophies can still speak to us with amazing freshness because of this discipline-specific character. It is not 'imprisoned' in the culture of ancient Greece and 'untranslatable'.

84. Berger echoed many in feeling that recent religious revivalism is a serious counter to the *general* socio-historical claim of the secularization-as-decline thesis. See P. Berger, 'Some Second Thoughts'.

However, *prevalence* of religious beliefs and practices must not be confused with *importance*. Berger is, himself, as in so many areas, more nuanced than others. Since religion is for the individual 'the religious experience', if secularization-as-decline holds then fewer people are having such experiences. Alternatively, people are having such experiences but under social pressure are denying it, i.e. religion is not so much in decline as suffering delegitimation. Berger believed that both are probably happening but that the second trend might be stronger.

85. B.S. Turner, *Religion and Social Theory*, argues for just such 'coexistences' and 'combinations' of consolidating and declining religious (and specifically Christian) influences in respect of rich and poor, pagan and Christian 'spaces', atrabilious and attritionist accounts of secularization.

86. M. Lienesch, 'Rightwing Religion: Christian Conservatism as a Political Movement', in *Political Science Quarterly*, No. 31, 1982–83.

The late seventies–early eighties were supposed to have been the period of rapid rightwing Christian revivalism in the USA. According to Lienesch, the claims of such movements/organizations were greatly exaggerated. At their peak, listeners to the 'electronic church' numbered 10 million, not the claimed 130 million. Jerry Falwell's Moral Majority had at most half-a-million members, not the claimed 3 million. Nor have rightwing evangelists that significant an impact on elections.

See also M.E. Marty, 'Religion in America since Mid-Century', in *Daedalus*, Vol. III, 1982; and R.K. Fenn, 'Religion, Identity and Authority', in R. Robertson and B. Holzner (eds), *Identity and Authority*, Oxford, 1980.

87. See S. Chandra, 'Secularism and Indian Polity', in B. Chakrabarty (ed.), *Secularism and Indian Polity*, New Delhi, 1990; H. Mukhia, 'Communalism: A Study in its Socio-Historical Perspective', in *Social Scientist*, Vol. 1, No.1, August 1972; H. Mukhia, 'Communalism and the Indian Polity', in *South Asia Bulletin*, Vol. XI, 1991.

88. See among others F. Braudel, *Civilization and Capitalism*, 3 vols, London, 1985; S. Amin, *Eurocentrism*, London, 1989; S. Eisenstadt, *European Civilization in a Comparative Perspective*, Oslo, 1987, and 'The Protestant Ethic Thesis', in R. Robertson (ed.), *Sociology of Religion*; M. Rodinson, *Islam and Capitalism*, Harmondsworth, 1974; P. Anderson, *Lineages of the Absolutist State*, London, 1979.

89. P. Anderson, *Lineages of the Absolutist State*.

90. P. Berger, *The Social Reality of Religion*.

91. For a corrective to the idea that 'ancient Indian culture', even its 'high

culture', lacked a strong secular dose, see A. Sen, 'India and the West' (the Lionel Trilling Memorial Lecture at Columbia University, 18 February 1993) and 'The Threats to Secular India', in *New York Review*, 8 April 1993.

92. P.C. Upadhyaya, 'The Politics of Indian Secularism', in *Modern Asian Studies*, Vol. 26, 1992.

93. A. Beteille, 'Secularism and Intellectuals', in *Economic and Political Weekly*, 5 March 1994. Beteille mounts a vigorous defence of secular institutions (both in civil society and the state) against critics of modernity and secularism like T.N. Madan. Beteille correctly points out that what is really at issue is not a rejection of secularism or secularization but the negotiation of the 'terms of coexistence' between the secular and the religious. What he does not add is that if a secular arrogance of ambition is to be avoided, so too must a religious arrogance of ambition. Indeed, the new 'terms of coexistence' will have to weighted in very decisive ways against religious claims.

94. S. Kaviraj, 'Political Culture in Independent India', in *Teaching Politics*, Vol. VII, Nos 1–2, 1989.

95. Ibid., pp. 5–7. The late Ashok Rudra, one of India's more eminent Marxist academics, was even sharper. In his 'Myth of Tolerance', in *Seminar*, No. 67, March 1965, he stated bluntly 'that Hinduism has been tolerant only of such other ways of life and systems of thought and values which consented to let themselves be Hinduised in their fundamentals' (p. 25).

96. While there are certainly numerous examples of Hindu kings destroying Buddhist, Jainist and Vaishnavite temples, Islam's origins as a religion of tribal warriors certainly gave it a 'conquistadorial' edge different from the Indic religions, and this affected the behaviour of Muslim marauder-kings and the scale of their depredations in the sub-continent in the period of transition to more settled dynastic rule. Hindu communalists not only ignore shrine destructions by Hindu kings (which were considerable, though not matching the scale of early Islamic marauders), they also ignore the partially 'secular' motives behind such assaults and usually elide the distinction between kings and ordinary Muslim subjects, implicitly holding the latter, as a community, historically responsible.

— 4 —

Communalism, Hindutva, Anti-Secularists: The Conceptual Battleground

Every discourse in India on communalism and fundamentalism, secularism and anti-secularism, Hindutva and its rejection operates with preconceived notions about culture, civilization, Hinduism, caste; and their inter-relationships. Since these notions are insufficiently probed they are often implicitly shared. It is not as if political and ideological opponents always or usually have markedly different understandings. Were that the case Hindu chauvinists and communalists would not so readily attempt to pass themselves off as genuine nationalists or as true secularists rather than Nehruvian 'pseudo-secularists'. Nor could they have succeeded to the extent they have in appropriating for their purposes anti-communal nationalist figures like Mahatma Gandhi. Nor indeed could that other breed hostile to secularism, the anti-secular anti-modernists (or the ambiguous modernists), have disguised so easily the modernity of their posturings.

Civilization and Culture

Civilization and culture emerge as general social science concepts (independent nouns) in the West in the mid-eighteenth century.[1] Initially culture was a synonym for civilization, and to this day a strongly culturalist understanding of civilization endures. This is particularly so for India, with distinctive consequences. Civilization contrasts with barbarism. The study of civilizations, then, has been the archaeological–historical study of how the first civilizations emerged and survived. It has also been the study of what sustains many a subsequent non-barbarous or civilized 'state of affairs'. The second type of study has a stronger tendency to use a broader notion of civilization, loosening it from the

130

study of highly specific social formations which characterizes the first approach.

That approach has been strongly historical and well rounded. Civilizations were seen as historical–geographical–economic–political–cultural–social complexes, and not primarily as cultural complexes. Indeed, the unities of such civilizations were seen as dependent on political, social and ecological–economic variables as much as on cultural ones. Such civilizations represent the first great harvest of the leap from ranked to stratified societies. Such social stratification emerges with a new kind of centralizing state in a still admittedly segmentary society; usually with alluvial agriculture helping to generate the necessary economic surpluses.

Renfrew's defining characteristics of a civilization belong very much to this tradition of study. A civilization is an insulation against nature carried out in three ways: (a) insulation against the unknown meaning a specific religio-ceremonial centre; (b) insulation against time – a writing script; (c) insulation against outsiders – urbanization, a city.[2] A civilization is necessarily characterized by significant asymmetry of power between centre and peripheries. While the cultural dimension of such civilizations can, and usually does, extend itself beyond the spatial and temporal confines of the civilizational cluster itself, it cannot do so ceaselessly. Even its *selective* continuity or reproduction–transformation must presuppose a material infrastructure related to its integrating factors of literacy, law, ritual.

Such civilizations emerge, rise, decline and fall. They are eminently historical entities. In such an approach it would be largely meaningless to talk of any *Indian* civilization, let alone one existing through millenniums. There have only been civilizations *in* India, where the India is not any 'natural' territorial entity but simply an extrapolation backwards in time of the geographical space that came to be defined by British colonial rule.

The second, looser notion of civilization is decisively marked by specific intellectual traditions and discourses in the Europe of the eighteenth, nineteenth and early twentieth century, above all by Orientalism, and within it by the German Idealist and Romantic current with its strong echoes later carried over to post-war American cultural anthropology. The Orientalism that emerges in the period of an ascendant imperialism represented a shift away from the Enlightenment principle of universal equality to the view of the Easterner as a separate Other. It was not a complete break. The Other was Europe in infancy. It had a potential for reaching equal adulthood through the grace of colonial paternalism.

131

But the overwhelming thrust of Orientalist thinking was to endorse the idea of different civilizations with different essences, each evolving in its allotted sphere. The search for such civilizational essences, which were also the cultural essences, led to specialized study of the ancient past, when civilizations supposedly existed in pristine form, revealing most clearly their essential properties. Two popular disciplines of the nineteenth century, the history of religions (dominated by Idealist philosophy) and comparative linguistics greatly encouraged this approach. It received a further stimulus from two other developing disciplines – biological evolutionism and physical anthropology, taking it in the direction of racial taxonomies.[3] The uniqueness of a civilization was related to the uniqueness of language and to the uniqueness of race, with religion the expressive core of culture–civilization. Language, race, religion, became the vital triad. In India it became Sanskrit, Aryan, Hinduism.

Max Weber was to provide new sociological insights into Hinduism. But he was first and foremost a theorist of culture–civilization and his notions were very much in the eighteenth- and nineteenth-century German tradition of understanding culture as intellectual development, spiritual and of the mind. The decisive element in a culture was its world-view, as provided by magic, religion or science. These world-views were the 'switchmen' of civilizations, giving them their respective directional logics. Their dynamics unfolded both through the meanings imparted and in the 'elective affinity' of these world-views with the interests of particular social groups, which then became the main vehicle for the expansion of that world-view. They also influenced the 'practical ethic' of the religion in question, which in turn helped shape the personality of believers.

Many a twentieth-century civilization theorist of Weberian cast saw civilizations as 'cultural visions' which shaped the activity of particular elites and established the premises of a society, its core values and beliefs. Culture/civilization here is more or less an intangible whole, supposedly built up over centuries around these core ideas and values. It has a soul or spirit or ethos or *mentalité* which remains basically unaltered. In a more materialist rendering which pays more attention to the infrastructure of culture and to the problems of cultural transmission, the virtual isomorphism of culture and civilization, is averted. Nonetheless, civilization, above everything else, is said to have a cultural structure, which is the most important aspect of tradition.[4] Civilization is a 'structure of tradition', that is to say, 'a persisting form of arrangements for the handing down of cultural substance (ideas and its products) within a great community'.[5] The transmission of the Great Tradition is by the literati and its schools and institutional networks; the transmission of the Little Tradition is by local societal structures. Civilization is a relationship between society and culture defined by the latter, but society is where the vehicles of cultural transmission are necessarily located.

At least throughout modern Western intellectual history there have also been significant contestations of the anthropological/cultural/relativist approach to the study of civilizations, an insistence that change (sometimes dramatic) is as basic as continuity to the cultural dimension of the civilizational entity in question; and that the continuity of political structures may often better explain the continuity of the cultural tradition itself. For example, it is the remarkable continuity of much of China as a political unit, only intermittently broken, that better explains what we call the continuity of Chinese civilization. In the discourse on Western–Christian civilization and its 'continuity' many would see Christianity as the enduring essence of Western civilization or society. But there would also be many dissenters from this view. Insofar as the notion of 'Western civilization' across its numerous internal differentiations is employed by them, it aims to suggest little more than a cultural homogeneity of sorts indebted undoubtedly to the centuries-long infrastructure of Christianity – a monastic–episcopal economy, dominant educational institutions, an army of missionaries – outlasting its association with the Roman Empire. But this approach refuses to elevate the concept of Western civilization into a primary tool for social understanding and historical investigation for that part of the world.

In modern India's intellectual history the painting of the notion of civilization has been much more monochrome for two reasons. First, there was no equivalent of the European experience of Enlightenment humanism and universalism which promoted more secular and multiform understandings of civilization. Second, the imperatives of colonial resistance decisively marked the terrain and direction of discourse and historical evaluation by Indian intellectuals. In the period before the emergence of a political national movement, cultural self-affirmation required some assertion of Indian 'superiority' in the only sphere where it could be plausibly asserted – that of its cultural–spiritual traditions originating, flowering and defining its ancient *and* enduring civilization. This was resistance to the West within the discourse of Orientalism: reversed Orientalism becoming an affirmative cultural nationalism.

Later on, for the practical purposes of developing a political (and cultural) nationalism, some discourse of commonness had to be constructed. The concept chosen to bear this burden, so umbrella-like that it could be endorsed by all despite their variant interpretations of its content and foundations, was 'Indian civilization'. The notions of India's civilizational unity and its cultural essence were constructions motivated by the political and cultural needs of a developing Indian elite. They did not emerge out of serious empirical historiography. Nor was there ever serious research to objectively corroborate or refute these themes.

Once the idea of the continuity of Indian civilization achieved the force of an axiom, its natural correlate was the idea of India's cultural coherence or unity. How else to explain this continuity in the absence of a coherence itself derived from an essence? The idea of an enduring and cohering essence was vital. Mere uniformities would not be enough to determine a unity. All pre-modern societies are segmentary ones but these still have their distinctive specificities, e.g. the capstone state in China, the more modest state systems in India. The search for essences in India focused on two candidates usually treated as deeply interconnected – the religion of India, and the caste system.

This search for essences was entirely characteristic of Orientalism and of the European Romantics. Societies and cultures had determinate natures just as Enlightenment science had disclosed a principle of order in the natural world. Human societies were essentialist, objective systems where the principle of order had to be designed and the designer uncovered. Since culture subsumed society (culture was the more important term) it was cultural essences that had to be discovered. These clearly lay in the pre-colonial past of India. Upon this Indian intellectuals, whether aware or unaware of the influence of Orientalist thinking on them, were also fully agreed.

But pre-colonial India is still an extraordinarily long stretch of time. Where was the essence to be located? In pre-British India? Pre-Islamic India? Aryan India? Or pre-Aryan India? In short, there have been competing essentialisms with no conclusive way of adjudicating between them. However, the major competition has been between those subscribing to Hinduism as the essence of Indian culture–civilization, howsoever the term 'Hinduism' has been conceived, and those claiming that India's essence is represented by a 'composite culture'.[6]

England was the birthplace of Indology and it was largely empirical. Early admiration for India's intellectual heritage by Orientalists like Jones, Colebrook and Wilkins gave way to the more negative appraisals of politicians and administrators like Mills and Macaulay, partly to justify the newer phase of post-conquest consolidation. So after 1850 enthusiasm for Indology shifts to France and particularly Germany, where it links with the Romantic reaction against the Enlightenment. It is this Orientalist discourse that most affects subsequent cultural discourse in India. Indology in Germany was closely connected to German Idealism, which focused on philosophy as the heart of culture. The Indian essence was to be found in its ancient philosophical texts, most notably the Upanishads. Or as in one succinct formulation: 'India is indebted to Schlegel for proclaiming it, with Greece and Germany, the most philosophical of nations.'[7] Unlike post-Enlightenment European philosophy, Indian philosophy had not separated itself from religion or metaphysics. Even its atheistic currents were reactions within this larger framework. European Romanticism prioritized the search for inwardness as the essence of religion. If religion was the natural essence of Indian culture, then a moving spirit, a mystical ethos, was the essence of Indian religion. Such a view not only promoted the belief that Hinduism was the essence of India's civilization–culture, but made Brahminism the defining characteristic of this Hinduism.

At any rate, Indian philosophy had become central to Indian culture. Like nowhere else it has remained so in the self-perception of most Indian intellectuals who declaim upon the uniqueness of the Indian experience and legacy. Even those subscribing to the composite culture view of fusion of multiple religio-cultural influences have often felt the need to invoke the notion of an enduring ethos expressing itself throughout Indian history, and perhaps most clearly articulated and understood in its ancient texts. India was and is the world's most spiritual nation![8]

The composite culture argument has never been an adequate counter to the thesis of an essentialist Hinduism. The idea of fusion brings in the Islamic and other experiences and thus more strongly allows Indian culture to be in part evolutionary. But it still leaves too many unanswered questions. Does the fused substance have more of the properties of one component than the other? What first made this fusion possible if not the unique and natural syncretic genius of its earliest and original component, Hinduism?[9] Furthermore, as a characterization of what we can call the Indian cultural space, it is no more accurate than its rival, an essentialist Hinduism.

The notion of a cultural space enables us to avoid talking of Indian culture as a unified singular entity. What we call a cultural space or zone is always comprised of numerous cultures coming together in complex yet distinctive ways. It is an open, historical, to-be-empirically-determined question as to which sub-space or component is more important and influential than others – for how long, for how far, and in what way? A cultural space in reality is always much more chaotic and messier than are the theories or abstractions about it. The wider the cultural space territorially or inhabitant-wise, the more this is so. The idea of a composite culture is simply too neat, too 'composed' a depiction.[10]

Even if we were to accept that a religious system was the single most important determining element in a cultural space or sub-space before the advent of modernity in India, this would still not result in the neat synthesis of different religio-cultural uniformities. What is today called Hinduism was itself so diverse that what existed were an enormous multiplicity of cultural spaces and sub-spaces influenced by the principles of behaviour associated with local sects, not by the ordering principles of wider (regional or trans-regional) religious systems. Though Islam possessed a greater degree of uniformity, here also it was the local manifestations of folk or lived Islam that were more important than the ordering principles of an abstract High Islam.

Yet folk Hinduism did not meaningfully synthesize with folk Islam. The artistic embodiments of India's 'cultural synthesis' as in art, architecture and music took place at the elite or Court level. There was interaction between Hinduism and Islam, between the caste order and the mass of indigenous Muslim converts. The public space of everyday economic and political–administrative transactions was decisively influenced in its norms and values by the social conjunction of high political authority in the hands of Muslim rulers and their allies, and Hindu controllers over craft, production and commerce. The family and domestic space was where religion and the sacred held effective dominance. For pre-modern entities the norms of the sacred are more important than the norms of the secular and mundane. This more private and meaningful sphere was largely insulated and remained so despite the efforts and achievements of Bhakti and Sufi saints and mystics. These were at best the exceptions proving the rule. Even their products were for the most part absorbed into a developing Hinduism.

Adjacency and insulation marked the coexistence of Muslims and Hindus, though the caste system always had more influence on Islam (Low and High) than Hindu philosophical doctrine ever did. This did not mean, however, any major merging of ritual patterns within castes. Rather, many Muslim groups (especially artisans) were incorporated as sub-castes, while certain elements of caste-related ritual also entered in a limited way into Muslim households. This was a world neither of sharp polarities and divisions nor of cultural synthesis or social merger.[11]

A cultural zone also has a distinct cultural infrastructure or network of organizational means whose efficacy cannot be separated from its relationship to state power. So a religious system also influences culture *because* it influences the state. Where religious power is concentrated it is more likely to shape the state and the cultural zone. As it is, Hinduism is such a diffused phenomenon. Separated from the Islamic Court, the claim that Hinduism, nonetheless, was a defining influence on Indian culture must imply its integration with caste, the one social organizational form that had a palpably significant effect on Indian life and even on 'outsiders'. The claim must also make of Hinduism's essence an ethos, which, as such, is therefore all-pervading and unstoppable.

Christianity probably had more accumulative influence in pre-modernity over its cultural zone than Hinduism over its 'home terrain' because of its relative doctrinal uniformity, its superior infrastructure and its generally closer connection with state power. It was more able to provide overarching values for Europe's segmentary societies than Hinduism for India's segmentary societies. Contrary to the conventional view, Christianity had more to do with 'preserving' that nebulous entity, Western civilization, than Hinduism with that even more nebulous entity, Indian civilization.[12]

Caste and Hinduism

Yet the case for the indissoluble connection between Hinduism and Indian civilization was made, first by Orientalists and then by nationalist intellectuals. If the civilization was to be seen as enduring, then the durability of a unified Hinduism had to be unarguably established. One effective way was convincing oneself and others that Hinduism was the 'oldest living faith' and thus India the oldest continuous civilization. What could be powerful and convincing evidence for this claim?

The discovery that the Vedas were the world's oldest texts transmitted through generations could certainly be a source of such affirmation, provided the pervasive and formative influence of its philosophical content on Hinduism through the ages could also be established. Of course, if the Vedas had been read with a more sociological eye in conjunction with other non-Brahminical or 'second-order' (as they were called) traditional texts, e.g. Puranas, Buddhist and Jaina texts, what emerges is a more accurate and complex picture of major conflict between Brahminism and Shramanism.[13] For the Vedas to play this promotional role for Hinduism they also had to have an essentialist interpretation. Not surprisingly, within philosophical Hinduism,

137

Vedanta was elevated in importance, and within Vedanta the monism of advaita (non-dualist) doctrine was elevated. This was more the preoccupation of nationalist Hindu intellectuals than of earlier Orientalists.

Even if, for the Idealist Orientalist, Hinduism was the mind or ethos of Indian civilization, further confirmatory evidence at the level of social organization was by no means unwelcome. This time, the enduring and 'living' evidence was presumed to be caste. In a parallel move to the construction of the category of Hinduism, caste, too, had to be constructed as a pan-Indian and unified category. Orientalists of the eighteenth and nineteenth century and modern Orientalists like the French structuralists Louis Dumont and Madeleine Biardeau linked this to the ideology of the Vedas. However, the Vedas talk of varna but don't mention what is widely understood as in practice the caste system – the system of hierarchical jati clusters.[14]

Hinduism, then, was above all the mentality associated with caste. The empiricists among Orientalists focused on jati, the idealists on varna. Both reinforced the idea of an essential, irrational or arational India, even if one perceived this as negative and the other as positive.[15] The essence of India was either external–tangible or internal–intangible. If the latter, then it is no longer subject to the danger of disconfirmation by 'adequate' verification. India's essence just is, and always has been.[16] An internalist essentialism of Hinduism is conjoined to an internalist rendering of the meaning and purpose of caste. Varna is the conceptual purity of caste with the core of caste being hierarchy. The next step is the idealization of hierarchy and varna. The tendency towards idealization of hierarchy found its most famous expression in Dumont's *Homo Hierarchicus*.[17] Caste as the jati system was the corruption or degeneration or the historically concrete evolution of varna. Caste, then, was essential to India and unique. But in its purest and truest sense it was also strongly positive.

Not all Indian advocates of an essentialist Hinduism accepted the centrality of caste to Hinduism. Some were prepared to accept its separate and prior genesis to varna and to see it as an unfortunate accretion which should in fact be categorically dissociated from Hinduism. Their version of an essentialist Hinduism would be even more mystical and ethereal for it could not even point at this unique social institution as its distorted expression. Caste is here ignored rather than rationalized.

The justification of varna has strengthened over the last two centuries, symptomizing the intellectual popularization of the Brahminical conception of Hinduism, itself the natural corollary of reform Hinduism.

Yet since the 1940s and the rise of more empirical studies the idea of caste as a unified and pan-India category of the country's past has become increasingly unconvincing and implausible. The fourfold classification schema of varna seems so obviously the typical stratification pattern attending the transition from ranked to stratified societies anywhere that it is difficult to believe in any specific connection to the Indian peculiarity of jati. That four-fold classification represents political–military elites, the religious elite, urban low status groups like merchants and artisans, rural low-status groups or the peasantry. A tension often emerges between the first two, expressing itself in variable institutional and ideological forms.

The view that caste is the precipitate of Hinduism's ideology, an all-encompassing Brahmin-dominated system of hierarchy, has immense problems. Even in our times, M.N. Srinivas reminds us, caste is local in character and its system of hierarchies is not only qualified by segmentation sideways but exists as a regional cluster. It is, says Srinivas, only by putting it into the 'Procrustean frame of varna' that one can try to make it national.[18] Caste as ideologically a unified whole based on the principle of hierarchy whose defining criterion is the purity–pollution relationship is an idealist construct of Dumont and his followers. Those observations of theirs which lend themselves to empirical verification do not receive such validation.[19]

The category of the wholly impure – untouchables – is a later accretion to caste, suggesting that the purity–pollution principle is itself a later accretion, and its authoritativeness and spread is linked to the spread and consolidation of Brahminical influence within a pre-existing as well as much wider and variable jati system. Nor does Dumont's claim of Brahmin opposition to and superiority over Kshatriya secular power (the superiority of a purity-defined status to a power-defined status) receive much empirical support. The record on the ground is too varied. Indeed, notions of purity are themselves diverse and not always expressive of a social hierarchy. They also express a direct relationship between worshipper and deity.[20]

Diverse patterns of caste hierarchies are accompanied by diverse caste ideologies. There is no overarching Brahminical ideology defining either Hinduism or caste, although that Brahminical ideology has in the last two hundred years spread wider and faster than others, in the process undergoing modification itself. A more materialist interpretation of caste privileging non-ideational factors is more appropriate. Romila Thapar has suggested that caste, as the dominant organizational structure of Indian society, changed in relation to changes in environment, access to technology, distribution of economic resources, kinship patterns. But the ideological rationale for it was relatively constant. Thapar plausibly suggests that the very strength of its ideology of hierarchy (uniquely linking inequality to birth and untouchability) probably reflects the depth of resistance to it.[21]

Where her argument needs further clarification is the claim that caste was the dominant organizational structure of ancient India and therefore even more so of medieval India. It is only in recent times that forest systems become socio-economically distorted forest systems incorporating other kinds of socio-economic relations, whether of the market or of caste. But for most of its history, caste relations are to be decisively distinguished from forest–tribal relations. The caste is not a tribe and emerges because of the transition from nomadic and tribal to settled agrarian systems. Territorially speaking, the 'dominance' of caste is more recent; population-wise, it has a longer history.

The tribe is above all a community of ancestry, real or mythical; the community of caste (jati) is not. It is a closed endogamous status group best understood as a community of function or more narrowly as a 'marriage circle', or perhaps in some other way. This remains an area of major dispute among even materialist investigators of the origins and nature of caste.[22] But the important thing is that caste must be distinguished from tribe (except in more recent times) and that the caste system belongs to settled agriculture.

The importance and spread of caste to India is, then, connected to the importance and spread of agrarian systems. This insight provides the possibility of moving towards a more accurate assessment of the historical significance of the caste system. Through the 1950s, 1960s and 1970s, Indian materialist historians were strongly influenced by prevailing currents of Marxism. They were preoccupied with understanding the conditions for the transition to capitalism from pre-industrial agrarian systems. Most histories of ancient India (from the late Vedic age onwards) and of medieval India assumed without much justification the actual and progressive dominance of settled agrarian systems and, therefore, the relative ubiquity of the caste system, or, more accurately, of caste systems.

A minority current in contemporary Indian historiography has correctly pointed out that the issue is wide open. Indeed, the balance of historical evidence suggests that the agrarian transformation of most of the area we now call India is only a few centuries old. Claims for the widespread dominance of the caste system are greatly exaggerated, at least until more recently.[23] More importantly, it exhibited fluidity, fuzziness and variety, though efforts at singularizing–unifying its hierarchies have long existed, becoming stronger in more recent times.

Caste, then, is unique to India. It precedes Brahminism and has had a wider spread. It is not a singular, all-encompassing system anymore than is Hinduism. It has been for most of its existence spatially limited with forest and nomadic India excluded from the jati system. But as caste has spread, developed and changed, so too has Brahminism, with the two partially and variably intertwining. Brahminism has provided ideological sustenances for caste formations; and the latter has impacted upon and altered (in the direction of greater inclusivity with regard to rituals, beliefs and practices) the former.

The greater adaptability and usefulness of Brahminism to caste in agrarian systems is part of the answer to its overcoming the challenge of Buddhism. It cannot be coincidental that Buddhism survived in the north, eastern and southernmost peripheries of the sub-continent but not in its more inegalitarian and settled heartlands. Similarly, it has thrived most in the egalitarian village systems of Southeast Asia but has been only a counter-tradition in the more stratified socio-economic systems of China and Japan. Yet caste, for all its variant forms of imbrication with Brahminical doctrine and values, has always been more important than the latter. Islam and Christianity have had to adapt much more to the caste system(s) than to Brahminism.

The history and historiography of Hinduism have long been closely connected. The hows and whys regarding the construction of the very category of Hinduism have helped shape the understanding of what it is and was. Basically there have been three approaches to characterizing Hinduism.[24] The first was shared by Orientalism and the nationalist Indian response to it. Both talked in terms of differences and essences, of essential differences. Orientalism created a spiritual Hinduism by using prior Brahminical discourse, but in doing so greatly valorized it and textual, philosophical Hinduism. Indian intellectuals made worthy the characteristics that Orientalist empiricists saw as unworthy. But they did not dispute the Brahminical and singular rendering of Hinduism as such. There was also a difference between the Romantics and many an Indianist. The former saw the essential India (or East) as the original depository of what had been lost, not just the Other of the West but its other part. The 'recovery' would help constitute a new wholeness of being. The Encounter with Hinduism was also a search by Western man for his other or inner self, not just an intellectual quest but a therapeutic one.

The initiative for this Encounter and earlier engagements never came

141

from India. It always came from the outside – Greek, Chinese, Arab, and then European. As Halbfass points out,

> There are no Hindu accounts of foreign nations and distant lands. The Indian cultural 'colonization' of East and Southeast Asia and the spread of Buddhism are not at all reflected in Sanskrit literature. Even the Muslims . . . appear in vague and marginal references.[25]

It is only after the impact of the British with the Encounter forced upon them that many Indians began exploring the possibility of some kind of cultural synthesis.

As earlier defensiveness gave way to a more aggressive affirmation against colonialism, the search for a synthesis along the lines followed by European Romanticists gave way to a much stronger assertion of India's intrinsic spiritual–cultural superiority, plain and simple. One current among Indianists – traditional Hinduism or orthodox Brahminism – had in any case never been that interested either in the Encounter itself, or in responding to the West. Reform Hinduism or neo-Hinduism (which reinforced a Brahminical-leaning understanding of the nature of Hinduism) was much more concerned with so responding, and it did so in a discourse partly shaped by Western precepts. Often, the universalist claims of the West brought forth universalist claims on Hinduism's behalf. There is more Western thought and influence in neo-Hinduism than vice versa.[26]

Faced with a vast range of rituals, worship and beliefs not readily explainable through Brahminical discourse, there were and are differences on how best to understand the relationship between a Brahminical and lay Hinduism. How inclusive was Brahminism? How did it dominate? Through an ethos discoverable in the ancient and sacred texts and expressed in a true Brahminism which need not be identical with the current practices and beliefs of existing Brahmins? The origins of popular Hinduism were also in dispute. Was it a degeneration of textual Hinduism, or could it have existed separately from and even prior to Aryan-Brahminism but gradually coming into a broadly unified cultural–religious field marked by the 'spirit of Hinduism'?

The lowest common denominator in this understanding of Hinduism was that it was a Brahmin-dominated religious system paternalistically gathering sects to itself so that multiple texts, doctrines, deities and rituals could flourish. But there was nonetheless an overall coherence making of Hinduism both now and for centuries past a 'single religious fabric'. Such an understanding promoted a certain kind of history of

Hinduism. This was philosophical and art history or the study of iconography and symbolism. It did not stimulate a sociological study of Hinduism and only later anthropological research somewhat qualifies this established research perspective by bringing popular Hinduism closer to the forestage.[27]

A second approach concedes more ground to folk or popular Hinduism. In most versions there is talk of a Great Tradition, which is more doctrinal, uniform and pertains to upper strata; and of a Little Tradition, encompassing the diversity of folk or lived Hinduism. But the Great and Little Traditions interact and the former influences the latter more than vice versa, so that, ideologically speaking, a graduated hierarchy of religious values, practices, beliefs, even deities, emerges. Here the metaphor of the 'jungle of Hinduism' is more widely used and Brahmins seen as the forest guardians (equipped with the relatively more powerful tools of Brahminism) rather than as the gardeners of this jungle. While a more singularized Hinduism is emerging, this process is not best understood through categories like the Great and Little Traditions when applied to the past. Even today the degree of uniformity or coherence implied *within* the Great Tradition and *within* the Little Tradition just is not there.

Attempts at empirical validation in fact reveal variant and competing Great Traditions. Moreover, the so-called Little Tradition is so diverse that to categorize the variance under a single label, Little Tradition or Popular Hinduism, misleadingly implies that such diversity nonetheless 'belongs' to one religious field, itself broadly partitioned into two interlinked categories of the Great and the Little. A more radical version within this second approach expresses its unhappiness with these analytical terms, and is even more emphatic in its stress on the importance of popular Hinduism.[28]

This second way of understanding Hinduism differs from the first in rejecting the idea of a Brahminical–philosophical–mystical essence. It pays far more attention to the anthropology of 'Hindus' and thus to popular, lived Hinduism. In its most radical variant the heart of this popular Hinduism is considered to be worship of deities who can exercise power over humans in desired ways for the worshipper. Worship is a 'contract of power' with obligations on both sides. Here, Hinduism is an extremely worldly religion, though like all developed religious systems it will have its philosophies and its more ethereal speculations. But for all its differences with the first approach, here also there remains the rock-bottom insistence that Hinduism is a *comprehensible whole*. It does possess at the most fundamental level a necessarily

143

abstract but real unity which expresses itself in common organizing principles and structures.[29]

Only the third approach categorically rejects the idea that Hinduism, even today, can be understood as a comprehensible whole. It is simply too diverse not only regarding its range of beliefs and practices but also with respect to the variations in supposedly shared concepts, e.g. the existence of differing notions of karma and transmigration–reincarnation. The term 'Hinduism' is best seen by social scientists with no strong political or cultural axes to grind as a compendium label or category. That the very notion of Hinduism was quasi-political in origin has directed research on it, and made the compendium understanding of Hinduism the least popular (among Indianists) of contending interpretations.[30]

Having said this, however, it would be mistaken to leave it at that. The most important *process* that has been taking place over the last few centuries and greatly accelerated in this century has been the construction of a more singular Hinduism, or what Romila Thapar has called a 'syndicated Hinduism'. This syndication process is not the monopoly of any single cultural or political 'syndicate'. It has had a number of sources and those participating in its construction have had different understandings of how it had to be done, and why. But the most chauvinist construction of monolithic Hinduism existing today can trace an important part of its lineage to earlier currents of reform Hinduism and neo-Hinduism. For Thapar this syndicated Hinduism is a garbled form of Brahminism with a 'motley of values' from other sources, like the Bhakti movements and Puranic rituals.[31]

No assessment of contemporary Hinduism should ignore its intrinsic diversity, and hence the resources it possesses to counter this ongoing singularization. Nor should it fail to see that this process is taking place and has gathered pace. Indeed, on balance the centripetal efforts unleashed by those constructing a more essentialist and uniform Hinduism have made *significant* headway. Those content to emphasize the natural diversity of Hinduism, the insuperable obstacles to the construction of a Hindu community and therefore to the consolidation and growth of Hindu communalism need to think again. What has *already* been achieved in this respect is dangerous enough. Whether or not things can get worse is an eminently political question.

Modernity provides multiple possibilities. The forces of secularization and democratization lead to a more relativized Hindu identity, to an acceptance of a more modest social role for Hinduism, to greater plurality and choice in even religious behaviour, in keeping with

Hinduism's naturally large range of variations in this respect. A variety of other forces, communal and non-communal, push for a more singular religious system. Ultimately, this process is of less significance than the issue of secularization of civil society and the secularity of the Indian state. Even a singular Hinduism need not present a serious danger if accompanied by the diminished importance of religious identity in social life, i.e. greater secularization. The long-term evolution of what we call Hinduism is not, in itself, the most important political issue. What is are the ways in which distorted interpretations of Hinduism, and of India's past and present, are used to construct false and dangerous political, social, cultural ideals, and programmes for their achievement.

Hinduism's Mystique of Tolerance[32]

Hinduism's mystique of tolerance rests on two central pillars which on closer inspection disclose extremely shaky foundations. It is based on the plural coexistence of multiple faiths, religious practices and beliefs both within 'Hinduism' and across it, the 'non-Hindu' religious systems. It is based on philosophical doctrine. In neither case do 'facts' speak for themselves. Tolerance is neither axiomatic nor self-evident. 'Facts' were interpreted to mean as much and both the interpreters and the interpretations belong to the period of the Encounter between East and West and to its aftermath of reform Hinduism and neo-Hinduism. The mystique of tolerance is a modern construction to serve modern purposes.

The 'constructors' did recognize that if their judgement of overall tolerance was to stand, then it had to represent a balance between that religious system's ideology (here taken to mean simply beliefs, doctrines) and its social structure. What was remarkable, however, was the way in which obvious intolerances in both domains were ignored or rationalized away. If caste was the social structure associated with Hinduism, how could its obviously intolerant character be wished away? Yet it was, usually through rationalizing it as a degeneration of a pristine system of order – varna. Take this remarkable disclaimer by Sarvepalli Radhakrishnan:

> The institutions of caste illustrate the spirit of comprehensive synthesis characteristic of the Hindu mind with its faith in the collaboration of races and the cooperation of cultures. Paradoxical as it may seem, the system of caste is the outcome of tolerance and trust.[33]

145

Vivekananda, Gandhi, Radhakrishnan, all justified the historical references to caste and varna, claiming that caste later degenerated. They rejected caste in this form and insisted that only in its pure form (varna) was it central to Hinduism. But they remained silent about how varna, though a historical phenomenon, could nonetheless be conceptually pure. However necessary a system of order might be, and however useful and positive it might be deemed, all historical systems of order have their defects and their patterns of oppression, subordination and exploitation. Moreover, as historical systems they are necessarily subject to change and always encounter some degree of resistance from those subordinated. They can be stable but not harmonious. All ideological attempts to paint them as such result in a social bias towards the elites, i.e. to notions of tolerance on *their* terms.

Even when the claim made is only referring to religious tolerance and not to a wider social tolerance, this is still not sustainable. Strong rivalries between Brahminism, Buddhism and Jainism have been characterized wrongly as minor sectarian rivalries within a common fold. Thapar reminds us that

> [t]he insistence on the tradition of religious tolerance and non-violence as characteristic of Hinduism, which is built on a selection of normative values emphasising Ahimsa, is not borne out by historical evidence. The theory is so deeply ingrained among most Indians that there is the failure to see the reverse of it when it stares them in the face. The extremity of intolerance implicit in the notion of untouchability was glossed over by regarding it as a function of caste and society.[34]

What most distinguished pre-modern India from other parts of the world was not tolerance but the scale of its religious pluralism, where such pluralism has never meant much more than religious coexistence. Such coexistence was found elsewhere and in other histories but not to the same range nor in this intricate variety. However, everywhere the general terms of religious coexistence are substantially a function of the relationship between political and religious elites, for both strive for popular loyalties and are thus competitors for power, however much the arrangements for organizing that competition may vary. Those terms can and do change when that relationship changes. This has been the history of religious pluralism in India as much before as after the advent of Islam. Religious coexistence in India has been a sociological phenomenon not primarily a religious one. Ignoring this leads to improper conclusions.

Insofar as religious conversion is seen as some kind of obstacle to religious harmony and therefore to coexistence, much has been made of Hinduism's refusal to convert, said to derive from its doctrinally plural nature. Yet Brahminism and many a 'Hindu sect' have engaged in conversion. This is so obviously the case that the widespread insistence that classical Hinduism (pre-modern Hinduism) did not is another example of that wilful blindness that elsewhere leads many to proclaim the natural tolerance of Hinduism despite the existence of the caste system and untouchability. There is no way, for example, that Hinduism could have spread to Southeast Asia to become as influential as it did for centuries without such conversion. The ludicrous alternative is to believe that the overwhelming bulk of Southeast Asian followers of this Hinduism were the descendants of an original Hindu migration.

The point is not that Hinduism does not convert but that its conversion process is very different from that of the Prophetic religions. There is rarely a fixed point of conversion or a formal mechanism.[35] The will to convert existed but Hindu social arrangements – the absence of Church and Caliph – did not provide much of a basis for coercive mechanisms to emerge and carry out the ambition. Too much should not be made of this absence. Even for the Semitic religions, conversion was primarily through processes not involving coercion. But that Hinduism lacked such coercive arrangements and that conversion was more exemplary than emissary in character did make it different in important ways from Christianity and Islam. Hinduism did not require one to 'invade' another space or to 'reject' it. There is no equivalent, after all, to the Jihads and the Crusades!

Nonetheless, the connection of Hindu religious elites to secular political elites, i.e. the question of power, was certainly important for explaining the spread of Hinduism in Southeast Asia and elsewhere. The adoption of forms of Hinduism by local rulers would undoubtedly have hastened even the exemplary process of conversion among a king's subjects. And elite adoption of such Hinduism was often connected to calculations of how this could enhance their social, political and cultural authority.

No doubt other factors help to explain conversion at the popular level. These are all matters for historical–sociological investigation. But there is little room for the view that Hinduism lacked an impulse to spread and convert. Even within South Asia, Brahminism expanded through distinctive processes of accommodation and inclusion. Here again, provided the picture is not overdrawn (lived Christianity and Islam have also involved major accommodation to pagan and non-

147

Islamic practices, beliefs, rituals), there is an important difference between Brahminism and the Semitic faiths. The former had a much greater flexibility in its processes of incorporation.

But tolerance is not the other name for this flexibility, i.e. this internal coexistence of variant practices and beliefs, any more than it is the name for an external coexistence between sects and religions. The issue of coexistence of different religious communities is simply too complex to be adequately grasped by a notion of tolerance. Moreover, neither pluralism nor tolerance can have the same meaning in pre-modernity as they have when they are connected to modern notions of equality and democratic rights.[36] In pre-modern India, states may have been 'tolerant' of religions but justice was based on a principle of inequality. Religious and other minorities might have enjoyed protection and special rights but were not on a par with majorities. Under Islamic rule it would not be correct to see Hindus as a collectively oppressed 'majority' but Hinduism as itself comprising a world of many minorities.

Brahminical Hinduism's claim to doctrinal tolerance is based on its distinctive approach to the question of truth. Unlike the revelatory religions, it possesses no propositional truth. It has a much more flexible notion but does not do without a notion of truth altogether. Correlatively, it can avoid the sharp polarity of notions of good and evil more typical of the soteriologies of Christianity and Islam. Good and evil are seen as different facets of a common entity and ultimate quests are seen in terms not of the final triumph of good over evil but of the transcendence of both. This is a soteriology conducive to contemplation not activism.[37]

Doxa is not as important here. Hinduism is marked much more by a process of dialogue with itself, a kind of internal philosophical ecumenism.[38] But if this is a form of philosophical tolerance, it also expresses a form of philosophical intolerance. The internal dialogue is important but not dialogue with others or other 'truths'. What, then, is the notion of truth in Brahminical Hinduism? Are there elements or degrees of truth in other religions? Or are there equal, multiple truths? Though Vedantism can be interpreted as subscribing to the latter it most certainly plays around with the former notion. Indeed, there is a strongly held notion of truth being one, yet having many levels so that not all people can have the same perception of truth or of reality. An egalitarian relativism is here partnered, even subsumed, by an overriding arrogance.

This describes both philosophical Hinduism's understanding of society and its relationship to other religious doctrines. Thus different individuals (and groups) are at different 'levels' in relation to the ultimate truth, which is in principle an attainable quest. Different people are at different stages of spiritual growth in the quest for perfection and these differences are somehow connected to, and reflective of, the individual's actual condition of life.

Philosophical Hinduism is not religiously–doctrinally syncretic but essentialist. This Hinduism does not dialogue with other truths but avoids such dialogue or even the preparatory manoeuvres for a philosophical synthesis.[39] You have your truths and I have mine, and mine is the deepest truth! That is its credo. The essence of this Hinduism is also the essence of all religions! This 'doctrinal tolerance' does not seriously reflect on other 'truths' but merely includes them hierarchically or perspectivally. Halbfass, in describing the interface between traditional Hinduism and other religious doctrines, had it right.

> This process illustrates the potential and the limits of the traditional Hindu way of dealing with 'heterodox' teachings. It leaves room for many different views and standpoints, but always tends to include them in hierarchic or perspectivist schemes, and to subordinate them to one ultimate truth, frequently that of Advaita Vedanta. The 'other' teaching is usually not recognized in its otherness but claimed as an aspect of, approach to, or aberration from the truth contained in its own doctrine.[40]

Such a claim of doctrinal tolerance not only disguises its distinctive intolerance but justifies a belief in its own superiority. The claim that both Hinduism and Indian culture are uniquely characterized by a 'unity in diversity' is but another form of this mask.[41] Even the composite patriotism of Indian nationalists fed into this distorted catholicity of a Brahminical Hinduism.[42] The great redeeming grace of Hinduism lies not so much in its philosophy or in its Brahminism as in the simple ecumenism of its largely non-Brahminical and popular forms of existence.

Hindutva

The closest English translation of the term 'Hindutva' would be 'Hinduness'. As such it is a broader term than Hinduism and connects to the kind of answers given to the questions: Who is a Hindu? What are the properties that are constitutive of Hinduness? It was in the period of colonialism that religious communities began to be sharply defined.

149

Who did the defining and how they did it became major political issues serving definite political interests. If British colonialism had an interest in defining an India of different religious communities which shared few cultural characteristics and were often at loggerheads with each other, anti-colonial nationalists had their reasons for defining and understanding matters differently.

This issue was obviously connected to matters of nation and nationalism. Nationalists had many more reasons to claim that India had been a nation, culturally if not politically, submerged if not actually realized, long before British rule. To accept that it was this British rule that actually constituted an Indian nation in any meaningful, unified sense of the term would have been politically and emotionally disarming. Emerging nationalisms invariably invent a past for themselves. The first phase is the stipulation of a strong and enduring cultural nationalism. The 'Who is a Hindu?' and the 'Who is an Indian?' questions were inescapable aspects in this process of constructing competing versions of cultural nationalism.

Answers to the 'Who is a Hindu?' question had to be sought precisely because there was no self-evident and universally acceptable answer but multiple and overlapping ones.[43] But the question most preoccupied the Hindu cultural Right. This was a radical, modernist current to be distinguished from Hindu traditionalists and conservatives. They were out to remould the 'Hindu community' and 'Hindu society' not to conserve it. The operative term for them was not 'Indianness' but 'Hinduness' or 'Hindutva'. The 'foreigner' was not the non-Indian or simply the outsider beneficiary but all those not fully assimilated into Hinduness.

Many Indian nationalists, to a greater or lesser degree, saw Hinduism as a vital, indeed decisive, part of Indian culture and therefore of an Indian cultural nationalism. Like the Hindutva Right, they also sought to remould Indian society and even the 'Hindu community'. But there were significant differences regarding the exclusivity of their respective versions of cultural and political nationalism, and thus in their programmes and visions for India as an independent state.

The differences did not centre on the issue of Hinduism and how best to understand it. The first important synthesizer and proponent of Hindutva, Veer Savarkar, saw this as a racial, cultural, religious–spiritual unity, a unity of culture and territory.[44] Hinduism was a part of Hindutva but Savarkar would not give it as prominent a role as M.S. Golwalkar, the second head of the Rashtriya Swayamsevak Sangh (National Volunteer Corps), did.[45] What united the proponents of Hindutva before independence and unites them now is not agreement on specific definitions but common assent to a certain *chain of reasoning.*

Figures like Vivekananda and Gandhi, whose views, lives and teachings are in so many ways markedly different from, indeed opposed to, political Hindutva, can nonetheless be appropriated, with a degree of plausibility, to serve Hindutva interests. While such figures never sub-scribed to Hindutva's *full* chain of reasoning, they did implicitly or explicitly endorse some *links* in that broader chain.[46] Therein lies a major dilemma for all those who would promote an opposition to Hindutva from within the discourse of Hinduism and neo-Hinduism.

This basic chain of reasoning goes as follows: Ethos/spirit is the heart of, Hinduism, which is at the heart of, or coterminous with, Hindu culture (which defines Indian culture), which is at the heart of the Hindu nation (which defines the Indian nation). Four concepts – ethos, religion, culture, nation – are the key elements in this discourse. Not only is Hindutva's understanding of each extremely unsophisticated, but its understanding of the connections between them is absurdly determinist. Enough has surely been said so far about why this is so.

Cultural nationalism is always constructed. It is constructed with purposes in view. It is the judgement of these purposes – their value and their possibility of attainment – that provides us with a basis for assessing competing cultural nationalisms and for making alignments. Since there is no fixed entity called the *true* cultural nationalism, it cannot be 'uncovered' by historical study. But this does not mean there are not better, more accurate ways of understanding Indian culture and history. There clearly are, and these can provide no solace to the claims of Hindutva. But it is to say that an Indian cultural nationalism is neither 'naturally' a Hindu nationalism, nor 'naturally' a secular nationalism or a composite nationalism. What it is and will be is what we fight to make it be.

Hindutva operates with another tight reductionism. If India is to become strong, then it must acquire cultural confidence. This confi-dence comes from the people recognizing the country's true cultural roots. For all the crudity of these formulations, there is a hint of one noteworthy understanding. Cultural confidence may not be the key determinant but it is certainly conducive to the construction of a generally strong and healthy India. What we mean by 'strong and healthy' and what we mean by 'culture and cultural confidence' is precisely at issue. The best conception hinges on an understanding of culture (certainly culture in modernity) that is beyond the ken of Hindutva.

Strengthening the cultural resources of a country or society always preoccupied the late Raymond Williams. Throughout his life he constantly interrogated the notion of culture. In this process he began to draw a distinction between what he once treated as synonymous – 'culture in common' and 'common culture'. He came to endorse the latter and to argue that strengthening cultural resources meant moving closer to the deepening and institutionalization of a 'common culture'.[47] Where 'culture in common' could be read as a form of cultural essentialism, 'common culture' could be read as its opposite – always open, plural, ordinary, changing, expanding.

Hindutva is distinctively Indian, but in insisting that we possess a culture in common (a cultural essence) and that what prevents us becoming culturally stronger as a nation is our refusal (more accurately, the refusal of some – Muslims and secularists) to recognize this essence and build upon it, Hindutva is no different from the cultural chauvinisms of other countries, East or West. The political ideologies and implied threats to 'uncomprehending' minorities, of Thatcherite racism ('we are being swamped'), neo-Nazi anti-Semitism in Western Europe, Islamic fundamentalism and Hindutva forces are structurally isomorphic – 'If you do not recognize, understand or appreciate that this is our culture in common, then you are guilty of weakening, damaging, even betraying our nation/culture, and we don't like it and will not let you get away with it.'

The construction of a genuine common culture characterized by ever greater openness, plurality and ordinariness has a global dimension as well.

If Hindutva is anti-secular, there is also an anti-secularism that claims to be anti-Hindutva.

Anti-Secularism

The term 'anti-secularism' here refers not to all anti-secular forces, but to a much narrower grouping taking its distance from both communal–fundamentalist–Hindutva forces and from the secularists opposed to them. As such it is not a serious political force guiding any identifiable party, or organization of any major consequence. However, it does describe an intellectual current which has gained ground in Indian academia, among NGO activists, and has influenced the general public discourse on matters pertaining to communalism and secularism. It claims to represent a third position which opposes communalism and

its various manifestations but not in the name of a supposedly Westernized concept of secularism and the secular state. Instead it proposes an
'authentic' indigenism which seeks to oppose communalism and the
various forms of perversion of religion through endorsement and
utilization of the resources within India's religious traditions.

In the eyes of many a secularist, however, this anti-secularism is seen
as having a damaging political effect, as legitimizing implicitly when not
explicitly the assault by communal forces (above all political Hindutva)
against the current level of secularity of the state. It is seen as reinforcing
a false solution already pervading the public discourse – the idea that a
secular state should be one which enjoins and prescribes the showing of
'equal respect to all religions' (*sarva dharm sambhavam*) rather than
maintaining a basic separation of state apparatuses from religious
influence and religious institutions. And that a state which maintains
this principled distance is necessarily anti-religion or very likely to be so,
and is therefore repressive, totalitarian, etc.

L.K. Advani, the former head of the BJP (and currently party
president), has often publicly stated that a true as opposed to a pseudo-
secular state would be a state practising *sarva dharm sambhavam*, with the
added rider that a Hindu *rashtra* (nation) would be truly secular because
of the unique tolerance of Hinduism. Not all anti-secularists share this
vision of Hinduism's unique tolerance. But they do endorse the view
that if the notion of a secular state in India is to be meaningful, then it
must break away from the Enlightenment-inspired notion of impartial
religious abstinence to a more authentically indigenous notion of active
organization of religious toleration.

The three most important spokespersons for this anti-secularism are
Bhiku T. Parekh, T.N. Madan and Ashis Nandy.[48] If there are certain
similarities in their thinking and writing, they also have their important
differences and their distinctive ambiguities. Anti-secularism is not a
strongly consistent and coherent discourse. It is still united more by
what it is against than what it is for. But in this discourse, ranging over
six general themes, there are common points of reference. These six
general themes are: the issue of modernity; understandings of culture,
civilization, religion, Hinduism, in regard to Indian society past and
present; secularism and secularization; particularism and universalism;
individualism and communitarianism; neo-Gandhianism.

All three share similar basic understandings of culture and civilization
and of religion's relationship to Indian culture, though they differ in
their assessments of Hinduism (and Islam). All three express varying
levels of unease with modern concepts of democratic individualism and

stress (in varying degrees) the importance of religiously rooted communitarian values as a preferred counterpoint. All three express sympathy for Gandhi's vision and thought. They are neo-Gandhians but
differ over what Gandhiism is, and over the precise value of that legacy.
In seeking to explain the inapplicability of the Enlightenment inspired
notion of secularism Madan and Parekh flirt strongly with cultural
particularism–relativism, while Nandy relies more on an anti-modernist
'competing universalism'.

The most intransigent of these anti-secularists, the one who would not
hesitate to describe himself as such, is Ashis Nandy. He is also the most
uncompromising in his hostility to history, to the project of modernity,
and the one most determined to read Gandhi as an anti-modernist.
Neither Parekh nor Madan would go so far as to write off the project of
modernity altogether and seem more concerned to conjoin religion
and modernity. In contrast to Nandy's unremitting hostility to secularism, Madan is noticeably more ambiguous about it. Parekh is more
sober and judicious in assessing Gandhi and Gandhiism, and his own
preferences are more often to be read off from the sympathies and
reservations expressed in his explicatory narratives about political
leaders like Gandhi and Nehru. If many of Nandy's observations are
infuriating, extreme and unbalanced, many are also provocative, stimulating and insightful. Of the three, Nandy's views have been the most
influential, and in some ways politically the most dangerous.

Madan, Parekh and Nandy are cultural essentialists, and that essence
is religion. All the problems of double fusion (the cultural programming
of society with religion the cultural programmer) or analytical conflation of culture and society are faithfully replicated in their writings.[49] In
Parekh they can be gleaned from his treatment of Gandhi's thought. All
three immortalize and glorify religion. There is the standard bifurcation
of religion into good and bad, i.e. religion-as-faith and religion-as-
ideology, true religion and mere religiosity, enabling them to deflect all
criticism of religious failings as largely irrelevant because inapplicable
to what is the true subject matter. Culture is understood as a 'whole way
of life' but is also importantly connected to issues of cognition and
indigenous forms of knowledge. Each thinker varies in how he understands culture's 'structure of coherence'.

For Madan, culture has key themes or 'dynamic affirmations' which
are the principal source of the 'character, structure and direction' of a
cultural complex. They give it a 'civilizational distinctiveness'.[50] For all
three, civilization is understood only as a long enduring cultural
complex. Parekh sees civilization as 'a shared body of values, attitudes,

ways of looking at the world and forms of social relationship'. According to him, 'A common civilizational basis was thus not only available in India but formed the ineliminable substance of its collective life.'[51] For Nandy, Indian civilization is so inclusive of all other faiths that he avoids claiming special centrality for Hinduism; it is a 'confederation of cultures'. For Madan there is no disputing Hinduism's pivotal role in Indian civilization. Parekh's Gandhi also wishes to broaden the notion to include other religious–cultural contributions, but Hinduism clearly has a pre-eminent role.

Religion is either inescapably central to, or even constitutive of, Indian society, past and present. Both Madan and Nandy frequently endorse the second, more extreme formulation. But where Parekh is sceptical about Hinduism having an essence of its own and sees popular Hinduism as 'institutionalized bargains', as a power contract, Madan has a more forthrightly Brahminical understanding. Beneath diversity he sees a unity based on a common code of ethics, and on certain axial beliefs like dharma, karma, artha, kama. There is also a unifying syncretism at the level of action. But since 'civilizational distinctiveness' for Madan necessarily requires a world-view which certain favoured social strata are more likely to possess, there is no embarrassment in acknowledging Brahmin pre-eminence or the centrality of Brahminism and Vedic philosophy to Hindu thought. Like Dumont, Madan sees the 'secret of Hinduism' in the dialogue between renouncer and man-in-the-world.[52]

Madan's own studies on Muslims and Hindu Pandits in Kashmir have clearly shaped his understanding of Hinduism and Islam.[53] It is the former that possesses most resources for promoting the kind of secularism he most admires, namely inter-faith understanding and religious tolerance. The usual stereotypes regarding Hinduism's tolerance are echoed in his writings. Thus Madan does not talk of Hindu communalism, since there is for him no such thing as a Hindu community. He doesn't even consider that the politics of forging a Hindu community (which has been taking place) may legitimately be regarded as intimately connected to a developing politics of Hindu communalism. He rarely mentions Hindu nationalism, but is candid about his view that the Indian state 'panders' to the minorities. 'The notion of minority status as privilege is not slander in today's India but a social and political fact. And it is one of the very major reasons why Indian secularism has run into difficulties.'[54]

Nandy would never make such a statement. For him religious faith is the operative notion. Different religious systems may differ in the degree

155

of syncretism they encourage, but Nandy largely abstracts from the specificities of any particular religious system when seeking to explain the essentialism of Indian culture and civilization. He is content to understand Hinduism as a combination of classical and folk Hinduisms, where the inter-relationship is open to shifting balances. Similar strains are to be found between the classical and folk forms of other religions.

Madan's attitudes to secularism and secularization are marked by significant ambiguities, even confusions. He knows the kind of secularism he favours – *sarva dharm sambhavam*. But since he (and Parekh) seek to assert religion's centrality to modernity (at least in India) and he does not reject modernity (as Nandy does), Madan is conspicuously unsure what to make of secular humanism as an ideology, or secularization as a process. Madan does not successfully negotiate between the different meanings of secularization. Thus he can see it as having only a peripheral relation to religion. It is a process of 'empowering human agency' as contrasted to supra-human agency, and as such something that has been going on everywhere and throughout the ages. It would appear, then, to bear no special relationship either to modernity or to any particular religious system. Yet Madan also insists that secularization is the distinctive gift of Christianity.[55] What are to make of this?

The closest Madan gets to a clear definition of secularization is that it is a term

> useful in describing certain processes that are as old as human culture:
> the processes by which, step by step, human beings have reduced their
> dependence upon supra-human agency and narrowed down the areas
> of life in which religious ideas, symbols and institutions hold sway.[56]

However, the process of relative decline of religious influence is not as old as human culture but receives a qualitative acceleration with the emergence of modernity. Madan dodges this issue. Furthermore, in this definition there is, if not a stipulated connection, certainly a clearly implied conjunction between enhancement of human agency and reduction of religious influence.

Yet, elsewhere, Madan insists that religions enhance human agency by being the source of humanity's deepest values, and therefore are themselves an important expression of the secularization-empowering process. Perhaps Madan means that secularization is a capacious term describing a number of processes, some as old as human culture and to be judged positively (enhancing of human agency), and others not so old and not to be necessarily judged as positive (the relative decline of religious influence). But what happens, then, to his implied connection between the two? Madan never clearly states his view on these matters. Indeed, he seems unaware of such ambiguities. Certainly the definition does not square with his claim that secularization is a gift of Christianity.

In making this claim, Madan has in mind the tendencies towards greater privatization of religious concerns. Christian (Protestant) discourse legitimizes and endorses this privatization and thus promotes it. This is unlike the Indic religious discourses. But even if this is so it does not warrant the strong claim that secularization is the gift of Christianity.[57] It has multiple sources of birth and sustenance. Capitalist modernization and democratic discourses originating in the Enlightenment also come into the reckoning. Just how Enlightenment values, capitalist modernization and reform Christianity come together helps explain the emergence of processes of secularization. Given these multiple sources of birth and continuity, it cannot be complacently argued that the absence of a dominant Christian discourse means secularization is very weakly implanted in India, for both capitalism and democratic discourse have developed real roots in the country.

Madan can hardly deny that secularization has taken place in India and is continuing. This, he would say, is a value-neutral fact.[58] Insofar as it means more empowerment of human agency he can hardly be against it. Insofar as it also means a relative religious decline he cannot make it fully clear to his readers what he makes of this. This will remain so until he deals with the unresolved tension between the two themes of 'enhanced empowerment' and 'religious decline' within his own understanding of secularization. There are times when he expresses open hostility to secularization. Secularization as a process of privatizing religion acts to undermine the good society which must have religion and religious-based morality at its centre. Secularization creates, by way of a reaction, fundamentalism and religious fanaticism.

Logically, then, his position should be a clear opposition not just to the 'secularization thesis' or to what some secularists or forms of secularism say, but to the very process of secularization. Some way should be found either to halt and reverse it, or to separate its positive empowering aspect from its negative aspect of religious decline, presuming this is possible. This would require from Madan a much clearer, more coherent and consistent *attack* on secularization.

At other points Madan does suggest that promoting secularization or 'expanding human control over human lives' (which, he says, is proceeding weakly in India) does require a narrowing down of religious influence.[59] He further suggests that the Indic religions, not being revealed truths, are open to self-questioning and thus to such seculari-

157

zation. To promote it, then, requires not Christian-inspired secularism distinguishing between the secular and the sacred spheres of existence. Secularization in India, he says, needs to be promoted not by an anti-religious interpretation of secularism, but by a secularism meaning 'inter-religious understanding'.

But all this leaves unanswered questions. The Western notion of secularism is not, as Madan accepts, necessarily anti-religious. But by clearly delineating the secular and the sacred it insists that 'religion must be put in its place', which is narrower and more modest than in the past. If this interpretation of secularism is transported to India as part of democratic discourse, how does it thereby become anti-religious, even if (like democratic discourse itself) it is alien to indigenous traditions? Or is it that what is not an anti-religious ideology in Christian societies is automatically so in India where religious systems are more holistic?

Moreover, how does an ideology of inter-religious understanding *reinforce* a secularization process which demands that *all* religions in India accommodate to a more modest role and space? Promoting inter-religious understanding may help organize the terms of coexistence between religious systems. But secularization, insofar as it requires a reinforcing ideology, wants one to legitimize and justify its *gaining* of more 'secular' space at the expense of *all* forms of religious influence. This is about organizing the terms of coexistence between the secular and the religious and not about organizing the terms of coexistence between religious systems. There is no obvious passage from the latter to the former. These are *contending* interpretations of what secularism should mean pertaining either to contending interpretations of secularization or to contending stands (for or against) about an agreed interpretation of secularization. In Madan's writings the *real* Mr Secularization has still to stand up!

Thus similar ambiguities pervade his treatment of secularism. With more accuracy the ideology of secularism is said to have its roots in Christianity. But it is also, he says, the gift of the Enlightenment, which is not quite the same thing. How important the distinction is depends on how Madan understands the connection between Christianity and Enlightenment, itself a contentious historical issue. Since, as Madan notes correctly, in its origins and in most of its dominant versions the ideology of secularism was not, and is not, anti-religious, he has no reason to be against 'secular humanism'. He says he is more concerned to point out its limitations. When secularism is made out to be more important than it can or should be it creates problems. Moreover, 'extreme' secularists who are against faith or are obsessed about the importance of a scientific temper are the real danger. This caution is salutory but the ambiguities remain. Now it seems the problem is the immodesty of secularism and secularists. 'It is important to recognise that one of the major reasons for the rise of religious fundamentalism all over the world is the excesses of secularism, its emergence as a dogma, even as a religion.'[60] Presumably a more modest, undogmatic secularism would be fine. The problem in India, says Madan, is that the Western-inspired notion is an alien, unrooted ideology which has, furthermore, not received real backing from the state. A secularization process not receiving strong support from a popular ideology of secularism will be weakly institutionalized.

Here the villain of the piece would appear to be the inadequacy not the iniquity of secularism. It has been the naive imposition of a minority, according to Madan. But it is unclear how this can be so when the state has not strongly pushed it and in any case has confused notions about it. Is secularism a failure because it has been imposed and found wanting, indeed detrimental? Or because it has never been seriously pushed or institutionalized?

In other formulations, Madan is far more hostile to secularism. In India, secularism is impossible because of mass adherence to religion; it is impractical because neutrality of a secular state is not feasible; it is impotent because it cannot counteract fanaticism and fundamentalism. Secularism is also bereft of true morality, promoting only instrumental values. It is 'moral arrogance and political folly'. The careful reader of Madan is left confused whether he bemoans the fate of secularism understood in its Western sense or rejoices at its failure. Either way, he clearly feels vindicated.

And what of secularization? Has this, too, been a failure? Understood conventionally, this has clearly proceeded apace and Madan suggests as much. But he also misreads growing religiosity as indicating the failure of secularization. Here Nandy is closer to the mark, recognizing that modernist processes (including secularization), by 'de-permeating' religion and permitting its 'narrowing' institutionalization, can create the basis for more extravagant yet sharpened expressions of religiosity which serve to mark a religious identity and assert it against the 'Other'. Nandy goes further and insists that this is what modernity and seculari-zation will (not merely can) do. But the point is that, contrary to Madan, growing religiosity of this kind is compatible with (but not a logical outcome of) growing secularization. It is not a refutation of it. Perhaps Madan means that the 'failure' lies not in secularization failing to take place but that having taken place it has failed to do good.

159

Also, heavy propagation of any ideology or philosophy of secularism is not vital for extending the secularization–modernization process. The USA has maintained a secular state for well nigh two centuries without such ideological–philosophical affirmation. There is no paradox here. Secular-humanist values are a sub-set of a wider democratic–individualist framework of values. They institutionalize themselves as the latter do. But institutionalizing a strong secular state is much easier than institutionalizing a strong, secular civil society. Western social scientists advocating a stronger connection between religion and modern life are rarely, if ever, opponents of the secular state, which is correctly seen as a bulwark against religious fanaticism and fundamentalism. But they are also deeply sympathetic to the view that religion can provide a highly positive social and public input into coping with the 'plight of modernity'.

This is where the principal source of Madan's own uncertainties lie. He is justifiably deeply dissatisfied with the condition of modernity. He believes the discourse of rights is inadequate, indeed 'hedonist', because it does not speak of duties and obligations. It cannot give what religions provide – a collectively shared vision of the good and meaningful life based on commonly held ultimate values. This is a constant refrain to be found in Nandy as well, but one which leads him towards an intransigent anti-modernism. Madan, by contrast, has yet to adopt a strident anti-modernism.

Nevertheless, his intellectual and political posture is still extremely one-sided. Madan focuses on the presumed inadequacies of secularism and secularization, on the limitations of modern notions of liberalism and democracy. He does not focus on the profound inadequacies of religion and religious systems in coping with the problems of modern life. He attacks secularism for refusing to recognize that religion cannot be 'put in its place', or substantially privatized. It is by its very nature totalizing. But ironically enough, secularism is attacked for its own totalizations, for being both alien (Western in origin) and culturally arrogant, i.e. seeking to become part of the common sense of a culture in which it can have no roots. Other modernist notions like democracy and economic development have taken root for better or worse in India. But the speed and depth at which this has come about are issues he bypasses.

While Madan raises the problem of cultural untranslatability as a criticism of secular pretensions in Indian society, he doesn't seriously explore it. How does he justify his own essentialist understanding of culture and Hinduism, given contending traditions within a culture or

160

religious system? What about untranslatability between religious–cultural systems themselves? How does this square with assumptions of meaningful tolerance between such systems?

No religious system has natural to it the values of gender equality or citizenship democracy. The point is not to deny or decry this but to see religious systems and, more importantly, cultures as capable of evolving and changing. Such values, though originally external to religious discourse, can be 'translated' into and internalized within that discourse and into the larger culture. In much the same way, it is not enough to merely note the absence of values of secularism (once judged positive) in Indic religious discourses or cultures. Nor is it adequate to dismiss the struggle to internalize or 'indigenize' these values as something impossible or not worth the effort. This is not just to denigrate secularism, it is also to denigrate the open-ended possibilities in cultures and in a cultural space. Such determinism is always much more likely to arise from a perspective of cultural essentialism, with its usual corollary – the implicit or explicit, the more or less exuberant, defence of a cultural relativism.

Modern pluralism requires both secularism and religion 'knowing their places'. The issue is not outright rejection of one or the other but how best to negotiate their terms of coexistence. The totalizing claims of religious systems make it difficult though not impossible for it to move in this direction. This impulse to coexist is not internal to Indic religious systems. It comes primarily from the secular transformations that have been part of capitalist modernization in India.

Previous coexistence between religions in India is not because of, but despite, each religion's totalizing claims. This coexistence represents 'lived tolerances' in which there is neither mass understanding nor mass curiosity *across* faiths. One cannot simultaneously demonize the supposed totalizations of secular discourse and sanctify the totalizing claims of religion, all in the name of constructing a desirable pluralism.[61] Madan's desire, in some ways laudable, to resurrect a 'moral community' of the old Durkheimian kind (via the resources of religion) is reflective of the Nostalgia Paradigm shared in some significant degree by all anti-secularists. It is an unsophisticated replay of the present-day debate in political philosophy between liberalism and communitarianism, where best liberalism and best communitarianism find considerable meeting ground.

It is more unsophisticated because it fails to grapple adequately with modernist possibilities and transformations. The construction of a 'moral community' in a more secularized modern world is far more problematic because of the sharpening of social conflict, the emergence of competing ideologies, the range and depth of individual freedom, the great variety in conceptions of the good life. A moral consensus is attainable with respect to means (fair and impartial procedures, the values of compromise) rather than goals. Madan (and Nandy) fails to accept that religions are never unproblematically the source of the deepest or ultimate values. Religious systems have acted to stabilize and hierarchically organize from the *existing range* of values available. The deepest values are not self-evidently the same within a cultural space, or across its various social strata. Nor do different religious systems have the *same* ultimate values. These are never a fixed set discovered or grounded once and for all by the world religions. There is a historicity of the value systems associated with the respective world religions.

The search today for a commonly shared conception of the good is entirely legitimate. But it is a far more onerous task than the anti-secularist immortalizers of religion assume. And it is inconceivable without the healthy institutionalization of the much frowned upon (by them) modern discourse of rights.

Anti-Modernist Stridencies

Those who are not interested in conjoining religion to modernity but are stridently anti-modernist are not concerned about establishing the importance of tradition in, and to, modernity. They want to establish the incompatibility of modernity with tradition and culture. To accept modernity, however critically, is somehow to be anti-culture. Conversely, to be an anti-modernist is to be profoundly concerned with culture. And this stance of anti-modernism is a meaningful political choice today, because even in the face of the undoubted power of modernists and of modernizing processes, it speaks for a still enormously powerful constituency, the authentic Indian masses for whom culture and therefore tradition remains paramount.[62] This is the brief that Ashis Nandy has undertaken to argue.

Nandy's understandings of religion, culture, society, civilization, are not markedly different from many a culturalist or immortalizer of religion. But his distinctive twist lies in how he uses these notions to indict modernity as irredeemably tainted. 'Culture, however, is a way of life and it covers apart from "high culture", indigenous knowledge, including indigenous theories of science, education and social change.' Or elsewhere, 'a culture, in the sense of traditions, represents the accumulated wisdom of the people – empirical and rational in its architectonics, though not in every detail.'[63]

Here culture not society is the important term. Society is conceptualized in terms of culture. Culture may mean 'way of life' but what is most important about this 'way of life' is the various forms of 'indigenous knowledge' or 'traditions', meaning 'the accumulated wisdom'. Tradition, if you like, is a 'matter of the mind'.[64] Religion's strength is that it is a 'total theory of life' which has to invade public spaces and must have a theory of transcendence. What is civilization, or, more particularly, Indian civilization? For Nandy it means 'a culture dominated by religious consciousness that has not competed for the minds of men but offered itself as a lifestyle within which other lifestyles can be accommodated.'[65]

Civilization is above all a culture.[66] Culture is above all a distinctive sensibility, a mentality, a special sense of self (Nandy claims the premodern self is 'fluid'). It is accumulated wisdoms, including accumulated theories of all kinds – of indigenous science, culture, oppression, etc. It is a traditional world-view in which metaphysics is vital because it is perennial philosophy answering perennial problems in a way which situates individual and society as microcosmic expressions of the cosmic–universal order.[67]

And religion has been the source of this distinctive sensibility. Most of the time, Nandy sees religion as virtually isomorphic with culture. Occasionally he sees it as merely central to culture. But religion, too, is above all a matter of the mind and self, of experience and feeling or thought.[68] So to understand a civilization is to understand a culture(s) is to understand a religious system(s) is to understand the mind of an authentic inmate of that culture. Nandy's own discipline of psychology is thus privileged above all other disciplinary vantage points for developing a general understanding of culture, civilization, society, provided one follows him in recognizing that true psychology is not an engineering but a philosophical enterprise. It is the study of the art of self-realization. This is the psychologist as social thinker not social engineer.[69] But could it be that becoming a serious social thinker might require strenuous efforts to develop other disciplinary skills including those of history?

Not for the aggressively anti-historical Nandy. What holds for the study of traditional societies holds for the study of modern ones. Modernity is also, above all, a 'state of mind'. Indeed it is a diseased state of mind, a 'pathology' which has become particularly acute since the 1950s and 1960s. Colonialism, too, was above all a state of mind, which is why it has not ended. Modernizers represent the continuity of the colonized mind. Since modernity is a pathology, all forms are diseased beyond hope. Critical modernists are therefore feeble counter-players or 'ornamental dissenters' who should not ever be mistaken for serious critics.[70]

Since entities like culture or modernity possess 'typical' mentalities, they can be analysed and understood through the study of 'typical' representatives of that culture–mentality. The culture of 'critical tra-ditionality' (Nandy's ideal) is thus *represented* by the thought and personality of Gandhi. Time and again, Nandy uses this technique of making an individual personality or a personality-type *stand in* as an expression of larger social processes. These are his favoured taxonomies of culture and society. Such an approach has a long pedigree in post-Weberian Western social science. But this has not fazed Nandy, whose project is avowedly to 'recover' an indigenous social science.

Nandy is concerned most of all with the 'cultural psychology of Indian politics'.[71] Were this endeavour perceived only as a modest peep providing partial and limited insights into such complex matters as modernity, then one could even be highly grateful for some of the insights received. But instead it leads in his hands to the construction of a grandiose paradigm of anti-modernism, forging an Alternative Science, another theory of universalism which will compete with and oppose Enlightenment universalism itself!

Nobody can accuse Nandy of not thinking big. No doubt this 'large vision' has been one of his main attractions. But it is a form of big thinking which abjures the scholarly prerequisites of developing substantial expertise across disciplines. It is not the psychological or philosophical but the sociological approach to studying religion, culture, modernity, that has the strongest natural impulse to developing such inter-disciplinary skills. However, Nandy considers the sociology of religion to be like a theology of science, which suggests that though he may have thought about theology and science he hasn't thought much about sociology, let alone the sociology of religion.

It is not just that what Nandy does not know, or want to know, adversely affects his vision. There are problems enough in what he claims to know. Take his conception of religion and its relationship to culture. Our understanding of culture must recognize the distinction between religion-as-faith and religion-as-ideology. He says that this splitting may be inappropriate, indicating that he is aware that faith and ideology are not in real life, separate water-tight compartments. But this has never been more than a mere nod of the cap in the direction of a complex reality, because Nandy constructs a comprehensive intellectual edifice on the flimsy foundations of this being a real living distinction.

This point needs to be clarified. It is not illegitimate to make a conceptual distinction between religion-as-faith and religion-as ideology. But because in reality the two are not separable (any more than culture and society), the purpose and justification for making such conceptual abstractions or simplifications are that they can give us a handle to *better* understand the complexities of real life. If one takes recourse to abstractions like religion-as-faith and religion-as-ideology, it is only justified intellectually if one does so not merely to show how the two aspects of religion are different *but also to show how they are connected.*[72]

This Nandy has never seriously attempted to do. He cannot. It would wreck his intellectual project, devastating the foundations on which he has constructed his understandings of religion, culture, secularism. The *analytical* separation of faith and ideology must never be misrepresented as an *actual* dichotomy. But precisely because he does this, Nandy comfortably articulates a series of sharp dichotomies – religion-as-faith versus religion-as-ideology. The former is good, unblemished religion, the latter is bad, blemished, indeed not even genuine religion. There are the traditional masses with one kind of mind-set versus the modernizing-secularising elites with another kind of mind-set. Whatever the partial insights, this method is the enemy of sobriety and balance when it comes to assessing issues concerning religion, culture, society, secularism, secularization and modernity.

How Nandy defines his two concepts of religion is very revealing.

> By faith I mean religion as a way of life, a tradition which is definitionally non-monolithic and operationally plural. I say 'definitionally' because unless a religion is geographically confined to a small area, religion as a way of life has to in effect turn into a confederation of a number of ways of life, linked by a common faith having some theological space for the heterogeneity which everyday life introduces.[73]

A number of things strike the reader. To be 'non-monolithic' and 'operationally plural', to have 'space for heterogeneity', are all positive attributes. To possess these by *definition* is to render religion-as-faith impervious to negative criticism. There are no negative references or clauses serving as some kind of counterweight to the wholly positive appreciation of faith. This is not a neutral definition, but a positively loaded one ruling out *judgement* of faith. Since religion is a 'way of life',

165

indeed the larger religions are a 'confederation of a number of ways of life', religion is there where life and ways of life exist! This is, once again, to immortalize or near-immortalize religion. There is no entertaining the possibility even that religion could be a historically contingent phenomenon. If it is bad and unrewarding to assassinate religion by definition, is it justified to glorify and immortalize religion by definition?

Let us go further. Since culture, too, is a 'way of life' and a 'large' or 'world culture' is also a 'confederation of cultures', we have an understanding of religion that is virtually isomorphic with the understanding of culture. Is this a sensible way to go about grasping the relationship between religion and culture? In the case of religion, Nandy takes the analytically reasonable (though not necessary) step of distinguishing between religion-as-faith and religion-as-ideology but messes up his attempt to explain or understand reality by refusing to investigate the ways in which faith and ideology are connected or inseparable, as they undoubtedly also are.

But in the way he handles the relationship between religion and culture he makes the opposite error. Here, he analytically conflates two concepts, which not just reasonably but necessarily should be separated in order to better understand how in reality religion and culture are and are not fused. This is because the fusion is never total either spatially or depth-wise, and therefore is variably retractable. Analytical separation of the two is here a necessary but not sufficient condition for better understanding their relationship.

Since Nandy recognizes that world religions span world cultures, he also operates with a notion of world culture which does not occupy the same space as a world religion, though both are understood as 'confederations of ways of life'. Thus he is fully prepared to speak of cultures divided by the same faith, e.g. Iranian Islam and Indonesian Islam. Nandy says these two Islams are not isomorphic but interlocking, a sensible enough formulation. But this does not follow with any logical clarity from his own theoretical precepts. On the one hand, there is the isomorphism or near-isomorphism of his definitions of religion and culture. On the other, there is a recognition that culture is broader than religion, so though the latter may be central to the former, culture shapes religion in their fusion as well; so different cultures can be divided by the same faith.

In brief, Nandy can certainly say some sensible things about cultural change but this is despite, not because of, his theoretical constructions. So in his handling of the relationship between religion and culture he veers between seeing them as isomorphic, and seeing religion as merely central to and inseparable from culture. This is still a cultural essentialism (hence incapable of dealing adequately with issues of cultural change) in which the religious essence is itself the cultural essence or an indispensable part of it.

However, Nandy wants also to allow for the one-time peripheral in a culture to have the capacity to become, in changed circumstances, newly central. So traditional cultures should also be seen as having such dynamic resources. And if traditional cultures have such a capacity, then, given his determinism about the link between religion and culture, traditional religious systems must also have this internalized capacity. This particular track of Nandy's thinking runs somewhat counter to his other tracks.[74]

These confusions and inconsistencies are never faced squarely nor are the difficulties and complexities in the handling of entities like religion and culture seriously negotiated. At most they are rationalized away via conceptions of the essential flexibility of faith systems, or the unique fluidity of the traditional self, etc. The reason is simple. Nandy's definitions and arguments about religion and culture do not aim to explore in as open-ended or as balanced a way as possible this immensely difficult terrain. They are basically conceptual sticks with which to beat the 'anti-culture' and 'anti-tradition' of modernity, which he identifies above all with politics/state and science/rationality.

As for his definition of religion-as-ideology:

> By ideology I mean religion as a sub-nation, national or cross-national identifier of populations contesting for, or protecting non-religious, usually political or socio-economic interests. Such religion-as-ideologies are usually identified with one or more texts which, rather than ways of life of the believers, then become the final identifiers of the 'pure' forms of the religion.[75]

This text-basing provides 'a set of manageable operational definitions'.[76]

Here, Nandy's definition is neutral. But religion-as-ideology is made, by definition, *non-religious*. It is a 'secular identifier' connected to the pursuit of secular interests. Such identifiers do their job of demarcating populations by linking themselves to the 'purity' or dogmatism of texts rather than to the openness of lived religion, i.e. religion-as-faith, as a way of life. Since the latter is definitionally good, religion-as-ideology, which contrasts so strongly with it, can be considered for most purposes as bad, though, strictly speaking, it is not defined as such. But of course, time and again, Nandy expresses his hostility to, and criticisms of religion-as-ideology. At the same time, this really has nothing to do with 'true' religion or faith. It is, moreover, a secular identifier.

Nandy uses the word 'usually' in two places in this definition, each time to cover his back, as it were, because he has avoided introduction of one very important word into this definition – culture. Nandy talks of how these identifications–demarcations are made for the purposes of contesting or protecting 'usually, political or socio-economic interests'. What about cultural interests? Can religion-as-ideology provide identifiers for contesting or pursuing non-religious cultural interests?

Since Nandy uses the word 'usually', it would seem that he has to concede that, at least occasionally, religion-as-ideology serves the purposes of relating to non-religious cultural interests. But is the absence of any specific reference to cultural interests accidental? Given Nandy's strong culturalism, his insistence on the umbilical cord between religion-as-faith and culture, his stance on the natural anti-culturalness of modernity, and his view that it is in modernity, especially late modernity, that religion-as-ideology becomes more widespread, he wants to concede as little ground as possible to such notions as the existence of significant non-religious or secular cultural interests.

When 'usually' appears on the second occasion referring to texts rather than ways of life, Nandy again exhibits an uncertainty. Could religion-as-ideology be at least occasionally identified not with one or more texts, but with the 'ways of life of the believers'? But if this were so, religion-as-ideology could be connected to aspects of faith and 'true' culture. Then this connection would have to be evaluated. If good, then he weakens the argumentative force of his asserted dualisms of religion-as-ideology/bad and religion-as-faith/good. If bad, then he can be read as allowing for the possibility that faith itself (and culture) can be deeply tainted with ideology.

In his defence of popular faith, Nandy also takes up the cause of myth. When believers (or non-believers) give increasing importance to the claims of science over myth they reinforce the ideologization of religion. They refuse to understand the power and value of myth, its role in the structure or system of faith. Nandy has a real point here, but the deeper problem is his own. When objects become sacred and mythical their secular meanings recede greatly. They never completely disappear and can resurface or affect manifest or latent meanings in peculiar ways. But when something becomes a mythical entity its significance is *overwhelmingly* derived from some transcendental presence.

This process of constructing sacredness is always a process of investing properties which can *only* belong to humans in something beyond humans, and this is always a 'false' construct, though this can have real and positive value. But this 'falseness', central to myth and faith, is supported by a network of institutions and practices which itself is always characterized by asymmetrical relations of power between real people. The construction of a structure or system of faith and its forms of expression cannot be separated from the construction of a system of ideological power, though it cannot be reduced to that either.[77]

Nandy might be able to 'resolve' these ambiguities and justify his symptomatic silences. But it is doubtful if he is even interested in trying since the logic of such a venture once embarked upon would put at risk the integrity of his anti-modernist project itself.

For someone as hostile to secularism and secularization as Nandy, his use of these terms is remarkably casual. He generally assumes that secularization and secularism have an invariant relationship. When secularization advances, so does the ideology of secularism.[78] So a criticism of the latter can stand in as criticism of the former. In reality it cannot. The secularization process and specific histories of modernization and nationalism have generally been more important for explaining the emergence of secular states than the ideology of secularism. This is why so many essentially secular states have religious–monarchial trappings, and why sentiments or traditions of anti-clericalism vary so much.

In India also, there has been a real disjunction between the two. It is one of the myths of many an anti-secularist that the Westernized concept of secularism has been too dominant in public and political discourse. This, they claim, has been the source of communal and other evils. But since India is more than Westernized elites, and its 'public space' wider than that defined by these elites, there is the 'revenge' of the masses against the elites, and of culture against politics. Elite hegemony is being contested. Nandy's own endeavour is to recover the still living traditions of religious and ethnic tolerance 'from the hegemonic language of secularism popularised by westernised intellectuals'.[79]

Actually, most Westernized intellectuals in India have been quite confused about what is or should be meant by the 'language of secularism', rarely negotiating clearly between the Indian and Western notions, nor possessing much clarity about the Western notion, seeing it more as some vague principle of statehood than as an ideology of morality centred on a humanist individualism. As for its popularization or its construction as a hegemonic political or public discourse, this is way off the mark. Neither the state nor the 'secular elite' has even seriously tried to make it popular, to vernacularize it, or to attempt to give it wider and deeper roots.[80]

Even in its Indian version calling for *sarva dharm sambhavam,* or equal respect to all religions, it has never been popularized. Those hostile to the Enlightenment-inspired notion of secularism and partial to the Indian version have simply assumed that the Indian masses (or at least Hindus) *naturally* believe and endorse such a meaning of secularism. This is not true, and 'lived tolerances' should not be construed as meaning that the ordinary Hindu or Muslim has *equal* respect for all religions or believes that this should be an important principle of statehood or that the Indian state can or does behave accordingly. This debate on what is the most appropriate notion of secularism is itself essentially an elite affair.

One of the areas in which the ideology of secularism (stressing the values of secular, humanist individualism) could have but has not been systematically promoted is in education. Even after 1947 Indian education, public or private, has never promoted seriously the attitude that religious authority could be questioned, even though religious authority (Hindu or Islamic) has no specific hierarchy or clergy. Secular education tries to put the learner at the centre of the learning process not the teacher. In India the teacher–pupil relationship reproduces the hierarchical 'learning' relationship sanctified by existing religious traditions. So when 'secular' values or principles are presented (primarily in textbooks), they serve only as a mark of distinction, a way of saying that secular India is different from non-secular Pakistan, or the properly educated Indian by being secular is different from the ignorant and superstitious masses. The notion of secular here serves as a political or social marker, little else.[81]

> The failure of secularism is hardly the failure of an ideology. It is essentially the failure of a ruling class that used secular ideals as means of seeking legitimacy but which largely ignored the social tasks associated with the development of a secular society.[82]

Had India's elites really tried to make secularism a *hegemonic* discourse, they would have behaved very differently. Post-independence education did not even promote 'Indianness' except as 'canned patriotism'.

How then can something so weakly implanted as secularism do so much damage? Does a suspicion by Nandy that this might be the case explain his failure to define secularism as precisely as he does his two concepts of religion? Nandy attacks secularism and secularization in two steps. First, he treats secularism as a synecdoche, seeing it not as a narrow ideology of morals but as a wider ideology of statehood, thus making the secular state complicit with the arrogances of the nation-state system. Second, he believes that 'to accept the ideology of secularism is to accept the ideologies of progress and modernity as the new justifications of domination.'[83] Secularism is an ideology which legitimizes both those who exercise state power and the structures of the state itself, because it promotes the view that the irrational, religious masses lack the rationality of modernizers and because for moderniza-tion the state is crucial. It is the modern ideology of statehood – nothing less![84]

This is not correct. There are a number of modern ideologies of statehood – perhaps the most important being nationalism. Most of them are secular, but not all. A religious nationalism or a religious pan-nationalism are also modern ideologies and can be ideologies of statehood. But secularism itself is not an ideology of statehood. It is an ideology which endorses a particular *principle* of modern statehood, a principle that emerges historically as part of the *modern democratic revolution*. That is why, even etymologically, the word secularism comes much after the words 'secular' or 'state'. This is a new principle of democratic individualism and any consistent assault on secularism, e.g. by Nandy, will also assault modern notions of democracy and individualism.

Secularism is an ideology not of statehood but of ethics. It separates ethics and religion by grounding morality in the human individual and not in some transcendental sphere. It thus allows for a relationship between politics (state) and ethics separated from religion. This creates room for introducing new norms into state constitutions. A secular state is one which avoids legitimizing any particular set of ethics or moral codes associated with any particular religious system or world-view. Such a secular morality is possible because of common and universal features of humanity and is codified in the form of modern secular, not customary, law.

A secular state, then, would have three necessary and sufficient attributes. In the relationship between religion and the individual, it enshrines the right to freedom of worship. For the relationship of the state to the individual, there would be the primacy of the notion of citizenship, where this is not conceived of as linked to any fixed property or attribute of any particular individual or group. Regarding the relationship between religion and the state, the latter should be reli-giously non-affiliated and impartial. Formal non-affiliation is not as important as practical impartiality through basic separation of religious

171

and state power. These principles are so obviously conducive to democratic governance – a secular state is its necessary but not sufficient condition – that it is difficult to see what the fuss against it is all about.

The importance of such norms for good governance was clear to Gandhi, and in this sense he was all for the secular Indian state. But what Gandhi could not accept (nor indeed Nandy) is the *ethical premiss* of the secular state. Thus Nandy attacks this premiss, claiming that a secular public morality is greatly inferior to a religion-based public morality. He does not directly contest the validity of the three specific attributes that define the secular state. Gandhi was more explicitly in favour of such a secular state, and Madan, for one, pays more attention to this attitude of Gandhi than does Nandy.

Nandy focuses instead on the call for public space to be devoted to the dialogue between the religious and the secular. And he tries to make out that secularism, as an ideology of statehood, sees the state as 'the ultimate reservoir of sanity' and therefore as the 'ultimate arbiter among different religions and communities'.[85] This is an unsubtle caricature. The modern secular state claims ultimate arbitration powers only in matters of conflict between religious claims and secular constitutional law, on the assumption that such law (on which the state is constituted) is humane and just. Such secular–democratic law does not make the state the 'ultimate arbiter' but establishes a new equilibrium between state and civil society.

This represents a *redistribution* of powers of arbitration where *finality of authority* is no longer absolute (because sacred) or singularly or oligarchically located. The secular–democratic state is part of a new political arrangement of checks and balances fundamentally different from the balancing principles and institutions of pre-modern, segmentary societies dominated by customary law. Both the state and the institutions of an emerging civil society become more important. Much of political life is represented by the shifting relationship of forces between the two. Furthermore, mass forms of cultural politics become more powerful and more possible in modernity, especially in late modernity.

How does Nandy argue against the ethics of secularism and the ethical premiss of the secular state? How does he defend the claim that a religion-based public morality is superior to modern secular notions of public and political morality? He does this by rejecting the idea of any moral progress, e.g. that the modern notion of equality is a new moral value of the utmost importance. It is the 'ultimate' moral values that are crucial and these are to be found in all the major religious systems.

They therefore pre-date modernity. The practical human and social expression of such ultimate value systems would be the principle of *tolerance*, and not some recent acquisition, such as the principle of equality.[86]

Religious systems are peculiarly gifted with the ability to promote and institutionalize tolerance because all such religious systems share a belief in the importance of *transcendence*. Belief in transcendence expresses a distinctive psychology of the believer. In vibrant religious–cultural systems the believer has a 'fluid self', a 'configuration of selves'. This is fluid because it incorporates the self, the non-self and the anti-self. There is an empirical, perishable self as well as an imperishable, transcendent self, thus a distinctive 'wholeness of the self' which the more well-bounded self of modernity undermines.[87]

Openness, tolerance, etc., are powerfully connected to the fluid self. Modernity and secularism, which are incompatible with the preservation of the fluid self because of their natural hostility to culture and to notions of the transcendent (or at least to its importance), cannot support a tolerant and humane existence. When modernity or science or secularism is merely a newly arrived 'dissenting' principle in a traditional society, then it has a positive influence. But once it becomes too big for its boots, as it were, it is both dangerous and reprehensible. If India is to survive as a humane, tolerant society then it must turn its back on secularism, science, rationalist individualism, and all the other attributes, the goals and instruments, of modernity.

All that is valuable in modernity may be incorporated as a 'subset' in a reinvigorated and critical traditionality.[88] This is possible because India remains a traditional society and a traditional civilization/culture(s) with a modern, secular state whose further encroachment must be stopped and reversed. We must invest our hopes in inter- and intra-religious dialogue to lead us to a more worthwhile existence. So the religious community must be seen as a, if not the, principal political and social unit in the construction of the desired anti-modernist project.

After allowing for all qualifications and nuances, these last four paragraphs represent Nandy's basic credo.

It is a credo which in virtually every major respect rests on mistaken assumptions and understandings. While the principle of transcendence is central to all major religious systems, it is not confined to them. It is a part of all human cultures, including cultures not recognizably religious, as well as cultures in modernity.[89]

Furthermore, what religious systems mean by transcendence *differs*.

173

Religious systems, contrary to the view of anti-secularists, do not have the same ultimate goals, values, visions, but have different and often competing ultimaticities. This issue is repeatedly dodged by those who would invest so much in inter-faith dialogue and accommodation.[90] Religious systems have different metaphysics, different understandings of what are the 'perennial' questions themselves. In modernity, the notion of transcendence does not and cannot disappear. There are simply many more ways than ever before of thinking about and coping with it.

The psychology of the self does bear a determinate relationship with the society in which it is embedded. But the most important divide is not between the Eastern or Western self or between the Hindu and the Islamic self, but between the pre-modern and modern self. All talk by Nandy of the special fluidity of the pre-modern self is utterly mistaken.[91] The pre-modern self is not a more fluid but a more *diffuse* self because of the lack of sharp boundaries. But the range over which the self is diffuse is limited because of the much more *static* character of the world the pre-modern self inhabits.

The more static pre-modern world gives rise not to a more fluid or revisable self but to a more static and diffuse self, which precisely because it is diffuse allows the religious dimension and the religious idiom to dominate in ways that they cannot any longer nor should do in modernity. It is the more dynamized world of modernity which gives rise to the more dynamized self, which is more self-reflexive, more well bounded in its various selves, but also more fluid and revisable. The static self is not a more autonomous or flexible one. Its moral horizon is a more externally determined one and is constituted not by the abstract ultimate values of a large religious system but by the detailed and specific injunctions of local culture, and sect affiliation.

The modern self is more morally sceptical, flexible and questing. The complexity of self-perception and self-definition is necessarily linked to the complexity of social life itself. The moral horizon in modernity is more internally constituted than externally given. Even the faithful believer has to move in this direction.

Nandy is free to interpret the pre-modern self as a more wholesome self, conducive to the development of social tolerances.[92] But when he claims that the way forward in India is to try to recover those sources of tolerance in 'traditional ways of life', all he offers by way of a programmatic perspective is that we look seriously at the philosophies, theologies and symbolisms of such tolerances. What Nandy does not ask us to do is historically investigate the *contexts* in which those symbolisms and philosophies operated so as to get a better idea of their functions and purposes.

Nandy, for all his admiration of India's past, will not carry out a subaltern history to arrive at, for example, a Dalit's-eye-view of India's so-called tolerant past, or a gender view of patriarchal societies and patriarchal religions.[93] If he has to concede the fact of such traditional forms of oppression, he will in more conservative moments echo Ananda Coomaraswamy's claim that pre-modern caste oppression was never as bad as modern class oppression; or in his more radical moments endorse Gandhi's inversion of the traditional values associated with caste hierarchy, as the furthest one can go in fighting it.[94]

Among the weakest points in the anti-modernist and anti-secularist case is the programmatic alternative they offer. How is *sarva dharm sambhavam* to be institutionalized or to embody such multi-religiosity? Or can it practise 'equal respect to all religions' without embodying such multi-religiosity?[95] References to Gandhi's vision and injunctions to learn from him cannot compensate for this lack of a programmatic perspective. Nor will it do to cite the possibilities inherent in inter-faith/inter-community dialogue through its 'best' representative figures or institutions.[96] At most, they are sometimes a valuable source for inter-religious crisis-management.

If there is no common notion of transcendence, but only competing visions of it, and of 'true morality', and of the 'genuinely good life', then what reason is there to presume that inter-faith dialogue is more capable than the procedural principles of liberal-democratic individualism of providing commonly accepted standards for how to organize and participate in a public and political moral life? Even those modern-day communitarians wishing to accommodate different ways of religious reasoning through an 'overlapping consensus' insist that the state, to be humane and democratic, must have a *moral core* which is non-negotiable.[97]

The most fundamental mistake of anti-modernists like Nandy, or ambiguous modernists like Madan and Parekh, is their refusal to recognize that India was long ago 'condemned' to modernity. India is neither a traditional society nor one in transition from tradition to modernity. It has long been pursuing its own form of modernity shaped by its distinctive institutional and other legacies. But these 'traditional' legacies, e.g. of caste and religion, do not operate in traditional ways nor mean what they once did.

In a typical conceptual dualism, Nandy talks of the distinctive mindsets of the ordinary village Indian and of the Westernized–urbanized Indian. This is the obvious corollary of his claim that the typical inhabitant of traditional India has a distinctive psychology ('configuration of selves') separate from that of the no longer traditional Indian. That traditional Indian who thinks in fundamentally different, arationalist or non-rationalist ways from the secularized, rationalist Indian is 'authentic' and in tune with the enduring ethos and culture of India. This, again, is quite mistaken.

There is merit in the argument that the mind-sets of urban elites and rural masses are not quite the same in the weights attached to different ways of thinking and articulating. But there is no sharp dichotomy, only a weakly sloping trend line linking the two social poles of elites and masses. Thought or argument by analogy, axiom, assertion, or by logical procedures, coexist in the same person but they combine in different ways. Of these, only reasoned argument can operate according to commonly accepted standards of judgement and thus be the basis for genuine and uncoercive intellectual conversion. The elite mind-set is not distinguished from the popular mind-set by being 'rational' as opposed to 'arational'. Indeed, the middle-class professional can be equally 'arational' and dependent on axiom, assertion or analogical forms of thinking in certain spheres of life. Similarly, the popular mind-set can and does exhibit similar variations in ways of thinking in different spheres of existence and responsibility in everyday life.

The ordinary villager is, in fact, closer to the urban professional in her mind-set than she is to the mind-set of her foreparents. The mass awareness, unleashed by modernity, of the depth and range of possibilities for change in one's life makes certain of that. The ordinary Indian has internalized an awareness of the possibility of material progress (be it the value of literacy) that makes the values and goals, the very psychology and personality of the ordinary Indian fundamentally different from that of her ancestors.

That as a result of this there can be *levels of mass discontent* which have no equivalent in the past and which shape and influence Indian political and cultural life in ways bearing little comparison to what was conceivable in that past already testifies to the uniquely *modern* character of Indian society today and to the expectations it releases.[98] Gandhi could not be what he was and could not have the effect he had except in the context of a modernity which decisively shaped his own mind-set and that of the mass constituency he desired to influence. Gandhi introduced *completely new themes* into Indian cultural, and Hindu religious, discourse. He did this in a *very short span of time*. And he had *mass effect*. All the three aspects emphasized here are conceivable only within the framework of modernity.

Anti-modernism is *not* non-modern, and Critical Traditionality is an oxymoron. The resources for criticism within traditional societies are inherently limited. The unique character of tradition was its givenness and 'overwhelming' character; the impossibility of recognizing itself as just a tradition. Modernity de-traditionalizes tradition, leading defenders like Nandy to do what was never required even of traditional society's elites – rationalizing, justifying and defending tradition! The absence of any radical notion of change or progress meant no referential horizon (even imagined – even the utopias of tradition could not be so radical) by which to carry out serious criticism of traditionality.[99]

Nandy, of course, denies this. His is not just a lost cause, but a non-existent one. The only feasible choices available are either an arrogant, overbearing modernity, or a critical and modest one. Those rejecting both and insisting on the necessity of a mythology of Critical Traditionality or anti-modernity should at least acknowledge that this is (and can only be) a modern myth. They should not pretend that it represents some kind of continuity with the pre-modern past, and therefore there are long-enduring resources on which to build.[100] If Gandhi is the great exemplar of anti-modernity or Critical Traditionality, then search anywhere in India's pre-modernity – there will not, and cannot be a comparable figure.[101]

Nandy is so determined to preserve this illusion of a viable Critical Traditionality that he makes such brazen claims as that certain values like human dignity, freedom, non-violence, equality, are beyond history and culture. Are modern notions of freedom and equality even the same as pre-modern notions, let alone inferior? Or can what is good in modernity, e.g. civil liberties, survive as a sub-set within a more authentically Indian traditionalist setting? How is the modern principle of equality to survive as a 'respected' subset within a pre-modern casing whose defining substance is the principle of hierarchy, and an anti-liberal communitarianism?

The great irony in this defence is that Nandy displays a weaker understanding of traditionality and the past than he does of modernity and the present, even though his understanding of modernity is also deeply flawed. This is because the *critical edge* of his thinking applies overwhelmingly to modernity. At least he tells us what is bad about it. By contrast, despite all talk of a critical traditionalism, his weighing and assessment of the past is overwhelmingly positive. In justifiably attacking the arrogances of modernity, e.g. of Science, he ignores the arrogances of religion. Worse, he often pretends there are no such arrogances.

Modernity is not the enemy but the *accelerator* of cultural pluralism, of

177

all kinds of pluralism. Where, as in pre-modernity, there are few claimants to authority and the religious system often enjoys near-omnipotent status, then pluralism simply cannot mean what it means when there are multiple authority systems and none can claim the near-omnipotent status of a religious system.

Science with an S does represent a potential danger here. But opposing this danger does not mean swinging to the other extreme. Nandy's critique of Big Science is more useful than his criticisms of secularism. But when he denies that science has a special epistemological status, he is wrong. Science has rational and unique methods of reasoning but these operate more as values than as rules. They are also uniquely powerful in regard to the natural world. The material products of science are themselves one of the most powerful forms of evidence we have of a cross-cultural, anti-relativist and universalist system of knowledge. Yet the self-reflexive awareness of best science that knowledge cannot be entirely separated from interest, can also attenuate the claims of science itself. This self-reflexiveness comes from its strongly *theoretical* character. And theoretical forms of rationality, though certainly not the only nor always best forms of rationality, *are* a special form of it.

Compare this to the non-self-reflexiveness of non-science! One of Nandy's more delightful aphorisms is to point out that if astrology is the myth of the weak, science is the myth of the strong. More soberly reflected upon, the rejoinder would be 'well, not quite', and the 'not quite' is very important. Nandy says science must be put in its place and regarded as one among other imperfect traditions of humanity. One can only applaud in agreement (provided its epistemological uniqueness is not denied). But such modest pluralism is capable of becoming the dominant common sense only in modernity.

There is a special pluralism inherent in the discourse of reason, and any paradigm as hostile to rationality as Nandy's and yet insisting that it will be democratic is dangerously contradictory.

> Without reason, analogy, axiom and assertion can pass for argument. And assertions can be refuted only with other assertions. Thus such theories risk devolving into authoritarian non-theories more akin to religions. Far from being impenetrable, it is reason that has the potential to have an open texture and to be accessible to all who will participate in the discourse. It is faith and intuition that cannot be challenged.[102]

When Nandy insists he is immunized from professional criticism, that only more plausible myths can challenge his own myths, he is simply expressing his commitment to an authoritarian and deeply anti-democratic form of discourse.

Anti-secularists are religious communitarians who (like communalists and fundamentalists) see the relationship between individual and society as primarily based not on rights but on 'moral responsibility' and 'consensus'. Though they are generally less hostile to issues of individual rights, both are programmatically unspecific about how personal freedom will be organized in their respective social utopias.

One major difference, however, is that the anti-secularists are much more adamantly opposed to centralized state power, believing that a decentralized polity is vital. To check and unburden the encroaching state, there should be a looser federation of associations based on 'natural communities'. Among communitarians, religious or otherwise, there are significant variations on how anti-state or anti-modern such arrangements should be. But, in the Indian context, they generally agree on what these 'natural communities' are, though they may differ on which are more important.

These are jati, caste, religion, tribe, village; each treated as largely undifferentiated and subjected internally only to 'traditional' critique. These are key communities apparently, because each and every self is an embedded self and these are the most widespread and 'natural' forms of embeddedness. It is this embeddedness that gives purpose and meaning. The individualism (often caricatured as atomism) of modern life and political discourse would seek to destroy something profound and precious – this embeddedness. The religious community is one such natural community of embeddedness. Only by giving more responsibility to this community, already one of the organizing principles of social life in India, can we move towards a more tolerant, democratic and humane order.[103]

While every self is always an embedded self, modern life demands the ability to negotiate between different selves, to revise and change embedded selves, and respect for the right to do so. The communities one is born into represent our first contexts of choice, our original cultural set. It is important to have this but not vital that this remains unchanged for any given individual. Individual rights have ontological and ethical priority over collective rights and powers because collective rights to self-determination, or collectively binding consensus, must first presuppose individual freedom to decide whether and in what way to belong to a particular community.

That is the message of the modern discourse of freedom which proclaims its superiority over other (pre-modern) discourses of freedom

179

and autonomy. This does not deny the inescapability of being an embedded self, but expresses that, here too, a new freedom, a new pluralism, a new openness, operate. It is a message that will remain powerful and appealing. To endorse the value and importance of having a particular cultural community does not automatically mean endorsing the characteristics of any particular cultural community. Nor does it mean endorsing confinement within it.[104] Those who would struggle for a humane future must reject the siren song of anti-modernism. It leads to a dangerous and disastrous seduction.

The Curious Case of Subaltern Studies

Independently of anti-modernists or ambiguous modernists, key theorists of a school within Indian historiography – Subaltern Studies – have begun to beat a path to the door of Ashis Nandy and his brand of indigenism. There will not be total convergence, but, together, the machetes of anti-modernist anti-history and post-modernist bad history (or bad theories about history) are clearing a larger intellectual space for the arraignment of all kinds of Enlightenment-related values, including secularism. One such theorist, Partha Chatterjee, has launched a broadside against secularism, the first such direct attack from the Subaltern Studies Group.[105]

Given the remarkable popularity of Subaltern Studies in the USA, it possesses both the glamour and the academic–material resources to promote its influence in the third world, including another possible 'secondary' phase of expansion in India. It is important, therefore, to see what the fuss over Subaltern Studies is all about. An overview of the trajectory (or variant trajectories) of Subaltern Studies since its inception is followed by a specific focus on Chatterjee's latest views on Indian secularism.

Three striking aspects of the character and evolution of Subaltern Studies have been (a) the differential impact in India and in the West, particularly the USA; (b) the shift between early and later Subaltern Studies in its theoretical self-assessment of purpose and value; (c) the unmistakable gap (to this day) between the theorization of the practice and the practice itself as embodied in a whole host of concrete, empirically based micro-studies that have made up so much of the content of the volumes (eight so far) going under the name Subaltern Studies.[106]

When the Subaltern Studies project was launched in the early eighties, it was much discussed within India but not in the West. It is in the late eighties, really after Edward Said's and Gayatri Chakravorty Spivak's endorsement, and the theoretical articulation of the Subaltern Studies project by Partha Chatterjee in particular (himself significantly influenced by the Saidian framework of analysis), that it embarks on its meteoric career in that part of American academia concerned with 'Third World Studies' and 'Colonial Discourse Analysis'.[107] This later turn in the theory of Subaltern Studies, in which the founding figure, Ranajit Guha, would seem to have acquiesced (though its discontinuities with Guha's original project are much sharper than its continuities), has been accelerated in a clearly post-modernist direction by Dipesh Chakrabarty and Gyan Prakash.[108] Yet the freshness and importance of Subaltern Studies as a different kind of Indian historiography was established in those early years.

This contrast in reception and in career paths is understandable. The matrix of political and academic relationships in which Subaltern Studies has had to situate itself has been very different in India and the USA, indeed even between the USA and the UK, where it has enjoyed nothing like the prestige and popularity garnered across the Atlantic.[109] The original project defined itself as an 'epistemological break' with existing currents of Indian historiography, opposing the elitism of colonial, neo-colonial and liberal-nationalist historiography and the reductionism of orthodox Marxist treatments of the rise and nature of Indian nationalism.[110] It was, as Sumit Sarkar points out, born in a dissident Left milieu influenced by the growing disillusionment with existing Communist states and orthodoxies, the outburst of Marxist-influenced peasant and tribal insurgencies in India (late sixties and early seventies), the euphoria generated by the end of Mrs Gandhi's Emergency in 1977. Moreover, Thompsonian social history had a general impact on radical histories everywhere. In India this was reinforced by Thompson's trip to this country in 1976–77.

In this context, and inspired by Gramsci, Ranajit Guha theorized the project of a Subaltern Study. The terms 'subaltern' and 'subaltern autonomy' were taken from Gramsci but defined and handled in ways which even then departed from Gramsci's own usages.[111] Nonetheless, the Subaltern Studies project had nailed its flag firmly to the masthead of 'history from below', but with an important proviso. This was not just history from below but a project aiming to recover hitherto absent voices, to restore agency to the subaltern in a way which earlier forays into history from below in Indian historiography had presumably not attempted or achieved. Hence the great importance of reconstructing

181

peasant *consciousness* and its *autonomous* character, not otherwise easily discernible through the webs of domination constituting the normalized/routinized patterns of existence of the subaltern vis-à-vis the oppressor elite. Hence, also, the vital need to study abnormal periods, e.g. of insurgency, when such autonomy of consciousness would be strongest and most visible.

If this was one crucial new track, there was also supposed to be another of a recognizably Marxist provenance – explaining the failure that constituted the 'central problematic' of the National Movement. India's political freedom was not associated with social revolution of either a bourgeois democratic or Maoist New Democratic (led by workers and peasants) type. The bourgeoisie did not fulfil this historic role, the working class could not. Peasant struggles on their part could not transcend the limits of their localism because of the absence of a revolutionary bourgeois or proletarian leadership. In the Indian National Movement, therefore, the Indian bourgeoisie did not speak for the nation.[112] This second track was not seriously explored except for a major study by Sumit Sarkar.[113] (It is not altogether surprising that Sarkar should have emerged as the major critic from within the Group of its later theoretical development.) Such studies would have taken a very different direction from those operating on the first track and would not have been methodologically well served either by Guha's definition of the indigenous subaltern or by his insistence that while vertical linkages characterized the relationship between elite and subaltern, relationships within the subaltern category were essentially horizontal.[114]

The main engine of early Subaltern Studies, therefore, moved along the first track. Subalternists made commendable efforts to discover new sources – oral history, songs and poems, forgotten or ignored reports, personal diaries, etc. – as well as re-reading traditional archival sources to reconstruct and recover that most difficult of things, the subjective world of the insurgent rebel. Guha attempted to do more. He sought to theorize the process of development of subaltern consciousness.[115] The attempt was overly ambitious and flawed. It was based not on a study of peasants so much as on the more internally undifferentiated tribals.[116] Guha's typology was applauded by later Subaltern theorists but left no serious mark on the bulk of empirical work done by various contributors. What did leave its mark was the rejection of the notion of the *spontaneity* of subaltern rebellions, therefore committing the historian to try to 'enter the mind' of his subject of investigation, to try to see from a 'subaltern perspective'.

If the attempts to theoretically rationalize the importance of Subaltern Studies served largely to irritate others practising in, and familiar with, the broader field of Indian historiography, there was nonetheless a wide measure of respect for the new orientation – its emphasis on studying subaltern groups – and also for the actual quality of a host of micro-studies that emerged. The best of them did what all good history from below does – they provided wider and deeper insights because they explicated popular forms of behaviour as guided by local meaning systems in ways which also illuminated broader processes of change.

By the time Subaltern Studies was being 'discovered' and promoted in American academia as never before, a spectrum of evaluation had already been established amongst those long operating on the terrain of colonial Indian history. At the less generous end of this spectrum, Subaltern Studies was not credited with carrying out any paradigm shift in Indian historiography, or with making that much use of new sources. Its emphasis on studying the oppressed had merely accelerated a pre-existing tendency. Its theory was eclectic, pompously self-important and superficial. All it had done was to provide more pieces to the always three-dimensional jigsaw making up the overall historical picture of Indian society spanning the seventeenth century to the 1970s.[117]

At the more generous end, Subaltern Studies was seen as something of a breakthrough. It was attempting that most difficult of historical tasks – registering the consciousness of the unlettered. This is always more difficult than reconstructing the objective world of the downtrodden. Subaltern Studies did search for and use new historical sources as well as using old sources in new ways. It did represent an important change of direction and not just an acceleration of a pre-existing emphasis. Theoretically, its major contribution was to put to permanent rest the notion of subaltern spontaneity. Its efforts to develop a theory of subaltern consciousness was an overweening ambition and carried out on far too limited a repertoire of investigative knowledge. Nonetheless, like no other trend in Indian history writing, Subaltern Studies built up a formidable body of scholars producing good work of an essentially empirical–accumulative kind. To date, eight volumes of studies of albeit uneven quality have been brought out in its name. What other school of Indian historiography has done that much?[118] The positive impact of Subaltern Studies has long passed its meridian as it settles into its particular niche in the wider field of historical studies. Its various practitioners are now proceeding in different directions, testimony itself that the period of its most decisive contributions as a 'school' is over. In between these two ends of the spectrum there are others in

India who would see Subaltern Studies as simply a particular conceptual approach towards peasant and tribal movements with its own fair share of strengths and weaknesses.

In North America it was Said's famous imprimatur on Subaltern Studies that marked the turning point in its fortunes. Said's *Orientalism* had a massive impact in the West, especially in the USA.[119] It could not have anywhere near the same impact on Indian academia or more specifically on Indian historiography. The mainstream tradition in post-independence history writing was strongly anti-colonial and certainly alive, if not always fully immune, to problems posed by colonial complicity in Western scholarship. Effectively consigning all Indian historiography before Subaltern Studies into the dustbin of the 'colonized mind-set', as Said was wont to do, is absurd. It betrays Said's ignorance of India and Indian history writing.[120] If Said aligned himself with the Subaltern Studies Group it was not because of what it actually stood for or did for Indian history writing as for what Said believed it to stand for.

The one figure who had been strongly influenced by the Saidian framework was Partha Chatterjee, who had emerged by then as the pivotal theorist of the Group. His own background and academic training is in political theory not history, and his major contributions to the Subaltern Studies volumes have been self-consciously theoretical and methodological pieces. Early on he introduced the notion of a 'peasant-communal consciousness'. So even as he praised Guha's efforts to theorize the development of 'peasant consciousness', a subtle shift from the subaltern to community had been rehearsed.[121]

According to Sarkar, a Saidian ambience entered Subaltern Studies theory through an article by Chatterjee, 'Gandhi and the Critique of Civil Society' (in Volume III), and then the first major book to come out of and embody the theoretical turn in later Subaltern Studies, Chatterjee's widely acclaimed *Nationalist Thought and the Colonial World: A Derivative Discourse?*[122] A colonized intelligentsia was only capable, in true Saidian style, of a 'derivative discourse'. The elite/subaltern dichotomy had been partly supplanted by another binary contrast of colonial/indigenous community, which conveniently let pre-colonial oppressors off the hook. Early Subaltern Studies had focused its hostility on the colonial mind-set of the Indian bourgeoisie with its inflated sense of self-importance, and on a nationalist historiography reflecting this. Later Subaltern Studies was much more willing to apply the notion of a colonial mind-set to all modernizers and Enlightenment rationalists. Indigenism of concepts and values and the histories of fragments/

communities were now increasingly counterposed to Enlightenment concepts and values and universal histories.

What entered Subaltern Studies was not rigorous conceptualization or wide dissemination of Saidian categories but an 'ambience' and 'space' where the influences generally gaining ground in American academia could hospitably intervene. Said himself may not have rejected universalist discourses or the principle of objective representation *tout court*, but his critique of Orientalism did suggest that its failings necessarily flowed from the character of Western epistemology. The contemporary pull exercised by his writings had much to do with the fact that he seemed to fuse 'Foucaultian approaches to power, engaged "politics of difference", and post-modernist emphasis on the decentred and heterogeneous.'[123]

All this has fitted well into American academic-political culture, where multi-cultural studies, self-representation of third world peoples and cultural feminism were and are flourishing. Said's introduction of Subaltern Studies 'as an analogue of all those recent attempts in the West and the rest of the world to articulate the hidden or suppressed accounts of numerous groups – women, minorities, disadvantaged or dispossessed groups, refugees, exiles, etc.', authorized its relevance in that milieu.[124] Many in India agree when Sarkar says:

> Subaltern Studies does happen to be the first historiographical school whose reputation had come to be evaluated primarily in terms of audience response in the West. For many Indian readers, particularly those getting interested in post-modernistic trends for the first time, the sense of being 'with it' strongly conveyed by Subaltern Studies appears far more important than any possible insubstantiality of empirical content.[125]

Stretching its theory in post-modernist directions has further institutionalized and enhanced its status. The relativism of post-modernism seems particularly suited to the consumerism of American political, social, even cultural–educational life. Little surprise, then, that Subaltern Studies should now be sought after as a heavyweight recruit in the 'rage against humanism', against any project of universal human emancipation that might seek to mobilize, howsoever carefully, the power of science, technology or reason. In this 'rage', post-modernists are prone to suffer nostalgia for what has been lost, for a world-that-once-was and to whose remaining 'marginal' voices we must listen to since they alone have not been fully silenced by the imperialism of Reason or Progress.

So Dipesh Chakrabarty can now warn of a 'hyper rationalism' among

Indian intellectuals which makes them uncritical of Enlightenment Rationalism, modernity and progress. It also leads them to dangerously counterpose Rationalism and Science against Faith in India.[126] He seems to have Marxists particularly in mind. The problem with early Subaltern Studies was also its Marxist–humanist assumptions. It wanted to reconstruct the subaltern as its own subject but also to 'improve' its lot, where the criteria for judging such improvement was based on Enlightenment principles and values.

> In pedagogic histories, it is the subaltern's relationship to the world that ultimately calls for improvement. *Subaltern Studies*, the series, was founded within this gesture. Guha's insurgent peasants, for instance, fall short in their understanding of what is required for a 'comprehensive' reversal of relations of power in an exploitative society.[127]

Whatever its early value, it is now time, says Chakrabarty, to go beyond this approach towards a more truly democratic historical dialogue, to honour the fragment and its episodic vision. Of course the very notion of a fragment must now be challenged so that its implied relation to some whole is transcended. All 'wholes' are to be challenged and rejected, be it the state or universal progress or the idea of a good society. Each is an imposition, a 'monomania'. The future for Subaltern Studies is '[i]n other words to allow the subaltern position to challenge our own conceptions of what is universal'.[128] If Chakrabarty's hostility to the state, modernization, rationality, science, brings him close to Nandy, he is still resistant to the latter's search for a 'competing universalism'. His 'world' is one of incommensurable parts and of differences and so not a world at all.

For Sumit Sarkar, the original and most important dissident, it has all reflected a fatal transition. Subaltern Studies has shifted from 'Thompsonian social history' to 'post-structuralist cultural studies and Saidian critique of colonial discourse' – social history collapsing into cultural studies.[129] Along with this there has been the shift towards the dissection of elite discourses rather than field work on the subaltern.[130]

In the context of American political life, Subaltern Studies can appear radical. In India, there exist large and organized Left parties. There have been and continue to be strong anti-caste movements. Both organized Left-led movements of class struggle and explicit anti-caste movements have rarely featured in Subaltern Studies. These movements are joined by a range of ecological and women's struggles as well as by civil liberties groups and activists. Moreover, in a situation where the only serious defence against economic neo-liberalism in its Indian version (the World Bank/International Monetary Fund-inspired pack-age of economic reforms instituted in 1991) can come from an alert state committed to strategic control over the economy, the unbalanced anti-statism of late Subalternism helps those out to undermine this bulwark. The practical effect would be to further legitimize those transnational institutions standing 'above' the Indian state, i.e. the institutions/support structures of transnational capital (the World Bank, the IMF, GATT, etc.) and the institution of the unrestrained market standing 'below' it in civil society.

The latest anti-humanist and post-modernist turn of Subaltern Studies theory coming on top of its existing tendency to neglect class and caste struggles in a context of new global economic pressures makes its political impact altogether different in India. If this kind of Subaltern Studies grows in popularity in the catchment area of Indian radicalism, then its effect will be diversionary and detrimental. The agenda of *progressive* struggles, in the old-fashioned sense of what that terms means, needs to be widened and strengthened.

A Subalternist's View on Secularism

Partha Chatterjee's most direct attack on secularism in 'Secularism and Tolerance' carries forward the trajectory of a dynamic which had been well established in his latest book, *The Nation and Its Fragments*.[131] There, Chatterjee completed his slide into culturalism and through it towards ever greater sympathy for indigenism. To the binary contrast of coloni-alism/indigenous community were added other polar contrasts such as material/spiritual, outer/inner, world/home. In each of these binaries, the second term had become the more important, the realm of true autonomous thought and struggle, itself cultural as opposed to political or economic. Struggle on the terrain of the 'material' or 'outer' or 'world' had become a form of surrender to the defining principles of colonial discourse itself.[132] His last chapter on 'Communities and the Nation' constitutes Chatterjee's most sustained effort to date to theorize community and to counterpose the 'narrative of community' (not of class) to the 'narrative of capital', itself identified with and standing in for the narratives of universal history.

This has effectively paved the way for him to accept the 'religious community' as a primary political unit for the purposes of contesting the purportedly unjustified hegemony of the secular state. At the heart of Chatterjee's article on 'Secularism and Tolerance' is the attempt to

187

expose and then resolve a fundamental 'impasse' well expressed by the current dilemma of what to do about the issue of a Uniform Civil Code (UCC) given the communal Hindu Right's assault on the anomalous existence of Muslim Personal Law in a supposedly secular Indian state. This, says the Hindu Right, is evidence of the secular state's 'minorityist' bias towards Muslims.[133]

Chatterjee's stance, like that of Nandy's, is a third position against both the Hindu Right and Indian secularists. But he looks not to pre-modern indigenist arrangements for a solution but to as yet untried ones. Before explaining and justifying his proposed resolution of the problem, Chatterjee attacks Indian secularism, seeking to show that there is no incompatibility between the political agenda of the Hindu communal right and the preservation of a secular Indian state. The secularity of the state is not, therefore, a bulwark against this Hindu Right.

To dismiss the importance of one of the major gains of the National Movement and a fundamental pillar of Indian democracy, all Chatterjee latches onto by way of evidence is that the Hindu Right does not attack secularism as such but 'pseudo-secularists' and the 'pseudo-secular' state, showing that it is quite happy to live with a secular state.[134] This is a flimsy foundation on which to build a case. Chatterjee never entertains the idea that there may be other plausible reasons why the Hindu Right talks of 'pseudo-secularism'. He has no reason, therefore, to construct an argument other than by asserting the self-evident character of his claim. He does not contest other explanations as a way of defending and arriving at his own conclusions.

Is it not plausible that political Hindutva's talk of 'pseudo-secularism' is the tribute vice pays to virtue? That for all its flaws, Indian democracy has a real authority and prestige not easily challenged, and that for all the lack of clarity about what Indian secularism does or should mean it is generally realized that the preservation of the democratic state is in some crucial sense linked to its secular character? That to respect Indian democracy is in some way to respect secularism? Therefore, that the Hindu Right often seeks to redefine it rather than simply and always to frontally attack it? The Hindu Right does not say it is opposed to Indian democracy but that it is the genuinely democratic force representing the majority Hindus. Does this mean there is no incompatibility between the principle of a democratic state and its political project? With respect to the issues of both secularism and democracy, the Hindu Right prefers, not frontal attack, but to *redefine* democracy as majoritarianism and secularism as tolerance, in order to present itself as more truly secular and democratic.

As for the issue of Indian secularism, the Hindu Right can much more profitably seek to coopt for itself an existing notion of secularism already widespread within the public discourse, and use it to justify its political project. The notion of secularism as tolerance is thus appropriated by the Hindu Right and then used to justify the construction of a Hindu *rashtra*, since Hinduism is widely considered (not only by the Right) as the most tolerant of religions.

Chatterjee completely ignores such a line of explanation or the adoption of such a strategy by the Hindu Right. Had he taken this more seriously he might have been more inclined to question Hinduism's claim to a special tolerance as well. Insofar as he talks of defending 'the duty of the democratic state to ensure policies of religious tolerance', this plays into the hands of political Hindutva even if Chatterjee's own elaboration of what such tolerance should mean might not be acceptable on various counts to the Hindu Right. So the Hindu state or Hindu *rashtra* is not the real problem or danger. It is the secular state itself! But to make the secular state a problem and assign blanket responsibility for this to India's modernists–secularists, Chatterjee has to argue that this category of modernists–secularists possessed a consistent understanding of secularism when patently it did not.[135]

Different contexts did give rise to different meanings of secularism in India as distinct from the West, as Chatterjee also recognizes. These contentions, moreover, created confusion and affected the secular character and behaviour of the Indian state. It is not, as Chatterjee contends, that differences centred only on how applicable an agreed notion was. These confusions had pertinent effects. India's state laws were based on Western liberal-democratic and secular principles, but qualifications to it (absence of UCC) and the actual *behaviour* of the Indian state towards its religious communities have had not a little to do with conflicts about the most appropriate notion of secularism.

The Western notion was a guideline but there was little understanding of its core characteristics or of its incompatibility with National Movement-derived notions of secularism as a principle of tolerance uniting religious communities. Precisely because of such confusions, the word 'secular' was not included in the Constitution when first drawn up but only introduced by Mrs Gandhi in 1976 during the Emergency to legitimize her rule. In reality the secular state's behaviour has represented an admixture of Western and Indian notions.

Having correctly enunciated the basic principles of a secular state in terms of the founding values of liberty, equality and neutrality, Chatterjee sees the Hindu Right's pressure for a UCC as expressive of a dilemma the secular state cannot resolve. For is not the Hindu Right's demand for a UCC in the name of equality an encroachment on the principle of liberty in whose name the cultural rights and identity of Muslims should be respected? The secular pressure for a UCC thus plays into the hands of the Hindu Right; secularism is compatible with authoritarianism. Chatterjee never suggests that the establishment, piecemeal and accumulative, of the most gender-just laws, whether or not it is finally and formally embodied in a UCC, would itself represent the deepest threat to Hindu communalism's basic perspectives regarding the family; that such 'best' secular laws would in fact be incompatible with political Hindutva!

This dismissal of secular possibilities allows him to attack with a clearer conscience the very paradigm of Enlightenment democracy as incapable of handling cultural diversity and freedom because it is steeped in rights discourse. Chatterjee is fully cognizant of the individual–communitarian debate in modern political theory. But because he does not systematically argue his case out, he can only *assert* the failure or impasse confronting all efforts to resolve the individual–communitarian tension about 'collective rights' that operate within a framework accepting the ontological and ethical priority of universalist individual rights. He thus rules out the search for multi-culturalism on the basis of a fundamentally agreed set of universal values, or that a collective's right to its culture must also presume that the collective in question recognizes that it, too, must operate in a culture of rights. All such efforts at reconciling best liberalism with best communitarianism are, for Chatterjee, unconvincing and unacceptable. 'None of these liberal arguments seems to have enough strength to come to grips with the problems posed by the Indian situation.'[136]

The closest Chatterjee comes to an argument seems to be by way of a casual endorsement of the claim that since the very notion of the self or individual is itself to be questioned or rejected (the 'decentred self'), the individual cannot be the locus for anchoring a discourse of rights.[137] Since Chatterjee does not reject a rights discourse altogether, not only can a cultural community have its own distinct rights to do what it wants, it need not give reasons for this!

> Thus when a minority group demands a cultural right, it in fact says, 'we have our reasons for doing things the way we do, but since you don't share the fundamentals of our world-view, you will never come to understand or appreciate those reasons. Therefore, leave us alone and let us mind our own business.'[138]

This brazen defence of extreme group relativism is actually under-taken in the name of wanting to secure a truer democracy. To provide a theoretical gloss on what would otherwise be seen as an incoherent relativist free-for-all inimical to any notion of democratic political governance across communities and individuals, Chatterjee takes up a Foucauldian notion of 'governmentality' but frankly admits to using it in his own way. For Foucault governmentality was a specific form of disciplinary power cutting across the state–civil society divide, a 'modern regime no longer retains a distinct aspect of sovereignty'.[139]

But Chatterjee's purpose in reorganizing this concept is to argue something else: where governmental technologies don't hold sway, there you will not find applicable its 'juridicial sovereignty'. The 'inner' domain of the cultural community (or religious community where the identification of religion and culture is no longer considered problem-atic) can and should remain aloof from the tyranny of state-imposed laws. When a community refuses to give reasons to the state for 'not being like you', it is actually democratically resisting the incursion of the 'technologies of governmentality'.

The community, here the religious community, has become the desired locus for advancing the democratic process. Legislating inde-pendently on family and other matters the community need not give reasons to 'outsiders'. But to be tolerant it must give reasons to itself through some public and representative process, i.e. be accountable to its own constituency. However, the mechanisms of accountability here would seem to be no different from those operative elsewhere. Presum-ably some notion of universal, adult franchise would exist even if the 'universe' is the cultural community. Presumably each person's vote would count as much as another's – a smuggling in of the individual as the key political unit, at least for some public regulative purposes. Antipathy to the overbearingness of state forms has only resulted in the endorsement here of the overbearingness of a community form itself perceived in much the same way as a state-in-itself.[140]

The crucial issue in regard to such proposed 'legislative autonomy' for the religious community is the matter of the individual's right of exit. Does a Muslim woman, for example, have the right to reject the application of even an agreed internal consensus on Sharia, and opt for some other framework of non-community-based secular law? At this point of dispute what laws apply? This is the crux of the matter. And even many who would not wish for a UCC, and who insist that reforming Personal Law within a religious community should be the strategic 'line of march', would nonetheless agree that at a point of dispute by an uncoerced disputant secular laws should prevail where these be made as gender-just as possible.

Chatterjee does not directly address this issue, but the thrust of his argument opposes this as well as the (temporary, qualified or otherwise) right of exit. The religious community must be left to reform itself. To fears that this would mean endorsing existing relations of unequal and exploitative power, Chatterjee says history confirms the strong possibility of such reforms, and that such aloofness and non-interference is preferable to the unacceptable arrogances of state imposition.[141] Where once Chatterjee would emphasize, in opposition to all essentialisms, the constructed character of communities, he has now come close to politically essentializing and reifying the religious community.

The individual belongs to multiple communities and on various occasions communities and community values, norms and commitments clash and compete. This forces into the open issues of choice and judgement, and therefore raises questions about locating the unit which has the right of choice, and deciding a criterion (which must cut across communities) for judging such conflicts. In the name of an anti-individualist, anti-humanist so-called truer democracy, Chatterjee would have us, in effect, endorse the traditional networks of pre-Enlightenment collective oppressions, albeit with a modernist twist. He has joined forces with religious communitarians for whom the relationship between the individual and community is to be based not primarily on rights but on consensus.

In the specific area of Muslim Personal Law and the issue of a UCC, Chatterjee's strategic line is simply reactionary, contrary to the effort to widen the scope of application of gender-just laws, and a step backwards from what even many progressives working for internal reforms among Muslims would want. This is not the way to fight Muslim or Hindu communalism. It is, of course, a way to fight Indian secularism.

Communalism, Religious Fundamentalism and Religious Nationalism

The anti-secularist, anti-modern or post-modern, puts most blame for communalism or religious fundamentalism on secularism and modernity. These evils are the reactions to processes which have been mistakenly seen as solutions rather than for what they actually are – the causes. For the psychologically minded anti-modernist, communalism or fundamentalism (like so much else) is a particular state of mind or expression of a distinctive personality-type. Fundamentalism is the response of self-hating believers to a secular–desacralized world. And this self-hatred or 'inner threat' is projected as an 'outer oppression' by some identified group, the despised Other.

But whether it is the anti-secularist or the secularist, or the communal religious activist, their respective understandings of communalism represent different ways of navigating over a large terrain having common references or indicators. Some of them are like double-headed arrows, each pointing in opposite directions. The result is a wide variety of ways of defining or charting the phenomenon of communalism.

Choosing the best chart is more a matter of where one is trying to get to. How best to understand communalism is related to one's wider intellectual and political projects. This does not mean a complete relativism. There are better and worse charts. But no single chart will provide all the best possible angles for surveying the 'lay of the land'. This may become clearer when we look at these references – the dyads and binary contrasts – which have shaped the various constructions of the concept of communalism.

Certainly, a greater awareness of the complexities and difficulties involved in any such attempt at concept construction has made me more reluctant to put forward even a provisional or working definition of communalism in one or a few sentences.[142] I would now prefer to point out these dyads, look at some of the different choices of direction taken in each case, and simply explain my own preferences.

There are at least eight such dyads:

- *Modern–Non-modern*: Is communalism a modern or non-modern phenomenon?
- *Singular–Plural*: Is it a term applicable to a society with a single dominant religion or only to those with significant religious pluralities?
- *Political–Non-political*: Is it a political phenomenon or non-political? Or both but operating at different levels?
- *Individual–Collective*: Is it operative at the collective level only or at the individual as well?
- *Religious–Non-religious/secular*: Is it a secular phenomenon or is it significantly related to religion? And if so, what does this mean?
- *Religious–Ethnic*: Is it specifically religious or more generally ethnic?
- *Essentialist–Non-essentialist*: Is it an essentialist characteristic of India or the East, or non-essentialist?

- *Negative–Neutral*: Is it to be understood as negatively charged or should it preferably be evaluatively neutral?

Choices in respect of a particular dyad cannot be easily separated from biases and choices in respect of others, and are part of the overall framework of values and perceptions that define one's own intellectual–political alignments.

Take the question of communalism's modern or non-modern character. Anti-secularists would without hesitation insist on the modernity of communalism. Others would say it depends on what you mean by communalism, and suggest that certain dimensions of it have a significant pre-modern history. Still others would say the rise of communalism is associated not with modernity per se but with changes in the pattern of modernity. Communalism, then, is a modern phenomenon, but if modernity is its necessary condition it is not a sufficient one.

As adjective, the word 'communal' is mostly used with reference to consciousness and conflict, i.e. communal consciousness and communal conflict. For those who see modernity as constituting a profound and decisive rupture with the past, neither the forms of consciousness nor those of conflict within it can be seen in quite the same way as in pre-modernity. The use of communalism as a 'bridging' term, applicable with equal felicity to phenomena in that past as to our present, would not help us to grasp the distinctiveness of the problems of the present.

With some justification it could be argued that while communal conflict was a significant feature of the past, communal consciousness was not. This might seem comparable to saying that class conflict has been a feature of all stratified societies even if a strong class consciousness was infrequently associated with such struggle before the advent of industrialization. But the comparison is not tenable, unless one reduces 'communal' to being a synonym for the term 'religious', so that communal conflict and communal consciousness mean nothing other than religious conflict and religious consciousness. This would empty the concept of any distinctive value. Moreover, the actual emergence of the term and the development of a discourse of communalism is roughly concurrent with the constructions of the discourse of colonialism and then of nationalism. It is a modern construction meant to serve modern purposes, though different architects had different projects in mind.

The communal riot as an archetypal form of communal conflict precedes colonial rule but not by centuries.[143] It was also comparatively rare. Though references to the Muslim community and to defence of its interests are to be found under Mughal rule, the consciousness of belonging to a pan-Indian entity – the Muslim community – was for most Muslims extremely vague and weak, and subordinated to other, more local loyalties and forms of community consciousness. As communal consciousness sharpens during and after colonialism the character of communal conflict also changes significantly.[144]

To situate communalism as a modern phenomenon also raises a series of other issues and creates its own theoretical biases. It cannot then be an Indian essentialism. It was not a basic feature of India's past and is not equivalent to other kinds of supposedly essentialist factionalisms such as tribalism or casteism. British colonialists who saw it as such were making it part of an Orientalist discourse that justified their own civilizing mission. Not being an essentialism, communalism is a concept that in principle is generalizable to other shores and climes. There is no reason why it cannot be used to analyse the current travails in Bosnia except that the international relationship of political–intellectual forces that helps determine what discourses are used, and where, can hardly be expected to allow this.

There is also an existing Western usage of the term 'communalism', strongly positive and expressive of communitarian as opposed to individualist (self-centred) longings because the history of Western modernity has been different. Nationalism there was much more a secular phenomenon because it had already been preceded by the institutionalization of a democratic, secular discourse questioning the claims of Christianity and Church.

Even where a strong connection between religion and nationalism existed, the ideal of a secular state was not questioned.[145] Except for ex-Yugoslavia and Albania, Europe was uniformly Christian. Religious nationalism, not communalism, was the issue. The key contrast was between Europe's centre and peripheries, between the zone where national identity was less aggressive because more secure and where it was not. Religious identity as collective public consciousness was of much lesser import in the former.[146] Today's religious map of Europe is basically unchanged from 1648. No dynamic has risen from within Christianity to change this – significant evidence of Christianity's decline, and the emergence of a secular state and a more secularized society. For these rather than for any essentialist reasons, communalism has become a term confined primarily to South Asia.

Should it apply only to where two or more major religious systems exist or even where there is no such plurality? If the latter, then there are two likely corollaries. (1) Communalism is more likely to be a substitutable expression for religious fundamentalism or religious

195

nationalism. (2) It need not even refer specifically to a religious grouping but can be used to refer to some other ethnic grouping or even to an altogether neutral concept of 'community', ethnic or otherwise.

In both cases the special value of such a concept gets submerged. The moment communalism is seen as a term which applies when there is a plurality of religious (or other ethnic) groups, then it is likely to express some kind of tension *between* groups, to be a negative conception of communalism. It is something unpleasant, unwanted, even condemnable. This is the way Orientalists used it, the way most Indian nationalists perceived it. It is the direction even the Indian anti-essentialist and modernist construction of it (mainly in the 1920s and 1930s) took. There is no good reason why we should not continue to so use it, though there have been attempts to give it a more neutral imputation.[147]

A more debated theoretical or definitional issue, however, is whether communalism should be understood in ways which make it structurally modular. Can it not describe a range of group tensions? Here it becomes a term of ethnicity rather than of religion alone.[148] While there is no a priori reason for saying that this use is illegitimate, problems do arise. If we make communalism the equivalent for any kind of negative 'communitarianism', then certain theoretical tendencies surface. We are deprived of any specific term with which to analyse inter-religious tensions and conflicts in modernity. It becomes more difficult to think about how inter-religious tensions differ from other kinds of inter-ethnic tensions: the specificities of religious power and influence are obscured. The tendency, already strong, to believe that communalism really has very little to do with religion is reinforced. At most, religious identity becomes a boundary marker for the politics of communal mobilization. This is far and away the dominant tendency in the definitions and understandings of communalism held even by those committed to Enlightenment notions of secularism and the secular state.

Take these definitions of communalism, which, unlike the broad ethnic notion, do stipulate a connection to religion. It is 'the functioning of religious communities or organisations detrimental to the interests of other groups or the nation as a whole. The term usually invokes some kind of political involvement.'[149] Or, 'Communalism is taken here as a political doctrine which makes use of religio-cultural differences to achieve political ends.'[150] There is Jawaharlal Nehru's definition of communalism as 'a narrow group mentality basing itself on a religious community but in reality concerned with political power and patronage for the interested group'.[151] In this approach, the conceptual slide into notions like good and bad religion, true religion and false religiosity, religion-as-faith and religion-as-ideology, is greatly strengthened.

Communalism can, then, only be perceived as an overwhelmingly *secular* problem, having fundamentally secular sources, though opinion can be divided on whether there should be secular or anti-secular solutions. The central location for investigating the problems of communalism becomes simply the non-religious or contra-religious processes of modernity. This should not be the conclusion in an argument that rightly stresses the modernity of communalism. The true terrain is the changing relationship of religion and religious systems to other processes in modernity.

Both sides of the equation linking the religious and the non-religious have to be seriously investigated. It is not modernity per se but changing scenarios in modernity and the changing responses of religious systems that are the problems. The worldwide resurgence of religious fundamentalism, religious nationalism and of communalism is a feature of the fourth, not the third, quarter of this century. Temporally and spatially specific critiques of the forces operating within modernity, religious and non-religious, are called for, not general or ahistorical critiques of either religious systems or modernity.

Like other negative phenomenon (e.g. racism, sexism, casteism), communalism operates at the individual and collective levels. At the individual level it is an attitudinal problem which is socially derived. There are racial, sexist, casteist prejudices and communal consciousness/biases. But where caste identity presupposes the existence of a strongly institutionalised system of caste oppression, the existence of racial, sexual and religious identities and self-awarenesses does not axiomatically presuppose the existence of strongly institutionalized racism, sexism or communalism, though, concretely speaking, the institutionalization of patriarchy has been universal. In the case of racism and communalism, different societies can and do have different degrees of institutionalization of such evils, and the differences are often qualitatively significant.

It is at the collective or institutionalized level that the problem is most seriously posed and must be primarily confronted. Moreover, a collective resolution of the collective problem of communalism is not the sum of the individual resolutions of individual problems. An understanding or definition of communalism which sees it in more or less this fashion, which does not sufficiently distinguish between the individual and collective aspects as two different types of problem (with the line of causation running from the social to the individual), will not be that helpful in providing a programme for combating it.

This is a major problem with all 'state of mind' definitions of communalism. Since the problem has to be tackled at this wider, more public level, the Indian academic discourse has also, for the most part, seen communalism as a political phenomenon. This is eminently sensible because its political thrust makes it particularly dangerous. But it is also a social and cultural phenomenon, which is what gives it the political force it has. It operates not just in, and around, the state, but in civil society as well. It has to do not only with the constructions of politics but also with the constructions and affirmations of religious identity. It is not only political systems, structures, institutions, elites and personnel that are to blame but also religious systems, structures, institutions, elites and personnel. It is not just secularization in modernity but also competitive de-secularization in late modernity, or the striving to extend the reach, power and importance of religious institutions, ideologies and identities at the expense of secular equivalents that is the problem.[152]

Modernity makes communalism possible yet also carries the antidote for it. This is never a permanent cure, but it can be a stable and increasingly effective one. Communalism is the sharpest expression in a religiously plural society of the failure to establish a proper balance between the secular and the religious, i.e. the terms of coexistence. The initiative in this ongoing effort has always rested with secular forces.

It is not just the religious map of Europe that has remained unchanged for centuries. The religious map of the world will also no longer change. The era when any world religion could be said to possess the dynamism enabling it to greatly expand its sphere of influence is gone for good. The Christian, Islamic, Hindu and Buddhist worlds will no longer grow at the expense of each other, though within each of these spaces there certainly can be changes in the internal relationship of forces between churches, sects and branches.[153]

In brief, no world religion can any longer be said to possess a distinctive dynamism of its own. The exceptional power of the West and of Westernization does not give Christianity any reason to believe it can ride piggy-back to make newer conquests. It is not the distinctive gifts of religious systems that explain the recent (and fluctuating) resurgence of religio-political movements and ideologies but the specific weaknesses of secular processes in different parts of the world. Once, a world religion expanded because for both secular and religious reasons it was better able to address the needs of potential believers. Today, there is only the turning away from secular failures to whatever is at hand within an existing religious system. This indicates not the enduring power of religion but its new frailty (disguised by the fact of resurgence) in modernity.

This resurgence is, above all, a reaction to a failed modernization. Religion-related movements are usually most aggressively political, widespread and dangerous where the failure is most acute. That is why, though there is the rise of Christian fundamentalist movements in the advanced Western world, they do not represent as serious a threat for these societies as Islamic fundamentalist or Hindu communal or Buddhist revanchist movements do in their societies. This failure is a many-sided one expressed in inadequacies of socio-economic development, weaknesses of political democratization, ideological disarray. These religion-related movements take different forms varying in their explicitly political character and their obsession with state power. Not all are religio-political movements, and among the latter, political ambitions vary. Some others are religious revivalisms, and some have more to do with social reform. Yet others combine elements of some or all of the above.

Religious fundamentalism has become an inaccurate term of convenience to describe all such religion-related movements. Not all religious fundamentalisms are religio-political movements. A host of Christian fundamentalist currents are largely unconcerned about the public domain of politics. While all communalisms and religious nationalist movements are religio-political movements, they are not always religious fundamentalisms. And not all communalisms, e.g. Muslim communalism in India, are religious nationalisms. Where religious fundamentalisms and nationalisms need not posit hostility to a 'religious other', communalism does. So even when a communalism, e.g. Hindu communalism, is also a religious nationalism, it is not only that.

To properly handle these differences, religious fundamentalism must not be characterized too sweepingly. It need not be defined pejoratively. One person's fundamentalism is another's normality. Nor should it be perceived in an overly political fashion.[154] Where the secular state is secure, religious fundamentalism doesn't make state power its focus, or, even if it does, it has little scope for serious headway.[155]

Religious fundamentalism is best understood as a label for those movements stressing either a return to or reinterpretation of foundational sacred texts in order to resolve contemporary political, social or personal problems. Fundamentalism can be reactionary, i.e. 'radical backwards', but it is not conservative, i.e. seeking to conserve what

199

already exists. Hinduism and Buddhism, not being scriptural religions, could not, then, give rise to religious fundamentalisms. But the kind of religio-political movements that do arise – Hindu communalism or Buddhist communalism or nationalism – nonetheless share many similarities and resemblances with fundamentalist movements.

They both fight on the terrain of modernity itself and not on the ground between tradition and modernity. They are most certainly not atavisms. They both employ the mass politics of religious appeal. Their means of mobilization are invariably modern. They pursue goals which are modernist and anti-modernist but never non-modernist or pre-modernist. Their thrust is, on balance, directed against secularism and the secularizing process, and against political democracy. They share common attitudes to science, using science's own disclaimers about its provisionality, contingency and falsifiability to say that it cannot be true knowledge, which only religion can provide.[156] Much of what has been said here would apply to most religious nationalist movements and ideologies.

What is common to all these religio-political movements is that they are each greatly inspired in their reform agendas by religious faith (they are not just political manipulators of religious identity markers) and not only by secular hopes. They are, therefore, invariably far more precise in their programmatic injunctions concerning education and family life than they are in regard to reforming the macro-structures or systems of political and economic life. Even in modernity, the family is where religious influence remains greatest.

Religious nationalism contrasts with secular nationalism. It need not but can be a fundamentalism. It is relatively more benign than communalism. The 'Other' it opposes are secularists or secular nationalists, not necessarily a 'religious other', hostility to which is the basic characteristic of communalism. But most religious nationalisms today are strongly negative. They have a definite authoritarian thrust, but this is flexible and variable. There are shifting combinations of the religious and secular, the democratic and the authoritarian.

Religious nationalism is a distinctive hybrid in which the more important defining element is the noun. Religious or secular nationalism are two different forms of cultural nationalism, incompatible because of their irreconcilable differences with regard to the issue of individual rights. But religious nationalisms cannot be a *complete* replacement for a secular nationalism because of the nature of nationalism itself. The latter has not just a cultural dimension, which can be filled up by either a religious or a secular candidate, but also a political dimension which is secular in character. This usually, but not always, acts to temper the fervour and thrust of religious nationalisms, which is why the small minority of religious nationalist states that actually exist do not altogether outlaw secular values, institutions or laws, but incorporate them in variable ways.

Secular nationalism, especially if it is also a democratic nationalism, has resources of strength which are often underestimated. While the number of religious nationalist movements is growing, the number of religious nationalist states is not growing anywhere near as fast. Such movements do not have things all their own way. Religious loyalties are not equivalent to national loyalties, though religion and nationalism have in so many ways quite a similar structure.[157] Religious loyalty operates with a notion of believership. Nationalism does not just represent a community of believers, where the principle of believership can be religiously or secularly based; it is also a community of citizens operating with a uniquely powerful political (and secular) principle of legitimacy and empowerment – citizenship. It is the unique power of nationalism that explains why, in modernity, religious systems seek to co-opt rather than confront nationalism in the name of some 'higher' trans-national religious loyalty. Despite religion's 'transcendent' claims, should it seek through confrontation to 'transcend' nationalism it would lose out.

Of course, a fuller explanation of the unique power of nationalism would have to probe more deeply than has been done here. It would not be enough simply to point out the similar structures between nationalism and a religious system. To what extent is nationalism a replacement for religious affiliation made powerfully appealing precisely because the structures and symbols of this affiliation are akin to religion or kinship? However, if nationalism has been *more* powerful than a religious system in our times, the weight of explanation is more likely to fall on the fact that it is a *political* community as well as a culturally imagined one.[158] It has been suggested above that the empowering principle of citizenship has been one such crucial factor. But this hardly exhausts the exploration of the political sources of nationalism's unique strength.

Indeed, the intensity of belief and commitment that the nation can evoke, to the point of demanding and getting the sacrifice of one's life, may itself have as much to do with the fact of it being a nation-*state*, a 'community of political destiny', a 'community of life and death', because of the possibilities of wars between nation-states. Where membership is a matter of fate (belonging to a nation is not usually chosen and therefore is similar to religious and family membership), and where it also carries risk because such affiliation can demand the ultimate sacrifice, then such a community also possesses for its believers a distinctive purity. Here, the possibility of war gives the nation a special grandeur, and the fact of war gives it 'a precise, univocal and resolutely imagined identity'.[159]

Behind religion's inability to match the appeal of nationalism, then, are political weaknesses that go beyond merely the issue of citizenship. But this, nonetheless, remains a serious lacuna that needs to be registered.

Religious systems cannot override some kind of political arrangement in which the modern empowering principle of citizenship operates. The nation-state is not the only form such a political arrangement can take. Nor should we assume that the nation-state system will endure long into the future. But the search for alternatives is still in its infancy. Meanwhile, there are still progressive forms of nationalism that can be counterposed to religious nationalism. To reject religious nationalism, even in this era of globalization, does not require us, automatically or always, to reject nationalism itself.

But if nationalism provides resources to check the absolutist tendencies of religious systems, nationalism, because it usually legitimizes the authority of the state, can also promote the tendential absolutism of the state itself. Thus religious nationalism can also mean the dangerous marriage of two such absolutist-prone systems. It is not just any kind of secular nationalism that can effectively confront religious nationalism, but *democratic* nationalisms that can do the job. The struggle for democracy – the deepening institutionalization of human rights and the expansion of popular empowerment – are among the most powerful counters not only to religious nationalisms but also to religious fundamentalisms and communalisms.

All these religio-political movements have arisen in response to the many-sided failure of capitalist modernization. It is the resurrection of a more effective and sensitive modernization project that will most weaken the evils of such religio-political movements and ideologies. If the construction of such an alternative modernization project is considered inseparable from the task of deepening democracy and pursuing socialism, then the anti-communal struggle in India becomes an integral part of this wider anti-authoritarian and anti-capitalist project.

The most effective way to promote the various themes of secularism is not always to do it directly. The secular discourse is a subset of the wider discourse of democracy and equality. It is this discourse (with strong socialist references) that is most important and should be ideologically promoted. How the major principles of a secular outlook should be promoted is related to how best to organize propagation of a general democratic discourse. One major aspect of the discourse of secularism has to do with emphasizing and justifying the necessity of a secular state. This theme should be directly propagated in myriad ways. The message here is that the existence and strengthening of a secular state is the necessary but not sufficient condition for the existence and strengthening of a democratic system.

Another aspect of this discourse has to do with secularization of civil society, i.e. the ways in which religious loyalties must accept a more modest role and come to terms with secular institutions, affiliations and norms of functioning. Here, the motifs of privatizing and optionalizing religion mean more than merely a basic separation of religion and the state. These are not themes that fruitfully lend themselves to any direct agit-prop approach. Indeed, this would be counter-productive. Here, it is the actual institutionalization of greater democracy, social and gender equality and economic progress in civil society that is most important. The ideological complement to this is the propagation of a general discourse of democracy, welfare and equality (many would say that, in these times, only the discourse of socialism can meet these requirements) in which the specifically secular aspects are incorporated.

Any other approach reinforces the false accusation that the ideology of secularism is primarily anti-religious, when it is, above all, pro-democracy. And because this is its natural thrust, it demands that religious systems learn their place in this new dispensation. They have no inherent dynamic leading them to endorse or practically reinforce modern principles of pluralism and democracy. The world religions are historically shaped entities bearing the marks of that shaping. But this does not mean they are incompatible with these modern principles.

It does mean, however, that religions have to *learn* how to become compatible and to accept the costs and consequences of what this entails. That is what the ideology of secularism (insofar as it would deal with the issue of secularization of civil society) would demand, and it is easy to see how religious activists, from communalists to anti-secularists, can distort this message into a purportedly anti-religious one. This distortion is most effective when religions are directly exhorted to learn their place. They are least effective when religious systems are indirectly pushed to adopt more accommodating and modest postures because of the practical virtues and benefits that attend the progressive institutionalization of democracy and justice (in the widest sense) on the ground.

This is the best approach for India's secular activists to take in their confrontation with the various communalisms existing, at least in regard to their operations in civil society. Of these, Hindu communalism is far and away the most dangerous. Muslim communalism in India is more socially and spatially restricted, and not linked to any pan-Indian Islamic movement. Muslim communalism in a particular locale promotes the organizational growth of Hindu communalism there as well. The reverse does not necessarily happen.[160] But this should not justify a perspective of first tackling Hindu communalism and then worrying about the others. All communalisms have to be tackled together because they all feed on each other, even as we are aware of the special power of Hindu communalism to change the fabric of Indian society. It alone can bring about a highly authoritarian and centralized form of rule, the Hindu state. Moreover, the attempt to impose its specific view of pan-Hindu unity will greatly weaken the social fabric of India by reinforcing not just communal but also caste oppression, as well as weakening territorial unity.

This Hindu communalism, organizationally represented by the forces of the Sangh Combine, is not to be equated to Hindu nationalism. Nor is its ideology purely one of Hindu nationalism. Hindu communalism in its systematized hostility to the Muslim Other, and in its larger project for social and political change, is much more. It is a deeply reactionary and strongly authoritarian rightwing movement, having a corresponding ideological thrust, whereas Hindu nationalism comes in many kinds. It is entirely legitimate to talk of Gandhi's Hindu nationalism and that of other nationalist leaders and currents. But it would be utterly mistaken to brand Gandhi's perspectives as communal, or doubt his anti-communal credentials, or deny his remarkable anti-communal mobilizational capacities.

Many of Gandhi's perspectives were against modern conceptions of secularism, and to that extent weakened the struggle for it. But being anti-secular or behaving in ways that weaken secularism is not the same as being communal or behaving communally. Though, in a general and long-term sense, failing to strengthen the secular state or promote secularization strengthens the communal dynamic, there is still space for non-secular ways of discourse and behaviour (with their limitations and dangers) to contribute to the struggle against communalism. They cannot constitute the *strategic* perspective in the struggle against communalism, but can be a partial and important tactical resource.

Hindu communalism gives rise not just to any kind of Hindu nationalism but to the most vicious form of it going in India.[161] By using this term as a self-description, the forces of the Sangh Combine give themselves a more benign image than they can ever deserve, as well as imply continuities with other less pernicious forms of Hindu nationalism. As for Hindutva, it is an important part of the wider ideology of Hindu communalism, perhaps its most coherently organized part. But it is not the whole of that ideology.

Hindutva is the intellectual anchor of the ideology pursued by the most vicious form of Hindu nationalism, which is a major part of the overall project of Hindu communalism.[162]

Notes

1. R. Williams, *Keywords*, London, 1983, pp. 57–60.
2. C. Renfrew, *The Emergence of Civilization*, London, 1972. Also, M. Mann, *The Sources of Social Power*, Vol. I, Cambridge, 1988, p. 74.
3. M. Rodinson, 'The Western Image and Western Studies of Islam' (written in 1974), appearing in a collection of essays, J. Schacht and C.E. Bosworth (eds), *The Legacy of Islam*, Oxford, 1979.

   Four years before Said's *Orientalism* appeared, Rodinson synopsized the same theme in a way that was as remarkable for its sobriety and balance as for its brevity.
4. Mann, self-confessedly, is decisively influenced by Weber's 'general vision of the relationship between society, history and social action'. *The Sources of Social Power*, Vol. I, p. 32.

   So despite earlier avowal of Renfrew's understanding of civilization and his repeated avowal of the importance of multi-factor causality, Mann falls prey to a typically Weberian tendency to collapse civilization and culture, even if he pays more attention to the 'organizational power resources' of ideological movements (religion).

   Mann's understanding of Hinduism is not so much the result of an extensive and impartial study of Hinduism but reflects more his desire to 'fit' the study of India and Hinduism into a preconceived structure – his IEMP (ideological–economic–military–political) power model that is central to his book. So for Mann, Hinduism is essentially Brahminism, which was the most remarkable 'normative pacifier' in human social history. India, he feels, has long had a cultural unity. However, because of the attention he pays to cultural infrastructure, this unity, he argues, is due more to practical Brahmin power, especially over rituals, than to the distinctiveness of Brahminical ideas and values.

   But even his emphasis on the infrastructure of culture is lost on most Indian intellectuals who believe in the continuity of Indian

205

civilization. For them, Brahminism has been much more important than Brahmins in explaining India's cultural unity.

One of the most interesting efforts to theorize the notion of a continuous Indian civilization is by Ravindar Kumar, *India: A 'Nation-State' or A 'Civilization-State'?*, Occasional Papers, Nehru Memorial Museum and Library (NMML), May 1989. Kumar insists that a civilization be seen as an integrated economic, social, political and cultural phenomenon characterized by distinctive traits emerging out of the way its particular mechanisms of wealth creation, its particular principles of social and political organization, and its distinctive 'texture of moral values' all knit together. On closer inspection, however, most of the weight for establishing the distinctiveness of Indian civilization comes to rest on expected notions of the longevity and dominance of the caste system and on the uniqueness of the moral vision associated with Hinduism understood as a 'loosely structured religious system'. These are claims qualified or disputed in my text.

5. M. Singer, *When a Great Tradition Modernizes*, Delhi, 1972. Redfield shares Singer's view of civilization as a 'structure of tradition'. R. Redfield, 'The Social Organization of Tradition', in *Far Eastern Quarterly*, Vol. XV, 1955.

6. R. Khan (ed.), *Composite Culture of India and National Integration*, Ahmedabad, 1987; R. Khan, *Indigenous Intellectual Creativity: The Ethos of the Composite Culture of India*, Kyoto, 1978.

The Brahminical view of Hinduism has two versions of Hinduism's origins. It emerges with the rise of Aryans to prominence in North India (whether or not Aryan presence is explained as indigenous or through migration from the northwest); or in the interaction between Aryans and pre-Aryans.

7. R. Schwab, *The Oriental Renaissance*, New York, 1984, p. 165. For a critical look at Indian philosophy see the works of D.P. Chattopadhyay: *What is Living and What is Dead in Indian Philosophy*, Delhi, 1993; *Indian Philosophy*, Delhi, 1988; *Indian Atheism*, Delhi, 1991.

8. Even someone as committed to the compositeness of Indian culture as Nehru talked of the 'subconscious mind of India' striving centuries long for fulfilment–embodiment, and finding it periodically in the reign of 'great rulers' who understood this essentialist spirit–ethos of India. True to Nehru's ecumenism, such rulers were not only Hindu. They included Ashoka (Buddhist), Akbar and Sher Shah (Muslim), as well as Chandragupta and Harsha. J. Nehru, *The Discovery of India*, Delhi, London, 1956; *Glimpses of World History*, Delhi, 1982.

9. Gandhi is quoted (J. Nehru, *The Discovery of India*, New York, 1946, p. 136) as saying 'Indian culture is neither Hindu, Islamic or any other wholly. It is a fusion of all.' This gave Indian culture a broader base,

but for him, more than for Nehru, its foundations were unmistakably Hindu.

D.E. Smith, another believer in the compositeness of Indian culture, also says 'Hinduism has indeed provided the essential genius of Indian culture; this cannot be denied.' D.E. Smith, *India as Secular State*, Princeton, 1963, p. 378.

I am grateful to Javeed Alam for pointing out that the debate on composite culture begins in earnest in the 1940s in reaction to the movement for creating Pakistan. It resurfaces from 1959–62 onwards as responses to a series of nationalist studies brought out by the Bharatiya Vidhya Bhavan in India, and to official nationalist studies in Pakistan, notably the four-volume history of Pakistan's Freedom Struggle edited by I.A. Qureshi. The 1962 Indian History Congress devoted its annual session to the question of India's 'composite culture'.

I am also grateful to Kamal Mitra Chenoy for bringing to my notice how the Constitution, while endorsing the notion of composite culture, also privileges Hinduism and so-called Hindu culture as its core. Thus while Article 350A recognizes the necessity for instruction in mother tongues for linguistic minorities, Article 351 stipulates that the Union 'promote the spread of the Hindi language ... as a medium of expression for all the elements of the composite culture ... by drawing wherever necessary or desirable for its vocabulary, primarily on Sanskrit and secondarily on other languages'. A Sanskritized Hindi not Hindustani (which is shaped by the historic Hindu–Muslim interface) is made a principle medium for promoting a composite culture. K.M. Chenoy, 'Armed Forces in Northeast India', in *Cannons into Ploughshares: Militarization and Prospects of Peace in South Asia*, New Delhi, 1995.

10. See the sub-section in Chapter 3 on 'Culture and Society: The Problem of Order'. It may be noted that those holding to an essentialist Hinduism are cohorts in the 'double fusion' outlined in that subsection.

11. I am in general agreement with Sudipta Kaviraj's characterization of the everyday interface between Hindus and Muslims in pre-modernity. Kaviraj talks of 'fuzzy communities' and 'fuzzy identities', striking metaphorical generalizations, though the actual realities of a given cultural or social space could also reveal instances of less than 'fuzzy', and more than 'fuzzy', communities and identities. S. Kaviraj, 'Religion, Politics and Modernity', in U. Baxi and B. Parekh (eds), *Crisis and Change in Contemporary India*, New Delhi, 1995.

12. Prominent ideologues of Hindutva (not only them) assign the cause of 'continuity' of India's civilization–culture to the dominance of society over state (and the dominance of Hinduism in society). This is in contrast to the Chinese situation, where, far more plausibly, it is the

greater significance of the state in relation to society that is said to explain cultural (Confucian) civilizational continuity. The states of ancient India are illegitimately reduced to the status of being utterly 'residual' when it is far more sensible to recognize that within its range state power is never residual, though its importance vis-à-vis society and its institutions is always variable. In the cruder formulations of Hindutva ideologues, residuality of the state is said to obey a definite geographical or religious pattern, e.g. as between the state systems of East and West, or between Semitic and non-Semitic religious areas. J. Bajaj, 'Introduction'; K.N. Govindacharya, 'Future Vistas'; and S. Gurumurthy, 'The Inclusive and the Exclusive', in J. Bajaj (ed.), *Ayodhya and The Future India*, Madras, 1993.

13. Shramanism is a compendium term for a variety of Buddhist, Jaina and Ajvika sects, with a common opposition to Brahminism's beliefs and practices. By A.D. 1000 Brahminism advances at the expense of Shramanism but the latter continues in other forms – Puranic religions, Bhakti, Vaishnavism, Shaivism. R. Thapar, 'Imagined Religious Communities? Ancient History and the Modern Search for a Hindu Identity', in *Modern Asian Studies*, Vol. 23, 1989.

14. L. Dumont, *Homo Hierarchicus*, Delhi, 1988; M. Biardeau, *Hinduism: The Anthropology of a Civilization*, Delhi, 1994.

    Dumont and Biardeau are modern because they stress the universality of the structure of the mind; and are Orientalists because they see a diversity of cultural essences (themselves rooted in the mind). They see Hinduism's unity, despite its own diversity, as resting in core ideas of hierarchy.

15. Later Indian scholars promoting a neo-Hinduism, like Sarvepalli Radhakrishnan, former president of India, gave a more rationalist explanation of this essence while retaining its positive value. S. Radhakrishnan, *The Hindu View of Life*, London, 1964.

16. '[C]onstructions of "Hinduism" are indeed abstract models which never fit all the actual data of history and frequently appeal to the "Hindu spirit" or some other "reality" that must be found implied in the data or beneath the surface reality and beneath the surface meaning attributed to the data by believers, and are therefore also not empirically verifiable.' R.W. Baird, 'On Defining Hinduism as a Religious and Legal Category', in A.W. Baird (ed.), *Religion and Law in Independent India*, Delhi, 1993, p. 46.

17. See note 14. Dumont's notion of the relationship between hierarchical categories (that which encompasses and that which is encompassed, or between larger and smaller) cannot deal properly with asymmetries of power. His emphasis is on order not on oppression. Dumont's study was excessively sympathetic to caste hierarchy. Many Indian writings, though not as famous or influential, have been more idealizing of caste.

18. M.N. Srinivas, *Social Change and Modern India*, Delhi, 1966. 'Caste mainly exists and functions as a regional system' (p. 3).

19. Sanskritization means emulation by lower-ranked castes of the behaviour–rituals of upper-ranked castes to secure upward status mobility. M.N. Srinivas, who first postulated this with reference to a Brahminical model, has accepted that there are a variety of such models not only referring to Brahmin but to Kshatriya castes, at the apex. So Sanskritization does not mean confirmation of a singular Brahmin-dominated caste system, though it does suggest that a more singular Hinduism, strongly influenced by Brahminism, is steadily in-the-making. The spread of purity–pollution hierarchization is also only partial.

20. C.J. Fuller, 'Gods, Priests and Purity', in *Man*, No. 3, 1979.

    'Purity and pollution . . . define an *idiom* by which respect to Gods is shown' (p. 470). Concepts of purity–pollution are not exhausted by concepts of high and low status but are 'part of the conceptual apparatus of a highly developed religious tradition' (p. 473).

21. 'A caste society is characterised by hereditary groups ordered hier-archically, associated with particular marriage and kinship relations and often viewed as performing services for each other.' R. Thapar, 'Which One of Us are Aryans?', in *Seminar*, No. 364, December 1989, p. 17.

22. M. Klass, *Caste*, Philadelphia, 1980.

23. N. Bhattacharya, *The Great Agrarian Conquest*, forthcoming publication.

24. The sociological approach to the study of Hinduism owes one of its biggest debts to Weber, one of the first major thinkers to attempt a systematic investigation of the 'Hindu social system' and the evolution of Hinduism from ancient through medieval to current times. He looked at the orthodox and heterodox teachings of religious intellec-tuals, and sought to establish the general characteristics of the Indic religions. Weber spins a sociology out of three concepts – tradition, charisma, rationality. So he talks of three types of religious specialist, three modes of authority and three kinds of social action. He provided many useful and new sociological insights.

    But Weber did not aim to provide a definitive study of the Orient and its religion–culture. His researches were not presuppositionless but meant to illuminate and confirm what he already assumed – the uniqueness of Occidental rationalism, for which he had a clear line of explanation. The Orient was characterized, above all, by the absence of the 'spirit of capitalism' and explaining this absence was what Weber was most concerned about.

    Like the Romantics, Weber believed in an 'essential India' and in the 'unity of Indian culture–civilization'; a unity provided above all by the Brahminical belief-system. But unlike the Romantics he was sceptical of this essentialism surviving without grave disruption in the 'disenchanted world' of modernity. Though Weber was aware of popular Hinduism, he saw it as subordinated to overarching Brahminical beliefs of transmigration and karma and the caste system, which for him was an ubiquitous coherent whole. He was guilty of too much grand theorizing and too little empirical study. Since for him cultural change preceded and explained social change, the sources of cultural change had to be understood above all else. And this principle of change was pivoted on the question of the mentality of believers. As such it was non-verifiable.

Weber's is a study of how salvational strategies via the mentality of believers contributed to the promotion of rationalization processes, where rationalization was understood as disenchantment, specialization, knowledge accumulation. For Hinduism and the other Asian religions, Weber held that 'the world remained a great enchanted garden. . . . No path led from the magical religiosity . . . to a rational, methodical control of life. Nor did any path lead to that methodical control from the world accommodation of Confucianism, from the world-rejection of Buddhism, from the world conquest of Islam, or from the messianic expectations . . . of Judaism.' Thus Indian asceticism, unlike Calvinist Puritanism, was not an asceticism of work. M. Weber, *The Sociology of Religion*, London, p. 270.

Modern-day Weberians like Mann have followed Weber in generally seeing religion as a 'belief-system', and in assuming that for the Indian sub-continent: (a) caste was ubiquitous; (b) Hinduism is a singular religious system decisively shaped by a Brahminical contemplative soteriology; (c) that this soteriology, anchored by the caste system, has been the great 'normative pacifier' explaining India's continued vulnerability to outside political invasion, and its peculiar imperviousness to external cultural influence.

All these notions are eminently contestable. Mann's chapter on India and Hinduism in the first volume of his otherwise remarkable work, *The Sources of Social Power* is unsatisfactory.

Göran Therborn points out that Weber's sociology was born of the marriage of German historicism and Austrian marginalist economics, where the former was an idealist tendency promoting a notion of culture as above all a 'value concept'. G. Therborn, *Science, Class & Society*, London, 1980, pp. 279–83.

25. W. Halbfass, *India and Europe*, New York, 1988, p. 182.

'[W]e find no serious philosophical debate with Islam in traditional Hindu literature' (p. 182). There is only 'silence' and 'evasion'. Outsiders are neither a strong Other nor an inspiration.

'The "otherness" is a negative and abstract one; it does not contain any concrete cultural or religious challenges' (p. 187).

In the encounter between Islam and Hinduism, the major effort at mediation comes through Sufism, stronger in India than anywhere else that Islam has spread. Islam found it easier to engage in dialogue with non-Brahminic, Shramanic traditions than with Brahminism. The only major attempt (failed) at a philosophical synthesis of Islam and Brahminism comes from the initiative of the great Mughal ruler Akbar in his Din-e-Ilahi. British rule has far more dialogue with Brahminism and stresses its importance for the purpose of 'understanding Hinduism'.

26. Ibid. Halbfass distinguishes between traditional Hinduism and neo-Hinduism. 'What distinguishes Neo-Hinduism and Traditionalism are the different ways they appeal to the tradition, the structures they employ to inter-relate the indigenous and the foreign, and the degrees of receptivity vis-à-vis the West' (p. 220). Neo-Hinduism does much more reinterpretation and this is guided by Western models and values. It is striking that the major spokespersons on neo-Hinduism, Vivekananda, Aurobindo and Radhakrishnan, wrote primarily in English. Though Gandhi had neither a serious interest nor capability in philosophy, he felt compelled to philosophize since India's culture and identity were somehow supposed to be linked to its unique philosophy.

27. R. Thapar, 'Imagined Religious Communities?'

28. C.J. Fuller, *The Camphor Flame*, Delhi, 1992.

29. Ibid. Fuller's is a contemporary anthropological not historical study. He readily subscribes to the view that at its deepest level, where it embodies the unifying principle of Indian society–hierarchy–caste is pan-Indian. And he assumes that this has long been so. Fuller believes in a 'mainstream Hinduism' in which Brahminism is the single most important 'evaluative norm'. Bhakti is not an egalitarian deviation from it. It has the same quest for individual release–salvation but makes it more democratically available. It does not socially confront caste. It maintains the unequal guru–disciple relationship so common to mainstream Hinduism. Most of the founders of Bhakti sects and movements were ascetic renouncers, indicating its concurrence with traditional status values where the renouncer is evaluated higher than the Brahmin.

This is an interesting and provocative thesis. Certainly Bhakti has been incorporated over time in a more Brahminized Hinduism, itself undergoing a loosening–modification of its Brahminism. Whether Bhakti has always been like this is best left for historians to decide. The historian, Romila Thapar, has a much broader view of Bhakti, stressing its diversity of beliefs and practices. R. Thapar, 'Imagined Religion Communities'. Sudipra Kaviraj, the political scientist, sees Bhakti as the exception to mainstream forms of the Hindu–Muslim interface. S. Kaviraj, 'Religion, Politics and Modernity'.

30. Romila Thapar, ('Imagined Religious Communities'), is the most important representative of this school of interpretation.

'The position I would take is that there were Hindu religions (in the plural) using Hindu simply as a term that defines an area; and possibly up to a point defines the culture but not completely.' R. Thapar, 'Interpretations of Indian History', in G. Sen (ed.), *Perceiving India*, Delhi, 1993.

31. R. Thapar, 'Syndicated Moksha', in *Seminar*, No. 313, September, 1985. According to Thapar, Syndicated Hinduism draws largely on Gita, Vedantic thought and some aspects of the Dharmashastras, as well as from other sources.

32. See last sub-section of Chapter 3, 'Secularism as Tolerance'.

33. S. Radhakrishnan, *The Hindu View of Life*, p. 93.

34. R. Thapar, *Cultural Transaction and Early India*, Delhi, 1987, p. 15.

35. Currents in neo-Hinduism like the Arya Samaj, being a more Semitized form of Hinduism, have introduced a formalized system of conversion – the Shuddi or purification ceremony.

Proselytization is more a function of social factors than of doctrinal impulse. Which is why Indic religions have proselytized in their own fashion, while two revelatory religions have turned sharply inwards because of their distinctive histories – Judaism and Zoroastrianism. In the case of the latter, the strictures against conversion are so severe that the very survival of the Parsi–Zoroastrian community is at stake. There are fewer than 90,000 Parsis in the world today.

36. How can a traditional pluralism 'which does not involve any theory of consent or responsibility . . . be called even remotely democratic?' is the apt poser in S. Kaviraj, *Political Culture in Independent India*, seminar paper for the Indian Political Science Conference, Patiala, December 1978.

'Traditional Hinduism presupposes an irreducible cosmologically established inequality of human beings and a fundamentally hierarchical structure of society which leaves little room for the mutual recognition of free persons and their individual rights and choices.' W. Halbfass, *India and Europe*, pp. 410–11.

37. If the frame of mind this inspires among believers has its merits, it also has its demerits. Liberation theologies or indigenous equivalents remain alien to Brahminism with its authorization of varna and caste. But it is not alien to India. Ambedkar's Buddhism can be understood as an indigenous form of such liberation theology. See G. Omvedt, 'Hinduism, Social Inequality and the State', in D. Allen (ed.), *Religion and Political Conflict in South Asia*, Delhi, 1993.

Omvedt also points out that 'anti-Hinduization' movements, though widespread, tend to be invisible because they necessarily lack a single focus. They take a variety of forms – Dalit struggles, Veerashaivism, Sikhism, tribal movements, etc.

38. Javeed Alam has suggested to me that while Vivekananda, Aurobindo and Savarkar seek to effect a philosophical closure of sorts, Gandhi and Tagore are truer to this internal ecumenical philosophical tradition.

39. By the nineteenth century, European philosophy had been substantially secularized. 'True' philosophy was separate from religion and metaphysics. It was also open-ended. Not so for Indian philosophy. In the Hindu renaissance of the eighteenth and nineteenth centuries, even the earlier traditions of critical argumentation against religion and metaphysics were largely bypassed. Indian philosophy, with exceptions like Lokayata, contains finished doctrinal structures not open-endedly 'asking questions and pursuing knowledge'.

Of the ancient, enduring philosophies, Greek philosophy continues to be of far more contemporary relevance than Indian, undoubtedly because it is more secularly grounded. Ancient Greek religion had no notion of transcendence comparable to that in the Indic religions. See also D.P. Chattopadhyay, *What is Living and What is Dead in Indian Philosophy*.

40. W. Halbfass, *India and Europe*, p. 191.

Hinduism is 'all religions in one' not 'one religion among many'. Other religions accepting inter-religious differences of a fundamental kind may each claim to be the best. Philosophical Hinduism, especially in the hands of practitioners of neo-Hinduism, will simply not accept such fundamental differences. It therefore pushes not for any modern form of secular coexistence, nor for confrontation, but for an 'inter-religious understanding' on its *own* terms.

41. Sumit Sarkar has pointed out to me that the unity-in-diversity argument often endorses a hierarchical and ultimately Brahminized conception of unity. In Bengali there is the notion of *adhikari-bheda* or each caste, sect, religious community having its distinct norms (dharma) and niche in a hierarchical structure. Many religious intellectuals have played around with this perception, e.g. Ramakrishna and Rabrindran-ath Tagore in his Swadeshi phase. It was given a more philosophical cast by some writings of Vivekananda and Radhakrishnan. The 'composite culture' notion leans into this hierarchized conception of 'unity-in-diversity'.

42. Among proponents of neo-Hinduism there were also differences. For Vivekananda, the philosophical monism of Vedanta was decisive and the 'true' Brahmin remained his human ideal. For Radhakrishnan, Hinduism in its deepest sense was a 'feeling' beyond morality and metaphysics. For Gandhi, the essence of religion was morality and truth, though his understanding of the latter would undergo evolution. From an initial commitment to 'God is truth', he later committed himself to 'Truth is God'. He moved from a more personal notion of

the ultimate to a more impersonal one, closer to the Brahminical–philosophical tradition of belief in a Formless Essence or Cosmic Spirit – a non-embodied, all-pervasive consciousness beyond morality. This was Hinduism as the eternal, all-encompassing religion.

All three subscribed implicitly to notions of Hinduism's intrinsic, if unstated, religious superiority. All opposed conversion (though for different reasons), indicating their deep unease with modern notions of individual rights. Only Gandhi, the most self-questioning of the three, would seriously try to move away from his earlier position when he believed that 'Hinduism was the most tolerant of all religions' and that 'what of substance is contained in any other religion is to be found in Hinduism' to a more tortured self-realization that such claims were incompatible with any genuine notion of the equality of all religions. Looking for a common essence to all religions, Gandhi would find it in his constructions of truth and non-violence. But his understanding of these terms would remain imprisoned within the idiom of Hinduism. Nonetheless, with genuine sensitivity, Gandhi would say, 'Tolerance may imply a gratuitous assumption of the inferiority of other faiths to one's own and respect suggest a sense of patronizing whereas ahimsa teaches us to entertain the same respect for the religious faith of others as we accord to our own.' M. Gandhi, *Collected Works XLIV*, Ahmedabad, 1964, p. 166.

According to one biographer, after 1930 Gandhi forswore any statement that might suggest the superiority of Hinduism. J.F. Jordens, 'Gandhi and Religious Pluralism', in H.G. Coward (ed.), *Modern Indian Responses to Religious Pluralism*, New York, 1987.

43. G. Pandey, 'Who of Us are Hindus?', in G. Pandey (ed.), *Hindu and Others*, Delhi, 1993.

44. V.D. Savarkar, *Hindutva, Who is Hindu?*, Bombay, 1969. For Savarkar, Hinduism is the -ism of Hindus and applies to all the religions of the land of Hindus (e.g. Sikhism, Jainism, Buddhism), where a Hindu is defined as one whose holyland and fatherland is the same – Hindustan.

45. M.S. Golwalkar, *We or Our Nationhood Defined*, Nagpur, 1966.

46. Gandhi and Vivekananda both believed that a distinctive ethos constituted the essence of Hinduism.

Whereas the Hindu cultural right, e.g. the RSS, says it 'respects' Muslims because they were originally Hindus, i.e. *in spite* of their adherence to Islam, Gandhi respected Muslims *because* he respected Islam. At the same time, the source of Gandhi's respect was more his *abstract* commitment to, and respect for, all religions. When he retreated from the abstract to the concrete, Gandhi's observations about Muslims tended to fall into stereotypes. One extreme example of this tendency was his reference to the Muslim as a bully, at the time of the Moplah rebellion in Malabar in the 1920s.

47. R. Williams, *Resources of Hope*, London, 1989. See chapter on 'The Idea of a Common Culture'. Also R. Williams, *Culture*, London, 1981.

48. Bhiku T. Parekh is Professor of Political Science, University of Hull; T.N. Madan is Professor of Sociology at the Indian Institute of Economic Growth, New Delhi. Ashis Nandy is Senior Fellow at the Centre for the Study of Developing Societies, New Delhi.

49. See Chapter 3.

50. T.N. Madan, *Non-Renunciation: Themes and Interpretations of Hindu Culture*, Delhi, 1987.

   In this cultural–civilizational continuity, the principle of tradition is the principle of continuity, so, for Madan, '[m]odernity must be defined in relation to, and not in denial of tradition.' T.N. Madan, *Tradition and Modernity in the Sociology of D.P. Mukherjhee*, Lucknow, 1977, p. 23.

   As for secularism in India, 'in traditional or tradition-haunted societies they can only mean conversion and the loss of one's culture, and if you like, loss of one's soul.' T.N. Madan, 'Secularism in Its Place', in *Journal of Asian Studies*, Vol. 46, No. 4, November 1987, p. 754.

51. B.T. Parekh, 'Nehru and the National Philosophy of India', in *Economic and Political Weekly*, 5 January 1991, p. 39.

52. *Non-Renunciation*. The absence of this Brahminical slant in Nandy must partly explain the contrast in his and Madan's positions regarding the issue of caste reservations in the Mandal Report. Madan opposes Mandal, Nandy has rightly and courageously supported it.

53. T.N. Madan, 'Religious Ideology in a Plural Society: The Muslims and Hindus of Kashmir', in T.N. Madan (ed.), *Muslim Communities of South Asia*, Delhi, 1989; *Non-Renunciation, Family and Kingship*, Delhi, 1989; the Introduction in T.N. Madan (ed.), *Religion in India*, Delhi, 1991. From these studies Madan is convinced that peaceful coexistence of Hindus and Muslims, at least in Kashmir, is only possible by economic interdependence and functionality, political pragmatism and ideological compromise.

54. From the mimeograph of T.N. Madan's inaugural public lecture, 'There's Tricks i' th' World: Whither Indian Secularism?' at the International Conference on Religion, Identity and Politics: India in a Comparative Perspective, held at the University of Hull, 24–26 October, 1991. Also published as 'Whither Indian Secularism?', in *Modern Asian Studies*, Vol. 27, 1993, p. 667.

55. Madan endorses the views of Peter Berger and David Martin. (P. Berger, *The Social Reality of Religion*, London, 1973, and D. Martin, *A General Theory of Secularization*, Oxford, 1978). See 'Whither Indian Secularism?'

56. T.N. Madan, 'Whither Indian Secularism?', p. 669.

57. Madan is too influenced by Berger's understanding of Protestantism, individualism and secularization.

58. T.N. Madan, 'Whither Indian Secularism?'

59. Ibid.

60. Ibid, p. 695.

61. In a fine critique of Madan, André Beteille stresses the importance of negotiating the 'terms of coexistence' between the secular and the religious. He is not for dispensing with either. Does Madan really oppose the secularization of social institutions, e.g. universities, firms, administrative bodies? Does he really endorse the totalizations of religion? Is not this totalization more the ideal of the religious intellectual than a fact on the ground? Do not 'the totalising aims to which Madan has referred vary greatly from one religion to another, and within the same religious tradition; from one historical phase to the other'? A. Beteille, 'Secularism and Intellectuals', in *Economic and Political Weekly*, 5 March, 1994, p. 565.

Beteille also points out that secular institutions cannot show 'equal respect to all religions' by accommodating them equally or on an unlimited basis. This is simply unworkable.

In his reply, Madan clearly gives ground. He clarifies that he is attacking those secularists who believe religion is fake and evil. He also admits to overstating 'the holistic character of traditional religions'. But it was in the name of this holism that he attacked secularists and the standard notion of secularism, and not just the minuscule group who feel religion is fake or evil. T.N. Madan, 'Secularism and the Intellectuals', in *Economic and Political Weekly*, 30 April 1994.

62. Meera Nanda has called this posture of Nandy a neo-populism which is as old as modernity itself. Indeed, it is *only* as old as modernity. See her fine critique, M. Nanda, 'Is Modern Science a Western, Patriarchal Myth? A Critique of Populist Orthodoxy' in *South Asia Bulletin*, Vol. XI, Nos 1–2, 1991.

63. A. Nandy, 'Culture, State and the Rediscovery of Indian Politics', in *Economic and Political Weekly*, 8 December 1984. For a recent and confused attempt to deal with the various meanings of culture, see A. Nandy, 'Culture as Resistance', in *Times of India*, 10 December 1994. It highlights once again Nandy's determination to promote a notion of culture that is definitionally anti-modern, e.g. culture is itself a resistance escaping the discourse of resistance allowed by modernity.

See also the solid critique of the culturological approaches of anti-modernists by S. Joseph, 'Indigenous Social Science Project', in *Economic and Political Weekly*, 13 April 1991 and 'Culture and Political Analysis in India', in *Social Scientist*, October–November 1991.

64. A. Nandy, *At the Edge of Psychology*, Delhi, 1980.

65. Ibid., p. 113.

66. There are universal core values and they are found in those special, large accommodative traditional cultures we can call civilizations. What is distinctive about civilizations is how they synthesize the package containing these universal core values. See A. Nandy, *Traditions, Tyranny and Utopias*, Delhi, 1987.

   'All civilizations share some basic values and such cultural traditions as derive from man's biological self and social experience. The distinctiveness of a complex civilization lies not in the uniqueness of its values but in the gestalt which it imposes on these values and in the weights it assigns to its different values and sub-traditions' (p. 22).

   A culture also has a definite patterning. So cultural change operates within certain essentialist constraints. 'A culture is not a grocery store.... A culture is an interconnected whole with some strong interconnections and some weak.... Within it you have some options only if yet others are not exercised' (p. 120).

   Given this patterned and essentialist notion of culture, Nandy handles issues of cultural contestation *within* a tradition in expected ways which abstract from issues of power and ideology. Such tensions simply represent 'a dialectic between the classical and the folk, the past and the present, the dead and living'. A. Nandy, 'Culture, State and the Rediscovery of Indian Politics'. Both cultural conflicts and social tensions are underplayed in the interests of presenting a more or less harmonious picture of traditional societies.

67. A. Nandy, 'Cultural Frames for Transformative Politics: A Credo', in B.T. Parekh and T. Pantham (eds), *Political Discourse*, Delhi, 1987, p. 243.

68. For the immortalizer of religion, the religious consciousness is not so much a historical form of consciousness as an ineradicable element in the structure of consciousness. It is ineffable not because of the inescapable limitations in our cognitive powers concerning the workings of the mind, but because of its 'core' location in the psyche.

69. A. Nandy, 'The Politics of Application and Social Relevance in Contemporary Psychology', in U. Baxi and B.T. Parekh (eds), *Crisis and Change in Contemporary India*, Delhi, 1995.

   Personality encompasses identity but is not equivalent to it. Efforts to understand personality owe much to the insights of both the psychoanalytical and cognitive approaches to identity and personality formation. The psychoanalytical approach stresses 'objects of authority', the 'arational' roots of identity fixation and the 'fixity' of identities. It is more determinist than the cognitive approach, emphasizing the key role of typical authority figures in a typical family set-up, which in turn may be taken to express the typicality of the cultures in which such families are embedded. The psychoanalytical tradition has significant differences concerning how much importance to give to cognitive

217

understandings of personality and identity formation, and how much flexibility there is in personality construction. In the cognitive approach the family will not be so central a mediating link between culture/society and the personality, nor will the 'typicality' of a family set-up be so readily assumed.

The more determinist currents within psychoanalytically influenced psychology gravitate towards more determinist, essentialist and reductionist views about the relationship between culture/society and personality. For Nandy, there are distinctive personality configurations for distinctive cultures, and an Indian self which reveals its distinctiveness, e.g. non-violent ways of resisting, in crisis situations. For the distinctive Indian self to exist there has to be the distinctive Indian family cutting across such social categories as caste or class. So the gender division becomes all-important in personality formation and there will be a distinctive Indian way in which the Indian individual objectifies his or her relation, especially to the mother.

70. A. Nandy, *The Intimate Enemy*, Delhi, 1983. His characterization of critical modernism borders on caricature. He sees the range of such criticality as extremely limited. He claims it doesn't challenge the epistemology of science, when in fact there is an extremely lively dispute about what it is, how special and useful it is. Critical modernists are supposed to take the nation-states system for granted. What does this mean? Are modernists united in lauding it or believing it to be irreplaceable? Critical modernists are not supposed to have any serious problems with the urban–industrial vision and argue primarily about who should be the desirable elites! See 'Cultural Frames for a Transformative Politics: A Credo'.

71. A. Nandy, *At the Edge of Psychology*.

72. For a more thoughtful conceptual use of the distinction between religion-as-ideology and religion-as-faith, see R. Bharucha, *The Question of Faith*, 'Tracts for the Times' No. 3, Delhi, 1993.

73. A. Nandy, 'The Politics of Secularism and the Recovery of Religious Tolerance', in *Mirrors of Violence*, Delhi, 1990, p. 70.

74. While Nandy does not budge from a determinist notion of the religion–culture link, he does occasionally adopt an approach to cultural change that does not square with the essentialism of most of his formulations concerning culture. Interestingly, this surfaces most clearly when he deals with Gandhi's intervention into Hinduism and Indian cultural anti-colonialism. Nandy wants to appropriate Gandhi as a 'critical traditionalist' or 'critical insider'. Gandhi, says Nandy, tries to make central to Hinduism what was earlier peripheral. If this claim is true (which is disputable), then it represents an attempt at phenomenal religious or cultural upheaval. Hence a certain unease on Nandy's part with the adequacy of labelling Gandhi a 'critical

traditionalist'. Since Gandhi's dramatic intervention is to be seen as expressive of the internal resources for change possessed by Indian culture, this culture has to be redefined in the direction of greater flexibility. A cultural situation is now described as much more of a process. 'The two processes of inflow and outflow determine at a given point of time, Indian culture, rather than a rigidly defined set of practices or products surviving from the society's past.' *Traditions, Tyranny and Utopias*, p. 153.

75. 'The Politics of Secularism and the Recovery of Religious Tolerance', p. 70.

76. Ibid.

77. R. Bhargava, 'Objective Significance in Critical Theory', in B.T. Parekh and T. Pantham (eds), *Political Discourse.*

Myth transforms a world of facts into pure signs. It invests nature with properties belonging only to humanity. So the confrontation of science with nature was necessarily 'intercepted' by the confrontation of science and myth. Any attempt at an unbalanced (exaggerated) defence of the value of myth, such as Nandy's, has to launch an unbalanced attack on science.

Nandy would heartily endorse Clifford Geertz's mistaken claim that 'the ideologization of religion begins when the certainty of faith totters.' The ideology of religion was always there in pre-modernity when faith was not tottering. In the absence of competing ideologies and in the absence of serious doubt about religion's totalizing claims, the ideological dimension of religion was rarely seen as such. But it is also true that in modernity the ideological dimension of religion can become more important. There is a 'thinning' of the religious consciousness which enables mass mobilization through sharing of a few 'thinned' beliefs. This is not the replacement of faith by ideology, but a transformation of the nature of faith (and ideology), of the religious consciousness itself.

78. The advance of secularism here means some people or institutions (the state) push it more strongly, not that the ideology becomes more successful in securing adherents. For Nandy, as secularization advances in late modernity, the ideology of secularism becomes less successful, with people turning to religious faith to find meaning.

79. 'The Politics of Secularism and the Recovery of Religious Tolerance', p. 69.

80. S. Kaviraj, 'On the Discourse of Secularism', in B. Chakrabarty (ed.), *Secularism and Indian Polity*, New Delhi, 1990.

81. K. Kumar, 'Secularism: Its Politics and Pedagogy', in *Economic and Political Weekly*, 4 November 1989.

82. Ibid., p. 2476.

83. 'The Politics of Secularism and the Recovery of Religious Tolerance',

p. 90. Apparently, secularism and reasonable notions of progress and modernity cannot go hand in hand with rejection of justifications for domination!

84. Since specific states have been ethnophobic and ethnocidal, Nandy does not hesitate to claim that secularism is definitionally 'ethnophobic' and 'frequently ethnocidal'. Ibid.

The secular state ignores the difference between good and bad religion. Secularism limits the democratic process because it separates culture from politics, thereby 'truncating the political personality of the citizen'. Secularists are a sad lot who can be classified as follows: (a) secularists as elite modernisers; (b) innocent secularists who are what they are on ideological and moral grounds; (c) secularists as social climbers wanting to be au fait with the modern world; (d) the *genuine* secularists who cynically manipulate religion for expedient, secular purposes. Ibid.

Once again, the classification scheme simply comes out of Nandy's head and corresponds to a typology of character traits organized by him as psychologist–social critic.

85. Ibid.

86. Final authority in matters of inter- and intra-religious conflicts should rest with the appropriate religious authorities and not with the secular state.

87. Hans Mol and Georg Simmel would both meet with Nandy's approval since they hold that modern individualist rationalism makes the self 'brittle', weakening its sense of 'wholeness'. See sub-section on 'Religion in Modernity' in Chapter 3.

88. A. Nandy, 'Culture, State and the Rediscovery of Indian Politics', A. Nandy, 'Counter-Statement on Humanistic Temper', in *Mainstream*, 10 October 1981.

89. Life is about connectedness since death is the end of connectedness. The search for connectedness is what the principle of transcendence is about. As such, it is innate to humanness, but its forms are variable. Religion is but one form, and modern, more secularized culture also copes, albeit in different ways, with the issue of transcendence. What the best ways of dealing with it are is a question that is answered historically, not eternally, i.e. always through religion. See Z. Bauman, *Mortality, Immortality and Other Life Strategies*, Oxford, 1992.

90. Inter-faith dialogue is usually something undertaken by the most liberal elements among religious elites or intellectuals. The dialogue rarely goes beyond the level of platitudes – 'different paths to a common quest' etc. For the sake of harmony and ecumenism, the issue of conversion is usually skirted, for any aggressive defence of the importance and the right to convert would raise matters threatening such artificially constructed ecumenism–tolerance. The advocates of

neo-Hinduism like Gandhi, who had high hopes for what inter-faith dialogue can achieve, cannot accept a strong defence of the right or necessity to religiously convert. To convert is to convince, which demands shared agreement on norms of right and wrong, truth and falsehood. The impossibility of inter-faith dialogue ever arriving at such shared norms means the dialogue is confined to courtesies, to search for similarities in doctrinal meaning, listening to and respecting differences, but rarely involves vigorous argument, contestation, discussion or strong judgements. There is no democratic way of reaching a higher synthesis, for *democratic* dialogue means reasoned argument based on shared norms of judgement. The end result of such inter-faith dialogue may be a better understanding by participants of other faiths, and proclamations of overall harmony, but it invariably leaves the bulk of believers of any particular religion comfortably untouched.

91. 'The Politics of Secularism and the Recovery of Religious Tolerance'; 'Cultural Frames for Transformative Politics: A Credo'.

92. All that is required to sustain the 'authentic innocence' of a critical traditionality, Nandy feels, is to update the theories of evil/oppression that all major religions–cultures have. Such cultures have a language of continuity in which change is incorporated within a larger framework of continuity, which Nandy, for one, feels is desirable. There is a language of spiritualism containing idioms concerning oppression and its analysis. (It would be astonishing if religious systems didn't contain such idioms!) There is the language of self, concerned with matters of self-control, self-realization, power over the self. Nandy believes these languages provide enough resources to cope with life today and to create an adequate and meaningful existence.

93. Individualism erodes patriarchy. Nandy, who opposes modern individualism, has always sought to make light of patriarchy. One of the most important gains of modernity is how gender discourse, especially in recent times, has transformed notions of the good and desirable, and of acceptable social roles, beyond the ken of traditional societies.

See Nandy's convoluted attempt to condemn sati, yet attack modern feminism by defending the subtlety of the philosophy of sati, in A. Nandy, 'The Human Factor', in *Illustrated Weekly*, 13 March 1988.

94. 'Cultural frames for Transformative Politics: A Credo'.

For black anti-racists, as for anti-caste Dalits, the inversion of traditional values associated with racism and casteism has never been the ultimate goal, for the battle is not in the mind alone, and such inversion is itself a defensive posture. This inversion is but a means of affirmation and mobilization to eradicate racism and casteism as objective structures of oppression. Eventually there should no longer be the necessity for such an inversion. Eradicating racism and casteism are modern goals related to modern notions of equality. No wonder

Nandy is uneasy about this and supports the approach of Gandhi to caste rather than that of the fully modernist Ambedkar, who sought to abolish caste, not reform it. That Ambedkar, rather than Gandhi, is the more important figure for Indian Dalits does constitute a minor source of embarrassment for Nandy's self-positioning as an articulator of authentic Indian aspirations.

Nor is Nandy much interested in looking at the sources of tolerance in modernity itself, to see if they can better deal with modern-day intolerances.

95. Bhiku T. Parekh has some sense of the difficulties but does not delve seriously into the issue. B.T. Parekh, 'Nehru and the National Philosophy of India'.

96. See note 90.

97. C. Taylor; oral seminar presentation at Jawaharlal Nehru University, Delhi, autumn 1993.

98. It is only in modernity that education, leisure and health become 'basic needs'. It is only in our times that poverty becomes eliminable; that crime, sickness and madness become 'correctable', and, for better and worse, there emerge 'sequestrating' institutions for them. A. Giddens, *Modernity and Self-Identity*, Oxford, 1991. The authentic Indian masses seem to have no problems in welcoming and visiting good hospitals which do not practise only indigenous medicine.

99. Nandy has a baseless fear. If modernity is the only fate for India then the modernizer–Westerner becomes the privileged one who best knows India's future, as well as its past, since the West has been through that past (of tradition). This justifies an 'imperialism of categories' whereby the modern Westerner or its Indian clone seeks to understand India's past, present and future. A. Nandy, 'Self as a Political Concept', in P.C. Chatterjee (ed.), *Self-Images, Identity and Nationality*, Shimla, 1989.

India is pursuing its *own* form of modernity. The West holds no mirror to its past or future. Indeed, best Indian political science has always been preoccupied with the distinctiveness and peculiarities of the Indian political system, despite the Western origin of its democracy. Moreover, good conceptual tools, regardless of origins, can survive intelligent transfer and use elsewhere. The problematicity of applying 'Western' analytical categories is paralleled by the problematicity of applying 'Indian' analytical categories to India.

Kamal Chenoy has suggested to me that the Nandy type of indigenist anti-modernism enjoys popularity in Western academic circles partly because it constitutes an inverted form of privileging the West. By rejecting the idea that India has left traditional society behind and is pursuing its own kind of modernity, it reinforces the standard Western prejudices of India today as indeed a pre-modern society which can only either go its pre-modern way or ape the West. A *critical Indian* modernity is ruled out, to the comfort of old-fashioned Western conservatism.

100. In a pre-modern, timeless and repetitive world, ahistorical remedies can apply; the reinterpretation of myth to serve purposes of careful, slow and limited reform may work. It cannot be anywhere near adequate to cope with contemporary India's problems. Nandy's refusal to see this means he has immunized himself in his own mind against reasoned refutation. Either his myths are more plausible for the reconstruction of a more humane Indian society, or someone else's are. But since his audience both at home and in the West is influenced by reasoned argument, Nandy will, perforce, resort to such forms of logical discourse, even if he will not be bound by its conventions of propriety and judgement. *The Intimate Enemy.*

101. Parekh's understanding of Gandhi is superior to that of Nandy. Where Nandy sees him as a critical traditionalist, Parekh, more cautiously if still mistakenly, sees him straddling critical traditionality and critical modernity but closer to the first. He sees Gandhi's thrust as, in many ways, a 'secularized, activist Brahminism', whereas Nandy strongly underplays the influence of Brahminism on Gandhi. What for Parekh is a weakness is for Nandy (given his methodology) a strength. Gandhi sees groups as only a collection of individuals and therefore understands the dynamics of individual change as unproblematically applicable to the dynamics of group change. Self-improvement is the route to group improvement. Parekh is more sensitive to the failure, not of Gandhi, but of Gandhiism. Finally, Parekh is not so sanguine about the ahistorical Gandhi, especially in his perception of the Hindu–Muslim problem. 'A view of history that left out history itself could hardly be expected to unite those haunted by it.' B.T. Parekh, *Gandhi's Political Philosophy,* London, 1989, p. 190.

    Hind Swaraj, which Gandhi wrote in 1909 expressing his vision for India and which he never repudiated, is the most systematised expression of his anti-modernism. That Gandhi had an explicit anti-modern project does not make him a non-modern.

102. J. Grant, 'I Feel Therefore I Am: A Critique of Female Experience as the Basis for a Feminist Epistemology', in *Women and Politics,* Vol. 7, No. 3, 1987, p. 113.

103. Nandy's neo-Gandhianism means he shares his mentor's view of what constitutes proper justice. Customary law is said to be superior to modern law because the litigant is treated not as a 'passive object' but as an individual in a given community. Judgement of the litigant's behaviour should aim, above all, at promoting introspection and, therefore, self-correction. This is a conception of justice not as fairness but, above all, as a contributor to self-mastery.

104. W. Kymlicka, *Liberalism, Community and Culture*, Oxford, 1989; C. Gould, *Rethinking Democracy*, Cambridge, 1988; G. Mahajan, 'Cultural Embodiment and Histories', in U. Baxi and B.T. Parekh (eds), *Crisis and Change in Contemporary India.*

105. P. Chatterjee, 'Secularism and Tolerance' in *Economic and Political Weekly*, 9 July 1994.

106. I am grateful to Romila Thapar, Sumit Guha, Ravindar Kumar, Aijaz Ahmad, Prakash Upadhyay, Joya Chatterjee and Sumit Sarkar for sharing with me their views about the Subaltern Studies project. They have greatly enriched my own understanding. Aijaz Ahmad promises a major critique of Subaltern Studies in his forthcoming work on nationalism. For some illuminating observations on Subaltern Studies see his *In Theory*, London, 1992. Sumit Sarkar's various critiques of the Subaltern Studies School are simply the best and most comprehensive we have today. In addition to the logical force of his arguments, Sarkar's views have the additional authority of being the first and most sustained 'internalist' critique. He was one of the major figures and a former member of the editorial team. Anyone familiar with Sarkar's various writings on this subject will recognize the measure of my indebtedness to him. See S. Sarkar, 'An Anti-Secularist Critique of Hindutva', in *Germinal*, Journal of the Department of Germanic and Romantic Studies, Jawaharlal Nehru University, Vol. I, 1994; 'Orientalism Revisited: Saidian Frameworks in the Writing of Modern Indian History', in *Oxford Literary Review*, Vol. 16, Nos. 1–2, 1994; 'Subaltern Studies: Historiography and Thompsonian Social History', publication forthcoming.

   Ramchandra Guha, a contributor to the volume series of the Subaltern Studies Group, has recently come out with a scathing review of its latest volume (VIII). He, too, criticizes the nature of the theoretical turn undertaken by some of the key figures in the Group. See R. Guha, 'Subaltern and Bhadralok Studies', in *Economic and Political Weekly*, 19 August 1995. With reference to G. Prakash's 'Subaltern Studies as Post-colonial Criticism', in *American Historical Review*, December 1994, R. Guha correctly points out that to call Subaltern Studies 'criticism' is already to relocate its thrust from what its earlier intentions were. As for it being 'post-colonial' criticism, this is strange indeed since far and away most of the essays in the eight volumes of Subaltern Studies deal with the colonial and pre-colonial period.

107. See Edward Said's Foreword and Gayatri Chakravorthy Spivak's Introduction in *Selected Subaltern Studies*, New York and Oxford, 1988.

108. D. Chakrabarty, 'Marx after Marxism: Subaltern Histories and the Question of Difference', in *Polygraph*, Vol. 6/7, 1993; 'Radical Histories and Question of Enlightenment Rationalism: Some Recent Critiques

of Subaltern Studies', in *Economic and Political Weekly*, 8 April 1995. G. Prakash, 'Writing Post-Orientalist Histories of the Third World: Perspectives from Indian Historiography', in *Comparative Studies in Society and History*, Vol. 32, 1990; 'Can the Subaltern Ride? A Reply to O'Hanlon and Washbrook', in *Comparative Studies in Society and History*, Vol. 34, 1992.

109. This is for a number of reasons. For one thing there has always been a strong empiricist tradition among British historians either hostile to theory or more careful to integrate it within existing patterns of historiography. For another, on colonial India, the Cambridge School has had wide influence. Also, the two key British contributors to the Subaltern Studies series, David Hardiman and David Arnold, have carried on with their specific enquiries without being seduced by the Group's theoretical pretensions. Furthermore, the politics of British academia have been much more resistant to multi-culturalist pressures, whether of the more fashionable or more noteworthy kind. There has been nothing like the kind of multiple, short-term courses that American students enrol for and which encourage neatly packaged histories of other countries for quick academic consumption.

110. Neo-colonial historiography refers to the Namierite Cambridge School, which saw Indian nationalism as a 'learning process' for native elites who through principles of 'competition' and 'representation' fitted into a political process built by the British Raj. Indian nationalism here was the 'sign board of elite groups' with the entry of the masses taking place only when the 1935 Act enlarged the electorate. Liberal-nationalist historiography, according to Guha, unproblematically accepted the idea of a Congress eventually establishing its hegemony over the National Movement, thus whitewashing the inadequacies and failures of the indigenous bourgeoisie in whose interest this hegemony was supposedly exercised. Conventional Marxist historiography emphasized economic privations as the source of peasant and labour struggles and the importance of the presence or absence of Left leadership/organization.

In all cases the subaltern in its own right was ignored, as was its contribution to the making of the Indian nation. Similarly, the relationship between elite and subalterns or 'leaders' and 'led' was variously seen as manipulative, representative or charismatic.

111. S. Sarkar, 'Subaltern Studies.' Sarkar points out how Subaltern Studies broke from Gramsci's six-point 'methodological criteria', which was supposed to be Guha's guiding ideal. Gramsci gave variant meanings to the notion of 'subaltern autonomy', emphasizing interpenetration between elites and subalterns in contrast to the Subaltern Studies Group's increasing emphasis on the distinctiveness and separateness of subaltern autonomy. Gramsci's subaltern groups were very much

imbricated in wider socio-economic relationships, changes in which would affect the very construction of subaltern groups themselves.

Only rarely did Subaltern Studies contributors attempt to study such wider connections. Mostly, the various micro-studies fell into a fairly set pattern of analysis – exploring the conditions of oppression and exploitation, locating the triggers of rebellion or the 'factors of dislocation'; detailing the cultural and symbolic challenges to existing signs of authority and the ways in which new symbols were created, or older ones invested with newer meanings, for the purposes of organization and mobilization. See R. O'Hanlon, 'Recovering the Subject: Subaltern Studies and Histories of Resistance in Colonial South Asia', in *Modern Asian Studies*, Vol. 22, No. 1, 1988. In this critique, O'Hanlon, influenced by Foucauldian notions of power and deconstructionism, seems determined to rescue Subaltern Studies from its earlier incarnations, i.e. from its Marxist residues and its tendency, in classical liberal-humanist fashion, to treat an insufficiently 'decentred' subaltern as subject in its own right. By 1992, in a critique co-authored with D. Washbrook, 'After Orientalism: Culture, Criticism and Politics in the Third World', in *Comparative Studies in Society and History*, Vol. 34, O'Hanlon appears disillusioned with post-modernism and therefore more critical of the later theoretical turn of Subaltern Studies. But she was not wrong in earlier (1988) discerning post-modernist 'potentialities'.

112. R. Guha, 'On Some Aspects of the Historiography of Colonial India', in R. Guha (ed.), *Subaltern Studies, Vol. I,* Delhi, 1982.

113. S. Sarkar, *'Popular' Movements and 'Middle Class' Leadership in Late Colonial India,* S.G. Deuskar Lectures, Calcutta, 1980.

114. Ibid. For Guha, the subaltern could include rural gentry, impoverished landlords, rich and upper-middle peasants. Guha's determination to reject interest-based aggregation meant he could seriously address neither problems concerning the heterogeneity of the peasantry or those large-scale mobilizations in which different sections of the peasantry come together for different reasons, or clash and go their separate ways; nor how urban elites and the Congress could indirectly link with various sections of the peasantry in ways that went beyond simple domination to build an assemblage of struggles against colonial rule. See I. Habib, *Theories of Social Change in South Asia,* The Nizmul Karim Memorial Lecture, Dhaka, 1986; Also, L.S. Vishwanath, 'Peasant Movements in Colonial India: An Examination of Some Conceptual Frameworks', in *Economic and Political Weekly,* 13 January 1990.

Ultimately this inability to transcend the limitations of its concept of 'subaltern autonomy' so as to reconstruct a better history of the National Movement was to lead not a few Subalternists to reinstitute Gandhi as the central inspirational figure of the Nationalist Movement.

What began as an attempt to attack elite nationalist historiography and to explain the absence of a social revolution (for which failure Gandhi would surely have to suffer some indictment) ended up with the restoration of the 'iconic figure of official nationalism', Gandhi, by Guha's theoretical heirs, this time as the signifier of subaltern codes of resistance. See S. Sarkar, 'Orientalism Revisited . . .', and 'Subaltern Studies'.

115. See his highly structuralist attempt to define six stages – negations, ambiguity, modality, solidarity, transmission, territoriality – in *Elementary Aspects of Peasant Insurgency in Colonial India*, Delhi, 1983.

116. Studies of the urban working class have been conspicuous by their rarity. Even less than the peasant would they have lent themselves to Guha's particular typology of progression of consciousness.

117. P. Robb, 'New Directions in South Asian History', in *South Asian Research*, Vol. 7, No. 2, November 1987; C.A. Bayly, 'Rallying Around the Subaltern', in *Journal of Peasant Studies*, Vol. 16, No. 1, October 1988. 'What appears to distinguish the Subalterns from their predecessors and co-workers in the field of popular and rural history is a theoretical device, the term "subaltern" itself and a populist idiom' (p. 112). Bayly believes that a calmer and more authoritative historical hindsight will evaluate Subaltern Studies as nothing more than a 'vignette' in the intellectual history of modern Indian historiography.

118. Ravindar Kumar, one of the most respected historians of modern India, has suggested (privately) that the paradigm shift launched by Irfan Habib's own seminal works focusing on the centrality of production relations has been, theoretically speaking, far and away the most influential for Indian historiography; much more so than Subaltern Studies. But neither Habib nor anyone else brought together under one rubric such a large body of undoubtedly talented scholars producing such a range of good scholarly work.

119. For one of the best critiques of *Orientalism* anywhere, see the essay by Aijaz Ahmad, 'Orientalism and After: Ambivalence and Metropolitan Location in the Work of Edward Said', in A. Ahmad, *In Theory*. Ahmad's observations here are particularly pertinent to explaining why Said should have seen Subaltern Studies as representative of the kind of intellectual alignments he was looking for.

120. In the famous Foreword (see note 107) Said casually states that the British held India for three hundred years. No less!

121. P. Chatterjee, 'More on Modes of Power and the Peasantry', in R. Guha (ed.), *Subaltern Studies, Vol. II*, Delhi, 1983. I have relied heavily here on S. Sarkar, 'Subaltern Studies'.

122. S. Sarkar, 'Subaltern Studies'. Another article by Chatterjee, 'For an Indian History of Peasant Struggle', in *Social Scientist*, No.11, November 1988, was noteworthy for its casual denigration of Indian histori-

ography for being state-centric. Chatterjee emphasized more strongly the idea of 'two domains', related but nonetheless resolutely distinct. Now the 'single unifying idea which gives to peasant insurgency its fundamental social character ... is the notion of community' (p. 10). Publication of this article in a journal so closely associated with the CPM indicated some sense still of self-affiliation with the Marxist Left, although the article carried an implied critique of Enlightenment modernity.

123. R. O'Hanlon and D. Washbrook, 'After Orientalism', p. 141.
124. E. Said, 'Foreword', p. vi.
125. S. Sarkar, 'Subaltern Studies'.
126. D. Chakrabarty, 'Radical Histories and Question of Enlightenment Rationalism'. The article indicates yet again how close the post-modernist can get to the anti-modernist positions of someone like Nandy. An article whose title would suggest that a systematic rebuttal of 'recent critiques of Subaltern Studies' is in store does nothing of the sort. Sumit Sarkar is mentioned by name as one such critic but his recent writings elaborating his views are not even addressed. Instead, a much earlier writing is cited in order to criticize Sarkar's approach to religion. Apart from this, there is a general broadside of a by now very conventional kind against modernists and 'hyper rationalism'.
127. Ibid., p. 757.
128. Ibid.
129. S. Sarkar, 'Subaltern Studies'.
130. Ibid. In Vols I and II, all fourteen essays focused on subaltern groups. In Vols VII and VIII, only three out of eleven do so and this includes Terence Ranger's article on Africa. Ramchandra Guha ('Subaltern and Bhadralok Studies'), makes the same point and calls this trend, rather aptly, 'post-Subaltern Studies', of which he sees Chatterjee's latest book, *The Nation and Its Fragments: Colonial and Post-colonial Histories*, Delhi, 1994, as emblematic. A study of Bengali intellectual life is here passed off as 'histories'. Subaltern Studies has moved from what Guha, following the social historian Hans Medick, calls 'history-as-craft' to 'writing-desk history'. Field study, the archives, law courts, police stations and newspaper offices are being abandoned for the library.
131. P. Chatterjee, 'Secularism and Tolerance' (see note 105); *The Nation and Its Fragments* (see note 130).
132. S. Sarkar, 'Subaltern Studies'. Sarkar points out that even while elevating struggle by protagonists within the 'inner domain', Chatterjee does not take up the struggle against indigenous patriarchy or say anything about the rich history of anti-caste movements of Periyar, Phule and Ambedkar in his long chapter 'The Nation and Its Out-castes'. Similarly, neither workers nor capitalists constitute 'fragments'

of the 'Indian nation' worthy enough to be given the independent attention he otherwise gives to women, peasants, outcastes.

133. After independence, though the Indian state insisted on reforming Hindu codes regarding divorce, marriage, inheritance rights for women, custody of children, adoption, etc, i.e. family-related laws and their impact on women, it did not set up a Common or Uniform Civil Code. Muslims would still be ruled by Muslim Personal Law, in effect by various Qur'anic interpretations of the Sharia. This was a concession by Nehru and other proponents of a secular Indian state to the orthodox clerical leadership among Muslims, partly because of the nature of the Congress party's relationship to Muslims, which was mediated via this leadership.

Thus the goal of eventually establishing a UCC was not made part of the Fundamental Rights section of the Constitution but consigned to its Directive Principles. In the mid-eighties, the Hindu Right began to communalize the issue of Muslim Personal Law and UCC in order to push its case against state 'minorityism' or 'favouring of religious minorities'. This campaign has gained considerable ground, though it can hardly be said to exemplify 'favouritism' since Muslim women are the principal sufferers of the absence of reform in their Personal Law. For further discussion of the UCC issue and its political impact, see Chapter 6.

134. '[The] Hindu Right is directed not against the principle of the secular state, but rather towards mobilising the legal powers of the state', 'Secularism and Tolerance', p. 1768. Or elsewhere, 'The majoritarian-ism of the Hindu Right, it seems to me, is perfectly at peace with the institutions and procedures of the "western" or "modern" state'. Ibid., p. 1768.

135. '[T]he the proponents of the secular state in India never had any doubts at all about the meaning of the concept of secularism; all the doubts were about whether that concept would find a congenial field of application in the Indian social and political context'. Ibid., p. 1769.

136. Ibid., p. 1774.

137. Ibid. '[A]rguments about the need to hold on to a universalist frameworks of reason ... tend to sound like pious homilies because they ignore the strategic context of power in which identity or difference is often asserted', p. 1774.

138. Ibid.

139. Ibid., p. 1775.

140. S. Sarkar, 'Subaltern Studies'.

141. Chatterjee cites in his own support the history of the Shiromani Gurudwara Prabhandak Committee (SGPC), an elected lay body which has emerged as a major public regulatory force for Sikhs. The growing power of the SGPC among Sikhs has been part of a process whereby

the very definition of a Sikh and of a Sikh community has become more exclusive and undemocratic. The growing importance of the SGPC has reflected and promoted the process whereby the values and beliefs of one section – the Khalsa (unshorn) Sikhs – have become more dominant.

142. This is something I was more prepared to do earlier. A. Vanaik, *The Painful Transition*, London, 1990, p. 157.

143. C.A. Bayly, 'The Pre-History of Communalism? Religion, Conflict in India, 1700–1860', in *Modern Asian Studies*, Vol. 19, 1985; H. Mukhia, 'Communalism and the Indian Polity', in *South Asia Bulletin*, Vol. XI, Nos 1–2, 1991.

144. H. Mukhia, 'Communalism and the Indian Polity'. Mukhia points out that communal consciousness is not simply the creation of colonialism but that its first stirrings emerge earlier in medieval Mughal rule. This is to equate communal consciousness to community consciousness and to allow for a neutral evaluation of the terms 'communal' and 'communalism'. His article can also be read as affirming that such communal consciousness cannot have the sharpened and mass character that it has in modernity.

145. In India, '[w]e are secular not because we had begun to question the rule of religious injunctions but because we saw in secularism a way of holding our many religious identities together.' M.S. Gore, 'Secularism and Equal Regard for All Religions', in B. Chakrabarty (ed.), *Secularism and Indian Polity*, p. 158. In India it was the presumed commonality of religions, not the frank recognition of differences between religious sects, that justified the secular state.

146. Religion connects with nationalism through origin myths of the nation. This was strong in Scotland, Poland, Belgium, Ireland, Iberia, Serbia, Bulgaria, Romania, Greece. In France, Italy, Czechoslovakia, it had to contend with liberal secular nationalism. Where the origin myth is old and there has been little external threat, as in England and Holland, religious consciousness is more dormant. The relaxed unions between nation and religion are where this is based on glory – Holland, Spain, Sweden, Austria, England. It is not so when the union is based on threat and suffering – Greece, Cyprus, Poland, Belgium, Ireland, Croatia. There is more ambiguity where there are plural religions (much of ex-Yugoslavia, Albania) and where ecclesiastical authority was opposed to national unification – Germany, Italy. D. Martin, *A General Theory of Secularization*, Oxford, 1978, Chapter 3.

147. Communalism is 'that phenomenon we might define as a politicized community identity'. S. Freitag, *Collective Action and Community*, Delhi, 1990, p. 6.

Communalism is an 'exclusive identification with and commitment to one's religious or social community'. This is the definition by K.W.

Jones cited in J.W. Bjorkman (ed.), *Fundamentalism, Revivalists and Violence in South Asia*, Delhi, 1988, p. 78. Another definition by Jones is of communalism as the 'consciously shared religious heritage which becomes the dominant form of identity for a given segment of society.' K.W. Jones, 'Communalism in the Punjab', in *Journal of Asian Studies*, Vol. 28, No. 1, November 1968, p. 39.

But as Gyan Pandey points out, 'In its common Indian usage the word "communalism" refers to a condition of suspicion, fear and hostility between members of different religious communities.' Here communalism is both a state of mind and a state of affairs. G. Pandey, *The Construction of Communalism in Colonial North India*, Delhi, 1990, p. 6.

148. Khushwant Singh and Bipan Chandra see communalism on the individual level as a 'state of mind', which for the latter, is also a false consciousness. It is 'a feeling of belonging to a particular community which has a sense of exclusion towards all others and an unfair preference for your own community'. K. Singh, 'Dangers of Communalism in Contemporary India', in K. Singh and B. Chandra, *Many Faces of Communalism*, Chandigarh, 1985, p. 35. Singh also feels such a definition is adequate at the collective level, i.e. expressing a collective state of mind.

Chandra sees communalism at the collective level as an ideology or a specific doctrine whose communal character depends on the degree of separateness and hostility it postulates towards the 'Other'. So there are the beginnings of a communal ideology when there is a consciousness only of collective secular interests. There is a liberal communalism when these are seen as separate and distinct from other communities; and a full-blown communalism when such interests are seen as opposed to, and threatened by, other communities. B. Chandra, 'Communalism – The Way Out', in ibid., pp. 45–6. By making communalism an ideology, Chandra depersonalizes it. It can now become the property of a more impersonal entity like a party, i.e. it can become institutionalized. This is an advance on the 'state of mind' notion of communalism.

Also, 'Communalism in the contemporary Indian context is a deep, almost visceral form of antagonism and antipathy between communities of differing cultural, ethnic, linguistic and/or religious identities.' R.E. Frykenberg, 'Hindu Fundamentalism and the Structural Stability of India', in M.E. Marty and R.S. Appleby (eds), *Fundamentalism and the State*, Chicago, 1993, p. 236.

For Dipankar Gupta, communalism is not a religio-political phenomenon but an ethnic–separatist one. Which is why he believes Hindutva as the form of Hindu communalism is actually 'Hindustanitva' or Hindustan-ness, i.e. primarily about keeping India united. D. Gupta,

'Communalism and Fundamentalism', in *Economic and Political Weekly*, Annual No., Vol. XXVI, 1991.

149. D.E. Smith, *India as a Secular State*, p. 454.
150. P. Dixit, *Communalism – A Struggle for Power*, Delhi, 1974, p. 1.
151. J. Nehru, *The Discovery of India*, London, 1956, p. 387.
152. Religious discourse is not communal discourse. It only provides the alphabet or perhaps some words from which the ugly sentences of communal discourse are constructed. But religious discourse must also be seen as only one kind of discourse or language or alphabet system among others in a modern, secular society. It is a discourse that must recognize its limited applicability. When it intrudes into other domains where other languages (and alphabets) are more fitted, i.e. when it becomes legitimized as an acceptable discourse in the terrain of modern politics, then it widens the field over which communal discourse operates. This is true even when in that domain it can be used to fight communal constructions of its 'alphabet'.
153. Protestantism has made dramatic gains in Latin America over the last two decades. At current rates of conversion (mainly to rightwing American-based evangelical sects) Latin America by the middle of the next century would become a predominantly Protestant continent. According to one estimate, 9,000 to 10,000 Catholics are converting daily to Protestantism. J. Haynes, *Religion in Third World Politics*, Buckingham, 1993, p. 95.
154. Mark Juergensmeyer feels the political dimension must be brought into the centre of any conception of religious fundamentalism. But this seems largely because of his preoccupation with religious nationalism and his unconcern with less political forms of religious fundamentalisms. M. Juergensmeyer, 'Why Religious Nationalists are Not Fundamentalists', in *Religion*, No. 23, 1993.
155. '[T]he success of fundamentalisms in reimagining the nation and remaking the state have occurred primarily if not exclusively in states in which the public–private distinction ... has not been written into the Constitution and protected by laws and judicial rulings ... in polities in which some form of church–state separation has been adopted, fundamentalism seems less likely to dictate the course of national self-definition – unless and until the fundamentalists undergo a process of moderation. This is most apparent in the case of Christian fundamentalists in the USA.' M.E. Marty and R.S. Appleby (eds) *Fundamentalism and the State*, p. 640.
156. The more extreme elements would advocate at least supplementing secular science with Islamic or Vedic science.
157. Such a 'structure' comprises doctrines, myths, ethics, ritual, experience, social organization. Both religion and nationalism have the power to invoke martyrdom and sacrifice on a large scale. M. Juergens-

meyer, *Religious Nationalism Confronts the Secular State*, Delhi, 1994. Juergensmeyer mistakenly sees 'secular' nationalism as having the same structure as a religious system, when it is actually nationalism itself that has this. Similarly, in the term 'religious nationalism', he sees the adjective as the defining element. The result is a failure to address adequately the unique power of nationalism.

158. B. Anderson, *Imagined Communities*, London, 1991. In Anderson's phrase, the nation was an 'imagined political community'. But most of his own efforts went into the exploration of the nation as an imagined cultural artefact.

159. See G. Balakrishnan, 'The National Imagination', in *New Left Review*, No. 211, May–June 1995 (p. 68) for a thoughtful discussion on the strengths and weaknesses of Anderson's justly famous work.

160. J. Alam, 'Muslim Communalism', in *Economic and Political Weekly*, 2 June 1984.

161. In my previous formulations I was inclined to see this rampant Hindu nationalism as the principal form taken by Hindu communalism itself. I did not sufficiently stress that Hindu communalism is a deeper and wider phenomenon. Hence my willingness to adopt the term 'Hindu nationalist' as an adequate characterization of Hindu communal forces.

162. The Sangh Combine is also pragmatic. The sentiments cultivated amongst Hindus against the Muslim 'Other' range from a sense of righteousness to a sense of deprivation to a sense of fear. When the first is cultivated, then the open text of the message is religious solidarity, and the submerged text is antagonism. K.N. Pannikar, 'Conceptualising Communalism', in *Seminar*, No. 394, June 1992.

Given the different though related conceptions of Hindutva, I have preferred not to align myself with Savarkar's particular definition but to see Hindutva (as laid out in the earlier sub-section in this chapter) as a wider, more abstract intellectual construct having political resonances. Political Hindutva is a term I've used to describe the forces of the Sangh Combine, whose ideology, being more politically driven, is guided by but different from Hindutva. (See Chapter 6, sub-section on 'Deconstructing Sangh Ideology'.) I make no claim that this is the only useful way to deal with the notion of Hindutva or to draw appropriate relationships between it and the forces of the Sangh Combine.

PART III

Situating the Threat of Hindu Communalism: Problems with the Fascist Paradigm

Contending Paradigms

Any attempt to render the historical phenomenon of fascism conceptually serviceable for contemporary purposes, e.g. analysing Hindu communalism, must cope with the necessity and difficulty of establishing a 'fascist minimum' embodying its main dynamics. A set of defining characteristics – properties/preconditions – and methodological injunctions has to be articulated. This 'set' must in part or whole constitute a core and heuristic recognized as such by social scientists and general analysts. Along with supplementary theories it should be accepted as a dominant model amidst competing theories and paradigms, i.e. vindicate itself as a fascist paradigm. If total consensus is not demanded for the heuristic or 'fascist minimum' (because we are dealing with a research programme in the *social* sciences), too little agreement will not do either – to be just one among numerous angles of vision of fascism.

Stanley Payne has listed eleven different ways of attempting to theorize the phenomenon of fascism. The list is reflexive and open enough to include the approach of those scholars sceptical about even seeing fascism as a generic phenomenon. They would abjure the theorization of it altogether.[1] One can impose taxonomic discipline on this methodological largesse. Broadly speaking there are Marxist and non-Marxist approaches each with their intra-paradigm divergencies. This is especially so for the latter, which lacks any positive theoretical principle of unification. Yet there is some large and important ground of agreement in both research programmes:

1. Fascism in power, the fascist state, is a distinctive form of the modern state.[2] Its distinctiveness lies in its extreme centralization

of political power and, as a logical corollary, its exceptional degree of autonomy from other major power actors and forces.[3]

2. The two undisputed examples of fascism in power were Italy and Germany, though the latter had a unique Nazi twist.[4] These two regimes and states with their antecedent movements plus the plethora of National Socialist and fascist movements, parties and groups in Europe during the inter-war period constitute the primary empirical data for all attempts at theorizing fascism.

3. Fascism is a strong form of authoritarian nationalism. Fascism is always an authoritarian nationalism but the reverse does not hold.

There are fascist movements and fascist states, fascism in opposition and fascism in power. The first major difference between non-Marxist and Marxist approaches has been that the former, in seeking to draw up a 'fascist minimum' or 'essence', has focused much more sharply on movements while the latter has focused on the characteristics of the fascist state, fascism in its presumably matured form. Since ideology and ideological appeal is much more central to the existence and growth of fascism as movement, it is hardly surprising that non-Marxist approaches are much more strongly pivoted on the elucidation of fascism's distinctive ideological themes and organizational principles. Ideology, organization, even philosophy, become the principal criteria and obsession of such theorizations.[5]

The 'true' nature of a movement lies in its aspirations, not in its practices, which necessarily involve compromises. To be fascist is, above all, to have an ideology which in its pristine form qualifies as fascist. This still does not fully resolve the problem of establishing a 'fascist minimum' capable of achieving a strong consensus. What ideological elements or themes to count in and count out? But the problem has been made more manageable.

Payne has outlined a viable method for establishing a 'fascist minimum' in such a framework, 'the right way to go about things'. His three-part model comprises (a) fascist negations, (b) generic ideological motifs and goals, (c) special and common features of style and organization. With regard to the first, all fascisms would have to incorporate explicitly in their ideologies anti-liberalism, anti-democracy and anti-Communism or anti-Marxism. The shorter the list of negations the more extended the list of qualifying candidates for the status of fascism is likely to be. However, some theorists have insisted on including other negations such as anti-conservatism and anti-pacificism.

What would be the indispensable ideological motifs and goals? These might be (i) treating the state as an 'absolute' or near-absolute; (ii) the goal of empire or an aggressively expansionist foreign policy; (iii) the primacy of some collective principle or unit of belonging subsuming individual autonomy and universalist values and generally requiring construction of some collective 'Other' as the enemy;[6] (iv) extreme authoritarian nationalism; (v) an apocalyptic perception of deep 'civilizational crisis' requiring construction of the 'new man', which is more important than any new programme. It is the *mystique* of a fascist movement rather than its programme that makes it a radical inspirational project.

These are the following common features of style and organization:

(i) Charismatic leadership would seem to be central to all fascisms. The leader embodies the inspirational ideal. Indeed, it is precisely the relationship of *the* leader to the masses that embodies the superior, because more 'direct' and plebiscitary, democracy of fascism.[7]

(ii) There is the exaltation of youth and the youthfulness (relative to leaders of the traditional Right parties) of fascist leaders. A real generational gap prevails.[8]

(iii) Violence is glorified and there is the militarization of political behaviour and relationships.

(iv) Political meetings are carefully choreographed to arouse mass emotions through evocative symbols.

(v) Masculinity is stressed.

As this example of an elaborated 'fascist minimum' might suggest, such a non-Marxist approach has attractions for many a Marxist who has also made similar ideological–organizational comparisons to justify the designation of fascism in a given case. But even such a worked out fascist minimum leaves enough scope for never-ending disagreements over how best to characterize a specific movement, party or group. The content of the postulated minimum will be continuously disputed with demands for revision/amendment/deletion, i.e. that the minimum be filled out differently.

Fascist movements have more in common with each other than fascist or semi-fascist/neo-fascist/proto-fascist regimes. There have also been many more fascist movements than regimes. This provides a more confident basis for generic speculation or theory-building. But if non-Marxists in one sense find it easier to make generic claims, they are also in another sense less pressured to do so. No indissociable link is postulated between the capitalist accumulation process and the fascist phenomenon. As it is, the bourgeois state as an autonomous entity 'above' classes (whatever its possible class biases) renders nugatory the search for some distinctive relationship between class power and fascist state power. Non-Marxists readily concede the importance of recognizing the class or social base of the fascist movement or state, i.e. the refracted influence on the fascist entity of the petty bourgeoisie or middle classes; but that is a different matter.[9]

Some will readily recognize the importance of incorporating a significant 'socio-economic dimension' into the study of fascism, but it is overwhelmingly Marxists who subscribe to an agency theory of fascism, i.e. that it serves the interests, especially and decisively when in power, of dominant classes other than the petty bourgeoisie. In the best Marxist expositions it is recognized that fascist agents are *self-appointed* and far from being the pliable servitors of the big bourgeoisie.

Non-Marxist approaches to the study of fascism, then, are highly flexible and employ a variety of modes. They can perceive it as a generic phenomenon, or refuse altogether to see it as such. If the latter, they can insist that fascism is the result of unique national histories, e.g. of Italy and Germany, where contingency and the unforeseeable accidents of history play a decisive role. So Nazism peaked by 1932 and was then declining but for the contingently explained rise of Hitler to chancellorship, hence the reversal of fortunes for Nazism and its accession to power. But even if fascism is accepted as something generic expressing itself in 'varieties of fascism', there can still be a whole range of answers to the question of 'how generic?' Variously, it has been seen as an inter-war European phenomenon and only that.[10] It has been seen as a political phenomenon linked decisively either to political ideology or to problems of development/modernisation. If the first, then it is easy to conclude that fascism itself is a sub-set of a larger political phenomenon of totalitarianism. This is a widely held view among non-Marxist analysts of fascism.[11] If the second, then in principle fascism is of more general world significance and could well surface in other times and other places than inter-war Europe.

The non-Marxist attempt to construct a paradigm of fascism therefore offers, a series of differently positioned windows from which to view the phenomenon. This, it could be claimed, is one of the strengths of this kind of intellectual tradition. Even where fascism is considered a generic entity and building theories about it apt, the multiplicities of causations and correlations in history are more likely to be respected when there is no single comprehensive theory of fascism, no attempt at building a meta-narrative. Less grand theories, narrower in their scope, often supplementary to each other, illuminating this or that dimension of the phenomenon, are both the best that one can hope for and the most that one should strive for.

Whatever the merits of such a position, it has not satisfied Marxists. Though generous and skilled non-Marxist practitioners can acknowledge the value of the insights provided by the more sociologically and economically oriented investigations of Marxists into fascism, they can never assign quite the same weight to socio-economic factors in their overall explanatory framework.

The fulcrum of a Marxist approach rests on the economic function of fascism and on the fragile nature of the relationship of class forces that make the 'fascist option' available and its success possible or probable. Common ideological referents gleaned from the movement phase of fascism before it emerges as a new form of the bourgeois state can certainly feature in the delineation of a Marxist fascist minimum. But they are the second level of clinching arguments for characterizing the 'fascist danger'. Analysis of the economic preconditions for fascism has to be given pride of place. Additionally, and just as important, there is the precise evaluation of the social balance – the class relationship of forces in a context of prolonged economic crisis of extraordinary depth, between capital and labour, and of the relationship of forces between class fractions/constituents of the ruling class bloc/coalition/alliance.

That this should be the central focus for investigating the possibilities of fascist victory when potential candidates for such status are in opposition, i.e. in the movement phase, must seem at first glance a major aberration. Surely it is ideological appeal that most explains the continuing growth of a mass movement and of a fascist political formation? Surely it is this growth that then alters and destabilizes the class relationship of forces and not an existing instability or crisis in class relations that explains the rise of a fascist movement? Isn't that putting the cart before the horse?

Not so! Certainly the growing power of a fascist movement is itself a powerful input into the forcible and sometimes drastic rearrangement in the distribution of class power even at the apex. But it is the existence of a prior crisis in class relationships both within capital and between capital and labour, (which must necessarily play itself out on the social and political terrain) that gives a decisive fillip to fascism. Whatever the mediations, refractions and lags, the crisis must reveal itself in class tensions and antagonisms and in the turmoils of political parties, both internally and in their relationships with each other. It is this prior crisis that creates the 'space' for rapid growth of fascist formations, even

241

though their origins and initial growth can, and usually does, take place independently of these developments. The latter operate backstage, as it were, from the more visible terrain of political contestation. The rapid acceleration and growth of fascist political formations is never a straight-forward function of its ideological message but feeds powerfully on pre-existing social dislocations of an abnormally serious kind.

These socio-economic preconditions are not simply to be listed dis-cretely in the set of defining criteria. They largely constitute the principal dynamics of fascism, the point of departure for theory construction. Indeed, it is on this terrain of the balance of class forces that the decisive battles – whether fascism will triumph or not – will be fought. Any autonomy of the state is ultimately relative. Fascism is so extreme a form of the bourgeois state, one where its 'freedom of action' vis-à-vis dominant classes is greatest, that only the most extreme crisis conditions drive the dominant class(es) or sections thereof to endorse this 'solution'.

An enduring criticism by non-Marxists and sometimes by 'unorthodox Marxists' is that such a perspective can never give adequate weight to ideology or politics or to the principal fascist actor itself. Considering that much of the best post-war work by Marxists has been in the area of ideology and politics, this charge is not strong. But there is a point beyond which fewer Marxists than non-Marxists will go in elevating the importance of the ideological–political. Most charitably one can simply acknowledge that both Marxist and non-Marxist approaches have their distinct virtues and vices. A non-Marxist can argue that political move-ments, especially one like fascism, are no doubt influenced by but autonomous of class forces. It may be difficult but possible for them to arrive at power regardless of what ruling classes decide. In a democratic order this is even easier than otherwise, given the mass character of such a movement and thus its legitimacy.

The weakness of this proposition is that if a fascist movement can arrive at governmental power 'against the wishes' of dominant classes or class fractions, it can hardly rule except within constraints set by the necessity of reproducing capitalist social relations on an expanded scale. Beyond a point it cannot go 'against the wishes' of the dominant classes and expect to stabilize the fascist state, i.e. its own existence. Fascist movement aspirations do not automatically become fascist regime policies or even options. Fascism is as fascism does, and for the fascist party in power this is not endogenously or unilaterally determined.

In the end, choice of paradigm is determined by one's balance-sheet judgement regarding the comparative merits of the two basic approaches.

Marxist theorizations of fascism have a definite cast. They are 'agency' theories (however sophisticated) of a strongly functionalist kind. Fascist formations are perceived as conscious or inadvertent agents for some section of ruling capitalists, more inadvertently in the movement phase, more consciously so when in power. In striving for, coming to and staying in power, fascist formations carry out a crucial economic (and social–political–ideological) function for the favoured classes or class fractions and for the capitalist system as a whole. The problem with functionalist argument is well known. They are rarely decisive except where the mechanism which 'functionally explains' is specified. They are usually, at best, persuasive secondary evidence for the validity of a stipulated proposition.

It is hardly surprising, then, that non- or anti-Marxists remain sceptical of the Marxist approach. These sentiments are reciprocated by their Marxist counterparts and with good reason. Bourgeois theories have never provided so compelling a picture of the socio-economic dynamics of fascism. The dialogue between Marxists and non-Marxists over fascism, more than half-a-century after its appearance, remains a dialogue of the deaf, whatever the limited exchange of insights. The roots of this deadlock are clear enough. Marxists are inescapably committed to the idea of social existence as a 'complexly structured totality' which includes the notion of intention and directionality in the weak sense. The economy influences other 'levels' in ways not equivalently reciprocated, at least in capitalism, even though the 'level of the economic' can never be purely economic. It 'determines' where determination is akin to the conception of Raymond Williams as 'exerting pressures and setting limits'. No more perhaps? But certainly no less. This does not necessarily lead to an economic reductionism but it does mean a special weightage, however qualified or mediated, to economic and class factors.

This is alien to the methodological habits and traditions of non-Marxists. Also for Marxists, states in capitalist societies, at least, are axiomatically class states. So, too, the fascist state. If non-Marxists disagree with the Marxist theorization of the fascist state it is because they disagree fundamentally with the Marxist theorization of any bourgeois state or state in capitalist society. Unless Marxists develop the conceptual tools which establish the capitalist and class character of the state independently of functionalist argument and are able to empirically validate this analysis in concrete cases, they cannot decisively win the argumentative battle vis-à-vis unbelieving liberal or conservative theorists of the modern state, even if they won't lose the argument either.

Marxists may believe that the balance of plausibility rests strongly with

243

them. But the grey area of theoretical and empirical uncertainty that exists provides a not dishonourable escape route for those against the caricature of Marxism, but genuinely unconvinced of the legitimacy and efficacy of the Marxist approach. Marxists may be justified in believing their approach to be superior. But they do have an enduring difficulty sustaining this claim to superiority beyond all reasonable objection in the court of intellectual appeal. It is likely, given the nature of the social sciences (the impossibility of controlled experimentation), that conclusive 'proof' of the validity of the notion of the class state is impossible. But this methodological impossibility is not the same as logical impossibility. Better Marxist theory should be able to persuade non-Marxists not because it will offer conclusive proof but because it offers qualitatively better explanation and the possibility of better prediction.

To opt for the Marxist paradigm in the analysis of fascism is to have already opted intellectually for a Marxist approach in the social sciences. Since no eclectic mishmash of methodologies or approaches will do, and would not constitute an improvement, the Marxist paradigm has at least a 50 per cent chance of being the better one. It is within the Marxist paradigm or, more correctly, the historical attempts to construct such a paradigm that the rest of the discussion will be situated.

The Marxist Paradigm: The Tensions Within

The insistence on the indissoluble link between capitalism and fascism means Marxists are naturally predisposed to discover a theory of fascism, to be inveterate genericists, to treat it as a phenomenon fully capable of recurring/occurring beyond the temporal and spatial confines of inter-war Europe. It may not actually so recur, but it is capable of doing so. However, the global historical record since 1945 has created a certain inadequately explored tension.

The first fascisms appeared, assumed power or achieved threatening proportions in inter-war Europe. For Marxists there was a clear association between advanced capitalisms and imperialisms and the danger of fascism. But after 1945, despite the occasional emergence of 'fascistic' or 'fascist-like' organizations in the OECD countries, it is precisely this zone that has seemed most inoculated against anti-democratic authoritarianisms, let alone fascisms. This is especially so after the transition to bourgeois democracy of Portugal and Spain in the late seventies. Fascist-like formations have been pressure groups helping to shift the political centre of gravity rightwards (especially in regard to certain policies, e.g.

race, immigration) in certain advanced democracies during certain periods, but little else.

The zone where capitalist authoritarian nationalisms have flourished has been the third world. Hence the question raised – can there be third world fascisms? If so, what are their preconditions and principal characteristics? In the light of such experiences what modifications are required when elaborating a fascist minimum (otherwise based heavily on the properties of classical fascism) to make the notion of fascism more relevant to the second half of the twentieth century? Is such a step legitimate? Are we dealing with 'functional substitutes for fascism' rather than fascism proper? How significant anyway is the difference between the two?

An important Marxist tradition remains hostile to such spatial extension. Fascism is a feature not just of capitalism in crisis but of capitalism in crisis in its imperialist stage and prevails among imperialist countries only. Brutal authoritarianism in an advanced, imperialist country has a global and historical significance of a *qualitatively* different order than in a non-imperialist, dependent capitalist country. Fascism is a form of 'international reaction' in a context of close correspondence between national capitals led by their big battalions, i.e. monopoly capital and the nation-state. Fascist rivalry flows from and exacerbates inter-imperialist rivalry. Trotsky/Mandel, Gramsci/Togliatti and Poulantzas all saw militarism and an expansionist foreign policy as intrinsic to fascism.[12] The fascist temptation was strongest where the link in the imperialist chain was weakest, i.e. among the weaker latecomer imperialisms.[13] Not just economic imperatives but ideology also promoted such expansionist politico-military behaviour.

There is an enormous difficulty in establishing a fascist minimum that encompasses the central dynamics of classical inter-war European fascism and also post-1945 third world candidates for fascist status. This partly explains why within the Marxist tradition theories of a third world or 'universalist' fascist threat or possibility are undeveloped and scarce. The continent where authoritarian nationalist capitalist regimes have emerged time and again, enjoying a fairly long run, has been Latin America. Yet the generic concept that seems most appropriate to explaining the Latin American experience, whether authoritarian or quasi-democratic, has been 'populism' not 'fascism'. The term 'populism' has no single accepted meaning and is the site of much dispute. But in all versions the differences with classical fascism are marked.[14] The crucial point of contrast, however, is that the middle class of post-1945 third world countries is located in a qualitatively different class matrix compared to that of inter-war Europe and has a different character. The Latin American experience has given rise to a different kind of political movement and regime. Hence the generic label of populism.

For a Marxist wishing to justify the possibility of third world fascisms one possible theoretical route to take would be to see it as a political outcome which emerges in certain cases and for certain reasons but is a potential embedded in the general dynamics of the capitalist modernization process. Fascism is not, then, the 'specific conjuncture of the class struggle' (Poulantzas). It need not share most of the characteristics of classical European fascism that went into the making of the classical Marxist theories, of which the most outstanding were those of Trotsky, Gramsci, Thalheimer and Bauer. The fascist phenomenon becomes not so much a *recurring temptation* of a capitalist system in periodic crisis as a *moment of transition* in the historical development of capitalism. Such an approach rescues and enhances the possibility of third world fascisms in our times but greatly minimizes (if not negating) the possibility of its recurrence in the advanced metropolitan countries.[15]

Such an approach sacrifices the complexities of a multi-causal explanation of fascism for a more single-minded focus on the socio-economic necessities of capitalist industrialization and the imperatives imposed on the modernizing state. But in the hands of its most skilled practitioner to date, Barrington Moore Jr, it has been fruitful. Moore replaced the wide fish-eye lens of analysis with a deep-focus lens – he greatly extended the time-span for studying the possible emergence of fascism in a particular case. The study of its preconditions is stretched backwards well beyond the vision of even the most reputed Marxist students of classical fascism. Moore might not qualify as a 'Marxist' historian–sociologist. But he is taken as the most eminent representative of a Left approach with very strong affinities to Marxism because he shared a similar commitment to rooting the story of political evolution/state transformations in class struggles and imbalances.

For Moore, fascism was a latent possibility in almost all the major societies (except the USA) and also in societies undergoing modernization today.[16] Though he employs the comparative method, he still generalizes on the basis of too few case studies (England, France, USA, China, Japan and India), even if these be major ones. Moore has excused himself from providing similar case studies for Germany and Russia (as well as for Italy), citing the excellent material already available, and stresses that he does refer to them to illustrate his comparative case studies. Latin America and Africa are completely excluded, which certainly damages any effort to theorize the broad principles, landmarks and contours of the development process and its associated political–state forms. Even so, he provides rich and thought provoking fare.

Moore designates pre-war Japan an Asian fascism instituted between 1938 and 1940. What were the distinguishing points of fascism, the points in common between Germany and Japan?

> National mobilisation was decreed, radicals were arrested, political parties were dissolved and replaced by the Imperial Rule Assistance Association; a rather unsuccessful copy of a Western totalitarian party. Shortly afterward, Japan joined the anti-Comintern Triple Alliance and dissolved all trade unions, replacing them with an association for the 'service to the nation through industry'. Thus by the end of 1940 Japan displayed the principal external traits of European fascism.[17]

Fundamental anatomical commonalities are also elucidated.

> Both Germany and Japan entered the industrial world at a late stage. In both countries, regimes emerged whose main policies were repression at home and expansion abroad. In both cases, the main social basis for this program was a coalition between the commercial–industrial elites (who started from a weak position) and the traditional ruling classes in the countryside, directed against the peasants and the industrial workers. Finally, in both cases, a form of rightist radicalism emerged out of the plight of the petty bourgeoisie and peasants under advancing capitalism. This right-wing radicalism provided some of the slogans for repressive regimes in both countries but was sacrificed in practice to the requirements of profit and 'efficiency'.[18]

For Moore, the key to understanding all twentieth-century fascisms is the scope provided for 'plebeian anti-capitalism'. The three routes of successful modernization have been: (a) capitalist development via a bourgeois revolution 'from below', which is most conducive to establishing strong democracies; (b) peasant revolutions (Russia and China) leading to Communist modernization; and (c) reactionary capitalism leading to authoritarian states, culminating in certain cases in fascism (Italy, Germany, Japan) and carrying out a revolution 'from above'. India is a fourth route fitting into neither of these courses and negatively confirms Moore's thesis. It has a weak bourgeois democracy with a weak economy – stagnant modernization.[19]

The solution to the riddle of development/modernization (with its associated political forms from democracy to the spectrum of authoritarianisms ending in fascism) is found in the countryside. Lord and peasant not bourgeois and worker are the key actors in the story. Always and everywhere the peasant and the countryside pay the highest price (dislocation, transformation and contribution) for industrialization and the rise of the modernizing state.

The economic compulsions behind the rise of fascism lie not in the imperatives of surplus extraction from the worker in the city but elsewhere. There must exist a labour-repressive agrarian system and the crucial preconditions for democracy (spelt out elsewhere by Moore) must be absent.[20] These are the necessary though not sufficient conditions for the emergence of fascism. Such labour-repressive systems can be of two types: either capitalist extraction of necessary surplus from the countryside keeps traditional peasant society intact but squeezes more out by using servile or semi-servile labour in larger units of cultivation; or there is plantation slavery or its functional equivalent. In Eastern Europe the reintroduction of serfdom was a 'halfway form'. Where there are American-style family farms or a mobile agricultural labour force, or where a pre-industrial/pre-commercial agrarian system exists but there is a 'rough balance between the overlord's contribution to justice and security and the cultivator's contribution in the form of crops', there is no labour-repressive system.

India does not fit into the category of any of Moore's labour-repressive agrarian systems. Moore's chapter on India is particularly weak on its post-independence agrarian structure and evolution.[21] The rural petty bourgeoisie (rich farmers and aspiring capitalist family farmers) may be susceptible to Hindu communalist demagogy but they can hardly constitute the base for 'plebeian anti-capitalism' or be strongly responsive to pseudo-radical pre-capitalist appeals glorifying the idealized peasant of the past. The Bharat versus India motif does glorify the 'free peasant on free land' but in wanting it to have the freedom to develop in a direction which is firmly capitalist. The farmer demands that the state intervene against the urban trader or industrialist who want to subordinate capitalist development in agriculture to their needs.

The most remarkable thing about India is the persistence of the peasantry, the huge size relative to other rural classes of family farmers, and the limited and slow polarization of classes in the countryside. There is no Indian equivalent of the small German peasant in hock to city-based middle-men and brokers. The only serious candidate for fascist status in India – the Sangh Combine – has felt no need to orient its ideology specifically to the small peasantry. The peasant is not a key motif in its ideology.

Moore's second necessary condition for the emergence of fascism is a reactionary coalition between an industrial/commercial class (too weak to take power itself) with a landed aristocracy and the bureaucracy of an authoritarian, e.g. monarchial, state. Competition from more technically advanced capitalist rivals throws the landed upper class into crisis and pushes it to use 'political levers' to preserve its rule. This leads to an authoritarianism (with some democratic features) but not yet fascism. It is the *failure* of these authoritarian regimes to solve the burning problems of the day – specifically, rapid capital accumulation – that is decisive. They are unable or unwilling to carry out fundamental structural changes, most importantly the dramatic overhaul and modernization of agriculture in ways incompatible ultimately with the preservation in the old form of the 'reactionary' coalition or the earlier 'labour-repressive agrarian system'. Where a regime seeks to modernize but is not able to transform the social structure, then, provided the other preconditions for fascism exist, the fascist state is the 'solution' to this problem. It is the developmentalist 'revolution from above'.

While remaining an outstanding work of comparative historical sociology, time has not been kind to Moore's overall perspective. The sources of capitalist development, of political democratization and of a variety of forms of authoritarianism have been too many and too complexly inter-related to be covered by Moore's broad yet patchy brush-strokes. The uneven spread of democracies, the numerically limited but nonetheless dramatic successes of capitalism in the third world, and the collapse of Communism in the second world all suggest that many more 'basic' forces are at work than allowed for by Moore's framework of analysis.

Not only is the specificity of the phenomenon of fascism lost in his model, but it is also a step backward from those Marxist analyses of fascism which, although also pivoted on class power and extraction of economic surplus, were urban oriented as well as insistent that other non-economic factors and social relationships had to be part of any derived fascist minimum. For Moore fascism is a 'revolution from above' rather than a 'counter-revolution from below'. Thus he can see it as a reactionary but forward movement in resolving the historical problems of modernization. Not surprisingly, Moore, unlike Marxists, is unconcerned with the programmatic perspectives (strengths and weaknesses) of forces opposing fascism or whether they could have triumphed and fascism avoided. In that sense his is an academic rather than political engagement with fascism. Had he included case studies of Italy and Germany this omission would have been near-impossible. Choosing not to include these two paradigmatic examples of fascism says much about the teleological and objectivist bias in his methodology.

Being a revolution from above, there is little reason for him to consider the 'movement' or popular character of fascism as crucial to the emergence of fascism. The 'revolution from above' may be facilitated and significantly marked by a 'fascism from below'. But this is not crucial to it. In his scheme of things there can be 'fascisms from above' as in Japan.

For all his sensitivity to socio-economic factors, Moore's approach has a serious problem which tends to align him with non-Marxists like Nolte whose method otherwise could not be more distant from his own. Moore rejects the idea of fascism as a counter-revolution, which all Marxists aver. They may not all agree on distinctions between conservatives, reactionaries, radical Right and fascists. But to call fascism a counter-revolution is, above all, to insist that it is a rescue operation. It is the most radical form of social and political surgery whose primary goal is to *protect* the most crucial existing ligaments of class power. That which is already the most powerful segment of the capitalist class (or alliance) is to remain so. It might be legitimate to stretch the classical notion of fascism (always a fascism from below) to incorporate the possibility of a 'fascism from above'. Chile after the coup against Allende could be a candidate. But this would still have to be a 'counter-revolution from above' and not a 'revolution from above'.

The notion of third world fascisms may be valid but it still awaits theorization that is a qualitative step forward from Moore's model. Moreover, the latter is at a tangent to the existing tradition of serious Marxist analysis of fascism where it indubitably emerged. Moore does not build on these perceptions but bypasses them. It is doubtful if that is the most promising way forward for those insisting on the contemporary validity of the concept of fascism in both the developing and developed world.

The Classical Marxist Views

In historical retrospect the analyses of Trotsky, Gramsci, Thalheimer and Bauer stand up best. They grasped more accurately than others the properties of the phenomenon they were dealing with, gauged the threat more seriously and put forward the best programmatic perspectives of their times. It is hardly surprising that what is common to their respective analyses is more important than their differences. The most

250

serious effort at theorizing fascism in the post-war period was undertaken by Nicos Poulantzas. Perhaps his Greek origins had much to do
with his unusual sensitivity to the problem of authoritarianism and the
fragility of the democratic state in Western Europe, when others were
much more preoccupied with the question of the durability of bourgeois
democracy and its dampening effects on working-class revolutionary
fervour.

Trotsky's approach to fascism was the single most impressive effort by
any major Marxist thinker. The late Ernest Mandel, the most important
systematizer of Trotsky's thought after Isaac Deutscher, has presented
Trotsky's 'theory of fascism' as a unity of six elements, each having a
certain autonomy but forming a 'closed and dynamic totality'. It is worth
spelling this out in full.[22]

(1) The rise of fascism expresses a severe social crisis of capitalism
not necessarily coinciding with a conjunctural crisis. This is capitalism's
impossibility of accumulating in the 'old' way at a given level of real
wages, productivity, access to raw materials, markets, etc. The economic
function of a fascist seizure of power is to dramatically raise the
production and realization of surplus value for decisive sectors of
monopoly capital.

(2) Bourgeois democracy is a highly unstable form of rule resting on
a 'highly unstable equilibrium of economic and social forces'. When
this is disturbed, as it must eventually be, then there has to be greater
centralization of executive power. Fascism means an extreme degree of
centralization wherein the bourgeoisie is 'politically expropriated' to
serve the economic interests of the big bourgeoisie.

(3) However, neither a standard form of centralization of power, e.g.
a military dictatorship, nor a 'pure police state' or absolute monarchy
has the capacity to atomize or demoralize for long a conscious,
numerically strong working class, i.e. prevent elementary class struggles.
Only a fascist movement can do this by mass terror and systematized
physical assaults on the working class *before* the seizure of power. The
fascist dictatorship only *completes* the job of atomization, demoralization,
control and surveillance of the working class in civil society.

(4) Such a mass movement only arises on the basis of the petty
bourgeoisie, which has large sections falling into despair. The ideology
of such a movement must (a) be extremely nationalist, (b) be verbally
anti-capitalist, (c) have an intense hatred for the organized working
class. Such a movement grows by cutting its teeth on (physically
attacking) working-class organizations.

(5) The fight to decisively shift the relationship of forces between the

fascist and workers' movements must take place *before* the fascist seizure of power. In this civil war, the working class, fighting for its life, also has chances of victory. It is this 'openness' of the civil war situation and its 'risks', i.e. the 'all-or-nothing' character of the situation, that makes the big bourgeoisie accept 'political expropriation'. Civil war is a real possibility because the acuteness of the socio-economic crisis affords the working-class movement real possibilities of victory as well.

(6) The fascist seizure of power/dictatorship both *completes* the fascist project and *initiates* a transmutation of the state into a Bonapartist dictatorship requiring an abandonment of the demagoguery of the 'movement' phase as well as the assimilation of its cadres into a bureaucratized state apparatus. The petty bourgeois base systematically shrinks as the 'monopoly class character' of the fascist party becomes more evident. The all-or-nothing character of the fascist dictatorship leads to it seeking to do on the world market what it has done domestically – revising the conditions for surplus production/extraction/realization by the monopoly bourgeoisie. This necessarily leads to foreign military adventure.

Trotsky's theory of fascism applies only to considerably industrialized countries in late capitalism. It assumes the country in question is not a semi-colonial, backward or semi-capitalist country. The decisive class actor behind fascism is not foreign capital or its representative or subordinate fractions but the domestic 'big bourgeoisie' or sections thereof.

Social democracy saw aggressive counter-mobilization against fascism as 'too provocative' and counter-productive. It also gave too much explanatory weight to the conjunctural economic crisis and too little to the structural crisis of capitalism. Third-period Stalinism did not recognize the independent character of the fascist mass movement and was too inclined towards a conspiracy view of fascism as the result of the machinations of the most 'aggressive sections of the big bourgeoisie'. Its false theory of 'gradual fascisization' of the state under Weimar rule or 'creeping fascism' disregarded the 'ruptural' character of the fascist victory and was first cousin to the now discredited 'social fascist' view of social democracy.

The post-1935 Comintern perspective underlying the Popular Front strategy saw fascism as the 'open dictatorship of monopoly capital'. Fascism was viewed as a new stage in the process of the expansion of executive power when in fact it was a *special form* of the strong executive or 'open dictatorship', characterized not just by 'traditional' repression but by the destruction of *all* workers' organizations. The Dimitroff thesis still saw fascism as a 'defensive' measure, a 'counter-offensive', thus underestimating its staying power and failing to realize that its victory presumes the decisive defeat of the working class. Fascism was not a 'counter-offensive' but an 'offensive' of the big bourgeoisie. The Seventh Congress Communist International thesis viewed the relationship between big capital and the fascist party deterministically and so was ill prepared for the flexibility and freedom of the latter, particularly in foreign policy.

Gramsci shared most of Trotsky's propositions and conclusions. Gramsci (and Togliatti) saw fascism as a mass movement of the petty bourgeoisie violently attacking working-class organizations. Its strength was the consequence not the cause of working-class and Left defeats. Big property used but did not control the fascist movement. Once in power fascism attacks its own petty bourgeois base. But unlike Trotsky, Gramsci, like Thalheimer, sought the explanation for military expansionism abroad less in economic compulsions and more in the need for a diversionary and unifying policy to cope with the internal contradictions of the fascist state partly arising out of the tension between the aspirations of the petty bourgeois base and the interests of the big bourgeoisie.

While Gramsci never had as 'rounded' a theory of fascism as Trotsky's, he offered a more developed understanding of the ideological dimension of fascism via his notion of hegemony. Both Gramsci and the Frankfurt School-inspired studies on the mass psychology or social pathology of fascism help fill a lacuna in Trotsky's analysis which underestimated the strength of fascism's nationalist appeal.[23]

Bauer, and Thalheimer especially, were close to Trotsky's theory. Like Trotsky, both saw the victory of fascism as coming *after* the ebbing of the revolutionary flood.[24] Their major difference with Trotsky and with each other was over Bonapartism. Thalheimer had a view of Bonapartism closer to Marx's own, seeing it as the extreme power of the executive in special circumstances. Fascism and Bonapartism were different but had many similarities. So Bonapartism should be the starting point for developing a theory of fascism. He was also less certain about rejecting the 'creeping fascism' thesis and thus more prone to devaluing the capacity of the working class to resist it.[25]

Trotsky refined the notion of Bonapartism, arguing that there were two types – a highly unstable as well as a more stable one. The unstable preventive Bonapartisms were the Brüning and Papen governments preceding Hitler, which held the balance between Left and Right, i.e. trying to contain fascism's threat vis-à-vis the bourgeoisie (its political expropriation) while seeking to utilize it against the working class. The more stable Bonapartism was the Hitler regime. But this, too, is relatively unstable in the longer run because it must turn against its petty bourgeois base. Gramsci/Togliatti agreed but did not see it as a Bonapartism but as the unavoidable transformation of a *fascist* state in power.

These classical Marxist theories also have their enduring weaknesses. The most important was one they could not be blamed for, being denied the luxury of historical retrospect which alone could have enabled important refinements to their theories. Nazism was a distinctive form of fascism in which the importance of the 'Führer principle' was exceptional. Mussolini came to power within three years of the formation of the Italian Fascios. Hitler came to power after a much longer period of incubation, growth and consolidation of German fascism as a mass movement. Marxists like Trotsky were so keen to emphasize the 'agent' character of fascism, especially in power, that they laid more stress on the discontinuities between fascism as movement and when in power, downgrading important continuities.

This led to underestimating the importance of 'charismatic' authority and of the 'Führer principle' carried over from the Nazi party to the Nazi state. The stronger the fascist party, i.e. the stronger the movement it led, the easier for its 'personal authority' to make this transition. Gramsci's brief comments on 'Caesarism' offered more hints about the possibility of such an outcome in Germany. But these were hardly more than hints, a variation on the theme of Bonapartism that was the common currency of these classical Marxist theorists of fascism.[26]

These Marxist theories of classical European fascism operated within certain distinctive parameters which either no longer operate or can only do so in critically amended ways. These parameters have rarely been spelt out. But a general sense of unease with the validity of the classical theories of fascism certainly marks the work of Poulantzas. He has preserved the idea of fascism as a recurring tendency in advanced capitalist societies (and only there) but at the price of a 'dilution' of its force and threat. His key formulations are that fascism emerges from a 'specific conjuncture of the class struggle' and is a specific form of the regime in an 'exceptional state'. Exceptional here means not 'rare in occurrence' but 'emphatic in degree'. The exceptional capitalist state is exceptionally bureaucratized. It is that state in which physical repression and its apparatuses become relatively more important than legitimizing apparatuses. Repressive apparatuses also have their own legitimacy. Fascism differs from other forms of the exceptional state such as

Bonapartism or military dictatorship not by its relative autonomy (which, believed Poulantzas, is less than in Bonapartism) or by the urgency of its economic function 'but by the forms it used, the radical changes in the ideological state apparatuses, and their relationship to the repressive apparatuses of the state'.[27]

Poulantzas gives valuable emphasis to the idea of fascism as a response to an ideological crisis of legitimacy, but at the price of devaluing its economic function. His notion of fascism emerging as a serious option because of the crisis of the conjuncture without requiring a more prolonged structural crisis (e.g. Great Depression type) means it can emerge after 1945 and in the post-boom West. His concept of the exceptional state spanning the range from milder to the harsher varieties of authoritarianism makes it a more feasible possibility than otherwise in the advanced countries.

However, says Poulantzas, the kind of 'pure' political crisis of the conjuncture that is required for fascism to come to power is so rare that fascism proper is highly unlikely in the contemporary capitalisms of the advanced countries. Fascism is a 'live' tendency and a recurring factor. But realistically what emerges are different kinds of exceptional states having different combinations of the characteristics of fascism and non-fascist authoritarianisms.

The Basic Parameters

What were the basic parameters of classical fascism that in part or whole may no longer obtain? Eight such parameters can be listed.

(1) The enormous dislocation of a continental-scale modern war whose physical, ecological, social, economic and political devastation had till then no close historical approximation. The core cadres of all the most active European fascist movements and parties included the declassed, war veterans, lumpen and unemployed. World War I and the inter-war interregnum were widely perceived as the epitome of a deep 'civilizational crisis'.

The cultural nationalisms that emerged in inter-war Europe, the loss of self-confidence among large sections of the petty bourgeoisie and of the intelligentsia, were rooted in this palpable sense of civilizational decline – the end of the *Belle époque*, the run-up to World War I, its frenzied aftermath (the decade of the twenties) and the onset of the Great Depression. In contrast, the cultural nationalisms of the colonized world was the reaction of indigenous elite and middle-class intellectuals to the colonial experience itself. Though the cultural nationalisms of inter-war Europe manipulated themes that had emerged decades earlier, even before the turn of the century, the cultural nationalisms of the colonized countries (because of their link to a progressive project – the stirrings of anti-colonialism) were to have an organic growth, a wider spread and a more lasting appeal.

(2) The sense of 'civilizational decline' expressed itself in popular and elite disillusionment with liberalism and the liberal order. It was only through and after World War II that liberalism was to stage a remarkable and unexpected comeback.[28] Inter-war Europe was *uniquely* fertile ground for the message of anti-liberalism and anti-democracy so central to fascist ideology.

(3) This receptivity to anti-liberalism/anti-democracy was connected to a disbelief in the durability of bourgeois democratic structures. The stated or unstated assumption of all classical Marxist theories of fascism was that bourgeois democracy might be the most desirable and effective of all forms of bourgeois rule, but it was an exceptional state of affairs, inherently unstable. Nothing left Marxists as unprepared for the course of the post-war era in the metropolitan heartlands as this facile and utterly mistaken assumption.[29] While there is a relationship between economy and polity – the stronger the economy the more feasible a bourgeois democratic form of the state – this is not axiomatic.

In the weak, dependent economies of the third world the overall historical trend so far has been opposite to what Marxists should have anticipated if they believed in the instability and exceptionalism of bourgeois democratic rule, all the more so for backward economies. Authoritarian rule in third world countries has been increasingly punctuated by quasi- or controlled- or guided-democratic experiments. Inconceivable to pre-World War II Marxists, even military dictatorships have held largely unrigged elections and stepped down when their legitimacy or that of their political puppets has been repudiated.

In the last two decades over 800 million people in the former second and third world have moved towards quasi- or near-democracy.[30] Political liberalism has never enjoyed greater or more universal appeal and the democratic idea (albeit in bourgeois form) has become a material force of such strength that *explicit* anti-liberalism/anti-democracy has less chance than ever of popular, even middle-class endorsement.

In functioning democracies rightwing movements seeking popular support more often than not cloak their anti-democratic character, apologize for or disavow occasional 'excesses', rationalize their demands and behaviour as expressions not just of the popular will but of the *democratic* majority. Only to the detriment of their populist ambitions would such movements campaign on an openly anti-democratic platform. Where fascism promised to usher in authoritarianism in full sight through the front door, today's radical or 'fascistic' Right will bring it in surreptitiously through the back door.

This is an important point. The character and mood of a rightwing movement's social base (even among the petty bourgeoisie) is very different when its leading party campaigns openly on a comprehensively anti-liberal and anti-democratic programme and when it does not. This is so, even if the party trains its cadres in a spirit explicitly hostile to the ideology of liberalism and bourgeois democracy. The potential for mischief and evil of such rightwing formations is qualitatively greater when it wins popular support for what it actually is and not for what it pretends to be.

It is not an adequate counter-argument to point to the experiences of participation and involvement in democratic processes by fascist parties in the fascist era or to the examples of their dissimulation of an anti-democratic thrust and message. Propaganda about the essential bankruptcy of the liberal-democratic model, the believers in this notion and the *believability* of this notion were all of a qualitatively different order in the 'fascist era' than in the post-1945 era. Mussolini openly espoused totalitarianism, giving it a positive content. Hitler and others presented fascist *dictatorship* as a superior, transcending form of 'truer', more meaningful mass democracy/mass self-expression.

So much water has now flown under the bridge, so strong remain the negative historical memories of fascisms and 'totalitarianisms' in power and so strong the myriad contemporary re-creations of such memories that no putative fascist force in our times can pursue the ideological course adopted by the fascisms of the past. They cannot, to their mass base, openly proclaim their allegiance to an anti-democratic *fascism* or an anti-democratic *totalitarianism*, i.e. to a fundamentally anti-liberal, anti-democratic project. Nor can they pursue a second course, legitimizing use of such labels in public discourse by redefining these terms to give them a 'softer', 'more positive' or 'more *truly* democratic' content. Such is the historical discredit attached to them.

This differs sharply with the fate of such terms as socialism and Marxism. Here the historical record has pushed many subscribing to the transformative project labelled socialism to redefine the notion to make it 'softer' and 'more democratic', even to reduce it to a sub-set of democracy. But the label itself has not been abandoned. Indeed, can any kind of meaningful socialism ever be brought about without clinging to the term itself? Those influenced by Discourse Theory and the presumed importance of 'interpellation' should ask themselves what kind of fascism or totalitarianism can be brought about when the very use of such 'names' or terms has become impermissible. Why this impermissibility? What are its consequences for the construction of the transformative project that fascism promises?

The usual way out of this 'difficulty' for third world 'unorthodox Marxists' or 'post-Marxists' committed to the notion of third world and Indian fascisms but influenced by Discourse Theory and the presumed 'irreducibility of the ideological–cultural' is simply to ignore its existence, although it emerges from the very terms of their own theoretical framework. For all the emphasis of this school on the 'collective construction of identities' by culturally authoritarian mass movements and cultural discourse, the development of what is to all intents and purposes postulated to be a *fascist* mass movement owes nothing at all to the construction of a self-consciously *fascist* mass identity, which is clearly absent. Such movements are *objectively* fascist and totalitarian. This might be acceptable to Marxists or to others who take seriously the notion of objectivity but is certainly at odds with the biases and analytical practices of this school itself.

In those Left circles in India less influenced by Discourse Theory, preserving the validity of the fascist paradigm has involved a definite shift towards acceptance of the 'fascism from above' perspective. Such fascisms may be facilitated in certain cases by a mass movement from below which need not be openly anti-working class in its behaviour or self-perception, but is *objectively* so.

(4) The underestimation of the strength and durability of bourgeois democracy after 1945 by Marxists was, of course, the natural correlate of an obverse error – the overestimation of the 'structural crisis' of capitalism. The remarkable productivity of late capitalism and its ability to learn from its mistakes (preventing a repeat of anything approximating the Great Depression) has thrown all earlier anticipations out the window. Whatever its contradictions and problems, 'actually existing capitalism' has proved itself more capable of coping with them than 'actually existing socialism', its principal systemic rival, showed itself to be in coping with its own.

The kind of socio-economic dislocations that were the preconditions for the growth of fascism in inter-war Europe have not been approximated anywhere in the heartlands of advanced capitalism. Marxists of the inter-war period believed not just that there would be relative poverty and inequalities in the advanced countries but that there would be absolute impoverishment on a mass scale. Though cyclical upswings were likely and severe defeats for the working class via fascism could usher in a more sustained upturn, the longer term prospects for the global capitalist system were bleak, even though there would not be any inevitable breakdown.

Twenty years after the end of the 'long boom' (itself never anticipated), in the current declining phase of the 'long wave', the prospects of fascisms coming to power remain dim. Though new and stronger authoritarian pressures are visible in certain countries of Western Europe, the overall climate is still nowhere near as disturbing as in the 'fascist era'. It is more to the former second world and to the third world that fascism-watchers have shifted their gaze. Despite the incomparable strengths of the Marxist critique of capitalism as an economic system, it has still to properly grip late capitalism's sources of productivity and dynamism.

(5) It was this acuteness of the capitalist structural crisis between the wars that explained the attractions of the fascist option for sections of domestic big capital, particularly its finance wing. What is more, this crisis operated in a global framework where imperialist competition for expanded economic control over raw materials and markets was rife. Success in expanding economic control was crucial for coping effectively with the structural crisis in its national manifestations. And this effort by competing national capitals was inseparable from expanding political (therefore in the final analysis military) control by competing national states.

For the Marxist theorists of classical fascism, the typical form of inter-imperialist competition and conflict was territorial expansion through wars, particularly by imperialist latecomers. Fascism or military dictatorship with its much greater centralization of political and military power, was one of the more effective ways of preparing and conducting this inter-imperialist rivalry. The economic stake of World War II was global pre-eminence, and it was the USA which, coming out of that war, achieved and retained that status for perhaps two decades.

The usefulness of this vision of global economic imperatives did not outlive the inter-war period. Such have been the changes in global capitalism that territorial expansion through wars is not only atypical of modern inter-imperialist rivalry, but almost inconceivable. The presence of a powerful Soviet bloc rival which contained such inter-imperialist tensions was not the key factor. Even after the collapse of Communism, wars between imperialist powers and conquest of territory are processes clearly belonging to a bygone era.

Even Marxists sense as much but have to properly theorize why, as part of the larger task of adequately theorizing imperialism in its new phase. For Marxist theorists of fascism in this new phase of imperialism what are the strong compulsions, if any, for the fascist option to emerge and triumph in the metropolitan countries?

(6) The classical theory of fascism was linked to the classical theory of imperialism (Hobson, Hilferding, Lenin). The core principle of imperialism remains unchanged – the expansionist compulsions of monopoly capital. But the forms, mechanisms and correlates of this expansionism can and have varied. It is here that the assumptions of the classical theory of imperialism have proved inadequate. For Lenin, 'It is beyond doubt, therefore, that capitalism's transition to the stage of monopoly capitalism, to finance capitalism, is connected with the intensification of the struggle for the partition of the world.'[31]

What is this connection? Economic partition, in particular of raw materials' supply and markets, would require political partition.[32] The classical theory's over-emphasis on the importance of territorial expansion flowed from its under-emphasis and lack of recognition of finance capital's dynamism. In the classical theory, technical innovation as a source of profit was downgraded and subordinated to cartel agreements and manipulation of financial markets as far more important sources of profit.

The most important feature of late capitalism after World War II, however, has been the growing, indeed primary, importance of technical innovation. Control of know-how, not so much of raw materials or markets, has become central to the capitalist accumulation process on a global scale. Political stability and preserving capitalist social relations has become far more important for imperialism outside its territorial heartlands than direct political or military control. Control over technology and know-how has superseded in importance the expansion of control through direct ownership, thus allowing more complex forms of cooperation and competition between monopoly capitals, transnational corporations (TNCs) and smaller capitals, domestic and foreign. The attitudes of imperialist capital and states towards authoritarianism in the second and third world are diverse. When rolling back revolutions and the influence of the USSR was the primary obsession, imperialist support for third world authoritarianisms was often very strong. The key purpose was not specific economic compulsions of making profits in these countries but the more general purpose of preserving capitalist social relations and preventing political challenges to this order, i.e. making the world safe from Communism.

But political stability was often better served through the institution-alization of quasi-democratic or near-democratic regimes, especially when it became clearer that the threat of steady Communist expansion was greatly exaggerated. Neither authoritarianism nor democracy is the natural preference of imperialism in the third world but political stability, where this is a function not simply of strong rule by preferred dynastic leaders but also of the strength of popular democratic aspirations among the ruled.

Since Marxists hold that in most third world states domestic capitals are *dependent* capitals, the interests of the entities they are dependent upon, namely foreign capitals (more precisely complex segments of foreign ruling classes), becomes crucially important. Any Marxist attempt to theorize third world fascisms has to factor in this external dimension. Why should foreign capitals having controlling positions in the dominant-class coalitions or ruling-class alliances of specific third world countries want to encourage, not just the authoritarian option, but the specifically fascist one? If fascism is the 'resolution' of the acute economic–political–ideological dilemmas of the hegemonic component of the biggest and most powerful fraction/segment of capital in the ruling-class bloc/coalition/alliance, then it must be the resolution of the dilemmas of foreign capital or its representatives, which, even in the strongest of the third world capitalist states, plays this crucial hegemon-izing role! To be a *dependent* capitalist country means foreign capital plays the crucial hegemonizing role in the ruling power bloc or class alliance.[33]

Third world fascisms, it would appear, are ultimately rooted not in the needs of third world bourgeoisies but in those of the first world.[34] But the third world, while remaining an important source of profits for metropolitan-based capitals, has become secondary. It is the 'intensive' processes of accumulation within the OECD countries that has been central to the global accumulation processes of advanced capitalism.

There are great, perhaps insuperable, difficulties for any Marxist theory of third world fascism which at the same time wishes to remain faithful to the class dynamics elucidated by the classical theories. No wonder, then, that the most sustained if ultimately unsatisfactory effort in this direction – Barrington Moore's – took self-conscious leave of the classical Marxist approach.

(7) All mass Communist parties of the non-Maoist/non-Castroist type had their origins before World War I or between the two world wars. Not a single new mass Communist party of the orthodox type emerged after World War II. Only two such parties – the South African Commu-

nist Party (SACP) and the Communist Party of India (Marxist) or CPM – are still stable or growing. This is true of the Maoist or Castroist currents where they have emerged as mass parties. Nepal may be the only Maoist exception. It is a dismal picture contrasting sharply with the first half of the twentieth century, when, whatever its temporary vicissitudes, socialist-, Communist- and Marxist-inspired working-class movements were a powerful and growing force and Communism an ideology with a vibrant and strong appeal. The 'actuality of the revolution', to use Lukács's phrase, by which was certainly also meant its imminence, was no mere rhetorical slogan. There was justification for an equable revolutionary optimism. The fascist option made sense in the context of this powerful systemic threat to the rule of capital, especially where the working-class threat and the possibility of its rapid mass radicalization, was so real and strong.

In the post-war era, the overall historical trajectory has been the domestication and de-radicalization of the working-class movement worldwide with but few exceptions, e.g. Brazil. Social democracy and orthodox Communism are both in historic decline, with their political centre of gravity more to the right than at any time in their respective histories. The loss of élan in socialist ideology and the loss of self-confidence in all the organized currents of socialism–Communism is unmistakable, especially after the collapse of Communism in 1989 and China's new economic trajectory. The revival of the socialist agenda and restoring the 'actuality of the revolution' is clearly a matter of the 'long haul'.

In the first world the working-class movement is nowhere a systemic threat and has yet to replicate its earlier more radical credentials of the inter-war or immediate post-war period. This may not be a permanent situation but the prolonged absence of such a radical pressure on the system must affect one's evaluation of the prospects and possibilities of fascism now and in the foreseeable future.

In the former second world the general direction of a 'transition to capitalism' is unwavering, only its pace and manner in dispute. A 'transition to democracy' is much more problematic. An authoritarian involution of the state in many, perhaps most, cases can hardly be ruled out, nor barbaric forms of state behaviour which might warrant the label fascism (as a term of abuse). The re-formation of nation-states and the redrawing of territorial boundaries is on the agenda. But it is the similarities with the pre-World War I/pre-fascist rather than with the inter-war 'fascist era' that are more striking. There are no signs anywhere of the kind of working-class threat that might evoke an extreme fascist response. In no Eastern European country is there a working class that looks likely to be radicalized quickly. It is reformist parties that may even eschew the label of socialist or Communist that hegemonize the working class. These parties express whatever level of class unity and independence has been forged in the post-Communist phase. Even such minimal class political independence of a reformist type may not emerge in certain countries where the American model of two main bourgeois parties, liberal and conservative rather than conservative and social democratic, might be institutionalized.

In the third world, with few exceptions, the working class is divided in its political loyalties among an array of forces. Explicitly working-class or Left parties have to contend with populist parties which often have as strong a, if not stronger, working-class base. In few third world countries is an independent and fairly united working-class movement a major political threat to bourgeois rule. In some of the more industrialized third world countries, e.g. India, South Korea, they are little more than a significant pressure group.

Only in Latin America in the seventies did working-class power pose a grave threat to bourgeois domination. Chile under Allende was the foremost example. Pinochet's counter-revolutionary coup/dictatorship did not have many of the properties of a 'fascist option' or seizure of power. There was no mass fascist movement resting on the petty bourgeoisie defeating the working class decisively before ascending to power. There was no fascist party with a distinctly fascist ideology, which grew rapidly before making its bid for power. But one crucial function of fascism was certainly displayed. The working class was brutally crushed with all its organs smashed because the hegemony of the ruling classes was gravely threatened by the logic of Allende's reforms and the rapidly mobilizing social base of his government. This crushing took place not via a movement but by the military, not before but after a coup. The precise designation of this experience and of the Pinochet dictatorship – whether semi-fascist or fascist or simply brutal military authoritarianism – clearly takes second place to the function carried out by the new post-Allende regime.

But the 'fascistic' traits in the political process culminating in Pinochet's coup were in direct proportion to the strength of the revolutionary threat posed by the Chilean working class. If the Chilean counter-revolution carries one lesson it is that the character and behaviour of authoritarian states not provoked by the rising power of a unified and independent working class will be different in very significant respects from those that are so provoked. Repressing and subordinating the working class within a one-party state may be one property of fascism. As such, a number of third world regimes, e.g. Iraq, might fulfil this condition, but these are not fascist dictatorships. Many developmentalist dictatorships have had much the same relationship with the working class. Here, it has usually been the *prior* weakness of the working-class movement, its relative isolation and limited spread in a largely backward economy, that has facilitated the institutionalization of such a relationship when the party-state dictatorship or military dictatorship was formed. This is clearly quite different from the counter-revolutionary character, the 'last-ditch rescue operation', of fascism.

However, the Chilean experience does suggest that *perhaps* the only fruitful way to generalise a theory of fascism to the third world and yet remain broadly faithful to classical Marxist theories would be to abandon two elements in that classical 'fascist minimum'. The working class need not be decisively demoralized by a mass movement before fascist seizure of power but can be so after a 'fascist-like' seizure of power. There also need not be any fundamental impulse to external territorial expansion. Such a 'pared-down' fascist minimum would only preserve the idea of a basic dynamic of class forces operating at the bottom and top of the given society where the fascist threat supposedly exists.

Such a fascist minimum is *solely* pivoted on socio-economic factors in an even more extreme or sparse way than Barrington Moore's model. But with one crucial difference. It would be a 'counter-revolution from above' and not a 'revolution from above'. But even this would not legitimize the notion of a third world fascism. At best it would endorse a third world *neo-fascism* or *semi-fascism* which by its extreme nature would also be characterized by its great rarity of occurrence. The 1965 Indonesian army coup, despite its crushing of what was then the third largest Communist party in the world, is still best seen as an especially brutal form of third world authoritarianism *outside* the distinctively fascist paradigm. Chile remains the strongest candidate since 1945 for some kind of 'variant of fascism' label.

(8) The eighth feature of fascism in inter-war Europe was the 'squeezing of the middle classes' of town and countryside. Two pressures kept the vice in place. First was the class-polarizing effect of capitalist industrialization. In the towns this would mean the steady proletarianization of the lower rungs of the petty bourgeoisie as the proportionate size and objective strength of the working class grew. In the countryside the small peasant would lose out. The peasantry would not persist.

The other factor behind the squeezing process was the growing conflict between capital and labour pushing the vacillating petty bourgeoisie to choose sides. Nonetheless, this shrinking middle class was the only mass base for the bourgeoisie. One of Trotsky's key insights was that the self-consciousness and self-confidence of this stratum would determine the particular *form* of bourgeois rule. Hence the crucial importance of fascism in shaping and directing the consciousness of the petty bourgeoisie.

The second half of the twentieth century has shown that here, too, the assumptions of the classical Marxist theories of fascism have been shaken. In much of the third world the most striking feature has been not the more or less rapid disappearance of the small landholding farmer but the remarkable 'persistence of the peasantry'. In the towns the middle classes have usually had little pressure from below from a working class that has been undeveloped and fragmented.

This middle class has been a major base for populist movements and important layers have often been the driving force behind progressive reform movements. Far from being squeezed, this middle class has been more easily incorporated into ruling oligarchies via the state bureau-cracy. As late industrializers, most third world countries had a higher proportion of the middle class within their overall class matrix than was the case with the early industrializers of the West at a comparable point in their modernizing process.

Insofar as populism is a more useful generic label to attach to a variety of political movements/regimes in the third world, it is surely because of the relatively greater role played by third world middle classes in the political evolution of their societies. The natural pattern of political development in the advanced societies has been the emergence and consolidation of sharply etched class parties, obviously so in programme and composition, because working class and peasant largely achieved class independence. Multi-class nationalist political formations have been the norm in much of the third world precisely because worker and peasant have not achieved the same degree of class political independence.

In the advanced countries the post-war developments have created an intellectual controversy about what has been called the 'embarrassment of the middle classes'. Is the sociological record such as to refute classical Marxism's polarization thesis – the dominant two-class model? There is no clear answer. According to one Marxist definition of class as necessarily structured by a relationship of exploitation, it is still possible to argue that the polarization thesis holds.[35]

But no Marxist will dispute that if the working class has grown absolutely and proportionately it is also more segmented internally than ever before by criteria of skill, education, gender, race, wages, conditions, etc. If indeed the petty bourgeoisie has objectively been squeezed by the processes of late capitalist accumulation in the first world, this also seems to mean much less than it did earlier. The growing segmentation of the working class beneath it, whose upper layers overlap with the lower reaches of the middle class, has immensely complicated the question of sustaining, let alone deepening, the unity and class independence of that proletariat. The subjective pressure of the working class on the petty bourgeoisie has been significantly defused no matter what its 'objective' constriction.

The social, economic and political evolution of late capitalism has made the usefulness of the fascist paradigm more problematic, not less. In the post-war era only the most blatantly 'neo-Nazi' and 'neo-fascist' groups have been referred to as fascist by a wide consensus within Marxist circles. These formations self-consciously trace their lineage to the inter-war fascisms. But the thrust of their public propaganda and campaigning is not the 'fascist solution' to the 'civilizational crisis' of their times or the construction of the 'new man', but a super-patriotism focused on racist and anti-immigrant xenophobia. Since their fascist potential is not to be gauged solely or even primarily by their internal ideology and organization, and since much of their base is working-class youth, they have also been characterized more cautiously and sensibly as pre-fascist or potentially fascist formations whose ideology contains dangerous fascist themes.

The memory and awareness of what the historic experience of fascism has meant and the practical experience of prolonged bourgeois democracy are powerful vaccines within the working class (and even the petty bourgeoisie) against the fascist temptation. Neo-fascist groups have got mass support for their racist and xenophobic programmes and activities, but there is no easy transition from this to widespread support for fascism proper.

If there is widespread but not total consensus on the characterization of some groups and parties in Europe as fascist there is no consensus on the characterization of movements or regimes as fascist. No single movement and no single authoritarian nationalist regime anywhere has secured such a consensually agreed label in the post-war period. The fascist era was, above all, an era of fascist movements, not regimes. If, in its heyday, it is the rarity of fascist victories that is so striking, what reason is there to believe that fascist movements or fascist regimes are likely to be less rare and more frequent in an era when the preconditions for its emergence, growth and victory are weaker or absent? Is not the absence of consensus over the validity of the fascist label for any single post-war movement or regime reflective of the absence of the fascist phenomenon itself?

The frequent resort by Marxists (and some non-Marxists) to adjectival qualifiers of fascism – semi-fascism, neo-fascism, quasi-fascism, proto-fascism or fascist-like – are revealing. They suggest both unease and pugnacious insistence. Fascism, Marxists are adamant, is a recurring phenomenon. But it has recurred in forms which leave one uncertain just how fascist it is or even whether it belongs to the genus. Such hyphenated fascisms are sometimes used simply to suggest that *some* characteristics of *some* fascist entities of the past exist in its contemporary look-alikes. This usage has descriptive value but hardly offers much in the search for a contemporaneously relevant theory of fascism.

There is a stronger interpretation of the meaning of such hyphenated fascisms. The political entities so described – parties/groups, movements, regimes – are seen as possessing the 'fascist essence', the 'inner logic' of fascism. It is another thing that this logic may be prevented from 'maturing' into the more recognizably fascist entities that are historically familiar.

To talk of the 'inner logic' of a fascist entity or of its degree of maturity is to perceive it as equivalent to a 'fascist organism'. This presumed homology of political or social entities with biological ones has often caused havoc in Marxist thought. It is misleading here as well. This 'inner logic' is not equivalent to the fascist minimum. The 'logic' or 'principal dynamics' of fascism subsumed by the notion of the fascist minimum are never the result of the evolution (unblocked or otherwise) of some 'organism' marked by its infant or adolescent or even adult characteristics. *The fascist minimum is always the complex structuration of characteristics both internal and external to the 'fascist protagonist' in a given context.* The contextual or 'shaping' factors are more important than any 'inner logic' or 'essence' of the 'fascist organism'. It is the fascist *situation* that 'matures', not the fascist entity.

Parties and movements may be pre-fascist or potentially fascist. It is difficult to see how they, or regimes, can be proto- or semi- or quasi-fascist except in a superficial descriptive sense. (Difficult but perhaps not impossible: see the earlier comments on Chile and theorization of third world neo- or semi-fascism.) Perhaps they could be called 'functional substitutes for fascism'? But which functions are fulfilled and which left out? And how effective the 'substitution' when these functions are left out? What are the forms of substitution and why? Is this not an attempt to salvage a thesis that is less and less defensible, where the refutation is redescribed as confirmation? For example, in order to explain the economic successes of far-east Asia, their Confucianist–cultural 'ethos' has been labelled a 'functional substitute' for the Protestant Ethic. Most of the movements and regimes likely to be so labelled are in the third world. Are we not in danger of getting lost in our own theoretical maze because determined to see things through some kind of fascist prism or its optical substitute? There is no developed theory of third world fascism except Moore's. And the classical theories cannot be transposed to the third world without distorting their essential character.

Fascism as a descriptive term of abuse will no doubt live on and have a certain rhetorical–political value. Fascism as a label for contemporary political phenomena claiming only that the phenomena so described share some (possibly important) properties with the fascist phenomena of the past can also be an acceptable usage. But Marxists might also ponder whether the time might not have arrived to abandon fascism as a conceptual tool of contemporary relevance.

From a different starting point, then, and following a very different route of historical self-evaluation, a 'Marxist theory of fascism' might end up with the same conclusion as some of the non-Marxist theories of fascism. Fascism was a generic phenomenon but one which was ulti-mately confined spatially and temporally to inter-war Europe. What we need is not a new, more developed or refined or universal theory of fascism but newer and better ways of understanding newer, even generic, phenomena thrown up by the late capitalism of our times. Knowing what to select and discard from the historic repertoire of Marxist concepts to better interrogate the present is always a tricky affair. Discarding the concept of fascism could risk serious error, but could also be a liberating decision.

Hindu Communalism and the Question of Fascism

It might appear strange that a text whose ostensible purpose is to 'situate' Hindu communalism so far has paid little attention to its concrete manifestation – the forces of the Sangh Combine and their collective ideology. But if the fascist paradigm itself is inappropriate or of very limited value for situating not just Hindu communalism but a whole host of political phenomena, particularly in the third world, then it hardly helps to delineate the 'essential' features of the Hindu communal Right to see how they 'fit' the fascist design or label.

Investigating the validity of the fascist paradigm is the primary level of exploration.

At the secondary level – investigating the 'fascistic' features of the organizational structure/style, behaviour and ideology of the Sangh Combine – the disputations are endless and assessment inconclusive. There are important dissimilarities as well as similarities. For example, the absence in the Sangh Combine of any truly charismatic leader; the absence of *explicitly* anti-liberal/anti-democratic and anti-working class themes in its campaigning; the absence of any verbal anti-capitalist demagogy (*swadeshi*, or emphasis on indigenous production, is not its equivalent); the absence of any orientation to the theme of a 'generational revolt'; and so on. No doubt a list of similarities can also be generated. When there is no accepted theory of fascism, no accepted set of objective criteria, the assignment of 'fascist' emphasis and weight must remain arbitrary, the method a solipsism.

Though all fascist formations and movements must compromise in propaganda and tactics, their pragmatism has definite limits. They draw support from all classes but are not multi-class formations or movements, nor a form of authoritarian populism. They do not 'loosely unify' but polarize society and politics. They have a mass but minority support. It is not a coincidence that where fascist parties did come to power – Italy, Germany and Spain – they did so in rightwing coalitions which they either subsequently dominated and destroyed (Germany, Italy) or to which they were subordinated and absorbed (the Falangists of Spain).

Fascist formations win ideological and political hegemony because their decisive victories are achieved on the non-ideological terrain. The tempo of their forward movement is convulsive and mercurial. They grow rapidly but also fade out fast if they don't achieve power, for the extreme crisis situation on which fascism feeds is by its very nature an unstable one crying out for a 'solution' and getting it in one form or the other – socialist, democratic, authoritarian or fascist. Extreme crisis can never be a durable or normal condition of any society. Once in power, however, the tenure of the fascist state can be much prolonged, even as the character lines dividing a fascist state from less extreme forms of authoritarianism get blurred.

In post-colonial societies, the political vehicles of religious fundamentalism or religious nationalism are not fascist formations but, at most, potential fascist formations. I have argued that the conditions for the realization of that potential do not exist and are not likely to surface. While the fascist state in India would necessarily be Hindu nationalist, the Hindu communal and nationalist state would not necessarily be fascist. It is noteworthy that of the range of Islamic states that do exist, from the 'harder' varieties in West Asia to the 'softer' variants in the Malay–Indonesian zone, it is very difficult to get away with classifying even one as properly fascist. This is not a clinching argument but it illustrates the variant possibilities regarding theocratic, confessional or denominationalist states, the range of combinations of the secular, the democratic and the authoritarian in structures, policies, laws and practices of states which are otherwise all religiously affiliated and therefore in some key respect institutionally discriminatory and undemocratic with respect to their non-Muslim citizens. Israel manages to combine functioning bourgeois democracy for Jews with institutionalized discrimination and often brutal repression of Palestinians. But it is not a fascist state.

If the weakness of the fascist paradigm calls for abjuring its use, this renunciation is made easier if one can see a plausible alternative paradigm. One can also see the rise of the Hindu communal Right as a specific Indian manifestation of a generic phenomenon but not one that belongs to the genus of fascism.

An Alternative Paradigm

Only the most rudimentary sketch lines of an alternative paradigm will be attempted here. In the last fifteen years, really from the late seventies, in all major zones – the first, the former second and third worlds – there has been the dramatic rise of the politics of cultural exclusivisms and xenophobia. Ethnic separatism or hatred or both have been the sentiments on the increase.

Across the globe the politics of cultural exclusivity have taken four forms. First, there has been the rise of religious fundamentalisms, not just Islamic but also, though less powerfully, Jewish and Christian fundamentalisms. Second, there has been the growth of Hindu nationalism and communalism and what with some caution might be called Buddhist nationalism and revanchism. Third, there has been the rise, especially in the former second world, of irredentist nationalisms – the unfinished business, it might appear, of the death throes of the Austro-Habsburg, Tsarist and Ottoman multinational empires put into deep freeze by Communist victories in the USSR, Yugoslavia, Eastern Europe and the post-Yalta Cold War glacis in Europe. Fourth, the spreading and swelling carbuncles of racist and anti-immigrant xenophobia in the first world have been evident.

In all these forms, the nation is either the focus or arena of contestation, the dominant point of reference. It is in the name of fulfilling the nation's destiny that the most barbarous political acts (those that most easily evoke the accusation of fascism) are justified. Why this centrality of the national unit? So international a phenomenon must have, to begin with, generic and global causes. Moreover, its irruption in these varied forms is too closely bunched in time to be dismissed as a temporal coincidence. Its primary roots are surely the crisis of late-twentieth-century modernity, be these differentially mediated via the dilemmas of late capitalism in its liberal-democratic guise in the first world; the collapse of Communism in the second; or the relative failure of developmentalism in the third.

Though an all-round crisis, it has a distinctive cultural dimension. The last half of this century has seen the rise, as never before, of cultural politics or contestation over norms, values and meanings. This in turn means conflicts over questions of identity since norms, values and meanings have to be felt and lived. Of course, both the content and frequency distributions of cultural politics have been variable and uneven. So, too, the lessons imbibed from a global historical experience – of world wars, fascism, the decline and rise of liberal democracy, anti-colonial movements, the rise and decline of Communism, the spread of consumer capitalism, the growth of mass communications systems and networks. But what, then, is the common and universal experience of modernity?

It is recognition of the unavoidability of constant flux, the permanence of change. Modernity institutionalizes the principle of radical doubt. It weakens where it does not destroy the absolute authorities of tradition, e.g. religion. It provides a plurality of claimants to authority. Modernity creates the self-reflexive personality for whom existential dilemmas can be more intense because there are no longer any easy answers. The certainties of custom and tradition are replaced by the uncertainties of reason and knowledge, the ambiguities of progress and of development/fulfilment, be it of the society one lives in or of the self. Even as religion and religious identity are relativized and compartmentalized, the preconditions for their resurgence are also created.

The devastation of older values, ways of life, forms of belonging, even of recently acquired values, ways of life, community, is traumatic enough. It is made bearable if what replaces the previous is 'better'; where the promise of greater fulfilment and empowerment and emancipation is believable. It is the fading of this Enlightenment promise of interrupted, uneven but nonetheless continuous progress that has

271

provoked a new kind of social disorientation and cultural despair, whose forms vary geographically, preceded by different histories, rooted in different combinations of the old and the new. The dangers and threats they pose differ in intensity. But everywhere the fall-back positions are the same.

When the future appears bleak, when neither steady generational progress nor the possibility of successful social transformation is believable, then the incorrigible past is the only source of guaranteed security. The imagined communities of ethnicity, nation and religion (of which the most important is nation) provide the most sought for continuities with that past. Of these it is the community of the nation that can subsume other identities because in its modern form, the nation-state, it is the prime locus of power. These three are the communities one is born into, that one can escape from only with the greatest difficulty, that one can belong to with greatest ease, without *doing* anything in order to belong.

Eric Hobsbawm had this to say about this kind of imagined belonging.

> After all, nobody can change the past from which one descends, and nobody can undo who one is. And how do men and women know that they belong to this community? Because they can define the others who do not belong. In other words by xenophobia. And because we live in an era when all other human relations and values are in crisis, or at least somewhere on a journey towards unknown and uncertain destinations, xenophobia looks like becoming the mass ideology of the 20th-century *fin de siècle*. What holds humanity together today is the denial of what the human race has in common.[36]

As with much else, the politics of cultural exclusivism, comparatively speaking, are qualitatively less destabilising in the first world than elsewhere. These negative cultural movements, primarily racism/anti-immigrant xenophobia, have come to the foreground recently. They were preceded (from the sixties to the mid-eighties) by an extraordinary and unparalleled flowering of progressive movements and struggles over ecological and peace issues, against race and gender discrimination, for freedom of sexual orientation and life-style. As Gramsci had suggested in his writings on Fordism, ideology and culture became more than ever the arenas of struggle in modern capitalism.

Unanticipated by him or by other Marxists, these struggles were accompanied by a relative quiescence of the traditional working-class movement. The politics of identity have overshadowed the politics of class. Culture had become a dominant, if not *the* dominant, terrain of social struggle, the preoccupation of the 'new social movements'. The end of the 'long boom', the transition from what some have called Fordism to post-Fordism, marked a new phase – the rise of conservatism and neo-liberalism, the partial containment and domestication of the new social movements, the growth of national xenophobia.

Part of the reason is the socio-economic decline. When the national cake no longer grows as fast or it stagnates (the collapse of the cake is no longer feared), then whether you 'belong' or not decides your entitlement to a share. Capitalism in its best liberal-democratic garb still delivers the goods but not enough of them and to not enough people. In the increasingly multi-ethnic societies of the West it is the inter-ethnic competitions that have grown fiercer. But the failure is not simply economic. Social disorientation also means a loss of sense of community. When the old links have been disrupted, what are the values that can bind people together?

In the more secularized West with its more settled nationalisms, the preferred options have been the ethnic communities of race and language. In the former socialist world, what else is there for the ordinary citizen to fall back onto except ethnicity and religion, separately or together? Here cultural chauvinism is not just nationally xenophobic, but often separatist. Great Serbian and Croatian nationalisms are not proto-fascisms, however barbaric their activities in Bosnia. They are the attempts to brutally forge new collectivities of meaning and political coherence along the lines of administrative convenience left by the collapsed socialist order, and so not the simple revival of the old, pre-World War I nationalisms. That socialist order ultimately failed to provide a stable new principle of collective belonging – loyalty to the socialist nation-state or to the socialist multinational state. It could not even provide the 'Fordist' prosperity of advanced capitalism or transit to a technologically more advanced 'post-Fordist' era.

The second world saw no equivalent to the cultural politics of the sixties to the eighties in the West. The politics of life choices could have no secure foothold when the agenda of the politics of life chances was so under-fulfilled.[37] And independent political life was not allowed to exist. When it was finally allowed to surface, cultural politics moved along the tracks already laid out – the formally legitimized, ostensibly self-determining 'nationalities' of ex-Yugoslavia, the ex-USSR, ex-Czechoslovakia.

In the third world the failure is the faded promise of the post-colonial project. The basic content of these anti-colonial nationalisms was negative, defined primarily by what they stood against rather than by

273

what they stood for. Since the colonized entities were rarely culturally 'homogeneous', neither for the most part were the emerging 'new' nations of the third world. The cultural content of these nationalisms was not a settled question. It would remain a part of the post-colonial agenda and its composition, organization and trajectory would be marked by the relative successes or failures of that project.

In India Hindu nationalism was already an important stream in the wider flow of anti-colonial cultural nationalism. But it is the decay of the post-colonial project as originally defined that best explains the subsequent rise of reactionary authoritarian populism embodied in the Sangh Combine.[38] It is not the newness of its ideological themes or messages, but the new receptivity to older, well-acquainted messages that most explains its rise. It is not the slow 'Long March' of Hindu communal ideology and its disseminating organizations that most explains its sudden popularity, but the factors outside the purview and control of the Sangh Combine. This new receptivity is grounded not in pre-fascist preparations or seedings of the economy (the New Economic Policy, whatever else it means, does not mean that) and polity, but in the collapse of the Nehruvian Consensus – the name that best defined the post-colonial project in India. The institutional embodiment of that project was the Congress, whose historic decline forms the crucial backdrop to the story of how and why Hindu communalism has grown.[39]

The guiding principles of that project were socialism, secularism, democracy. As the consensus collapses, the guiding principles themselves have been called into question, the first and second openly, the third surreptitiously. The first meant a vague but important commitment to social justice. The second meant a commitment to the preservation of a non-denominationalist and non-religiously affiliated state.

The danger, then, is the discarding not of the Nehruvian project but of the principles that underlaid it. Yet the appeal of Hindutva and its reactionary political encasement is precisely that it promises to provide a new project altogether based on very different guiding principles. It offers no *overall* socio-economic, political and cultural–ideological programme. Its focus is overwhelmingly on the last, its promise deceptively simple. If the nation is to be strong it must be culturally united through a clarification, recognition, acceptance and consolidation of its nationalist 'essence'. It is a new understanding of the past that provides the best means for handling the future. Knowing who we are, individually and collectively, somehow suffices for establishing, and guiding us to, our destination.

This is a perspective which seeks not to 'solve' the crisis of modernity as it applies to India, but only to cope. It offers neither revolution nor counter-revolution but a programme of cultural retrenchment. Cultural exclusivism and xenophobia are not the means to the creation of a new, more powerful and transformative project, they are the end or goal, the project itself.

Does It Make a Difference?

How *significant* a difference does accurate theoretical characterization of a phenomenon make? Given a bottom-line agreement that politically institutionalized Hindutva is a dangerous and pernicious phenomenon, that it is responsible for barbarous actions akin to those perpetrated by fascists of the past and that its coming to power would mean a new and more authoritarian form of the state, does it really matter if it is made out to be fully or partially fascist even if there is no strict theoretical warrant for either label?

This cannot be answered in any straightforward fashion. The significance of the difference between a more true and more false characterization, between political rhetoric and theoretical accuracy, varies according to the purposes of analysis. There are three aims that analysts separately can emphasize – explanation–understanding, prediction, practice, though all explanatory–interpretive frameworks have their own predictive and practical (policy) biases, even if implicit.

The first is in some ways the most important. The best test of a theory in the social sciences is its explanatory and interpretive power. Failure in prediction or in achieving a prescribed practice does not suffice to disqualify or discredit a theory or paradigm as long as its explanatory and interpretive power is greater than that of rivals. The very nature of the social sciences makes the link between the range and plausibility of explanation and efficacious application of its directives or orientations a much more tenuous affair than for the equivalent linkage between pure and applied in the natural sciences.[40] Whatever the failures of Marxism in prediction or as a guide for social transformation, its explanatory–interpretive power relative to other paradigms guarantees it a major presence in the social sciences.

To better know or understand phenomena is, in its own right, of great epistemological value, whatever the practical or other consequences might be. But when it comes to political phenomena and especially if these are of a contemporary kind, then the extra-explanatory consequences of different types of explanation are usually real enough, even if of uncertain and varying significance. A good social science theory or paradigm must above all explain and understand things better. The arguments laid out in this chapter have sought to show why the paradigm of fascism fails to perform well in this task. But better theories or paradigms should also have a reasonably strong tendency either to predict more or better or to do both better in comparison to worse theories or paradigms. And better predictions or assessments about the future behaviour patterns of the political phenomena in question should make it easier to find better means of coping with them. Whether we consider Hindu communalism and the forces that embody it to be fascist or not certainly makes some difference to political anticipations and practical perspectives.

Again, the differences in regard to anticipations are likely to be less significant, less diverse and less detailed than those on the level of explanatory–interpretive rivalry. The further one moves from 'pure' explanation to 'practice' (via predictions/anticipations), i.e. from theory to practice, the *less* likely are paradigm differences to matter significantly, though this does not mean these differences cannot be significant. It is only to point out a general tendency inherent in the nature of the differences between more theoretical and more practical endeavours.

The fascist and non-fascist views of self-described Hindu nationalism do have different analytical logics, giving rise to different conjectures and practical injunctions. Some of these differences will be looked at later after discussing the third aim – the practice that is derived from one's theory. A political practice aimed at combating a threatening phenomenon must have a shorter term as well as longer term perspective. Sometimes this can be seen as the division between tactics and strategy. On other occasions the short-term goal is of such paramount importance, e.g. preventing the Sangh Combine from achieving state power, that it, too, is seen as requiring a distinctive strategy.

The 'art' of political practice is different from the 'science' of theoretical analysis. The best theorists are rarely the best political strategists and there is no straightforward relationship between best or good theory and best or good strategy or practice. Theoretical differences are in an important sense less significant than programmatic differences and are usually secondary to the latter.[41] Programmatic agreement is more valuable than theoretical agreement. Precisely because there can be and often is such agreement despite theoretical–analytical differences, practical alliances between, and collective action by, disparate political forces is possible.

Programmatic perspective and practical strategy are a directed *distillation* of theoretical wisdoms. They involve a drastic reduction in the number of variables that have to be coped with in order to make theoretical insight *operational.* They also call for intellectual gifts of evaluation other than theoretical–analytical expertise of the usual kind. The operational significance of the theoretical differences may sometimes be small or even negligible.

Any political *strategy* must do certain things. It must first determine the principal aim, e.g. defeating the forces of political Hindutva. It must then break down this principal aim into a series of more specific objectives which are in some sense more strictly time-bound, e.g. preventing the reactionary Hindu Right from getting state power, or expanding further from its existing strongholds, or advancing on the ideological front, etc. Corresponding to these objectives, priorities have to be established. Actual and potential resources that can be deployed to achieve these priorities and objectives have to be assessed and rational courses or plans of action charted and adopted to connect means/ potential means and desired objectives. And all this must be done within an overall understanding of the constraints of the system, of what is possible and feasible at a given moment as well as over a longer time-span.

Over a longer period differences in theory become more important, being the *primary* and *general* way in which operational strategies, i.e. political programmes and practices, are affected. To prevent the Sangh Combine coming to power, theoretical rivalries may well translate into significant differences of political practice even in the short run. But perspectives for defeating the forces of political Hindutva for good, for destroying its social roots in the longer run, will likely be much more significantly affected by theoretical differences over the phenomenon's very *character.*

Some Political Conjectures

For a Marxist to believe that the forces of Hindu communalism embody the threat of an Indian fascism is to give the present struggle against it something more than an exceptional gravitas. It is to give it an apocalyptic charge, to believe that the working-class movement will be crushed before the accession of fascism to power, or *à la* Pinochet's Chile, that it will be so crushed immediately on or soon after fascism's seizure of state power. Fascist dominance in power may, however, be

277

preceded by a coalitionist interregnum where fascism briefly 'marks time'. In all Marxist notions of fascism, its accession to more or less full state power represents the *culmination* of the logic of fascism, not just an early transit point on a political dynamic which *ultimately* (later) *can* lead to fascism. That is too open-ended a formulation and is alien to any Marxist notion of fascism basing itself on the lessons of the fascist era. Such an open-ended formulation can be in consonance with an understanding of the forces of Hindu communalism as authoritarian, reactionary and anti-secular, and even as potentially fascist, but not as fascist already.

Clearly, a major difference of political perspective emerges from the two contesting (fascist and non-fascist) paradigms. One will more greatly emphasize the drastic curtailment or elimination of any democratic space for opposition once 'fascism' comes to power. It follows that the opposition, then, must resort to primarily clandestine forms of struggle and that mass and legal forms of resistance are near-impossible in the short and probably medium term. Only slow, molecular, underground forms of resistance can create the conditions for the subsequent and painful emergence of more collective and large-scale forms of resistance. In a very basic sense the 'political game is lost' if political Hindutva comes to state power. Its anti-Muslim character (even state-endorsed anti-Muslim pogroms) is secondary to a more fundamental logic – the destruction of even the possibility of *any* significantly scaled *organized* resistance whatsoever.

The logic of such a perspective should be to align the widest possible spectrum of 'anti-fascist' forces. In propaganda it would be a dereliction of political responsibility not to repeatedly highlight the 'fascist' threat *behind* the outward garb of political Hindutva, of selling this 'truth', howsoever reluctant its potential consumers (and fascism's prime victims, the working class) might be to see things this way. One of the most striking aspects of the fascist era was the lag in consciousness of the leadership behind the rank-and-file of the organized working-class movement, which had an intuitive hostility to the fascist threat, and was more 'aware' of its danger. (Even in Allende's Chile, the working class was much more sensitive to the imminent possibility of a military coup and clamoured for armed self-defence, which Allende and co-leaders opposed.) However, the organized working class in India does not see the forces of Hindu communalism in this way, though much of the leadership of the various leftwing political formations does. This does not lead these leaders to reject the notion of fascism but apparently makes the task of convincing the working-class movement and other

278

oppressed sectors of the danger of the specifically fascist danger all the more urgent, though extraordinarily difficult.

An alternative view might see the forces of Hindu communalism as viciously authoritarian and capable of launching anti-Muslim pogroms, fomenting civil strife at a hitherto unknown level, etc., but as non-fascist or at best pre- or potentially fascist. Such a view would be more inclined to believe that the scenario even after the formation of a Bharatiya Janata Party government would be very different. It would be more inclined to emphasize the significant domestic and international con-straints preventing any rapid elimination of all democratic space for open and mass forms of resistance. Precisely because the decisive battles to crush all democratic and working-class opposition have not been waged, there would continue to be significant prospects for delaying, halting and even reversing the extent of authoritarian degeneration. The securing of governmental power by political Hindutva would be a qualitative defeat for democratic, secular and anti-communal forces. But the political game would not have been lost and there would still be much to play for.

Such a perspective would have a more open-ended and flexible view of the range of outcomes and the degrees of authoritarianism possible. The state's authoritarian evolution would continue to depend on the unforeseeable outcome of continuing political struggles and pressures. At the same time those holding such a perspective would, as much as the anti-fascists, search for the widest possible secular and democratic front to prevent this reactionary rightwing populism from coming to power in the first place.

Apart from its rhetorical value the use (certainly the excessive use) of the label 'fascist' would be seen as misleading and possibly counter-productive. It would imply 'extreme' outcomes if political Hindutva were to continue rising rather than suggesting the longer menu of options that would presumably be the truer and more open-ended reflection of the reality on the ground. This could disorient the organization of opposition to the Hindu communal Right.

In a longer time-span the differing paradigms would also tend to suggest something else. The focus of the fascist paradigm is the question of state power – its loss to fascism (with all its baleful consequences) or not. An alternative approach which refuses to situate these proponents of Hindu nationalism within the fascist paradigm is much more likely to see the principal danger not as residing in something that lies *behind* Hindu communalism or as residing in some fascist core *contained within* or *hidden* in Hindu communalism, but as Hindu communalism *itself* as the specific manifestation of the politics of cultural exclusivity and rightwing reaction.

The long-term and in a sense more basic focus would be not on its potential or likelihood for a 'fascist' suborning of the state but on politicized Hindutva's deep roots and growth in civil society well beyond the question of its capacity to appropriate the state. In a sense the phenomenon is *more deep-rooted* than fascism, *more enduring* and *more difficult* to completely or comprehensively destroy. The ultimate decay or defeat of the Hindu state would not have the same decisively damaging effect on Hindu communalism as the ultimate decay or defeat of the fascist state has on the forces of fascism. The effect of the demise of a Hindu nationalist and communal state on this Hindu communalism would almost certainly be less complete or total than that of the demise of the fascist state on fascism. Its 'traces' would be stronger and longer lasting; indeed they would not be just 'traces'.

Whereas fascism in civil society is the prelude and the *preparation* for fascism coming into power, the same relationship in the same 'tight' way does not hold for Hindu communalism in civil society and the Hindu state. The task of secularizing Indian society is a much more arduous one than just preserving or deepening the secular and democratic character of the Indian state.

The Problem of Alliances

The two kinds of strategic alliances (corresponding to the fascist and non-fascist paradigms) for stopping the rise of the Hindu communal Right are the 'anti-fascist' front and the 'secular, democratic' front. But each can mean something different to different people, even among Marxists. Within the Marxist tradition there have been two distinct and competing candidates for the best way to fight 'fascism'. There is the United Front, formulated in the course of the first four Congresses of the Third International, and developed further by Trotsky; and the Popular Front, developed in 1935 at the Seventh Congress of the Comintern.

The United Front concept envisioned a *unity in action* of the main working-class parties in a context where (unlike in the third world with its populist parties) the characterization of working-class parties (Communist or social democratic) was unproblematic. This unity (with the assent of their leaderships) could not be based on any 'common long-term programme' between revolutionary and reformist parties/forces, but was for common *specific* goals to defend common interests. Since 'unity in action' and 'common experiences in action' were crucial for developing greater self-awareness and self-confidence of the working class vis-à-vis class opponents, e.g. fascists, the United Front should extend to all forms of working-class organization like unions and not just parties.

Structures to facilitate such 'unity in action' should not be artificially imposed but be based on the forms of class unity that already exist or are periodically thrown up in struggle in specific contexts. Moreover the United Front must under no circumstances involve an 'ideological non-aggression pact'. Revolutionary organizations must remain free to carry out ideological warfare against reformist ideas. Such a proviso clearly creates practical difficulties and is more likely to be acceptable where the revolutionary wing of the labour movement is of significant weight.

In two countries of the third world, China and Nicaragua, where strategic fronts were instrumental in ensuring victorious socialist revolutions via nationalist and democratic struggles, these fronts, while true to one fundamental principle of the classical United Front, also violated another. The revolutionary party or force in the strategic front retained its organizational and military independence but at the same time the front incorporated a major bourgeois political formation. They were, in effect, Popular Fronts, but the significant weight and organizational independence of the revolutionary component was the guarantee against successful betrayal by the 'bourgeois partner'.

The Popular Front perspective was different from that of the United Front. It, too, sought at its core to unite the working-class movement with its divided political loyalties, but this was to be integrated with the effort to create the widest possible unity of all forces, including bourgeois political formations/parties opposed to fascism. Thus three concentric circles were envisioned, each with a different level of unity:[42] first, the front of working-class parties with strong unity; then a broader and looser anti-fascist front of parties; and then an even looser national front including all anti-fascist elements. A possible fourth circle was the idea of an even looser international front against fascism.

The problem with the Popular Front approach is its political underdetermination and therefore its capacity to encourage a variety of ways in which the notion of alliances could be perceived and organized. When used by Stalin as a subordinate instrument of his foreign policy goal of protecting 'socialism in one country', or in Spain, Popular Frontism justified disastrous opportunist alliances, especially when the

281

working class could strike for victory. And yet, as in China and Nicaragua, when interpreted and carried out differently (keeping in mind some of the key principles of the United Front policy), they proved remarkably fruitful.

One of the central problems of the United Front perspective is its limited usefulness in countries where the working class is not hegemonized in its large majority by working-class parties. In situations of political urgency or crisis where clearly working-class parties are not strong enough even in combination, to win out on their own it is not a serious strategy for meeting the *imminent* threat or changing the overall relationship of forces decisively in its favour, though it can be useful for the narrower purpose of revolutionary party-building.

Since in most third world countries such hegemonization of the proletariat (urban and rural) by specifically working-class parties is a rarity and the proletariat (understood even in the broadest sense as all wage earners) itself may not be a significant majority of the general population, the strategy is something of a non-starter. In the Indian context to believe that the working class parties (the CPI, the CPM, far Left Maoist splinters), even if they could get together in a United Front, could on their *own* alter *decisively* the relationship of forces against the reactionary Hindu Right's current political onslaught is frankly absurd.

The Popular Front is far more realistic. But it is a strategy fraught with dangers. Some dangers are grave enough to make the whole strategy in certain circumstances counter-productive. It is a double-edged strategy but in most third world countries, certainly in India, one cannot simply counterpose the United to the Popular Front. The latter, understood as operating at different levels or 'circles', leaves room for many on the Left or far Left to pursue a classical United Front strategy as *part* of a wider Popular Front strategy. But the bigger and more influential the Left party or organization, the more it has to seriously reckon with the question of alliances with considered bourgeois parties and organizations.

The Popular Front must be pursued by the big actors on the Left, but with their eyes open, in full recognition of the risks involved. First, a Popular Front must never be based on some 'common longer term programme' between working-class or Left and bourgeois parties. It is a unity only against a common enemy. Second, since such fronts are neither socially nor politically homogeneous, they are always tension-filled. Even the common goals specified will for some be an initial step in the quest for deeper unity while for others they will represent the furthest they are prepared to go.

Popular Fronts, then, are likely to be brief political interludes. Furthermore, the internal relationship of forces between Left and bourgeois parties affects its trajectory. The weaker the Left is politically and organizationally, the more the chances of it being used and discarded by its temporary allies; the greater the chances of the experience proving counter-productive for the Left and its social base. These are real dangers and real problems. The Popular Front is guaranteed neither to succeed nor to fail. But where working-class parties *on their own* are not strong enough to succeed solely through a United Front policy, properly articulated Popular Fronts cannot be ruled out purely on the basis of an abstract theoretical principle treated as a historical Holy Writ. Too much has happened in the last fifty years and more. Such Fronts are most likely to succeed where the goal is short term and specific and where the Left goes into them in some strength, with its organization independent, critical faculties alive, eyes open.

In India some concretized expression of the Popular Front strategy is unavoidable at both the extra-electoral and the electoral level in order to contain and push back the forces of the Hindu Right. Such a general strategic perspective could be endorsed by some who insist that the Sangh Combine embodies fascism and by those who believe it doesn't. Whether one subscribes to the fascist paradigm or not apparently does not have to make a significant difference to choice of strategy. In practical terms the 'anti-fascist Popular Front' and the 'secular and democratic front' can both converge at the same arrangement, even as the different nomenclatures indicate a different evaluation of the nature of the main threat.

The stumbling block here is the question of the bourgeois centrist parties, the Janata Dal, the Congress party and smaller regional parties. Are one or some or all to be part of the 'anti-fascist front' or 'secular front' or not? The Janata Dal is now a serious political force only in Bihar and Karnataka. The addition of the Janata Dal to the 'anti-fascist' or 'secular' front does not resolve the central strategic problem in the Indian context – the establishment of an *effective* all-India anti-communal or 'anti-fascist' pole of political reference. Regional bourgeois parties in Andhra Pradesh, Tamil Nadu, Uttar Pradesh, also have to be taken into account. Hence the issue of forging a strong popular front of anti-BJP and anti-Congress political parties or what was once called the National Front–Left Front (NF–LF) alliance and is now called the United Front, currently in governance.

There is also the question of the Congress. Marxists upholding the fascist paradigm are torn between seeing the Congress as a flabby, authoritarian-inclined but nonetheless anti-fascist force, and those seeing it as so much responsible for the rise of Indian fascism and so close to the Sangh Combine in its nature as to disqualify it from any involvement in a strategy to combat fascism.

Those (Marxists and non-Marxists) who reject the fascist paradigm as applicable to today's India have the task of assessing the 'secular' character of the Congress, or at least of judging its commitment to the preservation of India's non-religiously affiliated, non-denominationalist state. Since I have suggested that the rise of Hindu communalism is best seen not as the rise of an Indian fascism but as the consequence of the collapse of the post-colonial project institutionalized in 1947, my bias should be clear.

The decline of the Congress has been the condition for the rise of the Sangh Combine. Despite the considerable communalization of the Congress, the erosion of its commitment to bourgeois democracy, it is a political formation whose historic character is fundamentally different from that of the Sangh Combine. It is the political force primarily responsible for the institutionalization of the Indian state in 1947 and for its continued existence as a 'weakly secular' and as a weakly democratic state, despite its supervision of the weakly authoritarian interlude of 1975–77. It must 'die' first before it can fully metamorphose into a party which is the equivalent of the BJP.

The still unrepudiated Congress policies of the previous Narasimha Rao government – its peddling of a 'pale saffron' perspective – make it pointless to call for its participation in an anti-Hindutva and 'secular' front. The Congress must itself see the need for such a perspective and take meaningful steps to forge such an alliance. All that can be said is that the Congress should not be *excluded* as a matter of principle from involvement in such a front. A battle against the Sangh Combine's usurpation of the soul of Indian nationalism is *pari passu* also a battle for the withering soul of the Congress party. The current tension in its ranks is an indication of this ongoing battle. But the decline is now so dramatic and the weakness of the Congress so profound that in the near future it can easily sink into irrelevance. Only if it shows signs of some significant revival can it once again make itself an inescapable part of the strategic struggle against the Sangh Combine. To even begin the process of doing that it would have to reject Narasimha Rao even as its leader in opposition and resile from the pursuit of a 'pale saffron' politics.

In the longer term struggle for the secularization of civil society in India, the Congress cannot be a strategic ally. But whether in the now

284

crucial short-term struggle the Congress can be a strategic factor really depends on whether it is able to overcome its current and greatest crisis ever, a crisis so great as to threaten its very survival as a significant all-India political force.

Since the Sangh Combine's ascent to governmental power would most likely take an electoral route, the question of an effective United Front governance today and an effective electoral front of secular forces in the coming period (which promises to be turbulent) cannot be dodged. If secularists win the battle to prevent the Sangh Combine's accession to governance in the next general elections, they are still far away from accomplishing their longer term task. But if these forces appropriate the Indian state, that longer term task for secularists, democrats and socialists will become immeasurably more difficult as the dark night of an authoritarian and communal Hindu state descends upon us.

Notes

1. S.G. Payne, *Fascism*, London, 1980.
2. H.A. Turner Jr, 'Fascism and Modernization', in *World Politics*, Vol. 24, 1971–72. Turner insists on taking German fascism's pastoralist themes at face value. The Nazi regime, had it lasted, would have revealed its anti-modern thrust more clearly. Nazism wanted the products of industry but without becoming an industrial society and its policy of *Lebensraum* was aimed at achieving just such an 'authentic' folk-German anti-industrial society serviced by non-Germanic industrialized regions.

   Turner also sides with those (A. Hughes and M. Kolinsky, 'Paradigmatic Fascism and Modernization', in *Political Studies*, Vol. 24, No. 4, 1976) who argue that fascism in Italy was not an agent of modernization. As late as 1938 only 33 per cent of the national income came from industry while between 1921 and 1936 industrial employment rose only from 24 per cent to 28 per cent while agricultural employment fell only from 56 per cent to 48 per cent. However, Payne (*Fascism*) and A.J. Gregor in his rejoinder to Turner ('Fascism and Modernization', *World Politics*, Vol. 26, 1973–74) are much more persuasive. Even before Mussolini, Italy was sixth in the world economic ranking. Comparisons with pre-1913 and post-1949 growth rates do not take into consideration the enormous dislocation of World War I nor do they adequately credit Mussolini's significant performance in the context of the Great Depression. For Gregor, without Mussolini's modernization of agriculture and prior industrialization, the post-1945 Italian economic miracle would not have been possible.

Barrington Moore Jr insists that fascism protected the interests of big agriculture in Italy at the expense of agricultural labourers and small peasants. Owner-operators dropped by 500,000 between 1921 and 1931 while 'cash-and-share' tenants rose by 400,000. In Germany Nazism in power junked its pseudo-radical agrarian populism since building a strong war economy could only be on the basis of industry. B. Moore Jr, *Social Origins of Dictatorship and Democracy*, Harmondsworth, 1966, pp. 450–52.

This dispute over the modern/anti-modern character of fascism is confined to bourgeois analysts. Marxists all agree on the modernizing thrust of fascism even if as a movement it feeds on the anti-modern sentiments of deeply dislocated social layers. At bottom the existence of this dispute reflects a key problem area in bourgeois thinking on fascism – what weight to give to economic structures and goals in any assessment of fascist movements and regimes? This problem is exacerbated by the methodological presumption in favour of ideology–organizational style as the most important elements of fascism.

3. Most Marxists perceiving fascism as a 'solution' to an extreme form of capitalist crisis accept that the price capitalist ruling classes have to pay is their substantial 'political expropriation'. Certainly, the Nazi state's determination to carry the war beyond 1944 when it was clearly lost and Germany could have sued for reasonable peace terms (the motivation of the Officer's Plot against Hitler in that year) and the economic 'irrationality and costliness' of Hitler's unflinching pursuit of the Final Solution strongly confirm this fact of the Nazi state's exceptional autonomy from the class interests it was ultimately supposed to serve. Differences between Nazism and Italian fascism – the greater importance of Hitler's party in the party-state of German fascism added to the autonomy of the German state – expressed themselves in the particularly aggressive expansionism of Nazi foreign policy.

Nicos Poulantzas (*Fascism and Dictatorship*, London, 1974) is one Marxist not prepared to concede that much (relative) autonomy to the fascist state. This derives from his understanding the state not in 'organizational-realist' terms as a distinctive set of apparatuses but as a 'social relation', i.e. the condensation of the balance of various class forces. Accordingly, the fascist state expresses a realignment in the 'power bloc' whereby big monopoly capital achieves hegemony. Such a 'condensation' of class forces would not be possible if the state as a 'social relation' was not relatively autonomous from specific classes and class fractions. For all its theoretical fruitfulness the alternative approach, which, unlike Poulantzas, refused to dissolve state power into class power, has proved to be more insightful in understanding state relationship to class power.

4. E. Weber, *Varieties of Fascism*, New York, 1964. Weber insists on drawing

286

a qualitative distinction between Italian fascism and National Socialism, especially in its German form. But even for him there are enough common references to incorporate both under the rubric of 'varieties of fascism'. Where Mussolini's fascism is supremely pragmatic, Nazism is more theoretical and doctrinaire. 'Fascism is pragmatically activist. National Socialism theoretically motivated or, at least, expressed. Both aim to conquer power and that center of power which is the modern state' (p. 143).

5. See, for example, the metaphysical meanderings of E. Nolte, *Three Faces of Fascism*, London, 1963.

6. This is too loose a formulation for those analysts (Marxists and non-Marxists) who insist on some race theory, e.g. anti-Semitism as indispensable to fascist ideology, i.e. a race–culture–nation symbiosis. However, the 'original' fascism of Italy did not really fall into this category. Mussolini's Blackshirts prided themselves on not having an anti-Semitic strain in their fascism. Only in 1938 did Italy, under German pressure, introduce a formal anti-Semitism into the fascist programme. Jews were proportionately over-represented in Italian fascism.

    If there was an element of 'Catholic fascism' in Italy there was no equivalent of 'Christian fascism' in Nazism. Indeed, many European fascisms were explicitly secular in their thrust, just as others (the Iron Guard Movement of Romania) had a semi-religious mystical fascism. The Falangists of Spain produced no race ideology, taking their ideology from the church instead. The attempt to form a Fascist International in 1934 could not agree over racism/anti-Semitism. (S.G. Payne, *Fascism.*)

7. For E. Weber, *Varieties of Fascism*, the unifying element is *the* leader. He 'is not so much the representative of his people as its medium' (p. 81).

8. In 1933 Hitler and Mussolini were 44, Mosley of Britain 37, Doriot of France 35, Codreanu of Romania 31, José Antonio Primo de Rivera of Spain was 30, Degrelle of Belgium 24.

9. There is even a theory by Talcott Parsons of fascism as an autonomous middle-class movement, and this in its most developed form is Seymour Lipset's theory of the 'radicalism of the centre'; Chap. 5 of *Political Man*, New York, 1960. For the view that fascism is not a petty bourgeois movement, see M. Mann, 'Class Politics in the Twentieth Century', in *New Left Review*, No. 212, July–August 1995. Mann's approach is similar to those who would deny that the Chinese Communist Party was a proletarian party. He sees the character of a movement or party as determined by its social base and cadre membership, ignoring the third and probably most important criterion of programme.

10. This is the view of E. Nolte, *Three Faces of Fascism*, S.G. Payne, *Fascism* and Renzo de Felice, *Interpretations of Fascism*, Cambridge, MA, 1977.

11. The concept of totalitarianism had a decisive impact on historical and

political research. It uncoupled fascism from the nature of capitalism and bracketed the study of fascism with the study of Stalinism. Bourgeois theories now searched for *fundamental* similarities between the fascist and Soviet state (Stalinist and post-Stalinist), abstracting from their different socio-economic structures. Since Mussolini was the first political leader to self-consciously describe the Italian fascist state as 'totalitarian', this subsumption by the concept of totalitarianism could claim a certain historical legitimacy.

The other decisive step in identifying the Stalinist political system as totalitarian was more dubious. Trotsky first pointed to totalitarian similarities but only in a restricted sense. 'A totalitarian regime, whether of the Stalinist or fascist type, by its very essence, can only be a temporary transitional regime. Naked dictatorship in history has generally been the product and the symptom of an especially severe social crisis, and not at all of a stable regime. Severe crisis cannot be a permanent condition of society. A totalitarian state is capable of suppressing social contradictions during a certain period, but it is incapable of perpetuating itself.' (*In Defence of Marxism*, New York, 1940 p. 13.) For Trotsky the totalitarian dictatorship had to give way rapidly to the Bonapartist dictatorship.

An ex-Trotskyist, Hannah Arendt, took over Trotsky's use of the concept and allied it with the psychological insights of the Frankfurt School to make it a characterization of a prolonged and stable dictatorship. To protect post-1945 third world dictatorships befriended by the advanced democracies from a similar charge, other theoretical steps were taken by analysts from Carl Friedlich and Zbigniew Brzezinski to Karl Popper. First, the totalitarian state's existence was linked to existence of an official totalitarian ideology like fascism/Nazism or Marxism, unlike mere 'authoritarian' states. Second, the totalitarian state was invested with the property of extreme political immobilism. Unlike authoritarianisms there could be no transformation from within or above, while the potential for such endogenously inspired transformation did exist in authoritarian regimes.

The bankruptcy of the totalitarian paradigm was never more obvious than after 1989. But Western victory in the Cold War has led to rapid internalization of the concept of totalitarianism within the ranks of its former opponents in the ex-USSR and Eastern Europe. Only those who believe the authority or longevity of concepts is primarily a function of intrinsic merits or the protocols of intellectual and logical consistency need be surprised by this.

For a good critique of totalitarian theories see M. Kitchen, *Fascism*, London, 1976.

12. L. Trotsky, *The Struggle Against Fascism in Germany*, London, 1975, introduced by E. Mandel. P. Togliatti, *Lessons of Fascism*, Rome, 1970.

N. Poulantzas, *Fascism and Dictatorship*. Also D. Beetham, *Marxists in the Face of Fascism*, Manchester, 1983.

13. The weakness is the result of the overall effect of accumulating contradictions, economic–political–ideological and not just of relative economic backwardness vis-à-vis other imperialist powers.

14. Populism has been understood as political movement, as ideology or both. G. Germani (*Authoritarianism, Fascism and National Populism*, New Jersey, 1976) says the Latin American middle class supported various populisms because there was no threatening working class beneath it. Latin American authoritarianisms were quite different. 'The main difference between the Latin American variety and the classic type of fascism consists in the fact that the active role in promoting and eventually establishing an authoritarian regime was usually assumed by the military not by the middle classes, which, however, under certain conditions gave their support to it' (p. 73).

   Alistair Hennessy ('Fascism and Populism in Latin America', in W. Lacquer (ed.), *Fascism: A Reader's Guide*, London, 1976) says six distinctive features of European fascism are absent in Latin America. (1) There has been no total war in twentieth-century Latin America as a pre-fascist 'dislocator' of society. The absence of war means that soldiers lack a military function, are more involved in civilian affairs, and are less tolerant of armed rivals. Populism links up through patronage with the 'marginal men', hence fascism holds less appeal for the latter. (2) Catholic culture is ubiquitous and the Church happy with its links to 'traditional' conservatives. (3) There is a weak Left in Latin America. Moreoever, there is urbanization without much industrialization. Clientelism controls the urban discontented. (4) Reactions to cultural crisis after World War I (anti-liberal, anti-Europe, anti-US) moved to nativism (Indianismo) and Hispanismo. (5) The preconditions for fascist economic autarky were not there. Latin American countries were primarily exporters, having a limited domestic market. (6) Only in the seventies was there student/youth support for the Right.

   Michel Löwy ([ed.], *Populism in Latin America*, Notebooks for Study and Research, No. 6, Amsterdam, 1987) also gives a useful typology of theories of populism in Latin America. According to him, Gino Germani conceives of populism as the 'political manifestation of traditional and authoritarian masses out of step with modernisation' (p. 3). Torcuato di Tella, says Löwy, sees it as the product of a 'revolution of expectations'. A whole dependencia school (Francisco Weffort, Octavio Ianni, F.H. Cardoso, R.M. Marini) sees populism as the expression of a distinct economic cycle – the period of import-substituting industrialization.

   Ernesto Laclau (*Politics and Ideology in Marxist Theory*, London, 1979) sees it as a moment of ideological discourse where social forces contest the power bloc so that there can be variants, e.g. fascism using 'populist interpellations'. For Löwy, a provisional Marxist definition would be populism as a multi-class 'political movement expressed in diverse organisational forms (party, trade unions, various associations, etc.) – under a bourgeois/petty bourgeois leadership and the charismatic leadership of a caudillo.' *Populism in Latin America*, p. 3. Its ideology is anti-imperialist and anti-Communist. Such movements are ideologically heterogeneous with rightwing nationalists, sometimes crypto-fascist wings, a hegemonic nationalist reformist centre, and a crypto-socialist leftwing. Populist regimes are Bonapartist (posing as above classes), resting sometimes on employers and army, sometimes on trade unions and popular mobilization. They pursue nationalist industrial development. *Populism in Latin America*.

Whether understood as movement or ideology, populism remains an imprecise concept. Löwy's definition makes Latin American (and third world) populism very different from the original turn of the century rural populism of Russian Narodnism and North America and also rules out the possibility of first world populism with its clearly defined relationships between capital and labour.

15. Influenced by Barrington Moore's remarkable work *Social Origins of Dictatorship and Democracy*, this seems to be the view of Vasant Kaiwar in *Politics and Economy in the New Age*, unpublished seminar paper presented in Sri Lanka, January 1991. He pays more attention to the components of fascist ideology and the legitimacy it derives from cultural particularisms of various kinds such as 'reactionary humanist ideologies'. Kaiwar points out that the latter manipulates the 'remembered past', glorifying the autarkic village and the glorious villager before the arrival of iniquitous 'Westernization', while fascist ideology, the terminus in this continuum of cultural particularist thinking, manipulates the 'epic past' – creating the myth of national essences and past glories.

16. Moore, *Social Origins of Dictatorship and Democracy*, Chap. 8 'Revolution from Above and Fascism', pp. 433–52.

17. Ibid., p. 301.

18. Ibid., p. 305. Moore also cites differences between Japanese and European fascism. In Germany the army housed the traditional elite, who were unsympathetic to Nazism but did Hitler's bidding. In backward Japan the agrarian sector was more important and the army was more sensitive to pressures from the countryside and from urban small business. There was no 'sudden seizure of power', no rupture with constitutional democracy, because Japan had no democratic phase comparable to the Weimar Republic or pre-Mussolini Italy. Japanese fascism found existing political institutions more congenial and evolved more naturally within them. Japan had no plebeian supremo, though the Emperor served as an abstract national rallying point. Nor did it

have a mass party. Japanese fascism was not the culmination of the growth of a mass fascist movement but a 'respectable fascism' from above, respectable because in the takeover by high government officials, popular elements were excluded, namely the anti-capitalist popular Right. Finally, there was no policy of mass terror and extermination against any specific segment of the indigenous population. Loyalty and obedience was secured by a combination of coercion and traditional symbols of authority.

19. Moore's book takes us up only to the mid-sixties. It is debatable whether the subsequent durability of Indian democracy and its steady if unspectacular growth would have led him to a serious revision of his assessments.

20. Moore's famous five conditions for stable democratic development are as follows: (1) There should be a balance between Crown and landed aristocracy/nobility, i.e. neither too strong a Crown nor too independent a nobility. (2) There is a turn towards an appropriate form of commercial agriculture by peasantry or landed aristocracy. (3) The landed aristocracy is weakened – its political hegemony must be broken or transformed so that the peasant becomes the commercial-minded farmer and the landed upper classes part of the rising capitalist class, or be swept aside. (4) There is no aristocratic–bourgeois coalition against peasants and workers. (5) There is a revolutionary break with the past.

India has some of these features, notably (3) and (4), and hence only a weak and insecure democracy.

21. Daniel Thorner's writings were among the earliest accurate characterizations of India's agrarian structure. For a collection of his writings at various points of time, see *The Shaping of Modern India*, Bombay, 1980.

22. See E. Mandel's Introduction in L. Trotsky, *The Struggle Against Fascism in Germany*.

23. See M. Kitchen, *Fascism*, for a helpful analysis of the strengths and weaknesses of bourgeois psychological theories of fascism and those of the Frankfurt School. The latter had the merit of pursuing explanations of mass and not individual psychology. They also sought to uncover the socio-economic dynamics of mass psychology and the external roots of the 'authoritarian personality'. Those inclined to individual psychology (the 'fascism within us' school) were more preoccupied with the psychological make-up of fascist leaders.

For the sophisticated way in which Gramsci tries to grapple with Italian fascism's ideological–cultural specificity, to understand its mobilizational capacities in relation to the distinctive socio-cultural history and character of Italy, see A. Ahmad, 'Fascism and National Culture: Reading Gramsci in the Days of Hindutva', in *Social Scientist*, Vol. 21, Nos. 3–4, March–April 1993. In a parallel move to Gramsci, Ahmad looks at elements of Indian culture, past and present, that help account

291

for the 'nostalgias' and 'cravings' that can be manipulated to build what he considers an Indian fascism.

24. 'But in reality fascism did not triumph at the moment when the bourgeoisie was threatened by the proletarian revolution: it triumphed when the proletariat had long been weakened and forced onto the defensive, when the revolutionary flood had abated. The capitalists and large landowners did not entrust the fascist hordes with the power of the state so as to protect themselves against a threatening proletarian revolution, but so as to depress wages, to destroy the social gains of the working class, to eradicate the trade unions and positions of power gained by the working class.' O. Bauer in W. Abendroth (ed.), *Faschismus und Kapitalismus*, pp. 153–4.

Poulantzas makes the same point. The decisive defeats of the working class must come before the seizure of power. The bourgeoisie first attacks the 'real relationship of forces' on which working-class gains rest and only after this (via fascism) does it attack the gains themselves. Where Poulantzas can be faulted is in insisting that even the beginning of the rise of the fascist movement must presume a series of working-class defeats. Initially, a fascist phenomenon (e.g. in Italy) can grow and bring in a stratum of working-class unemployed, uprooted, etc., not because the organized working class is attacked or 'defeated' in certain confrontations but because it is too fragmented, demoralized or misled to realize the necessity of challenging it. See C. Sparks, 'Fascism and the Working Class', in *International Socialism*, Autumn 1978.

25. Kitchen (*Fascism*) has criticized Trotsky on Bonapartism, preferring Thalheimer. The key difference is that Trotsky in the course of theorizing fascism also began to develop the idea of Bonapartism in an independent direction. The value of this initiative is testified to by the subsequent and frequent use of Bonapartism by third world Marxists to examine a series of state forms which have extreme executive power, considerable autonomy from dominant classes, yet, unlike Marx's version, do not rest unproblematically on an internally incoherent petty bourgeoisie and peasantry. Marx's belief that such a peasantry had to plump for bourgeois or working-class political leadership or else seek Bonapartist identification is belied by the numerous examples of it finding its own forms of political expression and often following its own distinct course regardless of the pressures of the bourgeoisie and working class.

26. See I. Kershaw, 'The Nazi State: An Exceptional State?', in *New Left Review*, No. 176, July–August 1989. According to Kershaw, the traditional elites continue to be outflanked by the fascist party after it comes to power not only because of the mass popularity of the fascist party but because of their own relative weakness. Their power expressed through their support of fascism to crush the working class is a

destructive one. They have little capacity to construct a stable new state, hence their need for the fascist party in power if other rightwing parties are much weaker. Kershaw's argument does help to answer something that is otherwise a puzzle – the peculiar stability–instability as well as continuing and remarkable autonomy of the fascist executive, years after the fascist seizure of power.

Both Trotsky and Gramsci stressed that fascism in power attacks its own petty bourgeois mass base and merges itself into the state apparatuses, hence a growing instability as it prepares for its own transcendence. This is what underlay Trotsky's view (criticised by, e.g., Kitchen, *Fascism*) of fascism transmuting into another kind of Bonapartism of a more stable kind than the pre-fascist 'preventive' Bonapartisms. Trotsky's clumsy formula of a stable or relatively more stable Bonapartism reflected a remarkable intuition.

The fascist state might undermine its own base, the fascist party might merge into the state apparatus, and the traditional elites and the fascist party evolve a new partnership reflecting a stronger convergence of interests. Nevertheless the state under fascist leadership would still be a Bonapartism (more autonomous and with a much stronger, centralized executive power than the normal bourgeois state) and yet more 'stable' in its authority than Marx's use of the term 'Bonapartism' would convey. Kitchen (*Fascism*) fails to recognize the superiority of Trotsky's intuition compared to the more conventional usage of Bonapartism by Thalheimer and Bauer.

27. N. Poulantzas, *Fascism and Dictatorship*, p. 52.
28. See P. Anderson, *A Zone of Engagement*, London, 1992.
29. Pre-war Bernsteinian social democracy did have a more optimistic assessment of the durability of bourgeois democracy. But this anti-capitalist social democracy rapidly debouched into the anti-Marxist, pro-capitalist social democracy of the post-war period, its legacy briefly revived only with the emergence of Eurocommunism.
30. P. Anderson, *A Zone of Engagement*, p. 350. But as this democracy has spread it has also 'thinned'.
31. V.I. Lenin, *Imperialism, The Highest Form of Capitalism*, (1916), Moscow, n.d., p. 131.
32. Lenin stated this connection between economic and political partition but never actually *proved* its necessity. It assumed strong congruence of interests between finance capital and the state and the existence of finance capital in national blocs.
33. If India is not perceived as a dependent capitalist country, then the economic impetus to fascism, it could be argued, is solely internally derived. But where, then, is the *severity* of the economic crisis driving the Indian bourgeoisie or key sections of it towards fascism? Most leftwing critics of the New Economic Policy (NEP) correctly point out

that there was no deep structural crisis necessitating this turn. It was an attempted 'long-term solution' to a short-term crisis. And why the NEP, which is clearly a dramatic reversal of the whole post-independence trajectory of autonomous capitalist development? A fascist resolution of an economic crisis for the domestic big bourgeoisie seeks to strengthen its independence and its relative position vis-à-vis external competitors. It does not aim to increase economic dependence on outside capital nor to broker for more favourable terms of economic collaboration with transnational corporations. Or will political Hindutva be the attempt to resolve in a 'fascist' way a coming economic crisis of great magnitude, i.e. establish autonomous capitalist development once again but in a more ruthless way? Considering that the forces of the Hindu Right are themselves divided in their attitude to the NEP, is this a serious viewpoint? Whatever way one looks at India – as a dependent capitalist country or as a rare, independent capitalist country in the third world – there is no convincing economic rationale for emerging fascism, though there can be for emerging authoritarianism.

34. Why should the West led by the USA welcome the advent of a Hindu communal version of a so-called fascist state in India? If political stability is its prime requirement, such an outcome, it could be plausibly argued, would on balance destabilize India, South Asia and regions beyond through its impact on the Islamic states from West Asia to the Central Asian republics. If the rise of Islamic fundamentalisms is going to be a major preoccupation of the West in the coming period, then it is doubtful that it would see much promise in the offer of a Judaeo-Hindu–Christian 'civilizational alliance', even if made. I am grateful to Kamal Chenoy for this observation.

35. See E.O. Wright (ed.), *The Debate on Classes*, London, 1989, for detailed arguments in support of the 'polarization thesis', for the 'new class' theories and for Wright's 'contradictory class locations'.

36. E. Hobsbawm, 'Whose Fault-Line Is It Anyway?', in *New Statesman & Society*, 24 April 1992, p. 26.

37. See A. Giddens, *Modernity and Self-Identity*, Cambridge, 1991.

38. I have been persuaded by Zoya Hasan, Aijaz Ahmad, Sumit Sarkar and others that if I intend to abjure the term 'fascism', then it is all the more important for me not to simply concede to the Sangh Combine its own favoured self-description of embodying the 'forces of Hindu nationalism'. Sumit Sarkar has correctly insisted that one must distinguish political Hindutva from run-of-the-mill rightwing nationalism by its much greater authoritarian threat and popular appeal. I consider political Hindutva a reactionary rightwing and dangerously authoritarian form of populism.

39. See S Kaviraj, 'On State, Society and Discourse in India', in J. Manor (ed.), *Rethinking Third World Politics*, London, 1991, for a perceptive

critique of the Nehruvian Congress failure in the realm of 'cultural reproduction' of its guiding principles, i.e. the failure in making it the Gramscian 'common sense' at the base of Indian society.

40. None of this should be taken as endorsing the view that it is possible or even desirable to separate theory and practice. A theoretical orientation is invariably based on a prior practical orientation even if this is unarticulated. But as in the natural sciences, there is a difference between the 'context of discovery' or the more value-laden fixing of an agenda of theoretical–historical inquiry, and the 'context of justification', the existence of 'objective' protocols for evaluating better or worse theories/histories.

41. It is only sectarianism that prevents political forces having programmatic agreement but theoretical differences from working together in practice. Thus within Left circles, theoretical differences over the nature of the USSR and its ruling stratum/class should have been subordinated to the common programmatic agreement on opposing the Soviet system and believing that only a radical overthrow of its ruling stratum/class could release a sufficiently powerful forward momentum towards a socialist alternative.

42. See E. Hobsbawm, chapter on 'Fifty Years of Peoples' Fronts', in *Politics for a Rational Left*, London, 1989. See also P. Rousset, *The Chinese Revolution, Pt. II*, Notebooks for Study and Research, Amsterdam, 1986. Rousset uses the same metaphor of concentric circles to describe Mao's successful 'united front' strategy for defeating the Japanese and rapidly expanding the CCCP's mass base. He perceptively points out that, contrary to traditional Trotskyist criticism of anything that smacks of popular frontism, the danger inherent in Mao's strategy was not opportunism or conceding too much to bourgeois cohorts. It was sectarianism, since the CCCP was the nucleus of the whole concentric arrangement and would brook no fundamental challenge to its authority in the name of socialist or democratic principles of pluralism, whatever its tactical 'concessions'.

— 6 —

The Communalization of the Indian Polity

The Historic Decline of the Congress

Virtually every major political development in recent times bears the stamp imposed by a basic structural malady expressed in a double dilemma. There is the historic decline of the Congress party and the simultaneous inability of any political formation to replace its historical role. The overall result is an unprecedented political and ideological vacuum, and a politics of extreme flux as competitors strive to cannibalize the space hitherto occupied by the Congress. Whatever the partial or temporary successes enjoyed by one competitor or the other, these have proved neither stable nor significant enough to make any single force the new fulcrum of Indian political life in the way that the Congress was for so many years after independence.

If the era of 'one-party dominance' at the Centre is long gone, neither is there any visible prospect that a stable two- or three-party competitive system might institutionalize itself. Most importantly, it is no longer obvious that some kind of bourgeois centrist formation is fated by the sheer complexity and segmented character of Indian society to always rule at the Centre. Therein lies the principal danger. A decisive communalization of the Indian polity and its authoritarian transformation is now a distinct possibility.

It is not a certainty, but the basic mould of plebiscitary politics and centrist rule which encased the range of variant regime possibilities for so long is now so seriously weakened that the future has become far more open-ended and unpredictable.[1] The single most important reason for this turn of affairs is the scale and depth of Congress decline in the last few years. The general trajectory has been visible for a long time, beginning in the late sixties, but the gradient of its decline was not, till recently, steep. Moreover, the two alternatives to Congress rule at the Centre – the Janata Party (1977–80) and Janata Dal (1989–90) –

296

were also centrist formations, and on both occasions gave way to Congress rule again.[2]

It was plausible, therefore, to assume (a) that a generally non-polarized framework of plebiscitary centrist domination in some form would still hold sway; and (b) that the Congress, though weakened and no longer enjoying sole star billing, would nonetheless be very much around. The prospect of a post-Congress India still seemed a matter of more distant speculation than of imminent realization.

The actual depth and severity of the crisis facing the Congress party only became evident after 1989, upsetting all calculations and perspectives concerning the future direction of Indian politics. It was the 1991 elections, during which the leader of the Congress party and former prime minister, Rajiv Gandhi, was assassinated, which indicated that a new phase in Indian politics had been reached. Hitherto the endemic instability of the polity had been expressed in a series of wave elections bringing either the Congress or a patched-up centrist rival (the Janata Party and later the Janata Dal) to power. The increasing volatility of voter behaviour expressed itself in sharp swings behind one or the other centrist formation, motivated negatively, by disillusionment with one side, and positively, by receptivity to a new issue-based (rather than programme-based) appeal by the other side.[3]

The 1991 elections broke this pattern, though the accession to power of the Janata Dal in 1989 as a minority government indicated the shape of things to come. For the first time in its history, the Congress formed only a minority government. Where once wave elections and strong parliamentary majorities expressed underlying instabilities, the deepening political instabilities were now to express themselves through the emergence of parliamentary instabilities as well! The Congress party in power established a parliamentary majority by engineering defections but the writing was on the wall. Coalition governments or unstable minority governments could well become a marked feature of the coming period of national-level politics.

More importantly, Indian politics was getting more polarized, the space for traditional centrist politics was shrinking fast, and the Congress was declining rapidly, despite its rule since 1991. So serious has been the decline of the Congress that it is no longer out of place to wonder whether its crisis is terminal or whether India is entering a post-Congress future, although it would still be reckless and rash to answer these doubts with confident requiems for the Congress. Matters remain too much in flux and therefore inherently unpredictable.

However, the crisis of the Congress is sharper than most observers have hitherto perceived. It would be tempting but misconceived to draw reassuring parallels with the longevity of populist political formations, for example, in certain Latin American countries.[4] The Congress may still survive as a significant force in the Indian polity. A more than hundred years old party does not cave in so easily. And the segmented character of Indian society continues to favour broadly centrist formations more than other, more polarizing ones. But if the Congress is to survive it must do so in a new form and shape. The old Congress is dying even if it is too early to write definitive epitaphs. A new Congress has yet to emerge.

The evidence for the existence of such a decisive historical conjuncture is unmistakable. Electorally speaking, centrist dominance by the Congress had a distinct social and geographical cast. Socially, Congress pre-eminence rested on its ability to combine solid upper-caste support with enduring loyalty from the ranks of the 'core minorities' or scheduled castes, scheduled tribes and a large proportion of Muslims in many parts of the country. The rise of the backward or intermediate castes and the consolidation of their votes weakened the electoral impact of the traditional pattern of Congress support. But what really undermined the Congress was the progressive abandonment by those sections which had long supported it.

Upper-caste (Brahmins and forward castes) loyalty was most important in the north, especially in the all-important state of Uttar Pradesh, which provides the single largest number of seats (85) to the national parliament, the Lok Sabha. Twelve per cent of the population of Uttar Pradesh are Brahmins, who also make up some 40 per cent of the country's Brahmins. Together with the forward castes they constitute around 25 per cent of the electorate in the state. Generally, dominance at the Centre has required dominance in the northern states, whose order of importance is first Uttar Pradesh, then Bihar, followed by Madhya Pradesh and Rajasthan. There were periods in the eighties when the Congress could compensate for loss of support in the north by gains in the south. But this only disguised the seriousness of Congress's declining support among upper castes because they took place in the context of wave elections. With that era now receding, its dilemma is revealed in its truer and starker proportions.

Certainly in Uttar Pradesh the upper castes have shifted overwhelmingly to the Bharatiya Janata Party (BJP). This is true to a lesser but still significant extent in the other three states in the north – Bihar, Madhya Pradesh and Rajasthan. But it is the eroding hold on the core minorities that has dealt a body blow to the Congress claim of being the country's true national party. Today the electoral behaviour of these groups is characterized by considerable volatility, with non-Congress alternatives more often than not preferred.

After the demolition of the Babri Masjid and with the Congress ever more willing to accommodate itself to Hindu communalism, Muslim alienation from the Congress is greater than ever. But even besides this, one of the most important developments in recent times is the remarkable new ferment that is taking place within the Muslim community. The enormous pressure political Hindutva has exerted on Muslims has heightened internal frustrations. The failure of traditional (usually religious) authorities to provide necessary protection and succour has been cruelly exposed. The overall result is a greater willingness than ever to reject or outflank the traditional leadership elements of Muslims. This new willingness to question the traditional leaderships and the norms they have laid down for how Muslims must organize their lives is a major development in Indian political life. It does not yet amount to a major self-assertion of Muslims in the larger context of Indian politics. But it does mean a new independence in political thinking reflecting itself in a much greater willingness to change political alignments from what they have been in the past.

The social base for this new upsurge of reform has been, of course, the emergence and consolidation of a sizeable Muslim middle class substantially making up for the vacuum in north India created by the earlier migration of this stratum to Pakistan after Partition. There is now a significant layer of young Muslims born twenty to twenty-five years after independence for whom the issues of the pre-Partition era or the traditional concerns of the Muslim leadership mentally formed in that period and in the first decades of independence seem increasingly irrelevant. They constitute an important reservoir from where activists for social and political reform can be found.

This Muslim middle class began to flex its muscles in the early seventies, pressing towards secular issues of reform which could help their social, educational and economic advancement. Thus issues such as preserving the status of Urdu (which for various reasons related to the communalization of north Indian politics for over a century had come to be seen symbolically as a 'Muslim' issue) were of much less concern to them than the promotion of measures which, symbolically or otherwise, led not to a politics of self-conscious isolation and separateness, but towards greater integration in the secular institutions of market, polity and higher education.

This secularizing thrust was set back, to the benefit of the traditional leadership pursuing its usual politics of the 'Muslim community', precisely because of the upsurge of communal Hindu politics from the middle and late seventies onwards. A Muslim politics otherwise has little *raison d'être* in a country so diverse and varied as India in which the shared cultural characteristics amongst members of a local community (Hindu and Muslim) or region are far greater and deeper than those supposedly shared between members of a single religious community across such localities and regions.

Two factors stand as the prime obstacles to the steady dismantling of such a politics of Muslimness – the defensive self-consciousness and fear among Muslims created by the growth and impact of Hindu communalism (especially the polarizing effects of communal riots); and the 'unifying' issue of Muslim Personal Law. Precisely because political Hindutva has launched such a major onslaught on Muslim Personal Law, demanding its replacement by a Uniform Civil Code, this has made an issue of gender equality and social reform into one of 'Muslim identity'.[5] Finding how best to deal with the issue of community-based Personal Laws, where these communities can be religious, tribal, sect, etc., has become an important part of the current struggle to de-communalize Indian society and politics.

For scheduled castes, the Congress no longer stands for anything with which it can identify. Other regional formations are as capable of pushing a vote-catching populism, and of doing so with greater credibility. The very fact that scheduled castes gave their loyalty to the Congress for so long makes the Congress failure to adequately address their needs all the more reprehensible and is now a powerful barrier to Congress efforts to reclaim such support. Moreover, the recent phenomenon of Dalit assertion as never before also threatens to transform the parameters of Indian electoral politics as hitherto understood. The Congress has suffered most from this upsurge of Dalit power and independence.

Even support from scheduled tribes, whose numbers are around half of the country's Dalits, has proved to be impermanent. In states like Gujarat with disproportionately higher numbers of tribals, the Congress base has been greatly eroded, with the BJP gaining at its expense. In other states, too, other parties, whether regional or those having nationalist pretensions, have gained ground.

The historically accumulated prestige of Congress among the core minorities was an asset that many observers felt could not be easily squandered even by a feckless leadership. But that is exactly what has happened. It is what makes the crisis of the Congress so acute, and its revival on newer terms so urgent if it is to restore its status as a major actor impossible to ignore in the organization of Indian political life.

Ideological Disarray

The ideological disarray of the Congress has been the inevitable corollary of its political and electoral decline, part cause and part consequence. There is now an ideological vacuum at the heart of Indian politics. The old Nehruvian Consensus has collapsed but there is no other consensus available for, or capable of, replacing it. That consensus was based on a loose acceptance of four principles – socialism, democracy, secularism and non-alignment. Domestically, socialism represented a form of social democracy, i.e. a state-driven capitalism and a limited paternalist welfarism. But it also embodied a serious value commitment to social justice and greater equality which acted as a benchmark for judging policies – their selection and effects. Secularism meant, at a minimum, a commitment (despite variant interpretations of secularism) to preserving a non-denominationalist, non-religiously affiliated state. Externally, non-alignment represented the effort to maximize national independence in foreign policy by avoiding formal or serious informal alignments with either bloc in the Cold War era.

The collapse of the Nehruvian Consensus owes more to the failure to adequately implement these principles than to the recent doubts entertained about the value and feasibility of the principles themselves, or to the impact of changes in the international context. In that sense India's experience is only a particular expression of the widespread disillusionment created by the failed promise of developmentalism in most third world countries in the post-colonial era.

The specific internal reasons for the collapse of the Nehruvian Consensus, i.e. for Congress decline, include the following factors and processes:

- The rise of rich farmers looking for political expression outside the Congress and of a much larger category of aspiring capitalist farmers who followed their leadership
- The rise of significant tensions between the industrial and agrarian elites
- The growth and consolidation of an industrial elite lacking commitment to the development of an indigenous industrial base and

301

strong technological self-reliance, and on the look-out for greater collaboration with, and subordination to, foreign capital

- The shift within the dominant coalition with the big bourgeoisie becoming more powerful and successful in imposing its strategic vision on India's desirable future
- The support for this elite by a small but crucial section of the bureaucracy
- The rise of a criminalized lumpenized business class linked to the black economy, tax evasion and speculation
- The steady transformation of the urban middle class and professionals who lost progressivist inclinations as they became more self-centred, hedonistic and consumerist in their aspirations
- The rise of a lumpen political elite
- The generational change in the Congress leadership
- The rising (but unmet) expectations and the increasing electoral volatility of the core minorities
- The growing federalist pressures in the Indian polity leading to the rise of all kinds of non-Congress regional political formations
- The increasing lopsidedness of the Indian economy with its uneven growth pattern, sectorally and geographically
- Finally, the ever starker inability of the Indian economy to meet adequately the basic needs of the poor, whose absolute numbers have risen.

Ideologically, then, the Congress has simply drifted. It has accommodated itself to winds whose force and direction have had sources outside its own control. In two fundamental areas – secularism and the economy – the Congress has shifted significantly to the right and in doing so pushed the centre of gravity of Indian politics as a whole in that direction. On the issue of secularism, it is the BJP that has made the running and there is little doubt that the Congress, to its shame, has pursued a perspective that is accurately characterized as 'pale saffron', saffron being the emblematic colour of political Hindutva.

This has been more than just occasional Congress use of the 'Hindu card', a practice that surfaced significantly with Mrs Gandhi in regard to Punjab, Kashmir and elsewhere. Under Narasimha Rao, the Congress for the first time in its history organized a *de facto* alignment with the BJP (before the destruction of the Babri Masjid) to stabilize its rule at the Centre. This further legitimized Hindutva politics and encouraged the forces of political Hindutva in its Ayodhya campaign. Indirectly, the Congress bears a great deal of the blame for the destruction of Babri

Masjid. It could see what was coming, could have done much more to prevent it, and to legally and politically punish those responsible for these communal crimes, including the unleashing of widespread anti-Muslim pogroms that followed in the wake of the demolition.[6] That it did none of these things reflected its inordinate concern not to go against what it perceived were widespread pro-Hindutva sentiments among Hindus. The politics of expediency and cowardice were of greater consequence than any politics of principles precisely because the old Congress ideology had ceased to have any guiding relevance.

The New Economic Policy (NEP) inaugurated by the Congress in 1991 was not the outcome of a wide internal debate within Parliament, the Press or the general public. It was a *fait accompli* brought about by a narrow circle of top politicians and high-level bureaucrats in conjunction with key decision-makers within the IMF and World Bank. The NEP did not merely represent a rightwing shift in economic thinking but was inspired by the most conservative form of neo-classical economic thinking – neo-liberalism. A Congress leadership anyway bereft of all ideological moorings and further disarmed by the collapse of the Communist world, and therefore presumably of the socialist paradigm, responded to an immediate balance of payments crisis by endorsing a 'long-term solution' to this essentially short-term problem. This proposed 'solution' was itself highly ideological – a triumphalist neo-liberalism which in the Indian case demanded rapid privatization of the public sector, removal of strategic control over the domestic operations of the market by the state, external liberalization and removal of controls over all kinds of foreign capital flows, devaluation, reduction of trade barriers and renewed emphasis on exports (especially of primary commodities), reduced taxes and a decline in 'unproductive' (social welfare) government expenditure. The ideological recoil from bad socialism was so strong that it has led to the widespread endorsement of bad capitalism.

Searching for a New Centrism

The only serious attempt to establish a new strategic foundation for Indian centrism in this situation of political and ideological disarray in old centrism (dominated by the Congress) was made by V.P. Singh, the former prime minister of the short-lived (1989–90) Janata Dal minority government. He had the acumen to realize the nature of the problem and to propose the most feasible solution. But he has lacked the organizational ability to institutionalize a coherent force or party capable of carrying out this politics of a new centrism. However, he remains the one Indian political leader of any stature in recent times who had such a strategic vision because he understood the implications of what are perhaps the most important two developments in Indian politics to have emerged over the last two decades. This is Dalit assertion as never before; and the 'forward march' of the backward or intermediate castes, or Other Backward Classes (OBCs), as they are also called. Admittedly these OBCs are led for the most part by their upper layers.

V.P. Singh's platform of 'social justice', as symbolized by Mandalism, however much of an anathema it was for the Indian elite and the urban middle classes and professionals, was one expression of this new strategic vision. Though he and his party were brought down, the Mandalization of Indian politics was effected. No political party today, regardless of what this or that ideologue might say, can openly oppose Mandalism and what it represents, except to their grave disadvantage. The forward march of the backwards and the new assertiveness of Dalits are indisputable factors of great importance which any political party wishing to expand its authority and power must now take into account and try to come to terms with.

What V.P. Singh and his Janata Dal sought to do but did not succeed in doing was to consolidate a new electoral and social foundation for centrism. No longer should it rest, as the old Congress did, on an amalgam of upper castes and core minorities but on backwards and core minorities, and in doing so provide a stabler foundation for new centrism than even that enjoyed by the old centrism.

The principal strategic problem is that the category of backwards is socially differentiated and electorally heterogeneous. Ultimately, the most stable and powerful foundation for a new centrism whose fulcrum would correspond to the *natural* centre of gravity of Indian politics – left-of-centre – would have to rest on the non-antagonistic alliance of core minorities and the very sizeable lower and middling sections of the backwards. Instead, what has emerged has been an electoral alignment of sorts between the upper sections of the backwards and sizeable sections of the core minorities.

This is an unstable situation because the social and class relations between the two groups, particularly between the upper backwards and the Dalits, are, all too often, highly antagonistic. The upper sections of the backwards are in class terms usually rich farmers or aspiring capitalist family farmers coexisting uneasily with tenants and agricultural labourers coming from the most part from the core minorities and the lower sections of the OBCs. The project of constructing a new foundation for Indian centrism is, and will be, very much on the cards but its successful accomplishment is still a matter for conjecture. The direction that a new centrism has to take is clear. Whether it will reach there is uncertain.

To put it another way, while the natural centre of gravity of Indian political life is left-of-centre, the actual centre of gravity has rarely been so, and need not be so in the future. Social tendencies and pressures are not the same as political tendencies and pressures. The former determine the natural centre of gravity, the latter the actual. The direction a society takes is never decided by its average consciousness, i.e the consciousness of the people as some amorphous mass, but above all by the consciousness of its leading strata and elements, i.e. the articulate, the mobilizers of the mobilized, and secondarily of the minority among the masses who are the mobilized. This is precisely why capitalist and elitist development has taken place in India although the objective terrain is so favourable to socialism and egalitarianism.

Political mobilization and struggle decide the direction a society takes, so while the votes of rural India decide which force comes to power, urban and semi-urban India decides, by and large, what that force stands for and does. Unless the forces that represent this natural centre of gravity successfully fulfil their political responsibility, there is no good reason to believe that the fulcrum of Indian politics will come to rest where it should – at a left-of-centre position. This requires more than just an actual or purported left-of-centre force or coalition coming to power. It also requires them to carry out a successful socio-economic and political transformation, the institutionalization of what would be a New Social Democracy. This would be superior in its egalitarian thrust to the Old Social Democracy upheld by the Congress till the early seventies as its formal ideal, even if it was not followed in practice. This Social Democracy would differ from the old one in its social base, organizational forms, and programmatic perspectives.

What will happen if this fails to emerge is that the general thrust towards regionalization of Indian politics that has been operating for some time now will most likely be further reinforced. This assumes that a BJP-led authoritarian transformation of India's political structure does not take place, either because the BJP does not stabilize itself in central power, or because, even if it does, it cannot properly carry out its programme. The historical decline of the Congress first had its most obvious and sharpest expression at the level of the states. Rivals to the Congress emerged, came to power and in some cases displaced the

Congress as the natural party of governance or natural pole of reference.

In any case, a host of other factors have led (despite more laws justifying central intervention in the states, and despite inadequate decentralization of economic and financial powers) to a more federalist and decentralized practice of politics. Regional leaders and regional parties have begun to exercise greater national-level influence. Shifting coalitional arrangements and elected state governments failing to last their full term of office have already become commonplace features. Given the results of the eleventh Lok Sabha elections in 1996 and the formation of a United Front government comprising numerous regional parties, they seem to have made their appearance nationally.

It is in this wider framework that we must situate the rise of the BJP and of the forces of political Hindutva.

The Rise of the BJP and of the Sangh Combine

A distinction must be maintained between the party expression of political Hindutva – the BJP – and the wider array of forces comprising organized Hindu communalism. The BJP's fortunes have fluctuated and can do so in the future. Hindu communalism's impact and that of the ideology of Hindutva have had a more uniform upward trajectory. There have been periods of stasis, where the graph of its movement showed prolonged plateaus. But it is difficult to perceive any serious slump in its fortunes once the country got over the trauma of the assassination of Mahatma Gandhi in 1948, for which Hindu communal organizations and attitudes were held directly or indirectly responsible.

But despite the steady if slow rise of organized Hindutva (above all of the RSS) since 1950, it is only in the last ten years that the Sangh Combine (the RSS-controlled or influenced group of organizations like the BJP, the VHP, Bajrang Dal, etc.) has risen to seriously menacing proportions. Indeed, though the cadre strength of the RSS since its birth in 1925 has steadily risen, by the early eighties this growth was so far short of its historical expectations that the RSS had lost much of its élan, and was suffering from serious internal organizational problems. Its actual impact, culturally, politically or organizationally, on that Hindu society and India it was committed to totally transforming was still remarkably limited.

The narrative of the rising menace of Hindutva and Hindu communalism must undoubtedly pay attention to its roots in colonial India (the

306

first stirrings of cultural nationalism), the various currents of Hindu nationalism in the National Movement, the slow spread of the RSS after independence, as well as to the triumphs and vicissitudes of previous political incarnations of the BJP, such as the Bharatiya Jan Sangh. But the major factors behind the dramatic growth of political Hindutva belong to the last fifteen to twenty years.

These factors are extrinsic and intrinsic. The external, contextualizing factors have been and continue to be more important. It is not an accident that a whole array of movements representing various forms of the politics of cultural exclusivism have arisen all over the world in the last fifteen to twenty years.[7] Everywhere the general explanatory principle is that these political movements of cultural exclusiveness have been responses to the failed promise of modernization in capitalist or socialist forms and the ideological disarray attending on this failure.

In India failed developmentalism is obvious enough at the socio-economic level. Its major political reflex has been systemic instability, while ideologically it is symbolized by the collapse of the hegemony of the Nehruvian Consensus. The BJP and the forces of Hindu communalism have benefited most from the ensuing ideological and political vacuum partly because of certain intrinsic strengths. They possess the most ideologically coherent, organized and disciplined cadre force in the country in the shape of the RSS.[8] The RSS, moreover, has steadily burrowed its way into the pores of civil society in many parts of the country. BJP and Sangh ideology can claim some degree of legitimacy and continuity from the cluster of ideological values that guided and informed the National Movement.

Most of all, the BJP has benefited from being a coherent political and ideological alternative to the Congress. The Left has also been such an alternative but its more regional character and identification has been a handicap. The BJP has been more nationally dispersed, and has always been a more significant factor in the heartland of Hindi-speaking states, which have been disproportionately more important than other regions for determining the shape of national-level politics. In brief, it has been so positioned as to be the most likely beneficiary of the decline not just of the Congress but of the politics of old centrism.

What is new is not the Sangh Combine's ideology and message but the *receptivity* to an old and otherwise shopworn message and ideology. However, the Sangh Combine has to be credited with the ability to take advantage of the new, more favourable political environment in which it found itself. As we shall see subsequently, the political trajectory of the BJP and of its earlier incarnation as the Jan Sangh was not without fits and starts, detours and diversions since the mid-seventies. But first a look at the structure of Sangh ideology.

Deconstructing Sangh Ideology

Hindutva has already been structurally dissected.[9] It is the wider, more intellectualized and abstract construct to which the ideology of the Sangh Combine is related, but not congruent with. The ideology of the Sangh, though deriving inspiration and guidelines from Hindutva, has to have a simpler, more concrete and *politically* directed structure and content. It has to be capable of mobilizing on a large scale, and therefore of arousing passions/emotions or identifications of self-interest in ways that Hindutva proper would find much more difficult.

The fundamental premiss of Sangh ideology is that Indian resurgence/salvation can only be brought about by the self-conscious unity of Hindus as a religious–cultural grouping. How, then, to unite Hindus given the peculiar character of Hinduism? There are only two ways and both have been pursued. One establishes a principle of coherence and unification that is either *internal* to Hinduism or *external* to it. The only halfway plausible candidate for the first approach is the construction of a loose and accommodating Brahminism. But this kind of construction of a more singular Hinduism can only take the Sangh Combine so far. As a sought-for principle to cohere all Hindus, it is weak, and because of tensions with the more popular forms of practice and worship suffers from too many problems to be an effective social glue.

The other approach – to establish an external principle of coherence – is more promising because it does not intervene within Hinduism to make choices but posits an opponent for all Hindus regardless of their variant beliefs and practices. This approach is absolutely central to the Sangh Combine's task of constructing the desired Hindu unity. Hindus can now hopefully be united not by what they are supposed to share but what they oppose, even to the point of hostility. Indeed, the more strongly emotional the common opposition to the external 'Other' or 'enemy', the stronger is the desired unity likely to be.

The only feasible candidate for this status as the hostile Other to Hindus, given India's history, are Muslims and Islam. But the logic does not end here. How, after all, is this hostility to be constructed among Hindus in twentieth century pre- and post-independence India? For the last a hundred and fifty years, and particularly after 1947, it is impossible to argue that Muslims have directly dominated and oppressed Hindus and Hinduism.

The ideological strategies for constructing such hostility are limited. First, there is the strategem of pushing a particular historical interpretation of the past. After all, some kind of case can be made with some degree of plausibility about Muslim persecution of Hindus and denigration/desecration of the symbols and institutions of Hinduism in the past, *provided* the distinction between Muslim rulers and ordinary Muslims can be soft-pedalled or elided. That is to say, responsibility of some sort for past 'crimes' is transferred to today's Muslims and to the community as a whole. Hence the argument that today's Muslims must acknowledge the presumed iniquity of Babar at Ayodhya by themselves agreeing to its replacement by a temple. By refusing to endorse this, they themselves become 'guilty' of disrespecting and antagonizing today's Hindus who want to right this putative historical injustice.

What can be said to unite elite Muslim rulers and ordinary Muslims either in the past or now? It is Islam. Culpability, then, resides in the character of Islam and the way in which it constructs Muslimness and influences Muslim behaviour in India. Islam is not usually *directly* attacked. The Sangh Combine can even genuflect to the positive aspects of Islamic doctrine and life. But the charge against it is always there in disguised or undisguised forms. One decisive difference between the attitudes of Mahatma Gandhi and of the Sangh Combine to the Muslims of India is important and educative.

The Sangh insists that it is not against Muslims. How can it be? After all, Muslims are by birth and blood Hindus. (For those Sangh ideologues who believe culture is tied to matters of birth and blood, this is tantamount to saying that the 'true' culture of Muslims is Hindu.) In the view of the Sangh Combine it is, then, said to be 'unfortunate' that Muslims refuse to recognize this, and what it entails. The Sangh therefore 'respects' Muslims not because they are Muslims and believe in Islam but because, in a more fundamental sense, they are *not* Muslims! Where the Sangh Combine 'respects' Muslims *in spite* of Islam and Muslimness, Gandhi respected Muslims *because* he respected Islam and Muslimness.

An interpretation of India's past stressing its essential Hinduness and the iniquities wrought by Muslims can arouse a level of emotional hostility and a desire to construct a Hindu 'unity' but it can only go so far. A politics of historical revenge is certainly a part of the Sangh's current political–ideological armoury. But among contemporary Hindus the cultivation of a strong sense of anger against Muslims must be based primarily on issues of the *present*. Since it is difficult for even the most diehard RSS cadre to argue that Muslims directly dominate Hindus today, how is this to be done?

The Sangh can try to arouse a sense of fear or a sense of deprivation among Hindus. But given the subordinate position of the overwhelming bulk of Muslims in Indian society, this is more difficult and less successful than trying to arouse a sense of grievance or righteousness among Hindus against Muslims. Given the absence of direct dominance by even a small section of Muslims this can best be done by shifting the angle of attack. Muslims are not attacked for being directly oppressive of Hindus, just as racist whites do not attack the minority black community in Britain for being directly oppressive of whites. In both cases, the Hindu communal and white racist attack is launched against the *state/government* for *favouring* Muslims and blacks respectively.

The necessary sense of grievance or indignation is cultivated by invoking the principle of 'unfairness of treatment' by the state/government vis-à-vis a 'majority' community and a 'minority' community (communities) for which *partial* responsibility is transferred not just to the leaders of the minority community (communities) or to those in or outside the community (communities) in question who would justify such 'unbalanced treatment', e.g. secularists or white anti-racists, but also to the ordinary members of the community (communities). What angers here is not that Muslims benefit from such 'favouritism' but simply the fact of supposed favouritism. Thus L.K. Advani has no difficulty in arguing that the absence of a Uniform Civil Code or the general policy of 'minorityism' (as he calls it) by India's secular state doesn't help the Muslims but perpetuates their backwardness. He can also don the mask of being a 'more sincere friend' of Muslims than their so-called secularist and progressive allies.

The structural logic of Sangh ideology demands that the notion of minorityism and 'appeasement of Muslims' become central to the strategy for uniting Hindus psychologically–emotionally and therefore, it is to be hoped, culturally and politically. What remains, then, is to make the accusation persuasive through the selective appropriation and treatment of those issues wherein a plausible case of sorts can be constructed to show the state or particular parties guilty of minorityism. Hence the constant (and often innovative) search by the Sangh Combine for issues through which this basic message can be pushed.

The Trajectory of the BJP

Until the 1977 elections the Jan Sangh was peripheral in Indian politics. When the Jan Sangh became part of an anti-Congress, non-Left coalition, temporarily welded into a single centrist party called the Janata Party, it made a decisive break from its hitherto undistinguished political past. In fact, the role of the RSS in resisting Emergency (a role they were literally pushed into by Mrs Gandhi's attack on them in order to give the Emergency a 'progressive' image), and before that its cadre participation in the anti-corruption 1974–75 JP Movement (named after its leader, a revered Gandhian, Jay Prakash Narayan), helped the Jan Sangh to secure the single largest share of parliamentary seat allotments within the Janata Party.[10] When the Janata Party broke up over the issue of affiliation of Members of Parliament to the RSS, it was clear that if a centrist party was to be genuinely centrist, then it could not countenance the kind of political and organizational loyalties by its MPs to such an extra-party entity as the RSS which was not subject to the control of the Janata Party itself.

In the elections of 1980 which swept Mrs Gandhi back to power, all the former components of the Janata Party, now split into various formations, were marginalized. The Jan Sangh between 1977 and 1979 was able for the first time to place its own people in many key sections of the central bureaucracy, and to use state resources to benefit itself and its parent organization, the RSS. But the 1980 election results were a grave shock.

The lesson its leadership drew from this débâcle was that the pattern that had brought it into the framework of an anti-Congress centrist alternative needed to be further pursued, i.e. it needed to move towards the centre of the political spectrum. This was how it had gained widespread legitimacy and managed a share of central power before the contradictions within the Janata Party split asunder the experiment.

Between 1980 and the next Lok Sabha elections in 1984, the Jan Sangh consciously pursued a 'moderate' line, downplaying the RSS connection, seeking greater independence from it, and electing a leadership opposed to aggressive Hindu nationalist posturing. Its declared ideological perspective was now 'Gandhian Socialism'. As was noted in Chapter 2, the dilemma of the Jan Sangh (and later the BJP) has been characterized as its uncertain oscillation between wanting to be the party representing the Great Hindu Rally/*Rassemblement* and wanting to represent a wider cross-section of support by diluting its strong Hindu cultural nationalist identification.[11] The 1980–84 interregnum was a self-conscious effort by the Jan Sangh to present itself as more of a centrist political force willing to be more pragmatic in its alignments and in its ideological commitments.

The 1984 electoral rout of the Jan Sangh effectively put paid to this strategy. There was a change of top leadership (A.B. Vajpayee was replaced by L.K. Advani, who was closer to the RSS) which meant a reassertion of tighter control by the RSS over the party and a rejection of 'Gandhian Socialism' for traditional Sangh ideology, only this time propagated and pursued much more aggressively than ever before. From 1984 the JS/BJP was a party looking for issues on which to peg its messages. It would now seek to extend its social and political base by moving right, actively pursuing the politics of polarization on the issue of secularism and the cultural self-definition of the Indian nation and state.[12]

Moreover, the pivot of 'mainstream' Indian politics was open to being shifted quite considerably. Indeed, deeper social transformations had fertilized the ground for certain kinds of cultural–religious activities and identifications that could benefit the Sangh Combine. The BJP was aware of this but the shift in its political strategy after 1984 was determined more by the failure of the alternative politics it had pursued between 1980 and 1984 than by any deep-seated and calculated analysis it made of the potential dividends to be garnered by making such a strategic shift. Moreover, the 1980–84 failure greatly strengthened the control and influence of the RSS over the party, naturally pushing it towards a more communal politics.

Nonetheless, the underlying social transformations were important. Of these, the most important was the rise of the intermediate castes, now seeking greater economic and political power, and upward cultural mobility. One avenue of such upward cultural mobility is not just Sanskritization but identification with and reworking of a wider Hindu identity. This was reflected in the great appeal of a series of processual religious (Hindu)–cultural events and activities, the various *yagna yatras* that took place through the late seventies and early eighties. These long, trans-state processions and religious cavalcades and pilgrimages linked up rural with semi-urban and urban India around common symbols of reverence and loyalty. The Vishwa Hindu Parishad (VHP) or World Hindu Council, originally set up as another front organization of the RSS, was instrumental in organizing such *yatras*. The VHP, as it grew in power and strength, spectacularly so in the eighties, also developed a considerable authority of its own separate from that of the RSS. It is now seen as more aggressively cultural nationalist and explicitly anti-Muslim in its attitudes than the RSS.

The rise of the OBCs has had immensely complicating effects on the Indian polity. Though the search by upper layers of the OBCs for religious–cultural mobility makes it in some ways receptive to a more Hinduized politics, its rise also imposes serious obstacles to the Sangh Combine's particular brand, which has strong associations with Brahminical and upper-caste Hinduism. This problem for the Sangh has surfaced most clearly in the nineties after V.P. Singh's successful Mandalization of north Indian politics.

In the mid-eighties, however, the BJP was beginning to make its mark as 'the party of the future'. In a context of deepening uncertainty and flux the BJP and the Sangh Combine were the one collective force that had the organizational means, the ideological clarity and the inclination to pursue the politics of sustained mass mobilization. The aim was not simply to search for events and issues to mobilize around. There have been many such mass mobilizations since 1947. It was a search to highlight or create those events and issues which were, or could be, exemplary expressions of an already pre-conceived perspective and ideology for which there was now an environment of greater receptivity.

Major mass mobilizations and mass campaigns like the 1974 Railway Strike or the J.P. Movement (1974–75) or the electoral campaign to reject Emergency rule (1977) or V.P. Singh's anti-corruption (Bofors) campaign (1989) were issue- or event-based activities which essentially defined the character of the participants. The combatant parties could derive some overall ideological colouring but this was necessarily of a very loose kind. The politics of such mass mobilizations defined primarily what the instigators and organizers were against, not so much what they stood for; certainly not in any broad programmatic or ideological way.

This was not the case with the mobilizational politics of the Sangh Combine. As their acolytes and ideologues have repeatedly asserted, theirs was for the first time since the National Movement an ideological politics of mass scope, an attempt, partly successful, to alter the mainstream agenda itself. For once they were right. Far Left insurgency movements have also pursued intensely ideological politics, but these have operated at the margins of general political life.

In a narrowly partisan sense the Babri Masjid–Ram Janamabhoomi Ayodhya campaign did for the Sangh Combine and the BJP what the Dandi Salt March did for the Congress-led National Movement. But where the latter helped unite the country against colonial rule, the former polarized and divided the country as never before. Whatever the damaging consequences for the Sangh of the demolition of the Babri Masjid, the Ayodhya campaign itself (before the act of demolition) was a massive political 'success'. It propelled the BJP and the Sangh to national prominence and undoubtedly extended their mass support far beyond what they had hitherto achieved.

Apart from the Ayodhya campaign, the BJP has sought to capitalize on a number of issues. It has waxed eloquent about Article 370 in Kashmir.[13] It has called for a Uniform Civil Code. It has tried to make political capital about the issue of illegal Bangladeshi migrants.[14] Even as the BJP seeks to construct a monster-sized Hindu vote bank it has cried itself hoarse over minority (read Muslim) vote banks and 'appeasement'.[15]

The issue of a uniform or common civil code, in particular, promises to be a long-running sore. It has been a prime obstacle to weakening the 'politics of Muslimness'. At the time of independence the government was prepared to subordinate issues of women's rights to considerations of national unity. This affected its understanding of how to deal with the question of a UCC. Perceiving national integration as integration of communities it did not press for a UCC since it felt that the key communities of Hindus and Muslims were not ready for it. Had it done so, however, protest from conservatives within the Hindu and Muslim communities would most likely have been containable. Even an imperfect common civil code, not sufficiently advanced in ensuring full gender equality, would still have set a base-line for further reform in the future.

Today the issue has become so deeply communalized that secular progressives have become divided and ambivalent about this vexed issue. Part of the reason why the BJP has successfully peddled the view that the absence of a UCC is a sign of 'appeasement' of Muslims and indicates their disloyalty to a united nation which should have uniform laws is because national unity was the basic prism through which even the Indian judiciary has viewed the UCC issue. Moreover, by constantly evoking the issue of a UCC in judgements concerning disputes over Muslim personal law but rarely in disputes over Hindu personal law, the judiciary reinforced the communal view that Hindus have reformed their laws setting a standard for others while minority communities not carrying out such reform are somehow anti-national. The central issue of gender justice across all religious communities has been obscured. The emphasis was on uniformities across religious communities not on uniformity of legal support for women everywhere.

Political Hindutva has no commitment to a genuinely gender-just UCC. The kind of common civil code acceptable to it would be based on Hindu codes interpreted in a loosely Brahminical fashion. In such a situation, not surprisingly, the very idea of a common civil code is seen by large sections of Muslims as motivated by anti-Muslim sentiment.

Among progressives there are currently four different perspectives:

1. Have a compulsory common code irrespective of what it is called – a UCC, a common civil code, a gender-just code, or whatever. The anti-women aspects of all personal laws should be done away with while certain inoffensive customary and cultural practices can be retained. All persons would be governed by such a code.

2. Provide a UCC which would be optional not compulsory. In a first variation, the civil code exists alongside personal laws and there can be access to it at any time in one's adult life. A second variation assumes everyone is born into a common civil code but can at any time opt to be governed by a particular personal law. A third variation assumes persons are normally governed by personal laws but can opt for civil code provisions at a time of dispute, when secular laws will prevail.

3. Here, the focus is on amending existing personal laws in line with gender equality. Formulating a common civil code should be avoided. And these amendments should emerge from within the community in question when they are able to arouse widespread support.

4. The fourth perspective is not to do away with personal laws, not to have one common civil code, but to have a number of laws cutting across personal laws in specific areas, e.g. a common matrimonial property act applicable to everyone. A start in this direction can be made by taking up those areas where personal laws have nothing to offer, e.g. access to matrimonial property, matters of domestic violence, compulsory registration of marriages, etc.

Not all these positions are exclusive. One might want ultimately a compulsory UCC but prefer an optional UCC for the time being. Or one might prefer a phased piecemeal legislative approach rather than a package legislation. The common ground is that all progressives agree on changes in gender-unequal provisions whether in personal or in existing secular laws. This emphasis on having the 'best' secular and personal laws also undermines the perspectives of political Hindutva, which cannot tolerate such a dramatic transformation of Hindu codes, although these have been reformed to a greater extent than Muslim Personal Law.

There is less disagreement about how such laws and provisions can be formulated – the active involvement of feminists/progressive women's groups, women disputants with respect to personal laws, legally skilled personnel. There is more disagreement about how such laws – the agencies and the manner (phased or otherwise, scale of application) – are to be brought into force.

While all movements of social reform within a religious community should be encouraged, can this alone determine the availability and scope of best secular laws? The answer seems obvious – it cannot. If current circumstances make a compulsory common civil code communally counter-productive, as a transitional measure there certainly can be the institutionalization of a 'best' optional civil code whether legislated piecemeal or in a single package. Anyone can opt for it at any time, its provisions holding over personal law or tribal custom at a point of dispute. Such an approach is politically practical in the short term and a significant secular advance on what exists today.[16] It is a perspective that the Left and progressive parties, for example, could be brought around to support and mobilize for.

But the ultimate goal of a common civil code applicable to all must be maintained. Religious and customary laws (which are community-based), beyond a point, cannot be reformed to be compatible with modern notions of equality and liberty without losing their character as recognizably religious–traditional laws. Nor should the diversity and plurality of Indian society be made an excuse for justifying the existence of a permanent plurality of personal laws.

A universally applicable body of democratic law governing family life, gender and interpersonal relationships within a country can be progressively made more open, tolerant and accommodative of changing social mores. But this is a process of constant reform of a body of democratic law already made available and universally applicable because it has *replaced* the bulk of religious and customary laws. One cannot achieve such a 'body of law', i.e. an open-ended, tolerant and plural legal structure, through some other process of stitching together various personal laws, which can somehow each be reformed as to be compatible with modern democratic principles of jurisprudence. This is an illusion. Undertaken in the name of preserving plurality and diversity, it will rationalize and disguise the existence of the principles of hierarchy and patriarchy that found all non-modern systems of community laws and codes.

But none of these issues – Article 370 on Kashmir's autonomy, Bangladeshi migration, a Uniform Civil Code – could have had the political charge that the Ayodhya campaign carried. The temple–mosque issue did what no other issue could – it *directly connected* an admittedly constructed but nonetheless strong and widespread (pan-Indian) belief and desire among a significant section of Hindus to a notion of Muslim intransigence purportedly abetted by the state. Ayodhya could be presented as explicitly and centrally a Hindu–Muslim issue.

With the demolition of the Babri Masjid on 6 December 1992, the Sangh fulfilled its professed goal and maximized the political benefits to it of that campaign. Had it timed its demolition closer to the 1996 general elections might it not have made more gains? This is uncertain. Sustaining such a campaign for so long at the same level of intensity was problematic. In fact the accelerating intensity of the campaign through-out 1992 had already made further procrastination difficult. In short, there are too many imponderables to allow for confident speculation that the Sangh Combine did make a serious mistake in carrying out the demolition when it did.

What is clear is that the BJP and the rest of the Sangh Combine had to fulfil its promise at some time or else risk a serious erosion of its credibility. The actual demolition and the developments that followed in its aftermath revealed both the threat of the Sangh Combine as well as some of the obstacles to its further expansion.

The Threat of the BJP

Whatever the fascist characteristics in the BJP's ideology and organiz-ation (or that of the Sangh Combine), the danger it represents is not of a fascist takeover but of the coming to state power of a reactionary rightwing and authoritarian yet populist political party.[17] Whether it will come to power and stay there and what it can do if it does are still subject to a number of imponderables.[18] But it is the only political party in India that promises a *new* project, a comprehensive break with the past. It rejects not simply the Nehruvian Consensus as ineffective but the foundational principles of that Consensus itself. Domestically, there were three such principles – socialism, democracy and secularism.

The first was consciously undermined by the Rao Congress, a process initiated by the Rajiv Congress. The NEP constitutes a conscious rejection of the idea of a pattern of economic growth that puts social justice as an evaluative norm (however much economic practice may depart from this norm) in the forefront. It represents a dramatic rightward shift in capitalist economic thinking itself. The social values associated with this shift run counter to the social democratic aspirations of the Nehruvian Consensus.

The BJP has carried out the assault on democracy as a governing principle and value by seeking to redefine it as a species of majoritarianism, i.e. the fulfilment of the wishes and potential of a supposedly natural majority, the Hindus. It thus seeks to destroy the fundamental underpinning of political democracy – the concept of an Indian citizenship which must necessarily be abstracted from the possession of any particular attribute (religion, race, language, etc.) that is not in principle universally available and achievable regardless of specific communitarian loyalties. One of the crucial checks to prevent such 'natural' majorities from achieving undue influence is institutionalization of minority rights. The BJP, however, attacks the very principle of minority rights as unwarranted privilege. It is not specific abuses of such rights that is attacked, which is reasonable enough, but the very principle itself. Therein lies a clear warning of what minorities, specifically Muslims, have in store, should the BJP ever stabilize itself in power at the Centre.

Similarly, the BJP's assault on secularism and the secular state is also sought to be carried out through redefinition. Once secularism is redefined as tolerance, then the truly secular state comes to mean the truly tolerant state. From here it is an easy step to advocating a Hindu *rashtra*, and implicitly a Hindu state, or one which is in some basic sense affiliated to the 'majority religion'. After all, Hinduism, it is claimed, is the most tolerant of all religious systems and therefore most conducive to true secularism. Those who oppose the idea of a Hindu *rashtra* or a Hindu state but propose a redefinition or reinterpretation of secularism as tolerance provide powerful legitimacy to the overall project of the BJP and the Sangh Combine, even if they would themselves be shocked by the political denouement favoured by them.

Never before has there been such a comprehensive and single-minded assault on the founding principles of the Indian Constitution and state. Meanwhile the efforts of the Sangh Combine to transform civil society through constructing a Hindu monolithism goes on. Precisely because the Sangh's project is new it arouses so much passion. People tend to be passionately for or against it. It arouses committed support and committed hostility, although the size and segmentation of Indian society is such that it can only come to power through the electoral route if it is able to gather a significant degree of support from the uncommitted. While the BJP has benefited the most from the historic decline of the Congress, this is still not enough. In a basic sense, the future of the BJP lies not so much in its hands as in the factors external to it, and therefore in what its rivals do or not do. It is not the strengths of the BJP but the weaknesses and failures of its opponents that can propel the BJP to national power.

The Obstacle to BJP Politics

What pushed the BJP to put so many of its ideological eggs in the Ayodhya basket was its reaction to the emergence of another kind of ideological politics which it saw as a serious danger. This was V.P. Singh's turn to Mandalism after his Janata Dal government came to power in 1989. The BJP's decision to embark on the fateful *rath yatra* or re-enactment of Lord Rama's chariot march through a number of states culminating in a massive rally to be held at the site of the monument in Ayodhya was directly motivated by hostility to Mandalism. Mandal politics was seen by the Sangh Combine as highly divisive of the 'Hindu community' because it pitted lower castes against upper, and because caste identity is more strongly felt than religious identity.

The BJP launched the *rath yatra* in defiance of the government, thereby signalling its determination to bring the minority government down (the Janata Dal depended for its survival on both BJP and Left support) if it stopped the *yatra*. The *yatra* was halted but only after passing through many states causing bloodshed and riots in its wake, arousing communal passions and religious hysteria on a scale and to a depth never seen since the Partition holocaust. The Janata government, of course, fell and was replaced by a Chandrasekhar minority government totally dependent on Congress support. In due course, the Congress forced the 1991 elections and came to power. The Rao government's subsequent behind-the-scenes hobnobbing with the BJP gave a boost to the latter's Ayodhya campaign.

But the Mandal genie once out of the bottle could not be put back in. It is true that the BJP was the only non-Left party that pursued a coherent and systematic ideological alternative in a general situation of ideological–political vacuum. However, V.P. Singh and the Janata Dal had seized on an issue – Mandalism – that could be the van of a more coherently organized and systematized ideological politics – the politics of 'social justice here and now'. That V.P. Singh and the Janata Dal have

319

not been able so far to go beyond Mandalism to work out such a systematized programme and then actively pursue it through mass mobilization reflects that party's political and organizational weaknesses.

Yet such has been the power of Mandalism that no party wishing to be a major all-India force can openly oppose it. This power comes from the rising strength of the social forces behind it – the backwards and the Dalits. If the BJP is to continue its forward march it must work through and besides these forces, accommodating and outflanking, not directly confronting, them. Insofar as in the key northern state of Uttar Pradesh the BJP is widely seen as a party of the upper castes, then despite their consolidated support (assuring it of a major elect- oral presence), it must find ways to win over sizeable sections of backwards and/or Dalits, or neutralize the opposition based on these forces.

Though the backwards, particularly the upper echelons, are suscep- tible to calls for Hindu identification and cultural unity, this is firmly subordinated to the politics of backward-caste mobilization. The former can provide psychological and emotional upliftment. The latter can provide direct access to representative political power. Thus the 'Hin- duization' of the intermediate castes can never be a simple Brahminiza- tion or strongly Brahminized form of Sanskritization.

The BJP, then, has a major problem. It possesses an ideological distinctiveness that is its greatest asset. Insofar as it must stand for a certain kind of Hinduism and Hinduness and cannot simply be a purely anti-Muslim force, then it is the political expression of a Brahminical, upper-caste Hinduism even as it makes this Brahminism looser and more accommodating. This sets limits to its appeal. How far can the BJP go in diluting its upper-caste character? Backward-caste and Dalit power understandably enough seeks independent representation and forms of organization. There are also tensions within the Sangh Combine of three kinds – within the BJP, between the RSS and the BJP, within the RSS itself.

Though the BJP has made its gains by lurching to the right towards aggressive communal politics, it now faces serious problems. The demolition of the mosque deprives it of any comparable mobilizational focus to what it possessed prior to the demolition. It is much more difficult to arouse mass passions for building a Ram temple than for destroying a hated symbol. The 1993 assembly elections in the north shocked the BJP and exposed the limits of Ayodhya-type politics. The BJP barely retained Rajasthan, got nowhere in Bihar, was ousted in Madhya Pradesh by the Congress, and most importantly, lost out in

Uttar Pradesh to a Dalit–backwards–Muslim alliance symbolized by the coalition government of the Samajwadi Party (SP) or Socialist Party led by Mulayam Singh Yadav and the Bahujan Samaj Party (BSP) or Party of the Plebeian Majority led by Kanshi Ram.

Unless the BJP extends its influence to sizeable sections of the backwards and/or Dalits, how is it to assure itself of power? A large part of the internal tensions within the BJP are related to this problem. The median point of Indian politics has shifted closer to Sangh ideology, but the old dilemma of whether or not the BJP, to expand, should move towards the centre, still persists. It would then have to dilute its Hindutva politics and be more critical of the NEP. There are significant differences within the BJP on how far to go in these respects. The urban professionals and middle-middle and upper-middle classes (often highly Westernized) are a new acquisition for the BJP, affording it a modernist aura and a new legitimacy.

The BJP is loath to lose this newly acquired support base which gives it a new public image no longer simply that of a petty bourgeois or trader party. Opposition to the NEP is not the way to consolidate its support amongst these layers of the population. Nor is even a highly diluted or merely rhetorical Mandalism. But how is the BJP to acquire wider influence unless it takes up perspectives of relevance to backward- and lower-caste aspirations? On this terrain, however, the BJP loses its singular asset – its ideological distinctiveness. It must compete on a political–ideological terrain defined by other forces which have operated longer and with greater credibility. Moreover, in searching for new pastures may it not lose out where it has already consolidated?

The existing relationship of forces within the BJP suggests that if left to itself a majority would like to move the party socially towards a greater pragmatism, i.e. pursue a more 'centrist'–inclined politics of cross-caste, cross-class mobilization, but economically towards endorsing the NEP. But the BJP is not left to itself. Overlaying this internal tension is that between the RSS and the BJP.

This pressure pushes in the opposite direction. The RSS is more hostile to any dilution of the BJP's ideology caused by social or caste pragmatism. It takes Sangh ideology much more seriously, is more committed to a Brahminical Hinduism as the ideal to be striven for, and to a paternalist relationship to lower castes. Strong economic nationalism (*swadeshi*) is the natural correlate of its stronger commitment to cultural nationalism. The differences between the BJP and the RSS centre on two questions. (1) How much control and influence should the RSS have on the BJP? The latter wants the various benefits of this link but also wants the flexibility to independently decide most of its programme and tactics. (2) What is the degree of ideological and programmatic pragmatism that is allowable?

It is the difference between the defining goals and values of a party formation wanting the quick route to electoral power, and the ideological–transformative purposes that form the *raison d'être* and inspirational basis for a cadre-based, non-party formation like the RSS. The latter has always been the force that is supposed to represent an idealism beyond the hypocritical compromises of conventional electoral and party politics.

The effectiveness of the RSS as an inspirational and highly disciplined cadre organization rests on the mystique of the *pracharak* system, the self-sacrificing, ascetic and committed character of the pracharaks – the spinal cord of the whole organization.[19] The values associated with economic liberalism, such as consumerist aspirations, relative unconcern for indigenous values, and dilution of nationalist control and sovereignty, are incompatible with the nationalist commitment that is supposed to guide and inspire RSS cadres. The BJP may be able to make the necessary contortions to justify cultural nationalism and economic liberalization, not the RSS.

The tensions within the RSS and in its cultural fronts have emerged largely as a result of its very success in broadening its appeal and catchment area for recruitment. As its political clout has grown, and it seems closer to power than ever before, there has been a mass influx into the RSS and its cultural fronts of the kind of elements which are always attracted to power and form the ugly 'underbelly' of conventional politicking. This represents a great dilution of the ideological standards demanded by the RSS of its members (not so much for the VHP, which is neither as disciplined nor as concerned with ideological training). The RSS is faced with pressures for internal transformation that could in time, if they persist, significantly alter its historical character. Certainly many of its top leaders who have long been associated with the RSS have been worried by these trends.

The very growth in power and influence of the BJP and the Sangh Combine have created new and serious problems, contradictions and obstacles to its further qualitative advance. The consolation is that certainly these are preferable to the dilemmas of an earlier situation when the BJP was politically of marginal importance and the RSS and its various non-party fronts were in something of a cul-de-sac. The independent assertion of Dalit power also poses a difficult problem for the BJP.

Dalit Assertion

Dalit assertion, although building up over the years, has been a more recent development than the 'forward march' of the backwards, which has been visible and influential for much longer. Where the rise of the kulaks also expressed the rise of the intermediate castes, there has been a much closer correlation in the case of the Dalits between oppressed classes and oppressed castes. It is the more advanced sections of the Dalits that have provided the leadership for Dalit movements – the sub-caste Mahars in Maharashtra and the Jatavs in Uttar Pradesh. This creates certain problems in that the leadership is often prone to play opportunist politics reflecting its own self-interests as an advanced layer separate from the bulk of the Dalits. Thus the BSP's leadership is representative of a Dalit bureaucracy which emerged precisely as a result of post-independence policies of reservation in government jobs and government-run educational institutions.[20]

But despite this, Dalit assertion is nonetheless a very significant movement from below. Indeed, of all the anti-upper-caste movements in modern Indian history this is far and away the most important. Historically, the resistance to caste oppression has taken certain patterns. There have been efforts at corporate caste mobility upwards through forms of Sanskritization. There have been efforts at individual and corporate movement out, and away from, the caste system through the emergence of new, more egalitarian sects and orders, e.g. early Sikhism, Bhakti-type movements. The response to caste oppression has been either to move upwards within the caste system, or to move outwards away from it. Either way, the system itself has not been frontally challenged. It is the modern Dalit movement that has for the first time been prepared to fight *against* the system and seek its very eradication. Admittedly, Ambedkar's decision to take his followers into Buddhism had clear parallels with older efforts to move out of the caste system, but Ambedkarism nonetheless possesses a self-conscious and powerful charge against the caste system itself.[21] Central to this process has been the more aggressive assertion of Dalit self-pride. The Gandhian paternalist label of Harijan (children of God) is rejected for the more naked yet affirmative self-description as Dalits (the downtrodden).

In modern India there have been three types of caste mobilizations. The anti-Brahmin movements could enjoy the widest support because the line of demarcation was between Brahmins and others. Whatever the undoubted value of these movements, in the longer term sense, the social heterogeneity of such a large category limited its progressive potential, though the very narrowness of the enemy base confronting it assured it of significant practical successes. There have been a series of such movements in the south and west of India for over a century. Mandalism represents another kind of caste mobilization where the line of demarcation between 'us' and 'them' is drawn lower down than in the anti-Brahmin movements. Here, it has been the upper castes versus the rest. But only the Dalit movement can draw the line lowest down, between the untouchables and others, the outcastes versus the caste system itself. Potentially, its transformational power is the greatest. Therein lies its great promise.

Dalit consciousness-raising movements have a much longer history than the more recent flexing of independent Dalit political power. These consciousness-raising movements have generally been connected to Ambedkarism. Its expansion both to other Dalit sub-castes as well as geographically (in Uttar Pradesh) is testimony to the continuing vibrancy of such movements. Dalit efforts to extend their political influence have been less impressive. Till recently, Dalit political forma-tions like the various rumps of the Republican Party of India in Maharashtra (and Dalit leaders) have been little more than brokering mechanisms (and brokers), acting to channel Dalit support to centrist-type parties (Congress and Janata) in return for favours and some powers of patronage.

What made the rise of the BSP as a governing partner in Uttar Pradesh so significant was that this was the first time an *independent* Dalit formation exercised its authority and influence bypassing the traditional role allotted to it by Indian centrist parties. The quality of the BSP leadership leaves a great deal to be desired. But the historic significance of the BSP as a path-breaker remains. It is far too early to say whether it is a precursor of other independent Dalit parties in other states or that a larger regional, trans-state Dalit party might emerge.[22] The forms of Dalit assertion will vary and there will be ups and downs. The more traditional pattern of Dalit brokering with centrist parties may well remain in many parts of the country or even be extended to hitherto unconsidered parties as the latter realize the significance of Dalit support. Elsewhere, Dalits may prefer to support regional parties. Dalits have a rising awareness of their collective power and will seek to assert it in multiple ways.

The turn in Uttar Pradesh politics with the BSP ditching its former ally, the Samajwadi Party (SP) in mid-1995, was necessitated apparently by the attempt of the SP leader, Mulayam Singh Yadav, to cut into the

BSP's base. But the break benefited the BJP, which extended its support from outside to a minority government of the BSP headed by Ms Mayawati, a protégé of the leader, Kanshi Ram. This was a temporary marriage of convenience for both, faced with an SP that was gaining ground at the expense of both parties, largely through manipulation of the government administrative machinery.

Whatever the merits or consequences (short term or long term) of the BSP's decision to break its alliance with the SP, the subsequent developments were quite remarkable in their own way. They testify to this new found importance of Dalits. For the first time in the history of independent India, a Dalit (and a woman) occupied the premier position in India's premier province. Moreover, despite all the criticisms by other parties about the opportunism of the BSP–BJP link-up, no party openly voted against the formal installation of the BSP minority government in the state legislature in June 1995. The parties critical of the new arrangement reserved their anger for the BJP and for the BSP's willingness to depend on support from such an upper-caste and communal party. All parties, including the BJP, affirmed their concern for Dalits and declared their support for the value and importance of Dalits rising to political eminence, even if some of those who said as much would have preferred this rise to chief ministership to have taken place in other circumstances.

The alliance between the BJP and the BSP barely lasted three months and was replaced by temporary President's Rule by the central government. The BSP in power, though dependent on BJP support, consciously sought to use the official machinery to build up its mass support and install its own personnel in the state bureaucracy. Not willing to temper its anti-upper-caste biases before a point well past what the BJP wanted, this opportunist relationship broke up. But this does not mean the BSP and SP can come together in the short term. The SP has emerged as the single most important focus of resistance to the BJP in Uttar Pradesh. But the BJP will still benefit most from the fact of opposition disunity.

The SP has said it will have an electoral alliance with the Left (which counts for hardly anything in Uttar Pradesh) and the Janata Dal. But this cannot hope to approximate the strength that an SP–BSP tie-up would have. If the BSP leadership has put its own interests ahead of the need to forge a strong anti-BJP and anti-communal front, the same can be said of Mulayam Singh Yadav. The BSP in Uttar Pradesh has temporarily allied (as the senior partner) with the Congress. At a deeper level what has happened to the one-time alliance of SP-BSP reflects the tensions in any social arrangement that looks to promote both Dalit interests and those of the upper sections of the OBCs. The failure of this opposition in Uttar Pradesh to get its act together before the Lok Sabha elections in the state in May 1996 enabled the BJP in those elections to repeat its Lok Sabha performance of 1991 there.

It is quite possible that the consolidation of Dalit political independence and organization in Uttar Pradesh and north India might actually be hampered by the BSP's leadership's opportunism and refusal to take up class-based economic and social issues and not just 'symbolic' caste issues. But in an objective and long-term sense, regardless of the actual Dalit leaderships and the representative forms that might come about, this is a very positive development. It will constitute a major structural barrier to the efforts to institutionalize a Hindu *rashtra*, even though dangerous tactical alignments of the BJP–BSP kind have shown themselves to be quite possible. In a context of unstable segmented politics resulting from the absence of a strong centrist force, changing coalitional equations of even the most unusual kind should not come as a great surprise.

Radical Dilemmas

Any perspective tying the long-term struggle to decisively secularize Indian society to the struggle for socialist transformation has to assess the current state and future prospects of the Indian Left and other radical forces, and not only their responses to the problem of growing communalism. What follows is a brief overview of the mainstream Left of orthodox Communists and Socialists, the Maoist far Left and the women's movement, the one section within the new social movements which has taken the issue of communalism most seriously.

Has the socialist movement aged even before it had a chance to fully mature and prosper? As Eric Hobsbawm has pointed out, and as was noted in Chapter 5, all Communist parties of the orthodox Third International type which survive as *mass* parties today had their origins either before World War I or in the inter-war period.[23] Since 1945 only a handful of new parties influenced by Maoism or Castroism have acquired mass influence. Well before the collapse of the former Soviet bloc the signs of an overall and historical decline of mass Communist parties were evident.

The curve of descent of the orthodox (non-Maoist, non-Trotskyist, non-Castroist) Communist parties has now reached the point where only two such parties having a mass character can still claim to be growing or stable in respect of membership, electoral or popular base, and general political influence: the South African Communist Party (SACP), which owes its good fortune to the unique situation that has prevailed in South Africa, and the Communist Party of India (Marxist) or CPM. The other mass orthodox Communist party, the Communist Party of India (CPI), is still a significant force but seems to have joined the Chilean and Portuguese Communist parties, which have clearly peaked and are now in slow decline. The CPI has better chances of reviving.

Of international Maoism, with the decline of the Philippines Communist Party and Shining Path in Peru, the two Maoist movements which have grown are both in the sub-continent – Nepal and India. To the surprise of most Indians, after the defeat of Naxalism in the mid-seventies, Maoist organizations have not only stabilized at earlier levels but even enjoyed a modest growth in influence and membership.[24] The crisis of Communist organization so evident elsewhere has for the time being bypassed India. The major reason surely resides in an Indian exceptionalism. Testimony to the peculiarities of the Indian social formation is the peculiarity of the CPM, the most powerful force on the Indian Left.[25] The CPM is perhaps the only party of its kind anywhere in the world – Stalinist in its ideology and internal organization, increasingly social democratic in its practice, yet immune to the attractions of Eurocommunist- or Eurosocialist-type perspectives and development.

This exceptionalism cannot guarantee the future prosperity of mainstream Communism (CPM and CPI). Indeed, the Indian Left may eventually join its declining counterparts elsewhere. But it has been afforded a longer breathing space where the possibility of future advancement exists, provided it can respond perceptively, both programmatically and practically, to its challenges.

What, then, is meant by an Indian exceptionalism? Nowhere else in the 'third world' has there been the same combination of socioeconomic backwardness and durable though weak bourgeois democracy. Moreover, backwardness here describes a state of social, educational and economic mass impoverishment, not the overall character of India's capitalist industrial structure, whose depth and diversity bring it closer to the more backward of the OECD countries than to the average less developed country or LDC. If a composite assessment of Indian strengths is made by looking at the nature of its industrial structure, degree of economic and political autonomy, territorial size and population, natural resources, scientific and technical base, military prowess, then the Indian state is the strongest of all states in the capitalist third world.[26]

Indian poverty means Stalinism as an alternative developmentalist model continues to hold an attraction for large sections. Both the CPM and the Maoists have benefited from this. At the same time, the fundamentally democratic nature of the Indian polity (howsoever weak in comparison to the advanced democracies) has greatly influenced the evolution of much of the Left practice of Stalinists and Maoists. In no bourgeois democracy has any Communist party developed a truly mass base without making electoral politics a strategic orientation. In the Indian context the mass Communist parties have diluted their programme, modulated class struggle, consciously sought to develop a base among the urban middle classes and amongst the more prosperous upper strata in the countryside, and increasingly abided by constitutionalism in their political behaviour. The result is reformism of a kind that has moved towards co-optation in, and defence of, existing political and social structures. In the case of the CPM, about twenty years of unbroken governance (supervision of capitalist development) in West Bengal (45 million people) has only reinforced this momentum.

This operational background of backward yet significant capitalist development, weak yet durable democracy, a militarily sophisticated yet constitutionalist state, bourgeois governance more through consent than coercion, has shaped Maoist practice, prospects and perception, in major ways. Rural-based revolutionary mobilization is far less of an objective threat to the Indian state than it was to a weakly implanted and militarily much less powerful Chiang Kai-shek regime in China. Selective rather than generalized repression by the Indian state has been able to contain though not eliminate the Maoist threat. Furthermore, Indian Maoism, faced with a social formation, class structure and state form for which traditional Maoist strategies are utterly inadequate, is under constant pressure to fragment as some streams readjust 'strategically' or 'tactically'.[27]

Even the most diehard Maoist groups, whatever their strategic loyalties, have in practice utilized violence/armed assaults more as a tactic. There is no evidence of any serious movement towards building the infrastructure for large-scale partisan warfare, or even of systematic attacks against government forces on the same scale as in Peru or the Philippines. Violence has been primarily directed against local landlords/oppressors and has been scattered, occasional and limited in scope and purpose. The strategic simplicities of Maoism have been most attractive among the most deprived sections of rural India – tribals, agricultural proletariat and poor peasants in and around the jungle belt of central India, in Andhra Pradesh, and in the most backward state of India, Bihar.[28]

A non-Communist component deserving inclusion in the mainstream Left are the Socialists, even though they have been in steady political and organizational decline. Their enduring dilemma has been the absence of a distinct and sustainable identity. Politically and organizationally they are highly dispersed, loosely united by what they are against. They have never succeeded in securing an enduring or distinct programmatic coherence. There are Gandhian Sarvodayists (social workers) eschewing the rough and tumble of electoral politics for grassroots social welfare work. But this is a tradition that is fading away. Its legatees are to be found in the broad NGO sector. Of the more 'political' Socialists there is a small component within the Congress. But since most Socialists are defined by a common non-Congressism which for most shades into anti-Congressism, they are scattered in a number of centrist and middle-caste political formations in north India such as the Socialist Party of Mulayam Singh Yadav, the Samajwadi Janata Dal (Socialist Peoples' Party) of former interim prime minister Chandrasekhar; in the middle-caste/rich farmer-dominated parties like the Lok Dal (Peoples' Party); and in the Janata Dal. Every time a major non-Congress national alternative has emerged, e.g. the Janata Party forged by J.P. Narayan in 1977, or the Janata Dal led by V.P. Singh in 1989, these Socialists have invariably gravitated towards it.

The future of the Socialists is in many ways bleaker than that of the Communists. Their principal leaders are few and ageing with no second-line of prominent regional or national-level leaders. Their cadre base is not undergoing serious regeneration. Despite sporadic talk of all Socialists coming together there is little chance of this happening. The 'socialism' of some components, notably in Uttar Pradesh and Bihar, is fast eroding to be replaced by a single-minded obsession with caste politics, the arithmetic of electoral alliances, and opportunist power-seeking.

The Socialists have no unified party but their leading lights do have a parliamentary profile. Major trade union federations are under their influence at the top level.[29] While lacking a distinctive programmatic identity, they are in their general orientation well to the left of European social democracy. They are committed to public ownership of important sectors of the economy and to strategic state intervention, and also pursue a more vigorous anti-imperialism. They are strongly anti-upper caste and committed to a strong social-welfarist nationalism. On their own their energies and beliefs will dissipate in many directions. But like the Communists, they are part of the catchment area for the construction of a political force embodying a 'New Social Democracy', which is the subject matter of the last section in this chapter.

The collapse of Stalinism could not be expected to have any significant ideological effect on the Socialists, though the break-up of the Soviet bloc has clearly made things more difficult for an anti-imperialist politics generally. There has been some ideological impact on the CPI and CPM, more on the former. But the interesting development has been the absence of any significant negative effect in the short term on the practical standing of the two parties. Even before the Gorbachev reforms there was a sharp contrast between the position of India's two main Communist parties and orthodox pro-Moscow Stalinist parties in opposition which have fared badly in the rest of the third world. In Africa, Asia and the Middle East neither armed opposition to ruling regimes nor a posture of strategic support to the parties of the national bourgeoisie have prevented ruthless repression when regime or policy changes took place. In Latin America, even under quasi-democracies such parties have mostly been reduced to ineffectual rumps tailing populist parties or outflanked on their left by 'armed struggle' groups owing no allegiance to Moscow.

In Western Europe the Cold War was successfully presented to a majority public as the face-off between Stalinism and democracy. Mass reformist parties of the Left adapted to the terms of this discourse. Nowhere was any such party simultaneously and consistently anti-imperialist, anti-Stalinist and pro-democracy. Identification with the USSR was a profound handicap. Or else, repudiation of Moscow meant accommodation to imperialism. In India, neither identification with the USSR nor even identification with Stalinism has been a similar handicap. So the CPM was recognized as willing to defend the constitutional rules of political competition from assaults by the Right (BJP communalism), by the Centre (Congress authoritarianism – the Emergency), and by the Left (Naxalite 'extremism').

Nor did Stalinism imply lack of independence from Moscow. From its inception the CPM combined a more rigid adherence to Stalinism than Brezhnevism itself, with organizational and political autonomy from the CPSU. It was the less Stalinized CPI that aligned itself more closely to Moscow. But after the end of Emergency, despite the Soviet party-state's supportive stand for the Congress government (in keeping with Soviet foreign policy preoccupations), the CPI joined the CPM in pursuing a consistent anti-Congressism in domestic politics. The CPI could even de-Stalinize beyond Krushchevism without serious negative effects on its Soviet connection. The link between the mainstream Indian Communist parties and the USSR was neither particularly harmful nor particularly helpful, politically speaking. A broadly pro-Soviet orientation in international matters went along with an independent line in domestic politics.

The Gorbachev reforms and then the collapse of the Soviet bloc affected mainstream Communism in India, above all, in the realm of ideology, and, of course, in deepening public doubts about the validity of the long–term project of communist–socialist transformation or rule in India. But this long–term project anyway had little connection with the operative strategies of the CPI and CPM, so the fall-out has not been damaging to these perspectives. The CPM initially welcomed the Soviet reforms in 1985 and the broad line presented at the Twenty-Seventh Party Congress of the CPSU in 1986. According to the CPM, it was the ideological deviations between the Twenty-Seventh and Twenty-Eighth CPSU Party Congresses that were unacceptable – the abandonment of the 'leading role of the party' and the acceptance of international class collaboration with imperialism. By the Twenty-Ninth Party Congress, the CPSU had become a 'mere social-democratic party' which mistakenly reopened the nationalities question which had been successfully resolved. Gorbachev's ideological deviations were the prime cause of the disastrous break-up of Soviet bloc Communism.

The CPI is no longer a Stalinist party and is itself divided into three sections. The smallest group has long been committed to the idea of a 'historic compromise' with the Congress, even after the Emergency. The second wing is opposed to the Congress but is strongly inclined towards a 'revisionism' which would take the party towards social democracy of the European type. This current was least critical of the Gorbachev reforms and would probably abandon such notions as the 'dictatorship of the proletariat', 'democratic centralism' and 'proletarian internationalism'. But the dominant current has retained a fairly orthodox position. Shifts in the internal balance of forces between these currents were connected to the evolution of the reform process within the ex-USSR.

What began as a Gorbachevian 'renewal' welcomed by the CPI ended up as repudiation, collapse and a level of collaboration with imperialism (the Gulf War episode) which no section of the CPI could approve. The denouement in the Soviet bloc was enough to decide the result of the internal balance of forces within the CPI. For the time being the ideological social democratization of the CPI has decelerated. Unlike the CPM, the CPI has a stronger sense of the problems raised by the history of Stalinism and of the extent to which the ideal of socialism itself is damaged by the failure of the Soviet model.

The CPM supported the Chinese government's repression at Tiananmen Square in 1989 and applauded the coup attempt in August 1991 in Moscow. The CPI opposed both. The CPM recognized the growing alienation of the masses in China and in the ex-USSR but continued to uphold the ruling parties as the ultimate guide for socialist reconstruction. It was the tragedy of the CPSU that Gorbachevian deviationists obtained leadership ascendancy. Yet even the CPM was motivated by the post-1989 upheaval to undertake some ideological rethinking.[30] And it has been more concerned than ruling parties in China and Vietnam to establish some kind of international relationship between national Communist parties![31]

But its energies have been primarily focused at home. And as a mass electoralist party its strategic preoccupation is different from the classical Marxist debates. It is simply how to make an electoral breakthrough outside its ghetto – the three states of West Bengal, Kerala and Tripura. Particularly important is a breakthrough in the Hindi heartland of Uttar Pradesh, Madhya Pradesh, Bihar (the big three), and Rajasthan, Haryana, Himachal Pradesh. For all its regional eminence, the CPM has never become a national force to reckon with because of this failure.

The CPM has ruled out an early merger with the CPI, which has a significant cadre (though not a strong electoral) base in Bihar.[32] This has left it with but one option – to hang onto the coattails of some other non-Congress bourgeois centrist formation more able to gain mass electoral support in this region. It was only with the emergence of V.P. Singh's Janata Dal and for the first time ever of an anti-Congress National Front–Left Front Alliance that the CPM's wishes were answered. From 1979 the CPM has called for a 'left and democratic front' or a 'left and secular front'. The NF–LF alliance was the clearest embodiment so far of such a strategic perspective.

But ironically neither the CPM nor the CPI gained much (as far as their own growth is concerned) from the arrival of this long sought-for alliance. In two areas – on the economy and on the issue of communalism – the country's politics have been stretched in ways that squeeze the middle ground. If the CPM (and the Left Front) could put itself *at the head* of an aggressive defence of secularism and democracy and push for an economic perspective of mass welfarism and social justice then it could certainly grow. The problem with the CPM (and CPI) is that, though committed to such goals, it is not willing to take the risks of aggressively pursuing such a line.

This needs to be clarified. Left politics cannot institutionalize itself in the same way as rightwing or centrist politics. Electoralist politics bases itself on existing levels of consciousness and prejudices. A leftwing politics which wants to retain its distinctiveness and operates in a context where centrist populism is already strong cannot hope to expand (beyond a point) by shifting its politics towards the centre. It must pursue a transformative (which does not necessarily mean an extremist) politics to take the electoral risks of more frequently and determinedly going 'against the grain' of popular consciousness in order to change such 'normal' consciousness.

Its longer term electoral prospects are, therefore, much more intimately tied to the consistency and depth of such extra-electoral activities and influence. It cannot resort to the division of labour that characterizes the forces of political Hindutva. There, the RSS has institutionalized itself over decades in the 'pores of civil society', being the bedrock on which political Hindutva has grown. But the RSS is itself too well defined and distinctive in its Brahminism and its petty bourgeois cadre and social base to become a mass electoral force. That responsibility is entrusted to the BJP, which is more diffuse and flexible. The two can grow in tandem, or the RSS can grow while the BJP falters. Their rhythms and patterns of growth are different though interlocked. Considerations of electoral popularity do not decisively determine the strategic line of march of the RSS.

In contrast, each of the single jockeys of the CPM and of the CPI has not been able to ride the two horses of electoral populism and extra-parliamentary radicalism with anywhere near the same skill and determination. This is most evident in respect of the related issues of caste and religion. The organized Left has never led major anti-upper-caste movements expressive of low-caste dignity, though it has fought against caste oppressions as part of its class struggle mobilizations. The Left has not understood adequately the importance of caste in Indian society. It dithered over the Mandal Report before coming out in broad support. It did not perceive its potential in the anti-communal struggle till this became obvious. On the issue of Ayodhya, at no point did the mainstream Left organize counter-mobilizations. It is one thing to organize communal harmony marches which even BJP supporters can endorse; it is another to counter-mobilize over Ayodhya and risk being branded anti-Hindu. Had the secular parties done that (and the Left with its cadre base had the capacity if not the will to do this) it would have sent a completely different message from what was actually conveyed by the ground reality – repeated communal mobilizations on one side pitted against the official forces of law and order on the other. A mass counter-mobilization would have expressed a *popular* determination to defend the Babri Masjid as the heritage and symbol of all Indians, not a legal–constitutionalist commitment to defend Indian secularism to be carried out by state institutions such as the police, judiciary or state governments. As such it would have denied political Hindutva the credibility to claim that whereas theirs was a genuine popular movement, opponents were merely a small minority using the pseudo-secular state to defend minority appeasement. In polarized situations, the politics of the 'safe mean' does not pay dividends. Even from a narrowly partisan point of view, the CPI and CPM would have benefited significantly in political and organizational terms from a more courageous posture of direct street- and ground-level *confrontation.*

If the Sangh Combine could not garner as much mileage out of the Ayodhya campaign as in its fondest hopes, this was certainly not because of the effectiveness of the resistance put up by the Left and other secular political parties. In fact, the CPI and CPM were sufficiently disoriented by the impact of this campaign and the demolition of the Babri Masjid as to venture into propaganda terrain quite alien to their own traditions. Thus the two parties put out propaganda pamphlets which aimed to show how the forces of Hindu communalism were themselves anti-Hindu, resorting to quotations from venerable Hindu religious and religious–political reformers like Swami Vivekananda and Gandhi to express what was 'truly Hindu'. This was the Left trying to use the resources of 'good' Hinduism to fight 'bad' Hinduism.[33] Apart from causing widespread disdain and incredulity, it paid no dividends.

The Left has no credibility in taking this tack. It has been a secular force whose great strength has always been its effort to provide secular answers to secular problems, generally eschewing popular debates on the terrain of religious belief and behaviour itself. Those forces most equipped to take on political Hindutva in the name of a more 'authentic' Vivekananda or Gandhi/Gandhiism are progressive inter-preters of Vivekananda's message and progressive Gandhians. It is not that the Left needs to remain aloof from such tactical approaches to countering communalism in the name of the virtues of Hinduism, but that its participation here must be of a supportive kind where others more fitted take the lead. Then it becomes possible for the Left to retain its criticisms of Gandhi and Vivekananda and to credibly assert that these are nonetheless not figures who can legitimately be usurped by Hindu communalists.

Any struggle for secularizing Indian life has two objectives – the struggle to defend and deepen the secular character of the Indian state today under siege; the struggle to secularize civil society. The first struggle requires aggressive propaganda on the need to sustain a basic separation of religious influence from governance to preserve and deepen democracy. It requires aggressive extra-parliamentary mobilization against specific campaigns launched by Hindu communalists and, if need be, extra-legal defence against the perpetrators of communal violence and bullying.

The second struggle requires not aggressive ideological propaganda demanding the dimunition or confinement of religious influence (which is acceptable in elite intellectual discourse) but an aggressive effort to root democratic and secular counter-institutions which address the everyday social, cultural and educational needs of people in the 'pores of civil society', i.e. to provide greater economic well-being, social cohesion and political liberty. That has always been a large part of the classical agenda of the Left everywhere. There is no reason to abandon or weaken this thrust for some 'inspired religious resource' with which to combat communalism; some illusory short-cut supposedly in keeping with the 'religious temper' of the Indian people.

The best way for the Left to fight communalism is to be true to its own historic vision and responsibilities as an undeterred and principled force for democracy and socialism. Today, the pursuit of that vision requires the construction (with non-Congress, anti-communal Left–Centre forces) of a New Social Democracy or a new Indian centrism different from, and to the left of, the old Nehruvian 'Congress social-ism'. This New Social Democracy is not to be confused with the current process of gradual social democratization taking place in the CPM and CPI. A New Social Democracy requires a strong left turn, a reversal of current trends in the CPI and CPM. It would involve a newer and stronger commitment to transformative politics, a more serious engage-ment in mass activity and in the setting up of structures of popular empowerment not necessarily controlled by their own parties. It would mean a special responsibility on the CPM, presuming it remains in power in West Bengal, to radicalize the character of its own rule and to stop playing the often obstreperous and intransigent Big Brother of the Indian Left. The CPM would have to develop a much more ecumenical and democratic approach to forging practical alliances with other sections of the Left and with progressive forces in the new social movements.

Of these social movements, the single most important one, especially with reference to the struggle against communalism, has been the autonomous Indian women's movement. Of all third world countries the women's movement in India is easily the strongest and has the most diverse concerns. In most third world countries women and women's organizations are at the head of 'life' issues. In India the women's movement comprises not only this component but others which focus specifically on 'women's issues'.

The autonomous women's movement took shape after the mid-seventies. In the pre-independence period the women's movement was very much a part of the National Movement. In the roughly three decades following independence there was widespread optimism that the condition of women would steadily improve. The government's development perspectives and progressive legislation seemed to promise much. It was the decline of such hopes and the more clearly perceived gap between pious legal enactments and implementation that led to growing disillusionment. During the sixties large numbers of women participated in the Naxalite movement, the urban price-rise demonstrations, the student movements, the general struggles of the rural poor and industrial workers, and in certain important tribal movements such as the Shahada land grab movement in the Dhulia district of Maharashtra where tribal women mobilized against wife-beating and male alcoholism, and in the Chipko or 'tree-hugging' anti-deforestation struggle in Uttar Pradesh.

In the mid-seventies major catalysts were added to this general milieu of women in ferment. Urban middle-class women, (many of them educated professionals) were undoubtedly influenced by the literature and example of the Western women's liberation movement. There was also the impact of the UN-sponsored International Decade of Women (1975–85) which helped legitimize women's issues. The end of the Emergency in 1977 was like the bursting of a dam. The time was over-ripe for the emergence of a broad women's movement with a specifically feminist focus, needing just a trigger.

It was provided by the famous case of rape of a fourteen-year-old tribal girl, Mathura, in police custody. The Supreme Court reversed a High Court judgement sentencing the policemen for this crime, sparking an unprecedented furore. Rape as an issue came out of the closet and nationwide publicity and demonstrations forced the Supreme Court to review the matter and eventually reinstate the High Court judgement.

A new anti-rape law was drawn up. Other forms of violence against women, hitherto confined to the family, became public issues, including alcoholism, wife-beating and dowry deaths. Even today, the primary focus of specifically women's groups tends to be various forms of violence against women.

Other issues have emerged – denial of inheritance and land rights, marketing of dangerous contraceptives and sex-determination tests (pre-natal female foeticide), dowry, sati, forcible prostitution, inadequate divorce and maintenance rights, the oppressiveness of religiously sanctioned personal and family laws, child marriages, sexist treatment of women in the media, etc. Alongside these new issues remain all the older 'life' issues of housing, social welfare provisions, etc., in which women have so often been at the forefront of struggle.

In the West autonomy of the women's movement meant organizational hegemony rested exclusively with women and independence from political parties. The Indian women's movement is a looser and wider affair. It now comprises the following elements:

1. There are party-connected or controlled women's groups, e.g. the women's fronts of the mainstream Communist and Maoist Left parties as well as those of the centrist bourgeois parties. Such has been the impact of the autonomous women's movement that rightwing parties have been spurred to highlight women's fronts and the Left and Centre parties have been forced to view autonomous women's groups with greater courtesy and consideration than were extended to them in the beginning.
2. There are voluntary women's groups, usually part of the broader NGO structure, funded externally by the state or agencies abroad. Some are traditional social welfarist self-help-type organizations which do not necessarily encourage the development of a specifically feminist consciousness. Others are more specifically focused on women's issues but with a more service-oriented dimension complementing consciousness-raising or agitational mobilization.
3. There are the rural grassroots organizations, most often among tribal women (not exclusively controlled by women), where struggle around a central 'life' issue common to all has led to greater consciousness and struggle by women over specifically women's issues, e.g. alcoholism/wife beating.
4. There are women's wings of peasant movements, not all of which represent poor peasant and landless interests, e.g. the Shetkari Sangathana of Sharad Joshi in Maharashtra, which has raised

337

women's issues to maximize rural support for essentially rich farmer interests.

5. There has been a proliferation of urban-based women's research centres and institutions.

The government has reacted to the rise of the women's movement by promoting legislative reform and efforts at co-optation. This latter exercise is part of the general effort from the Seventh Plan period onwards to utilize the NGO sector as a more cost-effective transmission belt for a state-guided developmentalist drive. This pays dividends through social containment and defusion of potentials for confrontation, and also promotes privatization of health care and social welfare. These are not minor considerations for the central government.

In 1988 the government released two reports – the *National Perspective Plan for Women 1988–2000* and *Shramshakti: Report of the National Commission on Self-Employed Women and Women in the Informal Sector*. Both drew heavily on work done by a plethora of women's organizations. The reports contain far-reaching recommendations but falter on operational perspectives. This is hardly surprising. Working with the bureaucracy and not rocking the boat dominated by a variety of vested interests has to be the practical thrust of any government-sponsored reform path.

Where is the women's movement and its autonomous wing, in particular, heading? What are the current debates and problems engaging its attention? The all-India conferences of the autonomous women's movement give an idea of the speed with which it has grown, and the shift in its preoccupations. The first all-India conference was held in 1981, the second in 1983, the third in 1985, the fourth in 1988, when some seven hundred delegates attended. The fifth was held in 1991, with around a thousand delegates from all over the country. Its central theme was women and fundamentalism. The sixth in 1993 focused on the impact on women of the New Economic Policy, while the seventh in 1995 was a retrospect with the 'Search for Alternatives' as its theme.

Though the women's movement has come to stay, there continues to be a tension between party-connected women's organizations and the non-affiliated ones. The former feel that the latter lack a sufficiently wide focus, are too often elitist and divorced from the mass of working or ordinary women; furthermore, that there is no connection between their specific preoccupations and the larger question of social transformation, i.e. the institutionalization of the socialist project. Certainly, though socialist feminists have always been an important current within the autonomous women's movement in India, discussion about the practical and theoretical linkages between socialism and feminism has significantly declined as the movement has grown.

Possibly, this kind of discussion has been seen as too remote from everyday concerns and divisive. Moreover, despite all-India conferences and certain forms of networking, the women's movement is anyway dispersed and fragmented. There is no attempt at forming any collective charter, and much rationalization that if the movement is to reflect the actual condition of women it must necessarily be dispersed and segmented in character. Non-affiliated women's groups continue to be wary of what they would consider to be the manipulatively absorptive or centralizing tendencies of party-affiliated women's organizations. These fears cannot be brushed aside, but the declining interest in how feminism is to be linked to other kinds of socially transformative projects and agencies, and in developing an overall strategic perspective, is a real loss.

Though the fulcrum of the women's movement in India is to the left of its counterpart in, say, the USA, and though feminists who consider themselves socialists continue to constitute a goodly proportion of the leading activists, Indian feminism also seems increasingly less influenced by socialism than perhaps at anytime in its young history. Two 'Western' debates have had a certain resonance within the Indian women's movement. There is first the state versus civil society debate, which has connected with the general debate about the role of NGOs/social movements in social transformation. Second, there has been the debate about the 'naturally distinctive' character of femininity and its promotion of qualities of nurturance and non-violence that are at variance with the basic thrusts of male-dominated societies.

The criticism of state-centric strategies of social change was partly linked to the hostility against the traditional Left. This Left, it was argued, had all too often in its theory and practice subordinated the 'woman question' to its totalizing aims centred on a state-centric notion of revolution sanctioned by Marxism-Leninism. In the wider debate about the significance of the rise of social movements (and NGOs) the key strategic statement was that the transformation of the state was to be achieved through the transformation of civil society. This was the simplistic obverse of its supposed rival, that the state is the principal author of social transformation. This was a view wrongly imputed to classical Marxism, which emphasizes the complex ways in which the process of transformation of state and of civil society are connected, but more accurately imputed also to Left parties. This could then connect to critiques of vanguardism, of the unwarranted privileging of the male-dominated working class. According to those with a more generalist orientation within the new social movements, what was required was not a party-led revolutionary transformation centred on the seizure of state power but a prolonged and incremental process of systematic change which would be led by a genuinely democratic and pluralist coalition of social movements and grassroots struggles of all kinds.

But this Indian version of a radical pluralist strategy has not steadily gained in popularity. The 'long view' has simply become less important as the socialist project itself has become less of a preoccupation. The promise of the NGO sector has faded. The women's movement has lost some of its earlier élan as it has witnessed the repressive and co-optive capabilities of the Indian state, as well as the real limitations of reformism.

One of the more important current debates within the women's movement is on legalism. The Indian state has on its statute books some of the most advanced legislation anywhere regarding women's issues. State reaction to women-led campaigns has often been simply to enact more favourable laws. While this has been welcome, the victory has often been greatly undermined by the petering out of the campaign and the inability to get the new laws implemented properly. Thus many women have felt a real frustration with legally oriented campaigns directed at the state. But there has been no clear idea either of what alternative strategies might sustain campaigning work. Even for service-oriented grassroots work, how does one avoid entrapment in developmentalism/social work alone, or avoid co-optation into 'NGO business' via external funding and internal professionalization? The differences and clashes within the movement, the realization that small, formally non-hierarchized groups are not immune to internal manipulation and personal ambitions, has shown that even if many of the movement's criticisms of traditional Left functioning remain valid, it is not as if they themselves have found much better ways of functioning.

In regard to the discussion on the distinctiveness of feminist virtues and what this might presage for a new kind of politics, there has also been some disillusionment. The most important development here has been the rise of communalism, majority and minority. From 1986 and the Shah Bano case (referred to earlier in Chapter 2), there has been growing uncertainty on how best to cope with communalism. The fifth all-India conference focused specifically on the issue. If women have been the worst sufferers of growing communalism (especially in communal riots), far too many women have themselves been deeply involved in reactionary and communal campaigns aimed at denigrating other

340

religious communities. All too many women have been willing to endorse traditional–patriarchal conceptions of the family or religiously sanctioned ideals of what male–female relations should be like. For women belonging to the minority religions, the onslaught of Hindu communalism has promoted a retreat into religious identity politics with a concomitant unwillingness to strongly question oppressive religion-related codes of behaviour.

In short, the Indian women's movement is less certain and more divided about what secularism should mean, in what way it should be defended or promoted. It is also more evasive about directly addressing the issue of secularism and secularization, partly from fear of its divisive effects within the movement, partly from genuine confusion. Objectively speaking, the advancement and deepening of democratic norms should be seen as the most obvious ally of the struggle of women. Therefore, a strong commitment to the secular state and to secularization of civil society should be seen as the obvious corollary of any effort to preserve and deepen democracy. That this is not the case reveals how much confusion there is, fed by a variety of existing currents having their specific agendas.

Thus, those currents more strongly immersed in the politics of religious identity might press for reform of Muslim Personal Law but can be hostile to even the goal of a common civil code, attacking it as a secularist imposition. Also, a growing number of women activists are now more prepared than before to cite new virtues in the religious outlook, to reject Western-inspired notions of secularism in favour of what are thought to be more indigenously rooted and culturally authentic notions of tolerance; to see in Gandhi and Gandhiism strengths and virtues hitherto unsuspected. This bias among many activists (often urban and educated) is reinforced by the desire to be 'in tune' with the majority who do have a strong religious sensibility, and therefore to take greater distance from the secular and non-religious ethos of the urban educated women activists who have disproportionate influence.

Yet another current addressing questions of ecology which link up with the plight of tribal women also feeds into this romanticization of indigenism and condemnation of modernist principles of democracy and secularism.[34] Intellectual clarity about secularism and secularization, and recognizing the importance of adopting sensible political strategies to promote them, are matters which must intrude into the current terrain of debate within the Indian women's movement. A special responsibility devolves upon socialist feminists, and liberal feminists who are rightly critical of the essentialisms of 'cultural feminism' or 'biological feminism'.

The Eleventh Lok Sabha Elections: The Uncertain Panorama

The 1996 election results, when properly evaluated, provide a powerful though partial insight into the changing social and political anatomy of India.[35] Of the 545 Lok Sabha seats, 543 were contested. The BJP and its allies got 195 seats compared to 122 in the 1991 general elections, with the BJP accounting for 161, making it the single largest party. This contrasted favourably with the 119 it got in 1991. The BJP's percentage share of the vote between these two elections remained the same at around 20.8 per cent. But as an alliance it obtained 23.5 per cent, a 2.7 per cent gain.

The stagnation in the BJP's average national vote share, however, is somewhat deceptive. It is performance in the big twelve out of India's twenty-five states that determines national power. These twelve are Uttar Pradesh, Bihar, Rajasthan and Madhya Pradesh in the north, Gujarat and Maharashtra in the west, Karnataka, Tamil Nadu, Andhra Pradesh and Kerala in the south, Orissa and West Bengal in the east. The BJP got many more seats than last time not only because of the first-past-the-post electoral system, but because of the concentrated character of its support in the north and west of India. Here the average vote share of the BJP and allies was some 36 per cent compared to 23 per cent for the Congress. Out of the 195 seats obtained by the BJP and its allies, 156 came from this belt.

In two important states, Bihar and Maharashtra, the BJP made major inroads for the first time ever, registering voting swings in its favour of 12 per cent and 9 per cent respectively since 1991. In the twelve taken as a whole, though the BJP faces severe problems in breaking through in the south and east and though its electoral success in the north remains dependent on disunity amongst the non-Congress opposition, it is still the party that can most plausibly claim to be the single 'rising national' force while the Congress is clearly the declining one.

To be sure, it is still far from actually being a national force. Moreover, the social profile of BJP voters shows that 96 per cent are Hindus (when Hindus make up 82–83 per cent of the overall population) and that its vote share among the unlettered and the lower castes when compared to its principal rivals the Congress and the Third Front (the coalition of non-Congress parties) is low. The strongest support for the BJP and its allies comes from the small section of upper-castes and highly educated Hindus. Some 52 per cent of this section voted in their favour. The BJP success comes from the consolidation in its favour of the upper-caste vote and from the fracturing of the OBC vote. Of the OBCs, 25 per cent went with the Congress, 23 per cent to the BJP and allies, and the remaining 52 per cent went to the non-Congress, non-BJP regional parties, the Janata Dal and the Left Front. If the fact that younger voters seem to prefer the BJP augurs well for its future, the parallel fact that it remains an upper-caste and upper-class party continues to be a severe handicap.

The Congress performance was disastrous. From 232 seats in 1991 it fell to 139 seats in 1996. Its percentage share of the vote fell from 36.5 per cent to 28.1 per cent. Below the critical 30 per cent mark it becomes more difficult to translate voting share into actual seats unless there is massive fracturing of votes because of major multi-cornered contests. The Congress constituency is also ageing and only the Christian minority (around 2 per cent of the population) is still firmly supportive of it. Dalits have progressively abandoned it, especially in those states where 'Dalit politics' has emerged. Only 31 per cent of Dalits supported the Congress. Among Muslims (who constitute 12–13 per cent or 110–20 million of the population), only 28 per cent supported the Congress in 1996 compared to 46 per cent in 1991. The figure would have been less except that in some states (Maharashtra, Rajasthan, Madhya Pradesh) the Congress was the only viable opposition to the BJP. Support for the Congress among tribals has been more stable with 47 per cent still with it.

The basic social–electoral profile of the Congress remains what it has been – a rainbow coalition appealing to a wide cross-section of the people. But both its appeal and its support have greatly weakened. The swing against it is uniform rather than regionally concentrated. A geographical break-up of its tally shows 27 seats from the north, 40 from the south, 37 from the east and 35 from the west. But most disturbing to it must be its virtual decimation in the two most populous states in the north. It obtained 10 seats (5 each) from Uttar Pradesh (85) and Bihar (54) which together provide 139 seats to the Lok Sabha.

The Third Force, as it was called during the 1996 elections, comprised an informal alliance between the Janata Dal, the Samajwadi Party in Uttar Pradesh and the Left Front of CPM, CPI and smaller Left parties. After the elections, a host of regional parties, like the Telegu Desam Party (TDP) in Andhra Pradesh, the Tamil Nadu parties of Dravida Munnetra Kazhagam (DMK) and the Tamil Manilai Congress (TMC) which broke away from the Rao Congress, as well as the Asom Gana Parishad (AGP) in Assam, all joined the Third Force. The United Front (UF) led by Deve Gowda of the Janata Dal and former chief minister of Karnataka eventually formed the government in June 1996 relying on the outside support of the Congress. The UF comprises the Janata Dal, the regional parties listed above, a small breakaway group from the Rao Congress, and the CPI. Together they have 136 seats, with the Janata Dal and CPI accounting for 44 and 13 respectively. The CPM with 33 seats and the smaller Left parties in its tow (with 8 seats) have supported the UF from outside.

The Janata's tally was significantly less than the 56 seats it captured last time. The Left Front as a whole got 53 this time compared to 55 in 1991. They have remained virtually stagnant and have been unable to make any breakthrough into the Hindi heartland. The real gainers from the space evacuated by the Congress (besides the BJP) were the various regional parties (especially in the south) which till recently had no pretensions to playing a major role beyond the states in which they operate.

The United Front's coming to power at the Centre was taken as striking evidence that the regionalization of the Indian polity even at the national level is now a fact. In one sense, this is clearly correct and constitutes an affirmation and extension of a trend that has been visible for well over a decade and has multiple sources.[36] Nonetheless, one has to be careful about what this might portend for the future of national-electoral politics.

One rather hasty conclusion that has been drawn in the wake of the 1996 elections is that there is now no escape from a new kind of coalitional politics at the Centre never before evident since independence. This may prove correct, but it could also turn out to be mistaken. Certainly, it is neither inevitable nor inescapable. At one level regionalization of the polity has meant a growing disjunction between electoral politics at the Centre and in the states. But interestingly enough this has not led to the emergence of institutionalized coalitional politics in the states, except in Kerala and perhaps West Bengal. In the latter state the CPM so dominates the Left Front that to call this Front a form of institutionalized coalitional politics is probably a misnomer.

Instead, most states have witnessed the institutionalization of stable two- or three-party competitive systems. Disillusionment with one party sometimes leads to a third party carving out a significant space and emerging in due course as the major alternative. If, in some cases, one or both of the major parties are purely state-wise formations, in other cases one or both of the contenders have a trans-state presence with pretensions to being an extra-regional and aspiring national force, e.g. the BJP, Congress and Janata Dal. Such parties are now faced with a growing dilemma. They have to learn how to strike an appropriate balance in their political appeals so that they can present themselves as champions both of particularist regional needs and of non-parochial, supposedly national needs. Organizationally speaking, their internal structures must neither be over-centralized, as in the case of the BJP and Congress, nor over-federalized, as in the case of the Janata Dal.

At the national level the crucial dilemma is that there seems no chance that a stable two- or three-party competitive system can be stabilized. The emergence currently of coalitional politics is itself the expression of the new phase of political instability through which the country is passing. In this phase, parliamentary instabilities have come to reflect the deeper-lying processes of enormous flux and uncertainty. To recognize that there is an ongoing process of such turmoil is also to recognize that one cannot make confident predictions about future political patterns. Matters are simply too open-ended.

Should the Congress decline continue, it is quite conceivable that the BJP can make up enough ground in the future so that on its own it crosses the electoral barrier of 200 seats. Once it does this, it becomes qualitatively easier for it to secure the necessary alliances to stabilize itself in power. Alternatively, if the UF government is unable to stay in power long enough to give flesh to its promise of ushering in a new era of stable coalitional politics, either because of debilitating infighting or because the Congress pulls the rug out from under it, or for other reasons, then the BJP could well be the biggest beneficiary of this collapse. The BJP, moreover, has one special advantage over its rivals of a kind which can appeal strongly to a frustrated electorate. It is a *single* political force possessing a degree of discipline, coherence and unity (despite internal strains) which is the envy of all parties, barring perhaps the CPM.

This general uncertainty regarding political prognosis also emerges out of a deeper reality which has shaped the 1996 election outcome in its own way. Attention has been called to this deeper and determining reality at the end of Chapter 1. Mentioned there are the four fundamental processes whose complex interaction and intersection are shaping and will continue to shape the Indian polity for another decade and more. These are (1) the communalization of the Indian polity; (2) the ongoing forward march of the backward or intermediate castes; (3) Muslim ferment; (4) Dalit assertion as never before.

But there is no way that one can as easily identify the political trends and patterns that will emerge from the interplay of these indisputable social trends. This is because the political forms that this complex interplay can take are necessarily multifarious and open-ended. In the crucial state of Uttar Pradesh, which is so vital for the BJP's status as a major political player, it is only the social and political disunity of the middle- and lower-caste majority that enables the BJP to have the impact it has. Yet it survives and flourishes. Dalit assertion has given rise to the Bahujan Samaj Party, but it is not inevitable that this party and its leadership must or will pursue the seemingly natural politics of seeking alliances with the political representatives of other lower castes, classes and socio-economically backward minorities. As the break-up of the Samajwadi Party–Bahujan Samaj Party alliance showed, basic political factors such as the quality of leadership, the presence or absence of a strategic vision, the willingness to compromise, etc., can override supposedly deeper social compulsions. Living politics not abstract social trends determine actual political trajectories.

Thus Dalit assertion can express itself through the construction of independent political formations or through existing centrist parties, or even to some extent through brokered arrangements with upper-caste formations eager to woo them for confrontation with certain sections of the OBCs and their political representatives. The stronger collective political consciousness of upper castes and classes often more than compensates for the objective weakness of their being such a numerical minority. Dalit awakening is not the same as Dalit political consolidation. Nor is the latter always effective against its enemies. Moreover, the 1996 elections clearly showed that this awakening has led, as a reaction, to quite considerable and dramatic consolidation of the upper castes, both in Uttar Pradesh and in Bihar.

Following from the 1996 elections, the most apt summary evaluation of the BJP's performance and prospects is that it is proceeding on a slow but uncertain forward march! If further gains are a definite possibility, so too are future reverses. In this attempted march forward the BJP and Sangh Combine have seen the virtues of periodically donning the mask of moderation. Thus in order to attract potential supporters, the BJP shortly before the 1996 elections appointed Vajpayee (widely perceived as the 'softer face of the BJP') as its leader in place of Advani, who was made the party president. As the single largest party, the BJP was given the chance to form a government during a two-week interim stint but Vajpayee had to resign when it failed to do so. The failure indicated the party's still pariah status. What was noticeable during this interim was that (with the backing of a deliberately subdued RSS) it self-consciously sought to soft-pedal the more contentious parts of its programme such as its commitment to build a proper Rama temple in Ayodhya, to rescind Article 370 of the Constitution on Kashmir's autonomy, or to push through immediately a Uniform Civil Code. But no one should be deluded by this behaviour. There was never even a hint of any willingness to permanently give up its goals. Only the pace and manner in which they would be pursued was open to adjustment and compromise depending on the political circumstances prevailing. Underneath the mask of moderation remains the steel-hard determination and ruthlessness of the Sangh Combine and the RSS.

But what of the future prospects of the Congress? Is the party now clearly in terminal decline? Certainly the 1996 elections, disastrous as they were for the Congress, did not suggest quite so drastic a situation. Its geographic spread is still the widest. Though the Right has made ground, the overall picture is more complicated than conveyed by drawing a simple scenario of polarization to the left and right. The character of Indian society continues to favour centrist-type formations and to put steady pressure on the forces of the Right and Left to move towards more 'moderate' centrist positions on various issues. Of course, this pressure doesn't always succeed and the centre position on issues is also subject to movement and redefinition. But the pressure persists and its effects resurface periodically.

The Congress is not fated to disappear into insignificance. It can never again be what it was – the centrist party of dominance par excellence! But it can revive and remain an important player occupying a significant social and political space. Achieving this, however, will take real qualities of leadership, an honest evaluation of the severity of the problems it currently faces (this is the worst crisis in its history), an internal organizational overhaul, a sensible and realistic identification of the social base it must stabilize and appeal to, and a corresponding programmatic readjustment. If it continues on the path institutionalized by the Rao leadership of a pragmatic communalism and a rightwing programme of economic neo-liberalism, then its decline will continue.

There has always been a close correlation between the character of the Congress and the character of its principal leader. Leadership changes both reflect and significantly influence the direction the party is taking or is likely to take. Whether or not Narasimha Rao, who bears principal responsibility for the 1996 electoral debacle, remains as leader of the Congress is important. His removal is the necessary though not sufficient condition for a Congress revival. The Rao Congress has been the worst in living memory. Bereft of all ideals or redeeming values, ideologically adrift as never before, the Rao leadership has had one dominant preoccupation – to survive in power. It is as if the future of this historic party no longer mattered to that leadership itself. It has been the sad fate of the Congress that in the time of its greatest need it got the worst leader in its history.

A man who had groomed himself for a political lifetime to be a comfortable also-ran, a behind-the-scenes manipulator for the real powers-to-be in the party, a confidant at most to more serious prime ministerial figures and candidates, Narasimha Rao, by a quirk of circumstances, was the compromise choice (at the time of Rajiv Gandhi's assassination in mid-1991) to head the Congress party and the Indian government. Jawaharlal Nehru (1947–64) was not just a politician but a remarkable statesman. Lal Bahadur Shastri (1964–66) was an interim leader whose accession to prime ministership expressed the rising power of the kulaks in the country and within the Congress. Mrs Gandhi (1966–77, 1980–84) was no stateswoman but she was a remarkable politician. Her son, Rajiv Gandhi (1984–91), was neither a statesman nor much of a politician. In the period of the acceleration of Congress decline he was a figure outside the party's culture and tradition, touched neither by its virtues nor by its vices. Narasimha Rao, by contrast, has been very much a part of that tradition, one that has greatly degenerated from its halcyon days. Rao has represented nothing more than the archetypal characteristics of this deeply degenerated Congress.

It is not as if ordinary Congress member-activists are not aware of this crucial problem of leadership. After the débâcle of the 1996 elections this can hardly be hidden. But their dilemma is to find a figure who can convince of doing better. The Congress has become so used to being a party of governance rather than a party with a clear programmatic purpose and mission that there is a strong tendency to look for a leader who will promise retrieval of governmental power quickly rather than one who can provide programmatic vision and longer term strategy.

It is this that largely accounts for why despairing Congress members should have, from time to time, looked upon Sonia Gandhi, the Italian-born widow of Rajiv Gandhi, as 'a potential saviour. That she has been periodically so touted expresses the tragedies that have befallen the Congress. Her undeniable influence among party activists testifies to the party's organizational disarray and drift. Her only asset has been her association with the charisma attached to the Nehru–Gandhi family. When the discontented in a party can only search for a 'charismatic leader' to resolve its sinking fortunes then it clearly has little idea of how to cope with that party's fundamental problems. Sonia Gandhi is not the answer to the Congress dilemma.

The Congress decision to support the UF government and not to align itself with the BJP showed that it still has a survival instinct. Aligning with the BJP would have tolled the death-knell of the Congress, the terminal point in its degeneration. Such an act is not thereby ruled out in the future. But for the time being the Congress has not lost all its secular moorings. Indeed, the anticipation that it might be able to join the UF government in the future will for a time be more alluring than any idea of a 'historic compromise' with the BJP. This hope of sharing governance as well as the unwillingness of the Congress to risk another election soon gives some breathing space to the UF government and to the Third Force of the UF and its sympathizers outside.

But is the Third Force capable of conducting the necessary fight against Hindu communalism and the Sangh Combine? Clearly, within the Third Force, it is the Left which, with all its failings, stands as the core component of any possible formation that is to be constructed in order to effectively carry on this struggle.[37] The strategic perspective remains that of building a left-of-centre 'left and secular' front. However, serious reservations have to be entertained about the left-of-centre character, and even about the enduringly secular character, of some of the bourgeois formations that make up the UF and the Third Force.

They may have come together in 1996 to keep the BJP out. But this in itself does not express any deep-rooted commitment to secularism or abiding hostility to the BJP and Sangh Combine. The bourgeois regional parties (in which the Janata Dal can also be included) have other reasons to prefer a non-Congress, non-BJP formation like the Third Force. Most are rivals of the Congress and/or the BJP in their home states. It is also within a coalition like the Third Force or the UF government that the regional parties can exercise most influence at the Centre; certainly much more than if they aligned themselves with either the Congress or BJP.

The inchoate and uncertain political and programmatic nature of the Third Force carries definite implications for the struggle against the Sangh Combine. There is one perspective for the shorter term struggle to fight the BJP and Sangh Combine and another one for fighting it successfully in the medium and longer term. In the first case, the Third Force, even as it stands, can play a significant role. Stopping the immediate rise of the BJP and rolling it back does require the institutionalization of a stable form of coalition politics at the Centre. This is new and difficult terrain. Where the emergence of coalition politics (as in many European countries) is not the expression of underlying political instability (as in India), then it can itself take a stable and institutionalized form.

In such cases the map of the key social and political identifications of the electorate is clearer and less complex than in India. Parties have well-defined and well-established social bases. They have fairly distinct programmes and appeals. They are more prone to the politics of adjustment and compromise and eschew (at least in the short term) the effort to undermine or eat into the social bases of potential and actual political allies. Pre-election coalition arrangements have a better chance of prolonged survival even after coming to power because they were formed on some principled programmatic basis. Post-election coalition arrangements like the UF lack this glue.

The programmatic basis for unity in the Third Force – the so-called Common Minimum Programme (which broadly endorses the NEP) – was cobbled together after the elections to rationalize and justify the components coming together for reasons other than commitment to common policies. However, insofar as the major constituents of the Third Force are not for the most part rivals of each other at the regional level, there is space for a feasible and stabilized politics of compromise and adjustment. If the UF government and the Third Force can last two years, they will have dramatically increased their chances of lasting the full term of five years. Such a development can certainly weaken the prospects of the BJP by showing that a coalition of regional parties can be stable and viable. The naturally decentralized, plural and federalized society of India can then find a parallel political expression of these traits.

However, in the medium and longer term the problem is not just the BJP nor even the Sangh Combine but the wider problem of Hindu and minority communalism. Over a longer time span it is not the quality of internal management or control carried out by the UF government or by the Third Force that is decisive but what it can deliver to the wider populace. The warning bells were already sounded in the 1996 elections and they pealed loudly, especially in Bihar. An institutionalized left-of-centre politics must, above all, be a politics of social justice. And a politics of social justice must be more than a politics of lower-caste pride. Important as Mandalization has been, important though Dalit and OBC assertion have been, these will not be enough to stem and reverse the deeper process of communalization of the polity. They have to be joined with the class politics of reform, welfare and empowerment. This means a break from the NEP (which the UF and Third Force has not so far been prepared to carry out) and the institutionalization of a New Social Democracy as the concrete expression of a new centrism in Indian political life.

In the West, old-style Keynesian welfarism, i.e. old-style social democracy, has nowhere to go, while the possibilities of new-style social democracy seem very bleak. The term often used to describe the situation in the West – a 'two-thirds society' with one-third prospering, one-third coping and one-third more or less doomed – may be somewhat misleading conceptually, but it does capture some dominant trends in advanced Western democracies. Growing segmentation within the working class, by age, skill, gender, race, organization, wage levels, regions, etc., and growing political apathy have combined to greatly weaken the prospects of any centralized and coordinated political struggle against the dominance of capital, no matter what the 'social movements'.

If the collapse of Communism has weakened the 'external' opposition to capitalism, then developments ranging from the inadequacy of Keynesian economic prescriptions (but not of its diagnoses) in a more globalized economy to the objective and subjective transformations in working-class life have conspired to weaken the 'internal' resistance to capitalism in the advanced countries. Thus the swing to neo-liberalism and a redrawing of the boundaries of 'mainstream politics' to virtually exclude the social democratic agenda. Much work has to be done to rejig this mainstream spectrum so as to legitimize the desirability and feasibility of a new social democracy, similar to the old post-war version in its commitments to a more humanized and just form of society but different in the mechanisms it will rely upon, and the forms it will take.

In India, there is no 'two-thirds society' but an 'iceberg society' with one-eighth prospering or coping but seven-eighths not. Moreover, the vast mass of Indians are not sinking into greater political apathy, but the opposite. This is what makes the possibility of institutionalizing a New Social Democracy much greater in India than in the West. This Social Democracy would be new in its social base. In caste terms it would for the first time seek to rest its electoral appeal on the lower and middle sections of the backwards in conjunction with the core minorities. In class terms it would seek to mobilize the rural proletariat, marginal farmers and the urban organized and unorganized working class. Oppressed classes and oppressed castes broadly correspond.

The organizational forms would also be new. Its political expressions would most likely be found in the traditional parties of the Left as well as in the left-of-centre populist parties that operate at regional and/or national level, provided they self-consciously move in a more left and democratic direction. While the traditional mass organizations – the trade unions, the women, student and youth fronts of the progressive parties – obviously have a role, ways must be found to attract a range of non-party organizations and autonomous single-issue movements or specific sector formations (from women's organizations to civil liberties groups to environmental activists) to a unifying platform of New Social Democracy. These independent organizations overlap but are not congruent with the expanding NGO phenomenon. The more progressive kinds of rural cooperatives and the few (but slowly expanding) worker-run firms also come into consideration here.

Finally, the programme of New Social Democracy would be new and different from that of old centrism. Economically it would, as mentioned earlier, have to decisively break from the NEP and its theoretical rationale of neo-liberalism. Even more fundamentally, it would define economic aspirations in terms of an ecologically and socially sustainable form of development which consciously rejects the consumerist values of advanced capitalism and avoids the impossible and disastrous course of trying to reach the *average* living standards of the West. Selective uncoupling and careful integration with the global economy is an option available to a large economy like India.[38]

Socially and politically, a guiding principle would be the facilitation of all efforts that promote and help empower Dalits, tribals, women, agricultural labour, etc.; much greater emphasis on social welfare – social security, health and education (priority to primary and secondary schooling); greater efforts to decentralize power within the Indian Union and to promote a more ecumenical and less uniform notion of Indianness, one which can accommodate the sensitivities of those states and peoples in India's geographical periphery from Kashmir to the northeast. Such a New Social Democracy would have an unwavering commitment to maintain and deepen the secularity of the Indian state while also promoting the secularization of civil society.

If so much has been made of the need for a New Social Democracy it is because there is no alternative to a holistic and many-sided approach to the struggle against communalism. The unexpected upsurge of communalism from the seventies onwards is the product of a diseased and inadequate process of modernization, insufficiently just, insufficiently democratic, and more malignantly and unrestrainedly capitalist than it should be. New Social Democracy is the name given to a reorganized process of a self-critical and modest rather than arrogant modernization, that can once again on *lived* grounds restore the promise of a sensible, sustainable and humane socialist alternative to capitalism.

If this is not quite the politics of the transition to socialism, it is certainly the politics of the transition to that transition!

If a politically and programmatically remoulded Third Force at some stage in the not too distant future can succeed in making such a new centrism the 'common sense' of Indian political life, then the forces of Hindu communalism will receive a decisive setback. If the Third Force can at least make the new politics an unavoidable point of reference in public debate, then it will also have constructed powerful barriers against the further consolidation and expansion of Hindu communalism. Indeed, it will have provided major resources for a systematic counterattack.

What if the Third Force fails to do either? The BJP then will have good reasons for seeing the next general elections as the decisive round in its drive to capture enduringly central governance. This is not a certainty. The sheer size, diversity and complexity of India has been the nemesis of all political Cassandras. But the communal sextant fashioned by the Sangh Combine will be one of the more easily available navigational instruments, as India sails into uncharted seas towards the horizon marking the end of the second millennium, and beyond it into the third.

Notes

1. Indian politics remains plebiscitary in one sense – most parties, barring the BJP, base their appeal not on ideology but on issues which seem to be of current relevance.

   On the general plebiscitary character of Indian politics till 1989, see my *The Painful Transition*, London, 1990, Chapter 2.

2. The Charan Singh government in 1979 and the Chandrasekhar government of 1990–91 were purely interim arrangements of little consequence. They had no electoral mandate, emerging only as a result of parliamentary manoeuvrings.

3. A. Vanaik, *The Painful Transition*.

4. For the cyclical changes in the fortunes of Latin American populist parties see, M. Löwy (ed.), *Populism in Latin America*, Notebooks for Study and Research, No. 6, Amsterdam, 1987. Certain one-time populist formations like Argentinian Peronism have reorganized themselves (under Carlos Menem) on a totally different rightwing basis. They have made the transition to a new type of party while the Congress has not.

5. Political Hindutva would like a Uniform Civil Code compatible with

what it believes should be the fundamental principles governing Hindu family life and gender relations.

6. The Congress government and BJP both produced 'White Papers' which, as expected, absolved the Congress and the BJP/Sangh Combine respectively of responsibility for the demolition. For the only independent judgement of the event by three respected retired senior judges, see the report of the *Citizen's Tribunal on Ayodhya*, Delhi, May 1994.

   The Judgement found the Sangh Combine guilty of pre-meditated conspiracy in destroying the mosque, and the Congress central government guilty of failing to prevent this demolition when it had been forewarned by its intelligence agencies.

7. See Chapter 5.

8. Serious studies of the RSS have been surprisingly rare. The most up-to-date attempt at a comprehensive study is W.K. Anderson and S.D. Damle, *The Brotherhood of Saffron*, New Delhi, 1987.

   The CPI and CPM now lag behind the RSS as organizations with an ideologically trained cadre force. The CPM has been particularly corrupted by unbroken rule since 1977 in West Bengal.

9. See Chapter 4, the sub-section on Hindutva.

10. Close to 90 out of the Janata Party's total tally of 297 Lok Sabha MPs.

11. B.D. Graham, *Hindu Nationalism and Indian Politics*, Cambridge, 1990.

12. That the BJP advanced by moving to the right refuted the principal thesis concerning its future growth prospects proposed by Graham (ibid). However, Graham was not wrong in pointing out the existence and continuity of the basic tension between wanting to represent the Great Hindu Rally and wanting to dilute this thrust in search of central power.

13. The BJP and its predecessors have opposed Article 370, which constitutionally provides for Kashmir's autonomy, from its very inception. It has always been anathema since the Hindu nationalist 'loyalty test' for the Muslim majority province of Kashmir was that it should not claim special rights of autonomy. BJP hostility is not the outcome of frustration at the exercise of rights given by Article 370. In fact, such rights as assured have already been whittled down in practice and by dubious special legislation. The BJP has never been as hostile to the special autonomy rights given to the Christian northeast states.

14. The overwhelming bulk of illegal Bangladeshi migrants into India have come to escape economic deprivation. The spokespersons for the Sangh Combine have sought to give a false patriotic colouring to this problem by calling illegal Muslim migrants 'infiltrators' and demanding that the government expel them. Prominent Hindutva ideologues like Arun Shourie and Swapan Dasgupta, who, as journalists, are fully aware of the ways in which language can be distorted, have repeatedly used the

term 'infiltrators'. The connotations of such a label go beyond expressing mere illegality of presence to suggest intentions and acts of betrayal
on the part of these entrants. Such deliberate attempts at whipping up
emotions against these Muslim migrants through linguistic misuse is a
standard technique deployed by Sangh ideologues. Illegal Hindu
migrants from Bangladesh are referred to as 'refugees' and according
to the Sangh Combine should be allowed to stay in India.

The real tragedy is that, as in the case of Goebbelsian doublespeak,
through sheer repetition, the term 'infiltrators' (without quotes) has
now become an accepted part of the language of public print media.

15. The idea of a Muslim vote bank which supports the Congress has been
of limited accuracy for many parts of the country, e.g. West Bengal.
Muslims have often preferred non-Congress regional or national
alternatives. Moreover, the effort to establish secure vote banks is a
standard practice in democratic politics everywhere, e.g. black support
for Democrats in the USA or for Labour in the UK. The BJP does not
highlight the most important form of vote bank electoral politics in
India, which is not of religious communities but caste. This is because
the BJP itself engages (like all other parties) in such vote bank politics,
and because if it criticised this as a form of 'appeasement', it would
alienate those caste sections, undermining its efforts to build a monolithic Hindu vote bank.

16. 'Reverse optionality', i.e. assuming that one is born into secular family
and personal laws but having the right to 'opt out' for religious personal
laws, would legitimize a reactionary choice, whereas the conventional
notion of optionality would recognize that a person, despite being an
Indian citizen (and therefore possessing a secular birthright), is invol-
untarily subject to regressive community laws but can opt out of its
ambit. Moreover, it is not at all clear how workable 'reverse optionality'
is. There would seem to be all kinds of technical–legal problems. Nor is
it likely to get much popular and political support from progressive
forces.

17. See Chapter 5.

18. Ibid. After the 1996 elections, the BJP, as the single largest party, though
well short of a majority, was invited to form the government. It lasted
two weeks before resigning, since, despite efforts at political horse
trading, it could not muster enough support from other parties, which
continued to treat it as a pariah.

19. A few thousand *pracharaks* or full-time organizers dedicate their lives to
make the RSS function. They must be bachelors whose family is the
RSS. They must be ideologically totally committed and have a spartan,
ascetic existence since they are not just the key organizers but the living
exemplars of the ideals of the RSS itself, its 'new men'. They are
supposed to be the best and the most dedicated of cadres and become

pracharaks through the most careful selection. However, social transformations inside and outside the RSS have reduced the quality of potential recruits to this status as well as made the attractions of self-sacrificing *pracharak*-dom far less. Even the upsurge in RSS popularity over the last ten years has not been able to overcome this internal crisis of the *pracharak* system. This crisis is one of the better kept secrets in the 'brotherhood of saffron'.

20. The Bahujan Samaj Party (BSP), which was founded on 14 April 1984, emerged out of another party called DS4 or Dalit Shoshit Samaj Sangarsh Samiti (Struggle Group of Exploited Dalits), which itself emerged from the All-India Backwards and Minorities Communities Employees Federation of 1978. This was the union of government employees headed by Kanshi Ram in which Dalit bureaucrats took the lead.

21. Dr Bhimrao (Babasaheb) Ambedkar of Maharashtra was the first major modern leader of untouchables, and was himself an untouchable. For him national independence was meaningless unless it also meant liberation from the social yoke imposed by Brahminical Hinduism and he emphasized independent Dalit social and political mobilization. He had major differences with other nationalist leaders, particularly Gandhi, in respect of how the anti-colonial struggle should be waged and what the role of the Congress vis-à-vis Dalits should be. Progressively disillusioned with Hinduism and its possibilities regarding the elimination of the caste system, he led his followers out of the Hindu fold through mass conversion into Buddhism. An erudite and accomplished lawyer, he drafted the Indian Constitution.

22. The possibilities of forming a trans-state or extra-regional independent Dalit party are higher, but the failure of India's kulaks to build a trans-state kulak party of their own is salutory.

23. Eric Hobsbawm, 'Whither the Labour Movement?', in *New Left Review*, No. 173, January–February 1989.

24. There are around forty odd groups with a total membership of roughly fifty thousand, up from the thirty-five to forty thousand estimated officially in a government study of 1987. About nine groups make up. 75 per cent of the total, of which five are particularly important. These are the People's War Group operating in Andhra Pradesh, Maharashtra and Orissa; the Maoist Communist Centre in south and central Bihar; the Liberation Group in Bihar and West Bengal; the K. Ramchandra faction of the Chandra Pulla Reddy Group operating in Andhra Pradesh; the Party Unity Group in Bihar. See P. Singh, 'The Relevance of Naxalbari Today', in *Times of India*, 12 April 1994. Singh is former Director-General of Police of Uttar Pradesh and Assam and also of the Border Security Force.

Naxalbari was the region in West Bengal in which this Maoist-inspired movement erupted. Since then Naxalism and Naxalbari have been synonyms of sorts for Maoism in India.

25. Party membership is estimated at over 630,000 (1994 figures). But a substantial increase has been registered only in West Bengal, where membership rose from 189,732 in 1991 to 213,195 in 1994. In Kerala over the same period the increase is marginal from 227,422 to 228,165. Tamil Nadu, with around 50,000 members, comes next, followed by Andhra Pradesh, with approximately 27,000 (1991 figures). Increase in the Hindi belt has been negligible. In Uttar Pradesh, the most important state, membership has fallen from 7,750 to 7,000 members.

Claimed membership (different from verified membership) for the Centre of Indian Trade Unions (CITU), the federation controlled by the CPM, is 2,386,242 (1989); of the All-India Kisan Sabha (the peasant wing), 11,763,811, with West Bengal providing 9.5 million (1990–91 figures); of the All-India Agricultural Workers Union, 1,890,488, with Kerala providing 1.1 million; of the Students' Federation of India, 1,989,054 (1990 figures); of the All-India Democratic Women's Association, 3,119,234 (1990), with West Bengal providing over 2 million members.

The CPI, once the largest Left party, has seen a slow decline in its membership from a peak of 546,732 in 1978 to 460,883 in 1995. It has also experienced a slow decline in its student, peasant and trade union wings. In the last general elections out of a lower house of 545 seats, the CPM bagged 33 seats and the CPI got 13 seats.

26. Till the 1991 economic reforms ushered in a World Bank/International Monetary Fund-inspired 'structural adjustment programme' of internal deflation and external liberalization, India had the most insulated economy in the capitalist third world, barring some insignificant powers like Burma/Myanmar. As such, India could simultaneously sustain a close security relationship with the USSR and an economic tilt to the USA. There was a sense in which India was the most nonaligned of the nonaligned. This was testimony to the high degree of autonomy enjoyed by the Indian state and its ruling coalition.

27. The single largest of the Maoist groups, the Communist Party of India (Marxist–Leninist) 'Liberation' Group, is now an above-ground party participating in elections. It seeks a Confederation of the Left parties (CPI, CPM, etc.) in which each party commits to a common minimum programme even while retaining the freedom to criticize each other. The CPM has been most uneasy with this perspective, resenting Liberation's criticism of its ruling party's behaviour in West Bengal. Of the underground parties, the People's War Group has been the most notorious. It has suffered a serious internal split, and a rash recruitment policy has allowed in elements with little ideological training. Being armed with modern hand weaponry and land mines (through connec-

tions with the LTTE 'Tigers' of Sri Lanka), its cadre teams or '*dalams*' have resorted to private vendetta killings, alienating many supporters among tribals, as well as among students and intellectual in the cities.

28. The National Sampling Survey of 1987–88 reveals that over 90 per cent of the rural poor below the poverty line live in Andhra Pradesh, Bihar, Madhya Pradesh, Maharashtra, Orissa, West Bengal, Uttar Pradesh, Rajasthan, Tamil Nadu and Karnataka. The Maoists are strong in the first six of these states and have pockets of influence in the remaining four.

29. The Hind Mazdoor Sabha (HMS) and Hind Mazdoor Panchayat (HMP) are trade union federations controlled by socialist leaders. Both were once united under the same banner but have since split. Collectively, membership would be close to 3 million.

30. For the first time since 1978, at its fourteenth Party Congress in January 1992, it had a 'Resolution on Certain Ideological Issues'.

31. In Spring 1993 the CPM organized an international seminar of Communist parties. The Vietnamese and Chinese Communist parties were insistent that it not be called a Congress or Conference or anything else that might suggest an institutionalized organization or even a regular network of some sort.

32. The CPI's internal organization is more democratic and open than that of the CPM. But being a mass electoralist party its biggest failure is that it has never come to power on its own in any state and is nowhere an electoral force on the rise. This has given it a massive inferiority complex vis-à-vis the CPM. It has pressed more aggressively for a merger with the CPM but to no avail. Such a merger would be fully justified, giving a great boost to the short- and medium-term prospects of mainstream Communism. Left capacity to take the lead in the struggle against communalism would be greatly enhanced. It would also significantly strengthen Communist prospects in the Hindi heartland.

There are no major programmatic differences that justify this failure to merge. But the CPM wants this only on terms close to capitulation, believing the CPI is a fading force with nowhere else to go. There is a wing in the CPI that is ideologically close to the CPM, and one reason why internal debate is not more open is the fear that such open airing of differences would benefit the CPM. The non-Stalinism of all sections of the CPI is not an obstacle to a merger, nor does it lessen the gravitational pull of the CPM on sections of the CPI. After all, the CPI and the CPM share a common ancestry and it was not the issue of Stalinism that caused the break between them.

Regarding the CPM's Stalinism, there is now more willingness to rethink this legacy among a younger generation of leaders than at lower levels. This need not occasion surprise. The CPM's existence as a ruling party in West Bengal has attracted recruits for reasons other than ideology. Furthermore, there has been serious neglect in the provision and quality of ideological training.

33. In December 1992, after the demolition, A.B. Bardhan, a senior politburo member and the recently appointed general-secretary of the CPI, brought out a pamphlet whose title is self-explanatory: *Sangh Parivar's Hindutva versus the Real Hindu Ethos*. The selective quoting of Vivekananda to show the true Hindu ethos was easily countered by Hindutva ideologues like Arun Shourie, former editor of the *Indian Express*. He took other quotes from Vivekananda to show how explicitly anti-Muslim Vivekananda was.

   A month later, the CPM brought out a pamphlet whose first part quoted the Bhagavad Gita, Vivekananda and a first-millennium Brahmin philosopher–mystic, Shankaracharya, to emphasise the secular traditions of Hinduism.

34. Perhaps the best known spokesperson for an Indian version of eco-feminism is Vandana Shiva (*Staying Alive: Women, Ecology and Survival*, New Delhi, 1988). Developing on Western eco-feminism with its emphasis on the ideological construction of the symbiosis between women and nature, she, too, sees violence against women and nature as rooted in those ways of thought and life which see the woman–nature coupling as inferior to the man–culture coupling. Shiva links the 'virtues' of pre-colonial existence to the superior 'Hindu' way of preserving nature as related to the 'feminine principle' of nurturance and creativity. This was presumably destroyed by colonial and post-colonial Western notions of science and patriarchy. 'The ecological crisis is, at root, the death of the feminine principle' (p. 42). Shiva also notes the more material links between rural women and nature that is the source of their respect for and specialist knowledge of nature.

   A welcome opposition to Shiva comes from Bina Agarwal, 'The Gender and Environment Debate', in *Feminist Studies*, Vol. 18, No. 1, Spring 1992. Shiva is criticized for taking too unitary a view of women (at least third world women) and overly emphasizing the virtues of an unproblematic Hinduism. Not only is India religiously diverse but Hinduism is itself too pluralist and conflictual in its various ideological themes and discourses to sustain such a singular interpretation of its enduring commitment to the 'feminine principle'. Shiva also ignores how women are socially structured and therefore how structured their own responses are to nature. She is too uncritical of pre-colonial, pre-capitalist and non-Western social, economic and ideological relationships concerning women and nature.

   Agarwal prefers the term 'feminist environmentalism' to eco-feminism. She emphasizes much more the material reasons why poor peasant and tribal women react in the way they do to nature and environmental degradation. Women are mainly responsible for gathering fuel and fodder and in hill and tribal communities are also the main cultivators. This is not so of all rural women. Statization or privatization of rural resources and environmental degradation affect women differently according to their class/caste/tribal, etc., position and character.

The gender dimension must also be factored into any such evaluation: (a) the pre-existing gender division of labour; and (b) the gender differences in distribution of resources, like the weakness or absence of land rights for women. Agarwal's notion of 'class–gender effects' is counterposed to the idea of some biological essentialism wherein women as women, or some cultural essentialism wherein non-modern/ non-Western women, have some distinctive feminine sensibility that tends naturally to a distinctive 'ecological sensibility'.

35. For one of the more thoughtful analyses of the 1996 general elections from which I have drawn liberally, see Y. Yadav, 'How India Voted', in *India Today*, 31 May 1996.

36. For an earlier evaluation of this historical trend and of its sources, see Chapter 3 in A. Vanaik, *The Painful Transition*.

37. As an unrepentant anti-Stalinist Marxist, my relationship to the main formations of the Indian Left – CPM, CPI and CPI(ML) – is that of a determinedly sympathetic but determinedly critical outsider. Solidarity with this Left, as I understand it, does not preclude but insists upon principled, often sharp, criticism. However, in the times we live, solidarity is the key operative term. This Left, with all its failings, willingly shoulders the heavy responsibility associated with its deep commitment to fighting against communal and anti-democratic forces. It would be sectarian not to want to work for the greater unity and growth of this Left. This should be a unity forged on principled lines and a growth that is collective as well as individual; a growth that is at the expense of the forces outside the Left, not of each other.

38. A more comprehensive programme has been worked out by a group of activist-intellectuals who have formed the Initiative for National Renewal and Empowerment of People (INREP), of which the author is a member. The economic part of its programme focuses on employment generation and meeting basic needs, rejecting the existing model of over-consumption – over-accumulation – while continuing to affirm certain basic principles of economic development. These are mainten- ance of high domestic savings rates, tapping underutilized labour in the agricultural sector (through land reform, rural infrastructural works programmes and off-farm rural industries), and retaining the role of the state in providing strategic direction to the economy.

Similarly, the INREP programme envisages a new attitude to science and technology and R & D, relating it to Indian needs and resource endowments and not corporate and multinational corporation-driven technology growth.

Index